Audubon at Sea

EDITED BY CHRISTOPH IRMSCHER

AND RICHARD J. KING

Audubon at Sea

THE COASTAL & TRANSATLANTIC ADVENTURES OF JOHN JAMES AUDUBON

With a Foreword by Subhankar Banerjee

THE UNIVERSITY OF CHICAGO PRESS
Chicago and London

The University of Chicago Press, Chicago 60637
The University of Chicago Press, Ltd., London

Published 2022
Printed in the United States of America

31 30 29 28 27 26 25 24 23 22 1 2 3 4 5

ISBN-13: 978-0-226-75667-7 (cloth)
ISBN-13: 978-0-226-75670-7 (e-book)
DOI: https://doi.org/10.7208/chicago/9780226756707.001.0001

Publication of this book has been aided by a grant from Furthermore, a program of the J. M. Kaplan Fund.

Library of Congress Cataloging-in-Publication Data

Names: Audubon, John James, 1785–1851, author. | Irmscher, Christoph, editor. | King, Richard J., editor. | Banerjee, Subhankar, 1967– writer of foreword.
Title: Audubon at sea : the coastal and transatlantic adventures of John James Audubon / with a foreword by Subhankar Banerjee ; edited by Christoph Irmscher and Richard J. King.
Description: Chicago ; London : The University of Chicago Press, 2022. | Includes bibliographical references and index.
Identifiers: LCCN 2021054623 | ISBN 9780226756677 (cloth) | ISBN 9780226756707 (ebook)
Subjects: LCSH: Audubon, John James, 1785–1851—Travel. | Audubon, John James, 1785–1851—Diaries. | Ornithologists—United States—Biography. | Naturalists—United States—Biography. | Ocean travel. | Sea birds. | Aquatic animals. | LCGFT: Diaries. | Autobiographies.
Classification: LCC QL31.A9 A223 2022 | DDC 598.092 [B]—dc23/eng/20211115
LC record available at https://lccn.loc.gov/2021054623

∞ This paper meets the requirements of ANSI/NISO Z39.48-1992 (Permanence of Paper).

A long voyage would always be to me a continued source of suffering, were I restrained from gazing on the vast expanse of the waters, and on the ever-pleasing inhabitants of the air that now and then appear in the ship's wake. . . . When the first glimpse of day appears, I make my way on deck, where I stand not unlike a newly hatched bird, tottering on feeble legs. Let the wind blow high or not, I care little which, provided it waft me toward the shores of America.

JOHN JAMES AUDUBON, "Wilson's Petrel," 1835

Contents

Surf scoters over Beaufort Lagoon, with coastal plain and Brooks Range in the background, Arctic National Wildlife Refuge. Photograph by Subhankar Banerjee, July 2002.

Foreword

In September 2005, I participated in Drum-Sing-Dance to Protect the Arctic National Wildlife Refuge, a several-month vigil organized by the Indigenous Gwich'in Steering Committee. The vigil took place on a small triangular grassy space across from the recently opened National Museum of the American Indian, part of the Smithsonian Institution in Washington, DC. One morning, I quietly pulled myself away from the vigil and walked over to the nearby National Gallery of Art.

The exhibition *Audubon's Dream Realized: Selections from "The Birds of America"* had just opened at the National Gallery. It included fifty original hand-colored prints and one oil painting, "Osprey and Weakfish." The modest scale of the exhibition combined with very sparse attendance created what felt like a sacred space—an opening for me to be with and appreciate the gorgeous and meticulously rendered prints, which I was seeing for the first time.

The exhibit's web version provides digital images and captions for thirty-four prints. The selections include such famous works as "Carolina Parrot" (1827) and "Passenger Pigeon" (1829)—both depicting species that have since gone extinct. But not a single seabird is represented, not, for example, the "Great Auk" (1836; plate 19), which Audubon also painted and which, too, is extinct.

We should not consider the omission of seabirds a mere oversight. "In the popular imagination, Audubon's art and science are shaped by landbirds, not waterbirds," the editors write in the following introduction. Waterbirds include shore- as well as seabirds, with the latter being the most overlooked in Audubon's oeuvre.

Audubon at Sea fills a void by honoring Audubon's engagement with waterbirds. A fruitful collaboration between a noted Audubon scholar, Christoph Irmscher, and a noted writer on the sea and its creatures, Richard J. King, this extensively researched volume is a reliable guide to understanding John James Audubon's art and writing on waterbirds. It urges the readers to imagine a "different kind of Audubon, one challenged, on a deeply existential level, by an environment where he couldn't rely on the instincts that normally made him such an effective observer and hunter of birds." The editors support that imagining by presenting Audubon's writing on shore- and seabirds alongside close readings of his writing.

Why did an accomplished artist like Audubon also take up writing? Audubon turned to prose, the editors suggest, because "the visual medium couldn't encompass the richness of the natural world as he had experienced it in the field." As I read through his "Journal of a Sea Voyage," the first selection in this anthology, I found myself getting exasperated—there are so many idiosyncratic French-infused English words, inconsistent capitalizations, oddly structured sentences. Sixteen years ago, when I stood in front of original prints from *The Birds of America*, the words that came to mind were very different—precise, elegant, perfect. It dawned on me that Audubon's work, at least at the beginning of his career, wasn't about perfection, not yet. It was instead about engagement, about expressing keen observations, about the excitement that comes from using whatever skills you've got. Quick pencil sketches, words thrown on the page in quick succession—these are the techniques Audubon adopted when he found himself face to face with birds he coveted during his voyage to England.

In popular accounts, John James Audubon is primarily identified as an "American ornithologist." But wait a minute—shouldn't it be "American artist"? I'm inclined to think that any member of the general public who has ever heard of Audubon but is not a specialist on his work (this artist-writer included) would consider him first and foremost an artist. Irmscher and King, however, tell us that, at least when he was working on *Ornithological Biography*, his compilation of bird essays, "Audubon, in his own estimation, was first and foremost a scientist."

In *Ornithological Biography*, the editors write, Audubon describes a bird's habitat, offers "a personal account of how and when he captured the bird in question so that he could draw it for the reader's benefit," then discusses its ethology ("flight patterns, migration, courtship, song, breeding behaviors") and, finally, its morphology ("size, color, plumage"). This sounds like what a scientist would do, doesn't it? By the time Audubon started writing *Ornithological Biography*, he had honed his skill as a writer and, with assistance from a collaborator, his essays became serious contributions to ornithology and the canon of American nature writing.

Audubon at Sea ends with a selection of Audubon's writing from an 1833 sea voyage to Labrador, in which he expresses a curious mixture of despair and elation. The editors write of the "apocalyptic carnage inflicted on the colonies of nesting murres by eggers hoping to sell their loot in the markets of Halifax" and the "fishermen who killed thousands of guillemots in a day," painful for Audubon to witness. But they also point out that in Audubon's writing, such massacres, rather than events to be watched in disgust from a distance, become "grotesquely magnified versions of Audubon himself"—and for that matter, of ourselves today, as we continue to wreak destruction on our planet. In the name of precision in the visual depiction of bird species and their behavior in the wild, Audubon killed thousands of wild birds, nothing short of a massacre committed by one individual. This is why, I assume, one of the most frequently reproduced portraits of Audubon (fig. 5) shows him holding a rifle, not an artist's brushes or a field scientist's pencil and journal.

In one extraordinary passage, a favorite of mine, Audubon writes about the wonder of bird migration, to the north for nesting and back before the north freezes over:

> That the Creator should have ordered that millions of diminutive, tender creatures, should cross spaces of country, in all appearance a thousand times more congenial for all their purposes, to reach this poor,

> desolate, and deserted land . . . and to cause it to be enlivened with the songs of the sweetest of the feathered musicians, for only two months at most, and then, by the same extraordinary instinct, should cause them all to suddenly abandon the country, is as wonderful as it is beautiful and grand.

Tracking Audubon's writing from the 1826 voyage to England to the 1833 voyage to Labrador, as this volume allows us to do, we notice how his writing evolved, from rough notes to polished and lyrical prose—a testament to the value of staying engaged with a craft.

Audubon at Sea is focused exclusively on voyages by water. I, for one, have never been on a sea voyage or even on a cruise ship. How, then, do I, and others like me, encounter seabirds in the twenty-first century? And how can we speak competently about seabirds in our time when those avian creatures largely remain out of our field of *binocular vision*? One way is by venturing to the edge of the sea, where we will encounter not only shorebirds but also some of the more enterprising seabirds when they come ashore to nest or rest or pause in their migrations. Over the past two decades, I have spent time at the Arctic coast of Alaska; for a few years, I also lived along the Salish Sea coast of Washington. And I have witnessed the population declines suffered by both shore- and seabirds. I have privately mourned their deaths and publicly spoken out against threats to their survival.

My contribution to shore- and seabird conservation and more broadly to mitigating the biodiversity crisis started in 2002. In July of that year, I made a few photographs of surf scoters, a very beautiful seabird species, in the Arctic National Wildlife Refuge. One of those photos, reproduced here, graced the cover of an eight-page conservation report, "Birds and Oil Development in the Arctic Refuge," published by Audubon Alaska. Looking back, I can say that a significant part of my work (photography, writing, activism) over the past two decades has focused on protecting important biological nurseries and places culturally significant to the Indigenous peoples in the Arctic, including the Arctic National Wildlife Refuge, the Teshekpuk Lake wetland (the largest wetland complex in the circumpolar Arctic), and the Beaufort and Chukchi Seas (which provide home and food to many sea creatures).

But I have also witnessed mass species die-offs, including two overlapping ones when I lived along the Salish Sea. In 2013, news arrived that starfish (or sea stars) were dying in large numbers along the Pacific coast of the Olympic National Park. Within a year, more than twenty species of starfish, from Alaska to Mexico, had been devastated. By 2017, scientists assessed that the mass die-off of starfish was unprecedented in scale and scope. In many sites the population decline was more than 99 percent. At the same time, masses of seabirds were also dying along the Pacific coast, in what the US Geological Survey assessed as the largest die-off of seabirds ever recorded in the Pacific Ocean. These two simultaneous events broke my heart. In April 2020, I founded the Species in Peril project at the University of New Mexico, which involves support for creative production, public scholarship, and grassroots initiatives to bring attention to the intensifying biodiversity crisis.

While the havoc wrought on seabirds has renewed interest in Audubon's work, the recent racial awakening and movements for racial justice are drawing attention to him for a very different set of reasons and aims. Irmscher and King address this sensitive subject in the coda to this volume. Here is my own brief assessment: The National Audubon Society was established in 1905, fifty-four years after Audubon's death—a monument no less significant than a marble or bronze statue, perhaps even more so because of its wide public reach. One hundred sixteen years later, in its Spring 2021 issue, *Audubon* magazine, the flagship publication of the National Audubon Society, ran a significant reevaluation of Audubon's legacy by the Black ornithologist J. Drew Lanham, which opens with an illustration that includes at the bottom right a severed head of John James Audubon lying on the ground—a monument fallen. While Audubon did not ask that white conservationists who came half a century after him build a monument in his honor, he certainly would have appreciated the intense admiration his art has generated over the past two centuries. And while he couldn't have anticipated the fury his personal failings have provoked, even that may be seen as part of a vigorous and necessary debate about a shared, sustainable future.

Audubon at Sea shines a bright light on, and makes visible, three overlooked but significant aspects of Audubon's work and legacy: his writings on waterbirds as they evolved from imperfect to polished and lyrical prose; his seabird drawings, like the unforgettable "Gannet" (plate 12); and a new focus especially on the seabirds that are now in peril even if they remain out of our sight. The book adds a significant new chapter in our understanding and appreciation of Audubon as an imperfect and troubled nineteenth-century polymath—an artist, ornithologist, writer. Audubon's work will live on in new debates and conversations, in which *Audubon at Sea* will play an important role.

—Subhankar Banerjee
Albuquerque, New Mexico

Sources for the Texts

Part I of this book comprises excerpts from John James Audubon's 1826 journal aboard the *Delos*, transcribed directly from the original manuscript, held at the Field Museum in Chicago, with permission. To preserve the flavor of the original, we have retained Audubon's inconsistent punctuation and spelling. His erratic capitalizations are a feature of his style, and we have not attempted to fix them, although the difference between lower- and uppercase letters is not always clear, and we have occasionally had to rely on conjecture. Spellings that seem particularly counterintuitive are followed by [*sic*]. Where Audubon deleted a word or phrase or inserted or moved a passage, we have reproduced only his final wording. Later additions in pencil, if they seem likely to have been written by Audubon, appear in square brackets, as do our own edits or conjectures. Otherwise, our interventions have been light, limited to making dashes all the same length and converting underlined words and phrases to italics. Sections removed are indicated by bracketed ellipses.

The biographies and stories in part II are from the first editions of the five volumes of *Ornithological Biography, or, An Account of the Habits of the Birds of the United States of America; Accompanied by Descriptions of the Objects Represented in the Work entitled* The Birds of America, *and Interspersed with Delineations of American Scenery and Manners* (Edinburgh:

Adam Black, 1831–1839), abbreviated in the introductory essay and notes as *OB*. The anatomical sections added in volumes 4 and 5, written by his collaborator William MacGillivray, are not included here, except for the one that accompanied "Black-footed Albatross." We have edited only words that were obvious typographical errors and made cuts in Audubon's texts only when he is quoting another author or observer at length; those instances are mentioned in the notes.

The original manuscript journal from Audubon's expedition up to Labrador in 1833 is lost. The excerpts in part III follow the sections included in the first published American edition of Lucy Audubon's *The Life of John James Audubon, the Naturalist* (New York: G. P. Putnam and Sons, 1869). Omitted entries are indicated by ellipses; editorial interventions are limited to obvious typographical errors or misspelled place names. As Peter Logan has pointed out, Lucy (or her nemesis, editor Robert W. Buchanan) misdated several of the entries and occasionally had trouble deciphering Audubon's handwriting (*Audubon: America's Greatest Naturalist and His Voyage of Discovery to Labrador* [San Francisco: Ashbryn Press, 2016], 442n18). Such obvious mistakes, including garbled species names, have been silently amended.

The plates chosen for this edition are from the double elephant folio set of *The Birds of America* originally owned by Robert Ray, which was purchased, in the early 1940s, by J. K. Lilly and is now held by the Lilly Library, Indiana University Bloomington. In the notes, we occasionally refer to Audubon's original watercolors, held by the New-York Historical Society.

The introduction, headnotes for parts I, II, and III, and coda were written by Christoph Irmscher; Christoph Irmscher and Richard King co-authored the explanatory notes; and the selections from Audubon's work were made by Richard King. Despite some basic division of labor, the final product is the result of a true collaboration, extending to every detail in the volume.

The history of Audubon's artwork, including the watercolors and the various published editions of his prints, has been well documented by scholars such as Susanne M. Low, in *A Guide to Audubon's* Birds of America, 2nd ed. (1988; New Haven, CT: William Reese Co. and Donald A. Heald, 2002), and Roberta J. M. Olson, in *Audubon's Aviary: The*

Original Watercolors for The Birds of America (New York: New-York Historical Society/ Rizzoli, 2012). In listing Audubon's plates as published in the first double elephant folio of *The Birds of America*, we follow modern convention by using the engraver's surname (Havell) followed by the number of the plate.

In writing the notes, for biological, taxonomical, and migratory information on birds we referred most often to Low, *A Guide to Audubon's* Birds of America; David Allen Sibley, *The Sibley Guide to Birds* (New York: Random House, 2000); Chris Elphick, John B. Dunning Jr., and David Allen Sibley, *The Sibley Guide to Bird Life & Behavior* (New York: Knopf, 2001); Derek Onley and Paul Scofield, *Albatrosses, Petrels & Shearwaters of the World* (Princeton: Princeton University Press, 2007); Peter Harrison, *Seabirds: An Identification Guide* (Boston: Houghton Mifflin, 1985); and the Cornell Lab of Ornithology's online *Birds of the World* (birdsoftheworld.org), with its scholarly articles on individual species. For conservation status, we have primarily consulted the International Union of Conservation of Nature (IUCN) Red List of Threatened Species.

For biographical and historical information around Audubon, we have primarily consulted Peter Logan, *Audubon: America's Greatest Naturalist*; Richard Rhodes, *John James Audubon: The Making of an American* (New York: Knopf, 2004); Olson, *Audubon's Aviary*; and Christoph Irmscher, ed. *John James Audubon, Writings and Drawings* (New York: Library of America, 1999), abbreviated as *Writings*.

Introduction

For anyone who reads about it today, the scene is heartbreaking, difficult to imagine. The setting: Eldey, a rocky, lonely island ten miles off the coast of southwestern Iceland, reachable only by boat, a rugged chunk of granite rising out of the sea. The date: June 3, 1844, by some accounts at least, though the exact day, month, or year would not have mattered to the birds, including a pair of great auks, likely the last in the world, who had made their home here. They were true survivors, descended from survivors: a volcanic eruption had forced their ancestors to leave their last home (another islet further to the south) and settle here. But there was nothing that had taught these large, flightless birds how to survive what happened on that day: the arrival of three Icelandic fishermen, Jón Brandsson, Sigurður Isleifsson, and Ketil Ketilsson. Abandoning their egg, which was cracked in the process, the adult birds ran as fast as they could. Isleifsson later recalled that the bird he pursued "walked like a man." But the auks weren't fast enough: the men strangled them.[1]

Ten years earlier, the naturalist John James Audubon had drawn a pair of great auks. He was in London at the time, and all he had was a dead specimen and a sketchy report from his engraver's brother, Henry Havell, who, a few years earlier, traveling from New York to England, had "hooked" a great auk and kept the bird on board for a while, for his own private amusement: "It walked very awkwardly, often tumbling over, bit every one within reach of its powerful bill, and refused food of all kinds." Maybe it finally dawned on Henry that the bird, extracted roughly from its watery environment, was in distress. After a few days, he let it go.[2]

Based on little more than another person's memory and a museum specimen (fig. 1), Audubon's drawing of the auks represented an imaginary world. He left it unfinished; the engraver Robert Havell Jr., Henry's brother, fixed the position of the feet of the bird on the left and created an arctic landscape for the background (see plate 19). Audubon's auks are silent sentinels in this empty world, one drifting on the water, while the other stands stock-still on a slab of rock. The ocean's surface is ruffled, the waves cresting in elegant little hillocks, while the cliffs, leaning in and over the water, appear bathed in a light that seems to come from nowhere. Here the birds, not us, are the real residents. Except that they are not. Audubon already knew that these birds, killed first for their meat, then for down and pin feathers, and finally simply because they were rare, didn't stand a chance. Frozen in timelessness, great auks were, for all he knew, gone from nature; even in Audubon's fertile artistic imagination, they are little more than monuments to their own demise.[3]

What happened on Eldey is a scene Audubon had known well, as both observer and participant, and he kept revisiting elements of it in his writing and at least implicitly in his art. As an artist, he sought to preserve birds for eternity; as a naturalist, he hunted them, killed them (by the barrelful), and often ate them, too. But birds were notoriously elusive, and none evaded his grasp more than waterbirds, which, in Audubon's drama of frustrated possession, were a particular challenge and provocation: "The Land Bird flits from bush to bush, runs before you, and seldom extends its flight beyond the range of your vision," wrote Audubon in the introduction to the third volume of *Ornithological Biography*, devoted exclusively to sea- and shorebirds. "It is very different with the Water Bird, which sweeps afar over the wide ocean, hovers above the surges, or betakes itself for refuge to the inaccessible rocks on the shore" (*OB* 3 [1835], xi).

Audubon's reference here is to seabirds, waterbirds adapted to a marine environment: for sixty million years, they have circumnavigated

FIGURE 1. Audubon's great auk when at Vassar College. The 1830 specimen, said to have been used by Audubon to paint his "Great Auk" (plate 19; Havell 341), likely came from Icelandic waters and is now at the Royal Ontario Museum. Reproduced from Errol Fuller, *The Great Auk*. Courtesy of Errol Fuller.

the globe, survived the roughest weather on the planet, found their way over vast expanses of water with no landmarks to speak of, and hunted for food high in the skies and in the depths of the ocean. Comprising nearly 350 species worldwide, they are the most reliable indicators of the health of our oceans. Which is precisely why it was not an incidental fact when an assessment of population trends conducted in 2015 revealed a 69.7 percent decline of monitored populations over sixty years.[4] Other studies have confirmed that seabirds seem twice as likely as landbirds to be threatened with extinction (28 percent) or decline (47 percent).[5] Significantly, open-ocean birds such as the albatross, the frigatebird, the petrel, and the shearwater are generally worse off than birds that stick close to the coasts, a reflection of the fact that they have smaller clutch sizes and, thus, even small increases in mortality have bigger consequences.

The last auks of Eldey died at the hands of humans. We even know the names of the perpetrators. The killers of seabirds today are less visible, less identifiable. To single out only one of them: seabirds routinely mistake small bits of plastic for fish eggs. If half of the world's seabirds ingest marine debris today, it is predicted that 99 percent of them will do so by 2050.[6] Written almost two hundred years ago, Audubon's essays about waterbirds conjure a world on the verge of becoming lost permanently; now, more than ever, they are important reminders of what it is that we need to save, if we want to save ourselves. The possibility of loss haunts the trajectory of the selections in this anthology, ranging from Audubon's excitement over the richness of sea life during his 1826 voyage to England to the despair he felt during his 1833 voyage to Labrador, when he wrote, on July 21, "Nature herself is perishing."

* * *

Born on an island, the son of a sea captain, Audubon, over the course of a life lived on two continents, made a total of twelve ocean crossings and dozens of passages around England and France and along the coastlines of North America, from Galveston, Texas, to the Strait of Belle Isle between Newfoundland and Labrador. He did so even though he was prone to debilitating bouts of *mal de mer*, abject seasickness. No wonder, perhaps, that he was also prone to inventing an alternative origin for himself, one that placed him firmly on land and not within walking distance of an ocean. In an autobiographical essay titled "Myself," which he wrote around 1835 and never published, he claimed that his birth was an "enigma" to him and then fabricated a story that made Louisiana his birthplace, foreign enough to be credible, familiar enough to legitimize him as an American naturalist: "My father had large properties in Santo Domingo, and was in the habit of visiting frequently that portion of our Southern States called, and known by the name of, Louisiana, then owned by the French Government." In Louisiana, Jean Audubon had married, he went on, a beautiful "lady of Spanish extraction," who "bore my father three sons and a daughter,—I being the youngest of the sons and the only one who survived extreme youth." But their happiness didn't last long: "My mother, soon after my birth, accompanied my father to the estate of Aux Cayes, on the island of Santo Domingo, and she was one of the victims during the ever-to-be-lamented period of the negro insurrection of that island."[7]

Since all of that would have taken place long before the Louisiana Purchase, Audubon had, in effect, given himself license to play fast and loose with the truth. But "Jean Rabin," as he was then called, was in fact born *in* Saint-Domingue (now Haiti) on April 26, 1785, in the southern port city Les Cayes. We know that his mother was not Spanish but a twenty-seven-year-old white chambermaid from the village Les Mazures in northern France, and that she died of a fever, not because of the Haitian Revolution. There is no evidence that Audubon's father ever visited Louisiana.[8] Audubon's obfuscations did not stop with his imaginary birthplace. With one stroke of his pen, he also declared himself his father's only surviving son from his imaginary marriage. At least on paper, he thus legitimized not only himself but also his half-sister, Rose, born April 29, 1787, the product of his father's relationship with his mixed-race housekeeper, Catherine "Sanitte" Bouffard.[9] The specter of his illegitimacy haunted Audubon his entire life; the somewhat clumsy cover-up offered at the beginning of "Myself" was just another installment in a series of fantastical stories that have accumulated around Audubon's origins, one of which—that he was Louis XVII, the lost Dauphin of France—was perpetuated even after his death.[10] More and more facts have emerged thanks to the efforts of recent biographers and scholars, including the probable site of his father's plantation, about a half mile south of the southernmost tip of Étang Lachaux, or Lake Lachaux, in Haiti, eight miles north of the harbor of Les Cayes, and thus not close to the coast. But if you live on an island, the ocean determines all you do, and Saint-Domingue's slave economy, perhaps the most brutal in the world, was based on the water, on the ships that brought an endless supply of enslaved African men, women, and children to feed the sugar plantations that dotted the landscape.[11]

* * *

Audubon's coyness about his descent, and his propensity for fibbing about his birthplace, have preoccupied scholars, leading more recently to the claim that he (and perhaps some of his biographers, too) had engaged in an elaborate cover-up to disguise the fact that, like his sister Rose, he was, perhaps, mixed-race.[12] But Audubon's lies—in perhaps the most celebrated one, he maintained that he had studied with the famous French painter Jacques-Louis David[13]—were more instinctual than clever or well-considered, reflecting the casual relationship with facts often maintained by those who carry some unspeakable secret. Apart from official documents confirming his Haitian birth,[14] we do have proof that at least on occasion he was even proud of it. There is a telling marginal note in Audubon's set of *American Ornithology; or, The Natural History of Birds Inhabiting the United States, not given by Wilson* (Philadelphia, 1825–1833), written by Audubon's friend and colleague, the ornithologist Charles-Lucien Bonaparte, and now held by the Audubon Museum in Kentucky. Reading Bonaparte's description of the song of the "Great Crow Blackbird" (the great-tailed grackle), Audubon remembered another bird he knew well. "The very bout de Petun," he wrote, mixing languages as he often did, referring to the Creole name for the smooth-billed ani, a bird still common in Haiti today.[15] Somewhat gratuitously—why would you sign a marginal note in a volume you own?—he appended his name to the comment: "J. A. born in *Santo Domingue*." For good measure, he underlined the latter phrase (fig. 2).[16] Here was Audubon's admission, not in an official document but in conversation with himself, that he was in fact born in the New World—proof that that fact mattered to him. As an earlier note in the chapter

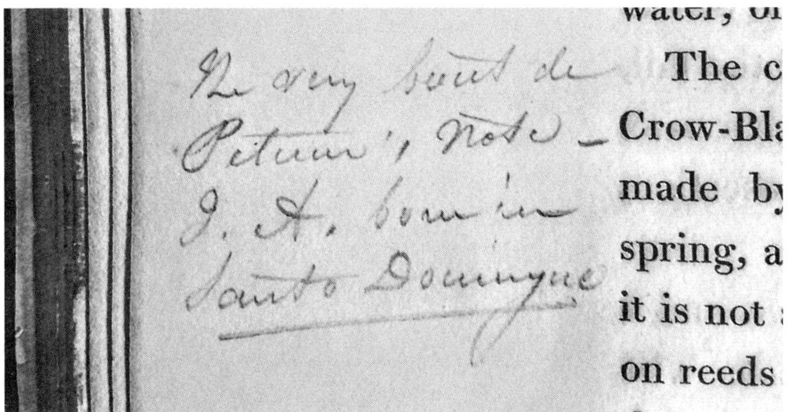

FIGURE 2. Audubon's birthplace. Marginal note in Audubon's copy of Charles-Lucien Bonaparte's *American Ornithology*, vol. 1 (1825). Courtesy of the Audubon Museum, Henderson, KY.

attests, he had been reading about the ani in Buffon's *Histoire naturelle des oiseaux* (1780). But the subsequent note clearly connects whatever Audubon had found in Buffon to his own childhood in Saint-Domingue, either because he remembered having heard that bird (unlikely, since he was so young when he left) or (more likely) because he felt he could claim special authority since he hailed from the same place as the bird.

If Audubon *fils* came from the New World, his father was as French as they come. Capitaine Jean Audubon (fig. 3) was born in Les-Sables-d'Olonne on the western coast of France, a cod-fishing port. But even this quaint seaside town had early connections to the Caribbean: it was in Les-Sables-d'Olonne that, likely around 1630, the infamous pirate Jean-David Nau, better known as François l'Olonnais, saw the light of the world. Sent across the ocean as an indentured servant around 1650, l'Olonnais, starting out in Saint-Domingue, raped, ransacked, and tortured his way through much of the Caribbean and Central America, until he was unceremoniously dispatched in 1669 by a band of Guna people in Panama, who fed his body, limb by limb, to the fire, to make sure nothing survived.[17]

The family of seasoned seamen into which Jean Audubon was born was more pacifically inclined. But like his pillaging predecessor, he early on felt the pull of distant places. When he was thirteen, young Jean accompanied his father Pierre on a trip to the Cape Breton Islands

FIGURE 3. Audubon's father. Capitaine Jean Audubon (1744–1818), after a portrait painted by Polk, ca. 1789. From Francis Hobart Herrick, *Audubon the Naturalist* (1917), facing p. 79.

and both got caught up in the hostilities between England and France. Pierre's ship, *La Marianne*, was taken, Jean was shot in the leg, and they spent three years in captivity in England. In 1770, Jean moved to Nantes and married Anne Moynet, a much-older widow with money and a near-infinite supply of tolerance, who didn't seem to mind that her husband spent as little time with her as possible. Having signed with the Coiron Brothers of France, Jean spent the next decade and a half shuttling back and forth between Nantes and the Caribbean, exporting fabrics, wine, and other luxury items to Les Cayes, bringing back sugar, coffee, and cotton. In a move not unusual for captains on these routes, he acquired a plantation in Les Cayes and soon began to trade slaves as well, either buying them for himself or selling them on commission for others. These were perilous voyages, not only because of pirates pursuing valuable cargo but because of the continuing threat posed by British buccaneers now fighting the Americans. Traveling to Nantes in the spring of 1779, Jean fell into the hands of the British once again and ended up jailed in New York. After his release, thirteen months later, he joined the American revolutionaries, captaining a variety of their vessels, perhaps his form of revenge.[18]

Capitaine Audubon was in his thirties when he began his residence in Les Cayes, a tough, sea-hardened man with only a fleeting sense of obligation to a wife back home whom he barely knew. Saint-Domingue was, as C. L. R. James put it, "the greatest individual market for the European slave trade," a place of incomprehensible brutality. Slavery was not an incidental fact here: on this island of mountain ranges and lush plains, under palm trees sixty or seventy feet high, day after day, year after year, on soil hardened by the sun, men, women, and children labored ceaselessly. Overworked and underfed, they had little expectation to live past their thirties.[19] We don't know when precisely Jean Audubon began to participate in the business of selling and buying human beings. Doing so would not have been unusual, given where he was from: Nantes, one of France's richest cities, was, for much of the eighteenth century, also its leading slave port; 34 percent of all slave transports to the West Indies originated from there. However, Jean seems to have limited his activities to buying and selling slaves in Les Cayes; his profits, therefore, were not subject to the risks involved in transatlantic voyages.[20]

Like the other whites in Saint-Domingue, he took what he felt was rightfully his. His household in Les Cayes was run by "Sanitte," the daughter of a fellow planter, Gabriel Bouffard. Their relationship quickly grew beyond that of employer and employee; it is not known how many children their "ménage" generated. And it seems that Capitaine Audubon's appetites did not stop there. It was this messy household that Jeanne Rabine, the servant girl from Mazures, joined, apparently after absconding from a nearby plantation. A few months later she was pregnant.

Jeanne was an "Extraordinary beautifull Woman," young John James was told (*Writings*, 30); he clearly owed some of his famous physical appeal to her. But she wasn't healthy. The itemized account left by her doctor, Monsieur Sanson, who also tended to Jean Audubon's slaves, showed that he treated her several times, before and after the birth of John James, for a variety of problems. It was with Sanson in attendance—he charged extra for spending the night—that little Jean Rabin was born on April 26, 1785. More visits to Jeanne followed, and more treatments, among them poultices soaked with *eau blanche*, a concentrated solution of acetate of lead, which didn't help, since Jeanne's infected breast turned into an abscess. These were rough months for the infant and even more so for the mother, who finally died on November 10, 1785, and was buried far from her home, in the cemetery of the Église de Notre-Dame de l'Assomption in Les Cayes. Audubon never mentioned her by name.[21]

* * *

The unrest and subsequent revolution in Saint-Domingue (fig. 4) brought Audubon's tropical childhood to a premature, sudden end. Even though he probably had no memories of Les Cayes, he would go on reliving the fact of his murky New World birth for the rest of his life. It might have occurred to him, too, that there was no absolute proof that Jeanne Rabine was his mother. Perhaps her name had served as a convenient cover for some unspeakable secret, an influx of black blood that would have complicated his racial identity, like that of his sister Rose. A confusing slip of the pen in his autobiography might point to just such an underlying identity conflict: after denouncing the slave rebellion as "that ever-to-be-lamented . . . insurrection," words that would have made sense to nineteenth-century white Americans, Audubon, a few pages later, as if he had forgotten his recent lament, characterizes that same uprising as the "liberation of the blacks" (*Writings*, 765, 767).

FIGURE 4. Burning of Cap Haïtien, Haiti. Frontispiece of *Saint-Domingue; ou, Histoire de ses révolutions* (Paris: Chez Tigre, [1820]), showing the revolution in Cap Français, Saint-Domingue (now Cap Haïtien, Haiti). Courtesy of the New York Public Library.

When political conditions on the island spun out of the French settlers' control, little Jean was sent across the ocean to Nantes to live with his father's family; his mixed-race sister followed later.[22] The voyage from Les Cayes to Nantes would have been young Jean's first experience of the open ocean. As miserable as being on choppy waters often made him, Audubon retained a lifelong fascination with ships and sailors, the efficiency required to make a wooden tub not only stay afloat but glide quickly and with seeming effortlessness to its destination. For the people enslaved by Capitaine Audubon, the transatlantic passage, during which they were "hurled from one side to another by the heaving vessel, held in position by the chains on their bleeding flesh,"[23] was the end of freedom; for many of them, it also meant death. For Audubon, ocean travel meant liberation: It was a ship that whisked him out of revolutionary turmoil in Haiti, and, after more than a decade amid another type of revolutionary turmoil in France, it was another ship that delivered him to the United States. The names of the vessels on which he traveled, from the *Delos* that took him to Liverpool in 1826, the official beginning of his ascent to fame, to the revenue cutters on which relied when crisscrossing the Florida Keys in the 1830s, to the *Omega* that ferried him up the Missouri in 1842, are threaded through the pages of his journals, essays, and letters. As are, for that matter, the observations of the sailors, pilots, fishermen, and captains Audubon consulted whenever he could about the habits and habitats of American waterbirds.

In 1796, Jean Audubon, a survivor who adapted well to the new realities of the French Revolution, enrolled his son in school on the naval base at Rochefort-sur-Mer, where he oversaw a training vessel. But much to his father's disappointment, "Jean Audubon, mousse," the cabin boy Jean Audubon (he had been formally adopted by the Audubons), was not cut out to be a sailor. Seasickness and despondency ended his naval career before it had even begun. On September 20, 1797, he failed the candidacy test for the School of Hydrography.[24]

Audubon never overcame his fear of travel on the high seas. But when he boarded the *Delos* in May 1826, he was, after more than two decades of working on his watercolors, full of happy anticipation. While the tedium of shipboard life would soon dull his excitement, it also sharpened his sense for the absurdity of his situation. The mini-menagerie kept on board the *Delos*, which included the cook's very entitled chicken as well as a confused small alligator Audubon had bought in New Orleans, served as a humorous foil for Audubon's own deep anxieties. As ill-adapted to life at sea as Audubon, the domestic fowl—far removed from Audubon's wild avian kingdom—developed an unfortunate hankering for fluttering overboard. After one spectacular rescue, the hen pushed her luck once more, in "squally weather," and, on the captain's orders, was left to the elements—a cautionary tale for Audubon, who could not shake his nervousness when he went for brief dips in the water. (The alligator, with one big final sigh, simply expired on board.) But look at the storm-petrels described in his June 20 entry, those tiny birds, popularly known as "Mother Carey's chickens," completely comfortable in the air and in the ocean, "Raising & falling with such beautifull ease to motions of the Waves that one might Suppose they receive a Special power to that Effect from the Element below them."

* * *

Audubon's stay in England and Scotland brought him the success he had coveted. Most dramatically, it marked the beginning of his long partnership with the world's best engraver, Robert Havell Jr. (1793–1878), in London, who became the co-creator of Audubon's *The Birds of America*. Havell began printing the massive portfolio in 1827, working from Audubon's watercolors: 435 hand-colored plates on gigantic sheets of paper, measuring 39½ by 26¼ inches, were released to subscribers over a period of eleven years. From the outset, Audubon's collection reflected only a portion of the North American bird world. Seabirds in particular were missing; more travel was needed. And Audubon made a second discovery: while in his art he had worked hard to undermine the conventions of scientific illustration, representing his birds in motion, their bodies turned this way or that, their beaks about to sink into their favorite prey or to caress their mates or to feed their young, the visual medium couldn't encompass the richness of the natural world as he had experienced it in the field. So he turned to prose, as his predecessor, the Scots poet-weaver turned American naturalist Alexander Wilson (1766–1813), had done before him. But if Wilson, in his *American Ornithology* (1808–1814), handled the format of the bird essay loosely, with his companionable narrative voice guiding the reader through an ever-changing panorama of observations, Audubon's essays in *Ornithological Biography* (1834–1839), for the most part, followed a consistent model.[25] Keyed to the plates in *The Birds of America*, his bird "biographies" are collection narratives, dramatic recreations of where and how he saw what he saw and how he approached and then got hold of the birds he desired. Their recurrent theme: violence is required to capture the birds we see represented in the plate before us or whose habits are revealed in the essay we are reading. Audubon carefully triangulates his stories—the initial encounter between him and an unsuspecting, fearful, or aggressive bird, or several birds, usually gives way to a three-way encounter, at the end of which the naturalist's and the reader's glances meet over the dead bird's body: mission accomplished. A final anatomical section (omitted in this volume), with notes about the bird's morphology, coloring, and wingspan, the length of its innards, and, starting with the third volume, the size of its egg, serves to confirm the bird's deadness.

* * *

Ocean-related selections from Audubon's *Ornithological Biography* are the centerpiece of our collection, framed by excerpts from two of Audubon's journals, which served as an aide-mémoire and a repository of raw field observations as he was writing the essays. *Audubon at Sea* maps the global reach of Audubon's oceanic imagination, from south to north, from Florida to the Carolinas to the Canadian Maritimes. Audubon never saw the Pacific; for birds such as the black-footed albatross, he had to rely on skins procured by fellow naturalists who had participated in western expeditions.

In the popular imagination, Audubon's art and science are shaped by landbirds, not waterbirds. *The Birds of America* begins with the American turkey, a bird Audubon made part of his personal seal. The original subscribers to the double elephant folio edition had to wait until plate 81 to encounter a genuine waterbird, Audubon's "Fish Hawk, or Osprey." Relishing his self-chosen role as "American Woodsman" (fig. 5), Audubon was well-equipped for stalking birds in the humid woods of the American south, his gun slung over his shoulder, carrying a paintbox and, at times, his multivolume set of Wilson's *American Ornithology*. Being

FIGURE 5. Audubon as the American woodsman. John Syme, *John James Audubon*, 1826. Oil on canvas. White House collection, Washington, DC. White House Historical Association.

on a boat in the middle of the ocean, with nothing but a few layers of wood and a captain's skill separating him from the loss of his collections or even death, was an entirely different experience. In this volume we are asking the reader to imagine this different kind of Audubon, one challenged, on a deeply existential level, by an environment where he couldn't rely on the instincts that normally made him such an effective observer and hunter of birds.[26]

In one of the sketches he inserted in *Ornithological Biography*, Audubon explores the land-sea contrast with a certain degree of irony. "The Bay of Fundy" effectively contrasts Audubon's happiness during a brief visit to a wooded island ("How often have I longed to converse with the feathered inhabitants of the forest") with the uncertainty of being on the water, encapsulated by the barely averted shipwreck Audubon witnesses. "On looking over the waters," notes Audubon after his safe return to Eastport, Maine, "and observing the dense masses of vapour that veiled the shores, we congratulated ourselves at having escaped from the Bay of Fundy." When Audubon was at sea, everything seemed larger, more dramatic, more overwhelming against a backdrop that defied conventional measurements.

Audubon had seen passenger pigeons travel in flocks so large that the sky darkened, but with seabirds, such immense numbers seemed to be the norm. They challenged his powers of perception. "I have seen not fewer than ten thousand of these birds in a single flock," he wrote about black skimmers. The sooty terns on Bird Key in Florida, when disturbed, pause for a moment in perfect silence, "as if to gather but meaning," and then rush forward, "like a huge wave breaking on a beach." Procuring specimens, with such masses of birds, often took the shape of a massacre. In the essays on waterbirds, we find very few of the one-on-one encounters that distinguish the more memorable descriptions of landbirds (for a nonlethal example, see "The Broad-winged Hawk," *OB* 1 [1831], 461–65). "Clouds of birds rise from the rock," Audubon reports in "The Eggers of Labrador," on his visit to the Murre Rocks, "and fill the air around, wheeling and screaming over their enemies. Yet thousands remain in an erect posture, each covering its single egg, the hope of both parents. The reports of several muskets loaded with heavy shot are now heard, while several dead and wounded birds fall heavily on the rock or into the water." Such parental solicitude served as a painful reminder to Audubon of the basic maleness of the world in which he moved during these expeditions, a world populated by hardened frontiersmen, hunters, sailors, and captains. Having abandoned, for prolonged periods of time, his own family so that he could pursue his art, Audubon found himself gazing wistfully after the osprey, his "Fish Hawk," as he set off to sea "to seek a favourite fish for her whom he loves."

Landbirds, overall, posed fewer problems for Audubon. He felt a clear affinity with them: if they stalked their prey, Audubon stalked them. Waterbirds, by contrast, obtain their food in ways uniquely theirs, inimitable by humans, with a machinelike determination marked by speed, efficiency, and pinpoint accuracy. Watch, for example, the oystercatcher use its bill to pry open the shells of crabs or the black skimmer insert only "its lower mandible at an angle of about 45 degrees into the water." If some of those behavioral patterns were somewhat predictable, others were certainly not. Oystercatchers in the Mid-Atlantic region, for instance, never sit on their eggs, letting the sun-warmed sand do the work of heating them, whereas in Labrador they were "found sitting as closely as any other bird." Had he not obtained specimens from both locations, he would not have thought them to be the same bird, notes Audubon, before giving us an account of how he once inserted a finger into an oystercatcher's muscular gullet, without being able to figure out "how this bird disposes of the hard particles of shells, pebbles, and other matters, with which its food is mixed."

* * *

If waterbirds were so unfathomable, Audubon had at least developed a predictable way of writing about them. A good example is his biography of the black skimmer. Audubon begins with notes about habitat ("a constant resident on all the sandy and marshy shores of our more southern States") and then creates a startling image to convey an impression of the vast numbers of these birds to be found by those who enter "the sinuous bayous intersecting the broad marshes along their coasts." Using the second-person singular, Audubon invites the reader to travel with him: "There, during the warm sunshine of the winter days, you will see thousands of Skimmers, covered as it were with their gloomy mantles, peaceably lying beside each other, and so crowded together as to present to your eye the appearance of an immense black pall accidentally spread on the sand."

In his essays, Audubon loves to capture the total effect conjured by large flocks of birds: it not only authenticates his experience but affords him a kind of bird's-eye perspective himself, allowing him to see them as a potential predator would. Distance turns into imminent capture as Audubon, the reader firmly at his side, swoops in for the kill: "Reader, judge of the deafening angry cries of such a multitude, and see them all over your head begging for mercy as it were, and earnestly urging you and your cruel sailors to retire and leave them in the peaceful charge of their young, or to settle on their lovely rounded eggs, should it rain or feel chilly." While the outcome, in this case, isn't mentioned, the existence of the finished plate leaves no doubt that the birds' pleas were ignored, as they must be, Audubon believes, in the service of science and art (and, of course, for the reader's sake).[27]

Many of the biographies of seabirds evoke the vastness of the regions they inhabit, the immense, shimmering canvas of the water and the wide canopy of the sky, traversed effortlessly by birds who are out of human reach: "How beautifully they performed their broad gyrations," writes Audubon about thousands of white pelicans he sees flying past him at the entrance of the St. Johns River, "and how matchless, after a while, was the marshalling of their files, as they flew past us!" Wishing that he and the reader be "furnished with equal powers of flight," Audubon notes, in "Common Gannet," that the birds can undertake "a journey of eighty or ninety miles without the slightest fatigue in a single hour." He is in awe of the sudden plunges into the water many seabirds perform to seize their prey: descending like meteors, they dive or dip, depending on the species, barely leaving a ripple or causing the water to foam. Birds live where humans shouldn't and survive where humans couldn't, as Audubon realizes during his 1833 trip to Labrador, "that inhospitable land," as he calls it in "The Puffin." "Stay on the deck of the Ripley by my side this clear and cold morning," he encourages the reader in "The Foolish Guillemot." "See how swiftly scuds our gallant bark, as she cuts her way through the foaming billows, now inclining to the right and again to the left." Soon it becomes clear that not all is well. Foul weather is ahead, the wind changes, the fog thickens, and the *Ripley* is tossed by furious waves: "the vessel quivers, while down along her deck violently pour the waters, rolling from side to side, seeking for a place by which they may escape." Everybody is in distress except the murres: "The sea is covered with these intrepid navigators of the deep. Over each tumultuous billow they swim unconcerned on the very spray at the bow of the vessel, and plunging as if with pleasure, up they come next moment at the rudder. Others fly around in large circles, while thousands contend with the breeze, moving directly against it in long lines, towards regions unknown to all, save themselves and some other species of sea-birds."

The alien land- and seascapes Audubon recreates tremble with the uncouth sounds of seabirds, further enhancing their strangeness: *cack*; *whip weep whip*; *cara, karew, karow*; *kee-re-kee kee*. In his plates, Audubon often represents birds with their beaks open, as he does with the female murre in Havell 218 (plate 13), leaving it to the viewers to hear

FIGURE 6. Robert Havell at sea. Robert Havell Jr., *Gulls over Rough Seas*, ca. 1830. Oil on artist's board. Courtesy of the Graham Arader Galleries.

sound where the silence of art reigns, pushing away from the experience even as he encourages them to share it with him. Consider the agitated waves Audubon included in his watercolor, which appear more sculpted and rounded in Havell's print. Surely it is no coincidence that tempest-tossed oceans had by now become a specialty of Havell's, who, prodded by his printing of *The Birds of America*, was turning into a credible painter in his own right (fig. 6).

* * *

The watercolors Audubon produced in Labrador paraded brilliantly plumed birds posing in crystalline seascapes emptied of human presence and seemingly exempt from the ravages of time. They betray little of the emotional rollercoaster this trip—recorded in the journal reprinted in this anthology's final section—entailed for him. Audubon was horrified by the destructiveness of the poachers his group encountered—rough, unthinking men hardened to the violence they unleashed when they raided the breeding grounds of birds with their clubs, oars, and guns, killing birds for bait, stealing their eggs, trampling the young. In earlier essays, Audubon had smoothly justified his lethal incursions into the lives of birds by the insights they provided for science, the benefits they brought for the reader's edification. In the Labrador essays, those explanations no longer cut it. Audubon seems almost eager to highlight how he and his men were complicit in the damage done to avian life. Thus, we see them stumbling through a landscape littered with the smelly carcasses of birds, many of them killed not by poachers but by his own party. Audubon's lyrical landscape descriptions become mere bookends to ornithological kill-fests, rendered in often excruciating detail.

Entering the harbor of the Ouapitagone Archipelago, for example, accompanied by the screams of cormorants, murres, and razorbills, Audubon perfunctorily evokes the beauties of the environment: "The mossy beds around us shone with a brilliant verdure, the lark piped its sweet notes on high, and thousands of young codfish leaped along the surface of the deep cove as if with joy. Such a harbour I had never seen before." But such delight turns out to be the prologue to slaughter. Leaving the *Ripley* at anchor, Audubon's party proceeds to an island where razorbills roost. Poking their hooked sticks into cracks in the rocks or inserting themselves into them, smashing eggs in the process, they extract the terrified birds, which then spiral right into the gunfire of the remaining men, causing Audubon to marvel at the razorbills' apparent stupidity. "Rare fun" this was for his men, who surrounded themselves with piles of dead birds, and Audubon himself even got a meal out of the experience. The birds' flesh was only "tolerable," but their eggs, the yolk a delicate pale orange, the white a pale blue, were lip-smackingly "excellent" ("The Razor-billed Auk").

Audubon's men participate in similar acts on the Murre Rocks, near Great Mecatina Harbor. Audubon's deliberate use of the second-person singular seems intended to involve the reader directly in the unsavory story that is about to unfold: "Now land," he encourages the reader as if they were right there with him on the boat and under his command, "and witness the consternation of the settlers" ("The Foolish Guillemot"). The somewhat surprising term "settler" casts the invasion of the Murre Rocks as an act of conquest, with the murres (who haven't even been mentioned yet) taking the place of the native population about to be brought into subjection. Ecocide becomes genocide, even more terrifying because it is so easy, since the adult birds readily leave their eggs and wait at a distance for the mayhem to be over. And over it is soon enough, the island turned into a landscape of death, which Audubon's men, too, are glad to abandon: "Eggs, green and white, and almost of every colour, are lying thick over the whole rock; the ordure of the birds mingled with feathers, with the refuse of half-hatched eggs partially sucked by rapacious Gulls, and with putrid or dried carcasses of Guillemots, produces an intolerable stench; and no sooner are all your baskets filled with eggs, than you are glad to abandon the isle to its proper owners." Note the reference to "proper owners," which appears to brand the excursion as an illicit act. Humans, in Audubon's Labrador essays, are no longer observers but active participants in the destruction of avian lives.

With his reference to the "rapacious gulls," Audubon fleetingly reminds us that birds are just as likely to become another bird's food as they are to be killed by the likes of him. At the approach of the black-backed gull, the largest of North American gulls, fish sink deeper into the water. As it happens, that tyrant of the open seas is particularly adept at murdering murres. The black-backed gull has all the markings of the villain; it kills indiscriminately and then eats to excess. Deaf to the desperate pleas of the parents, it delights in feeding on the eggs of other birds and their young. "Neither the cries of the parents, nor all their attempts to drive the plunderer away, can induce him to desist." A particular delicacy are the corpses of whales drifting in the sea.

If one, for the moment, ignores that last, unsettling detail, the black-backed gull could be seen as a kind of unsavory alter ego for Audubon, his avian equivalent, down to the "great size" and the "robust constitution" (Audubon was, or liked to think of himself as, tall and athletic).[28] Perhaps not unexpectedly, a few young gulls Audubon kept on the *Ripley* as pets quickly adjusted to life on board, where they ate nonstop and Audubon became "much attached" to them.

Yet Audubon himself had already undermined this attempt to use the alleged vileness of birds as a cover for his own killings. Havell 241 (plate 14), drawn a year before he traveled to Labrador, shows a black-backed gull collapsed on the ground, crumpled into a heap with one wing still pointed up in the air, its body, felled by a gunman's bullet, unnaturally twisted, blood oozing from the side, its beak open in agony, emitting a final, silent scream: a bitter parody of the rapid plunge after prey that bird likes to perform, which Audubon admiringly describes in his accompanying essay. This predator has become the ornithologist's prey. The anatomical detail, a severed foot included in the upper right corner, grimly foreshadows the bird's postmortem dismemberment. When confronted by humans, even the black-backed gull doesn't have a prayer.

Within the parameters of the violence Audubon evoked in his earlier essays, the killing sprees in Audubon's Labrador essays are *sui generis*. Labrador clarified for Audubon what he had always known but only now fully understood: birds are a provocation. They are like us and tantalizingly unlike us; they bring out the best in us and the worst. And if we can shoot them, that does not mean we can easily paint them. Take the loon, "a most difficult bird to imitate" (journal, July 9), which Audubon painted in Labrador as cold water dripped from the *Ripley*'s skylight right onto his sheet, as if the bird's natural element were spilling onto his picture, too. If Labrador froze Audubon's paintings, it bloodied his prose. According to novelist Katherine Govier, Audubon left Labrador "a mourner of birds."[29] But he also left it a mourner of himself, a mourner of the naturalist he once was. If previously he had always been able to tell himself that he killed birds so he could make them come alive again in his art, Audubon now found himself confronted with birds that were just dead. Surely it wasn't a coincidence that the only image in Audubon's oeuvre that shows a dead bird—a dead bird that's not another bird's meal but simply dead—originated in Labrador, the "Esquimaux Curlew" (Havell 208). He had managed to shoot seven of these curlews himself but, to his surprise, found he couldn't draw them properly. He finally settled for a mournful image, with the male bird, perched on a mossy mound, casting a melancholy glance at his prostrate dead mate on the ground. With the onset of death, her colors are beginning to fade—a nightmare for Audubon the painter and the reason he shunned stuffed birds and drew, when possible, from freshly killed specimens. Eskimo curlews were still plentiful then but are now believed to be extinct; Audubon's composition, in its revelatory intimacy, suggests he had foreseen their future. This was the visual equivalent to the warning expressed in his Labrador journal that, if humans didn't stop what they were doing there, soon all the "fish, and game, and birds" would be gone and nature would be "left alone like an old worn-out field" (July 21).

* * *

Audubon left us memorable accounts of birds that are no longer around, among them the Eskimo curlew and the Labrador duck. But he was more than a documentarian of loss. Charles Darwin crossed paths with Audubon in December 1826, when the wild-looking American naturalist with his flowing locks delivered "some interesting discourses on the habits of N. American birds."[30] If Audubon didn't make a big impression on Darwin at the time, he later became one of his primary sources. As Gerald Weissmann has demonstrated, Darwin cites Audubon more frequently than almost any other American or British naturalist—over two dozen times in *The Descent of Man* alone. When Darwin was in the process of formulating his theory of natural selection, it was Audubon's representation of a waterbird that caught his attention. Audubon's "Frigate Pelican" (magnificent frigatebird, plate 3; Havell 271) is one of the most dramatic in *The Birds of America*, though it's also one of the most starkly simplified: it shows an adult male bird descending upon prey, beak open, a dark, angular, menacing shape, deadly as the warship after which it was named, a true vulture of the sea. Audubon had observed them at Indian Key and was impressed by their sheer badness—they were, he wrote, "lazy, tyrannical, and rapacious, domineering over birds weaker than themselves, and devouring the young of every species." But watch them in action, and you can't help but think their "power of flight . . . superior to that of perhaps any other bird." Audubon related in awe how he saw such a frigatebird, in full flight, fight others for a fish it had snatched, inadvertently dropping it, then catching it again to swallow it greedily, all against the "deep green" canvas of the sea below.[31]

What really interested Audubon were the bird's pectinate claws, that is, claws covered with a comblike skin perfectly adapted to scratching insects from any part of the bird's body that "cannot be reached by the bill." The matter was so important to Audubon that he included representations of the bird's feet in the plate. They show distinctly the remnants of webs, typical of waterbirds. In his essay, Audubon affirmed that he had indeed seen frigatebirds sitting on the water, an observation that Darwin quoted, with some skepticism, in *The Origin of Species*: "no one but Audubon has seen the frigate bird, which has all its four toes webbed, alight on the water." That behavior is indeed rare: while frigatebirds are pelagic and can stay aloft over the ocean even for months, their feathers are not waterproof, and they definitely cannot swim or sit on the water, except briefly. But Audubon was right to focus on the peculiar appearance of the feet, which gave Darwin a detail useful for his theory. For natural selection to happen, incremental structural changes are necessary that give some organic beings advantages over others. In the universal struggle for survival, the frigatebird, a ferocious killing machine, has become so wonderfully adapted that it gets the best of both worlds—while living on land, it is still able to obtain its food from the water, without ever needing to land on it, with its webbed feet, now redundant, still serving as a reminder of its former existence—living proof that Darwin's theory of change by natural selection was more than just a hyped-up hypothesis.[32]

* * *

Birds, in Audubon's world, may be tender or tyrannical, prey or predator, murres or frigatebirds. Or, when humans enter the picture, they may be both, as his plate of the black-backed gull so vividly illustrates. But then there are those who, irritatingly, refuse to be categorized at all by simply rendering themselves unavailable. "American Flamingo" (plate 5; Havell 431) is one of Audubon's most famous plates and certainly one of the most expensive ones today. Ironically, it's also one of a handful that were not drawn from life. There is a reason: Audubon never was able to procure a specimen to serve as a model. This must have been particularly galling since he had, on several occasions, expressed his affinity for these birds. The flamingo is a large bird—five feet tall—a fact that would not have been lost on Audubon. It is possible that he saw something of himself in these birds' outsize, exotic bodies, so large that, in the watercolor and the print, he was forced to show the bird with its neck bent down as it strides past us—an opportunity also to represent its characteristic gait.

Although he must have observed it, Audubon does not represent the flamingo's characteristic upside-down feeding pose, perhaps in order not to disrupt the immediate eye contact between the bird and the viewer.[33]

In the essay accompanying the plate, Audubon speaks of his eagerness to procure a flamingo specimen for his art and of the many attempts that failed, beginning with the first time he saw a flock of the birds near Indian Key, on March 7, 1832, when the printing of *The Birds of America* was already well under way. He was so affected by the sight that, writing about it several years later, he lapses into poetic rapture: "It was on the afternoon of one of those sultry days which, in that portion of the country, exhibit towards evening the most glorious effulgence that can be conceived. The sun, now far advanced toward the horizon, still shone with full splendour, the ocean around glittered in its quiet beauty, and the light fleecy clouds that here and there spotted the heavens, seemed flakes of snow margined with gold. Our bark was propelled almost as if by magic, for scarcely was a ripple raised by her bows as we moved in silence." Had these birds taken him all the way back to his tropical island childhood?

Audubon's attempt at fanciful writing—some of which might also be the result of the ministrations of William MacGillivray, Audubon's Scottish editor—delivers the overture to the dramatic arrival of the birds, who move with balletic precision, "with well-spread wings, outstretched necks, and long legs directed backwards." But the deliberate overwriting creates an ironic framework for Audubon's repeated failure to obtain even a single specimen. For even as he followed the coveted birds with his eyes, "watching as it were every beat of their wings," while every man in his party "stowed away out of sight and our gunners in readiness," even as the birds came within a hundred and fifty yards of him, they remained provocatively out of reach: the bird in charge ("their chief"), anticipating the danger, abruptly turned, with the entire flock following. A second encounter proved equally disappointing: "alas! the Flamingoes were all, as I suppose, very old and experienced birds, . . . for on turning round the lower end of the Key, they spied our boat again, sailed away without flapping their wings." And a final confrontation, now in Key West, didn't lift his spirits either: observing a single flamingo cruising toward the mangrove copse where he was hiding, Audubon fired away, with no effect other than altering the bird's course. Chagrined, Audubon dispatched a letter to his most reliable specimen supplier, Dr. Bachman in Charleston, South Carolina, berating him for not being able to provide him with a flamingo either: "Indeed it will prove a curiosity to World of Science," wrote Audubon, "when that world will Know that John Bachman D D himself, . . . and about one half of a hundred persons besides have not been able to send me even a *Stuffed* Specimen in time for my Publication—So it is however and I drop the subject."[34] The specimens he ended up using for the drawing he made in London in 1838 were preserved skins sent to him from Cuba.[35] The flamingos had won—eluding their pursuer's grasp, they leave Audubon and the reader staring at each other in mutual disappointment.

While the American flamingo, thanks to its large habitat range, is a species of "least concern," its numbers in Haiti have dramatically decreased, the result of human disturbance, habitat degradation, and exploitation for trade. The last nesting colony there was seen in 1928.[36] The finished plate in Audubon's *The Birds of America*, based on a watercolor representation of a dead bird, is a fantasy; yet, given what is the inevitable fate of waterbirds in the real world, it is a welcome one. It shows Robert Havell, who had likely never seen a flamingo in the wild,[37] giving free rein to his imagination, adding flamingo after flamingo in the background, the watery landscape receding into the distance to where we might imagine it all began, where, far away, the island of Audubon's birth is still beckoning.

Notes

1. There are several accounts of the incident, with varying details, including one in Elizabeth Kolbert's *The Sixth Extinction: An Unnatural History* (New York: Holt, 2004), 65–67. Mine follows Errol Fuller, *The Great Auk: The Extinction of the Original Penguin* (Charlestown, MA: Bunker Hill, 2003), 36–37. A richly imagined version of the scene provides the opening to Peter Matthiessen's *Wildlife in America* (New York: Viking, 1959), 20–21.

2. Audubon recounts Havell's story in "Great Auk," in part II of this volume. The stuffed great auk he saw is now housed at the Royal Ontario Museum in Canada, behind double-pane glass, the only such specimen displayed in Canada. For the extraordinary history of that specimen, see http://omeka.tplcs.ca/virtual-exhibits/items/show/1563; Fuller, *Great Auk*, 154–60.

3. See William A. Montevecchi, H. Chaffey, and C. Burke, "Hunting for Security: Changes in the Exploitation of Marine Birds in Newfoundland and Labrador," in *Resetting the Kitchen Table: Food Security, Culture, Health, and Resilience in Coastal Communities*, ed. Christopher Parrish et al. (New York: Nova, 2007), 99–114, esp. 103–4.

4. See Jeremy Hance, "After 60 Million Years of Extreme Living, Seabirds Are Crashing," *Guardian*, September 22, 2015. See Michelle Paleczny, Edd Hammill, Vassiliki Karpouzi, and Daniel Pauly, "Population Trend of the World's Monitored Seabirds, 1950–2010," *PLOS ONE* 10, no. 6 (2015): e0129342.

5. John Croxall, Stuart H. M. Butchart, Ben Lascelles, Alisa J. Stattersfield, Ben Sullivan, Andy Symes, and Phil Taylor, "Seabird Conservation Status, Threats and Priority Actions: A Global Assessment," *Bird Conservation International* 22, no. 1 (2012): 1–34.

6. Lauren Roman, Britta Denise Hardesty, Mark A. Hindell, and Chris Wilcox, "A Quantitative Analysis Linking Seabird Mortality and Marine Debris Ingestion," *Scientific Reports* 9, no. 3202 (2019), https://doi.org/10.1038/s41598-018-36585-9.

7. Audubon, "Myself," in *John James Audubon, Writings and Drawings*, ed. Christoph Irmscher (New York: Library of America, 1999), 765.

8. Audubon's naturalization papers identify his birthplace as "San Domingue"; his father and his adoptive mother, in their wills, call him a "Créole de Saint Domingue," and his correct age was given on the rolls during his brief stint in naval school. See Alice Ford, *John James Audubon: A Biography*, 2nd ed. (New York: Abbeville, 1988), 38, 483–84, 486. For Capitaine Audubon's service record, see Ford, 468–69. The origin of Audubon's mother has been the source of much speculation, though it is in fact well-documented; see Chris Grégoire, "Jeanne Rabine et le mystère Audubon," *303: Arts, recherches, créations*, 82 (2004): 9. Jeanne and her seven siblings were born in Les Touches, diocese of Nantes, to the same parents, who spelled their last name "Rabine"; the variation "Rabin," the name given to Audubon at his birth to cover up his illegitimacy, reflects the fluidity of surname spellings in late eighteenth- and nineteenth-century France; Roberta J. M. Olson, personal communication, August 7, 2020. Audubon's descent is the subject of an essay by Roberta J. M. Olson, "Hiding in Plain Sight: New Evidence Regarding the Birth and Pseudonyms of John James Audubon," *Bulletin of the Museum of Comparative Zoology* 163, no. 4 (2021): 129–50, which contains several new revelations and which the editors were fortunate to see in manuscript. Olson, offering new archival evidence, definitively identifies Jeanne as Audubon's mother.

9. For more on Audubon's continuing relationship with Rose Bouffard, see Ford, *Audubon*, 62–63. On December 16, 1805, for example, Audubon was a witness at Rose's wedding in Couëron, France, to Gabriel Loyen Du Puigaudeau (see Ford, 479). Audubon also named one of his daughters, Rose Audubon (1819–1820), after her (see "Myself," in *Writings*, 791).

10. See Francis Hobart Herrick, "Audubon and the Dauphin," *Auk* 54, no. 4 (October 1837): 476–99.

11. See Christoph Irmscher, "Audubon's Haiti," *Public Domain Review*, March 6, 2019, http://publicomainreview.org/essay/audubons-haiti.

12. Gregory Nobles, *John James Audubon: The Nature of the American Woodsman* (Philadelphia: University of Pennsylvania Press, 2017), 17–18.

13. See Audubon, "My Style of Drawing Birds," in *Writings*, 760.

14. Francis James Dallett, "Citizen Audubon: A Documentary Discovery," *Princeton University Library Chronicle* 21, nos. 1–2 (Autumn 1959–Winter 1960): 89–93.

15. Apparently, the early colonists fancied that the ani's song sounded as if it were asking for *un petit bout de petun*, "a little roll of tobacco." Georges Louis Leclerc, comte de Buffon, *Histoire naturelle des oiseux* (Paris: Imprimerie Royale, 1780), 12:87.

16. Charles-Lucien Bonaparte, *American Ornithology; or the Natural History of Birds Inhabiting the United States, Not Given by Wilson* (Philadelphia: Mitchell, 1825), 1:40. Audubon's copy (referenced here) is held by the Audubon Museum, Henderson, KY. An enthusiastic ornithologist, Bonaparte, second Prince of Canino and Musignano (1803–1857) and nephew of Napoleon I, had unsuccessfully lobbied for Audubon's admission to the Academy of Natural Sciences.

17. David F. Marley, *Pirates of the Americas* (Santa Barbara: ABC-Clio, 2010), 1:285–89.

18. On Jean Audubon's captivity, see Francis Hobart Herrick, *Audubon the Naturalist: A History of His Life and Times*, 2nd ed., 2 vols. (1938; New York: Dover, 1968), 1:28–29. Ford offers the most detailed reconstruction of Jean Audubon's life available (*Audubon*, 14–20).

19. C. L. R. James, *The Black Jacobins: Toussaint L'Ouverture and the San Domingo Revolution*, 2nd ed. (1963; New York: Vintage, 1989), ix, 10; Pooja Bhatia, "The End of the Plantocracy," *London Review of Books* 42, no. 22 (November 19, 2020): 21.

20. Robert Stein, "Measuring the French Slave Trade, 1713–1792/3," *Journal of African History* 19, no. 4 (1978): 515–21.

21. On Sanson, see Herrick, *Audubon the Naturalist*, 2:314–25.

22. On the date for leaving Haiti, see Richard Rhodes, *John James Audubon: The Making of an American* (New York: Knopf, 2004), 21; Roberta J. M. Olson, "A Biographical Sketch of an American Icon," in Olson, *Audubon's Aviary* (New York: New York Historical Society/Rizzoli, 2012), 17–38, esp. 17–18. For greater detail than this introduction can offer regarding Audubon's life, readers are encouraged to consult Olson's succinct overview as well as her state-of-the-art chronology (432–35).

23. James, *Black Jacobins*, 8.

24. See Ford, *Audubon*, 36–37; Olson, "Biographical Sketch," 36n4.

25. For an emphatic defense of Wilson's "scientifically informed animal protectionist poetry," see Thomas Doran, "Alexander Wilson's 'Transcript from Living Nature': Biocentric Anthropomorphism and Animal Protectionist Poetics," *ISLE* 27, no. 1 (Winter 2020): 83–105. For a more general comparison of Wilson and Audubon, also in terms of their artistic differences, see Christoph Irmscher, *The Poetics of Natural History*, rev. ed., with a foreword and photographs by Rosamond Purcell (New Brunswick, NJ: Rutgers University Press, 2019), 204–7.

26. Audubon's personal set of Wilson's *American Ornithology*, with his notes, is now at the Audubon Museum, Henderson, KY.

27. For more on Audubon as a writer, see Irmscher, *Poetics*, 207–29.

28. On Audubon's boasts about his size, see Peter Logan, *Audubon: America's Greatest Naturalist and His Voyage of Discovery to Labrador* (San Francisco: Ashbryn Press, 2016), 450n11. Audubon's 1830 passport gives his height as 5 feet, 8½ inches (Dallett, "Citizen Audubon," 93).

29. Katherine Govier, *Creation* (Toronto: Random House, 2002), 25. For more on this topic, see Christoph Irmscher, "Audubon Goes North," in *Cultural Circulation: Dialogues between Canada and the American South*, ed. Waldemar Zacharasiewicz and Christoph Irmscher (Vienna: Austrian Academy of Sciences, 2013), 77–97, esp. 91–92.

30. *The Autobiography of Charles Darwin, 1809–1882*, ed. Nora Barlow (1958; New York: Norton, 1969), 51; Brian Desmond and James Moore, *Darwin* (New York: Norton, 1991), 37.

31. Gerald Weissmann, "Darwin's Audubon," in Weissmann, *Darwin's Audubon: Science and the Liberal Imagination. New and Selected Essays* (1998; Cambridge: Perseus, 2001), 9–24. Darwin's annotated copy of *Ornithological Biography* is in the Darwin Library, Cambridge University Library, and online at the Biodiversity Heritage Library, www.biodiversitylibrary.org/collection/darwinlibrary.

32. Charles Darwin, *On the Origin of Species by Means of Natural Selection; or, The Preservation of Favoured Races in the Struggle for Life* (London: Murray, 1859), 159.

33. See Stephen Jay Gould, "The Flamingo's Smile," in Gould, *The Flamingo's Smile: Reflections in Natural History* (1985; New York: Norton, 1987), 23–39.

34. Audubon to John Bachman, April 14, 1838, in *Writings*, 848–49. "D D" refers to the honorary Doctor of Divinity that Pennsylvania College conferred upon Bachman in 1835.

35. The flamingo skins were provided by Jean Chartrand of the coffee (later, sugar) plantation El Labirintero in Cuba in or around 1838. See the notes on "American Flamingo" and Olson, *Audubon's Aviary*, 364.

36. José A. Ottenwalder, Charles A. Woods, Galen B. Rathburn, and John B. Thorbjarnarson, "Status of the Greater Flamingo in Haiti," *Colonial Waterbirds* 13, no. 2 (1990): 115–23. Note that the American flamingo (*Phoenicopterus ruber*) was once considered the same species as the Old World greater flamingo (*Phoenicopterus roseus*), found in Africa, Asia, and parts of southern Europe.

37. Which is not to say that he couldn't have encountered them as exotic pets or in a menagerie. Sir Robert Walpole's pet flamingo warmed itself by the kitchen fire; see Christopher Plumb, *The Georgian Menagerie: Exotic Animals in Eighteenth-Century London* (London: Bloomsbury, 2015), 46.

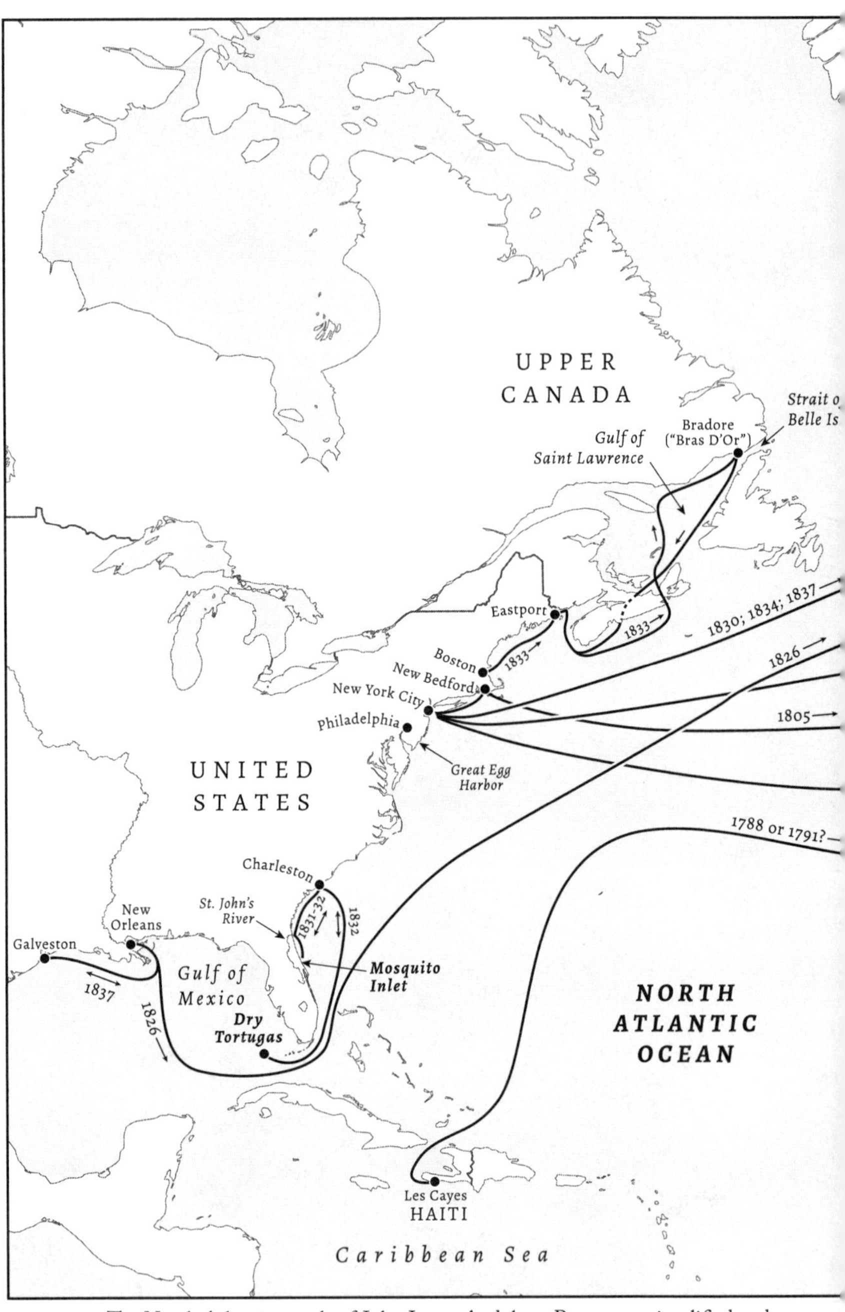

FIGURE 7. The North Atlantic travels of John James Audubon. Routes are simplified and approximated. Map does not include several of Audubon's coastal passages along the US East Coast and in Europe. Erin Greb Cartography.

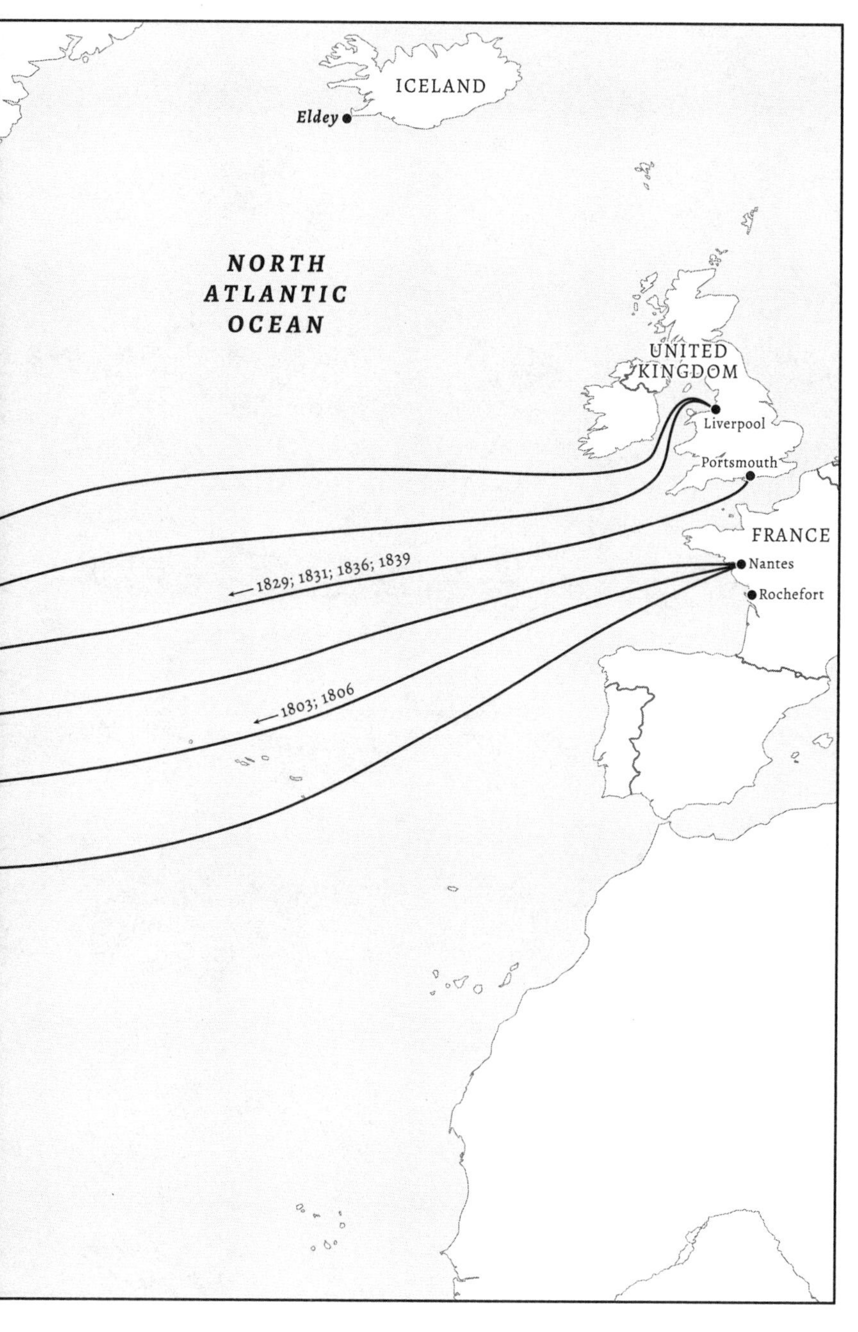

ICELAND
Eldey
NORTH
ATLANTIC
OCEAN
UNITED
KINGDOM
Liverpool
Portsmouth
FRANCE
Nantes
Rochefort
1829; 1831; 1836; 1839
1803; 1806

I

Journal of a Sea Voyage from New Orleans to Liverpool aboard the *Delos* (1826)

Early in the morning of April 26, 1826, Audubon left his wife, Lucy (fig. 8), and his two sons, sixteen-year-old Victor Gifford and thirteen-year-old John Woodhouse, at their home in St. Francisville, Louisiana, and traveled to New Orleans, where he boarded the Liverpool-bound brig *Delos*, laden with 924 bales of cotton, harvested and no doubt loaded by enslaved people. He would not see his family again for three years and eight months. At age forty-one, Audubon had reached a point of no return in his career: if his madcap plan to publish life-size engravings of all the birds of America, and thus to trump his predecessor Alexander Wilson, was to succeed, then England, well known for her support of the arts, was his last hope.

Audubon's journals served various purposes: they were field notes, reports to the family he had left back home, and an opportunity for self-analysis. "Journal of a Sea Voyage" (often simply called the 1826 Journal) is different in that Audubon wrote much of it to let his wife participate, vicariously, in his activities while he was abroad, as a kind of compensation for the sacrifices she was making so that he could chase his dreams (in Audubon's absence, Lucy continued to teach the daughters of wealthy plantation owners). The journal begins on April 26, with his departure from New Orleans, and ends with an upbeat entry written seven months

FIGURE 8. Lucy Audubon in old age. Unfinished, undated, and unsigned oil painting, found underneath an oil painting of an American bald eagle by John James Audubon. Lucy's portrait has been attributed by the family to John James Audubon, but Lucy's presumptive age and the style of the work point to John Woodhouse Audubon as the likely creator. Courtesy of the Audubon Museum, Henderson, KY.

later, on December 31, in Edinburgh. Audubon had accomplished much in the intervening months: his drawings had been displayed at the Royal Institution in Liverpool, the Manchester Exchange, and the Royal Institution in Edinburgh, and he had met and impressed important people, among them William H. Lizars (1788–1859), who would engrave the first ten plates of Audubon's *The Birds of America*. Getting ready to send the completed journal back to Lucy, Audubon felt he had every right to expect that she would be a sympathetic reader of his "heartfelt sentiments" (December 31, 1826; *Writings*, 192). In the months before, his journal had been his "faithfull uncomplaining friend" ("Journal of a Sea Voyage," Field Museum ms., July 17, 1826), an ideal listener, withholding judgment no matter what he had been up to, and he now expected Lucy to play a similar role.[1]

The excerpts that follow focus on the segments of Audubon's journal that deal with his experience of the Atlantic and that, at first blush, seem most like the field notes he was used to keeping. Audubon wrote these entries onboard as, despite the frequently uncomfortable motions of the ship (an "intended insult" on his entire system; July 15), he kept a sharp eye trained on the animal and human life around him. While he was frequently bored, he certainly wasn't idle: during his sixty-four days at sea, Audubon saw, caught, and dissected sharks, dolphins, mahi-mahi, and rudderfish. He saw and occasionally caught, drew, and dissected petrels, noddies, boobies, and frigatebirds. And he paid close attention to what happened onboard, adding finely executed sketches of the captain and his crew.

In "Journal of a Sea Voyage," Audubon first begins to experience himself as a writer. He had been keeping field notes for years. The notes he took in 1820–1821, when he traveled by flatboat down the Mississippi River to New Orleans, where he worked hard on becoming a painter, are saturated with fresh impressions of his environment, original observations on bird behavior, and quick sketches of the people he encountered. The journal he began on the *Delos* was different. The unavoidable tedium of a sea voyage ensured that writing became more than a means to an end. The mind-numbing sameness of his watery environment, the uniformity of the shipboard routine, prompted Audubon to turn inward and to write even when he had nothing to say, "scarce any new Incidents to relate." No longer bothered by his incomplete grasp of English grammar, he lets his words take him where they may, experimenting with increasingly complicated imagery: "The day past as I conceive One spent by a General who has Lost a Great advantage over an Ennemy," he complains on July 4, missing home and the noisy cheers associated with that holiday. If Audubon is a frustrated general, though, he is surrounded by rather lackluster troops: "My Compagnon passengers Lay strewed about the Deck and on the Cotton Bales, basking like Crocodiles during all the Intervals granted to the Sun to peep at them through the Smoacky heaziness that accompanied us" (July 9). The comparison undercuts the grandiosity of the military metaphor: no war has been lost; there's simply nothing for the passengers on a transatlantic voyage to do, and, from the perspective of sheer creature comforts, perhaps it is preferable to be a crocodile slumbering through a hazy day than a moping pretend general. Against that all-pervasive mist, even the sun, confined to intermittent glances, proves powerless.

Audubon's attention next turns to the seabirds—and what a contrast they are to the sluggish humans: "the Waves moved Magestically and thousands of Large Petrells displayed their elegant aerial Movements to Me—how much I envied their power of Flights to enable me to be here, there and all over the Globe comparatively Speaking in a Moment—throwing themselves Edge ways against the Breese as if a well sharpen[d] arrow just with the Strength and grace of One Sprung from the Bow of an Appollon." As if eager to prove his erudition, Audubon tacks a classical reference onto the end of the passage. And yet, that simile of Apollon's (single) bow seems jarring and even absurd when applied to an army of little seabirds: try to imagine thousands of little arrows hurtling back and forth across the surface of the ocean. But Audubon is thinking as an artist here: there is no adequate way of describing this spectacle of the dancing petrels, other than by acknowledging how utterly different the lives of such birds, unaffected by weather, heat, and boredom, are from those of idle, metaphor-making humans.

"Ah my Dear what strange incidents happen at Sea" (July 15). Just a few weeks into his journal, Audubon is no longer addressing Lucy only; his writing has become a much bigger thing—a tool for exploring the relationship between human observer and nonhuman environment that is nowhere stranger than on the high seas. And by far the strangest incidents are those that remind Audubon of the inevitable gap—one that no amount of scientific ambition can bridge—between him and that vast, teeming natural world out there that, like Melville's white whale, just wants to live—and to be left alone.

Take the human-size dolphin that the men drag out of the water and then leave writhing on the deck, where it flaps and groans before it dies. When Audubon cuts it open eight hours later, its intestines are still warm! Equally tenacious and unwilling to die is the baby shark whose head, severed from the body, appears to swim off on its own (April 26), an uncanny anticipation of Melville's later observation about the vitality that seems to reside in the shark's "very joints and bones, after what might be called the individual life had departed."[2] A brown noddy, snagged by the mate of the *Delos* and kept alive so that Audubon could draw it, offers passive resistance, remaining "Dull Looking and silent" as it is made to sit for its portrait until it, too, is ready for Audubon's knife ("the heart Large for the Bird"; June 22, fig. 15).

Although "Journal of a Sea Voyage" wasn't written for us, we feel we are sitting next to Audubon looking at that doomed bird. We even feel the dampness of the paper as we turn the page. And, most importantly, we hear his voice—Audubon's misspellings allow us to imagine his accent, the French language that always hovers in the back of his mind and causes his hand to write "anstant" instead of "instant" or, since the French *h* is silent, to omit it where it should occur and insert it where it shouldn't, turning, for example, the nautical hailings "Brig ho!" and "Ship hi!" into "Brig Oh! and Ship I!" (July 15). Audubon's foreignness liberated him from too precise a regard for his adopted language, allowing him to bend it to his needs, to let the words flow on the page unrestrainedly, the way his feelings did. In this journal, we will not find what the Romantics called "emotion recollected in tranquility." Instead, "Journal of a Sea Voyage" tells us plainly what kind of a man Audubon was: passionate, outrageous, salty, vain, and brutal, despondent, vulnerable, sentimental, self-ironical, and tender.[3]

The bound "Journal of a Sea Voyage," now held by the Field Museum, measures 12⅛ inches by 7¾ inches. It is 438 pages long, including the front and back endpapers (four pages) and six blank pages preceding the beginning of the journal, and contains twenty finely executed illustrations in ink and pencil, of which fourteen are full page and six on part of a page (one illustration is on the back paste-down). Twelve of these were made during the sea voyage, and nine are reproduced here. Among the extant Audubon journals, this manuscript is without a doubt the most consistently accomplished and the best written; it is also, from a purely physical point of view, the most beautiful (fig. 9).

Audubon never intended to publish his journal. But as with his other field notes, he went back to it when he needed material for his essays or narrative episodes. "A Long Calm at Sea," in part II of this anthology, offers a good example, incorporating the journal's description of the mahi-mahi that "glided by the side of the Vessel [the *Delos* in the Gulf of Mexico] like burnished Gold" into a new pleasing, atmospherically rich narrative.

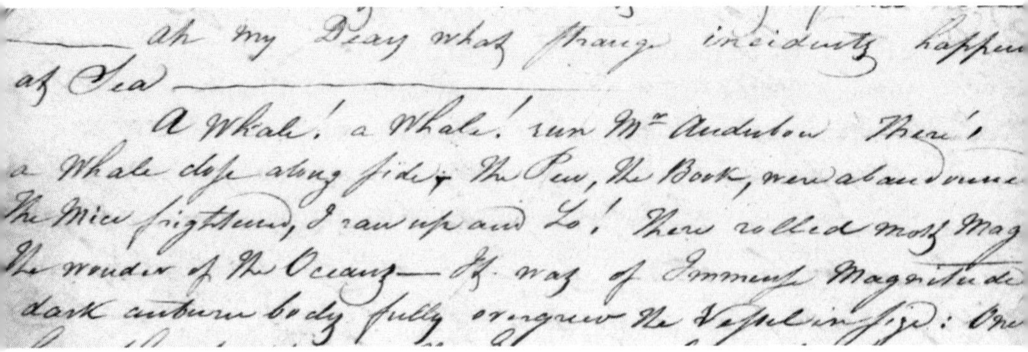

FIGURE 9. Detail from July 15, 1826, journal entry aboard the *Delos*, commenting on the captain's flatulence and then seeing a whale, in Audubon, "Journal of a Sea Voyage." Courtesy of the Field Museum, Chicago.

Audubon did not prize artistic originality over perfection of form. None of the drawings of birds that he had made in the field, with whatever was handy at the time—gouache, graphite, pencil, egg white, even his own saliva—were meant for public display (that was reserved for the engravings in *The Birds of America*). What seems charming, even revelatory, to the viewer of the original paintings, now held by the New-York Historical Society, poses problems for the reader of the original journal. "Journal of a Sea Voyage" presents enormous challenges especially to the editor—one might find three different versions of the same word ("Tail," "tail," "tale") within the same page or two. The first two editors of this text, Audubon's granddaughter Maria Rebecca Audubon (1843–1925) and biographer Alice Ford (1906–1997), didn't even attempt to be faithful to what they found. While Maria Audubon deleted or rewrote what did not satisfy her own Victorian standards of respectability, Alice Ford purified the writing itself.[4] But the beauty of this two-centuries-old manuscript, written with quills and iron pens onboard a rolling ship, is precisely that it is not pure, that it abounds in ambiguities, that it is often impossible to tell a comma from a period or an uppercase letter from a lowercase one. The journal's most recent editor, Daniel Patterson, states that, faced with "amorphous" textual evidence, he sometimes had to settle for the solution that was "more helpful in that place."[5] In this partial transcription, we have tried to preserve, as much as possible, Audubon's helter-skelter and unhelpful spellings, even the often arbitrary paragraph divisions, the capitals at the beginning of a paragraph, and periods in the middle of the sentence. These ambiguities are part of the deal, part of that journal's blistering intensity, written with, to use one of Audubon's favorite metaphors for the motions of birds, "the swiftness of thought."[6]

Notes

1. Information provided by Heidi L. Taylor-Caudill, curator, Audubon Museum, Henderson, KY.

2. Herman Melville, "The Shark Massacre," in *Moby-Dick; or, The Whale*, ed. Harrison Hayford, Hershel Parker, and G. Thomas Tanselle (Evanston, IL: Northwestern University Press/Newberry Library, 1988), 302.

3. On Audubon's "weird English," see Christoph Irmscher, "November 27, 1820: Landscape with Birds," in *A New Literary History of America*, ed. Greil Marcus and Werner Sollors (Cambridge, MA: Belknap, 2009), 154–60. On Romantic "emotion recollected," see William Wordsworth's preface to the second edition of *Lyrical Ballads* (1800).

4. For examples of their editorial interventions, see Christoph Irmscher, "Audubon the Writer," http://www.auduborroyaloctavos.com/SITE/pages/Irmscher.html.

5. See Daniel Patterson, ed., *John James Audubon's Journal of 1826: The Voyage to* The Birds of America (Lincoln: University of Nebraska Press, 2011), lvi.

6. See Christoph Irmscher, *The Poetics of Natural History*, rev. ed. (New Brunswick, NJ: Rutgers University Press, 2019), 215. In our selection, the metaphor occurs in "The Frigate Pelican" and "The Puffin." For other examples, see "The White-headed Eagle" and "The Ruffed Grouse," *OB* 1 (1831), 163, 218; "The American Sparrow-Hawk," *OB* 2 (1834), 247; "The Canada Goose," *OB* 3 (1835), 14; "Buffel-headed Duck," *OB* 4 (1838), 217.

Journal of a Sea Voyage from New Orleans to Liverpool aboard the Delos *(1826)*

26 APRIL 1826—

I Left My Beloved Wife Lucy Audubon and My Son John Woodhouse on Tuesday afternoon the 26th April, bound to England. remained at Doct^r Pope at St Francisville untill Wednesday 4 o'clock P.M.: in the Steam Boat Red River Capt^e Kimble—having for Compagnons Messrs D. Hall & John Holiday—reached New Orleans Thursday 27th at 12—Visited Many Vessels for My Passage and concluded to go in the Ship Delos of Kennebunk Capt^e Joseph Hatch bound to Liverpool, Loaded with Cotton entirely—[1]

[. . .]

On the 17th May my Baggage was put on Board—I had written 2 Letters to My Wife One to My Son Victor to whom I sent as present My Pencil Case with a handsome Knife—and also to Charles Bonaparte, apprising him of the Box of Bird Skins forward^d to him through Mr Currell—[2]

The Steam Boat Hercules came along side at 7 P.M. and in 10 hours put the Delos to sea—I wrote from her another letter to Lucy and in few Minutes found Myself severely afflicted with sea Sickness = This lasted however but a Short time, remaining on Deck Constantly, eating and Drinking without Inclination and forcing Myself to Exercise constantly—We Calculated our day of Departure from the 18th May at 12 o'clock when we first made an Observation—[3]

We are now the 27th and having nought else to do I put down the little incidents that have taken place between these two Dates—

The weather has generally being fair with light Winds and the first object that had any weight like diverting my Ideas from the objects left behind [me] Was the number of Beautifull Dolphins that glided by the side of the Vessel like burnished Gold during Day and bright meteors by night—Our Captᵉ and Mates proved all expert at alluring them with baited Hooks or dexterous at piercing them with a 5 prong Instrument generally called by Seamen Grains—If Hooked the Dolphin flunces desperately, slides off with all its natural Swiftness, oftentimes raises perpendicularly out of his element several feet shakes off the hook and Escapes partially hurt—if however the Dolphin is well hooked he is playᵈ about for a while Soon Drowned and hauled into the Vessel—some persons prefer pulling them in at once and are seldom successfull the great vigor with which the fish Shakes sideways as he assends generally being quite suficient to extricate him—they differ very much in their sizes being agreeably to age smaller or Larger, I saw some 4½ feet long but a fair average could reduce them to 3 = The Punch of all we caught contained more or Less Small fishes of various Species amongst which the flying fish is prevalint—the latter is apparently their congenial food, and is well adapted to exercise their phisical Powers—their flesh is firm, perhaps rather dry yet quite acceptable at Sea—Dolphins move in Compainies of 4 or 5 and sometimes of 20 or more; chase the flying fish that with astonishing rapidity after having avoided his Sharp pursuer a while in the water, emerges and goes through the air with the swiftness of an Arrow sometimes in a straight course and sometimes deviating by forming part of a Circle, yet frequently the whole is unavailing The Dolphin raises out of the sea in bunces of 10, 15 or 20 feet and so rapidly moves toward his pray that oftentimes the little fish just falls to be swallowed by his antagonist—[4]

You must not suppose that the Dolphin can however move through the seas without risk or danger to himself—he has as well as others, Violant and powerfull Ennemies—one is the *Ballocuda* in Shape much like a Pike growing sometimes to a Large size [fig. 10]—One of these Cut upward of a foot in length of the Tail of a Dolphin as if done With an ax as this Latter made for a Baited Hook—and I may say that We about devided the Bounty—there is a degree of Simpathy existing betwin Dolphins quite remarkable, the moment one of them is hooked or Grained, all those in company Imediately make up towards him and remains thus untill the unfortunate one is hoisted and generally then all move off and seldom will bite = when small and in large Scools they then bite and are caught perhaps to the last—the skin of these Fish is a tissue of Small scales softer in their substance than generally seen in scally fishes of such size, the skin is tough and torn off from their bodies when Cleaned =[5]

We also Caught a Porpoise about 7 feet in length this feat took place during the night, when the moon gave me a full view of all that happened—The Fish contrary to Custom Was *Grained* instead of being harpooned, but Grained in such a way and so effectually through the forehead that he was thus held and sufered to flunce and beat about the bow of the Ship, untill the very person that had secured it at first gave the Line holding the grains to our Capt[e], and slide down along the *(Bob Stays)* with a rope, then after some little time and perhaps some dificulties, The fish was secured imediatly above its tail and hoisted with that part upwards it arrived on the Deck, gave a deep groan, much alike the last from a large dying Hog, flap[d] Seferely on the deck and Died—I had never before seen one of these animals at hand and the Duck bill like snout, along with the Orisontal disposition of the tail with the body were new matters of observation—their large Black, sleek body, the Imensity of warm black blood issuing from the Wound, the Blowing apperture placed over the forehead, all attracted my Attention—I requested that it should remain untouch [*sic*] untill the next morning and this Was granted = On Opening of it, the Intestines were still Warm (say 8 hours after death) and resembled very much those of a Hog, they filled all the Inder [*sic*] Cavity; the Punch contained several *Scutle* fish partly decayed = the Carcass was cleaned of its flesh and left the Central bone Supported on its sides after the abdomen by 2 orisontal and one perpendicular giving it here the appearance of a 4-edged cutting Instrument = the Lower Jaw or as I would prefer Style it, Mandible exceeds the upper

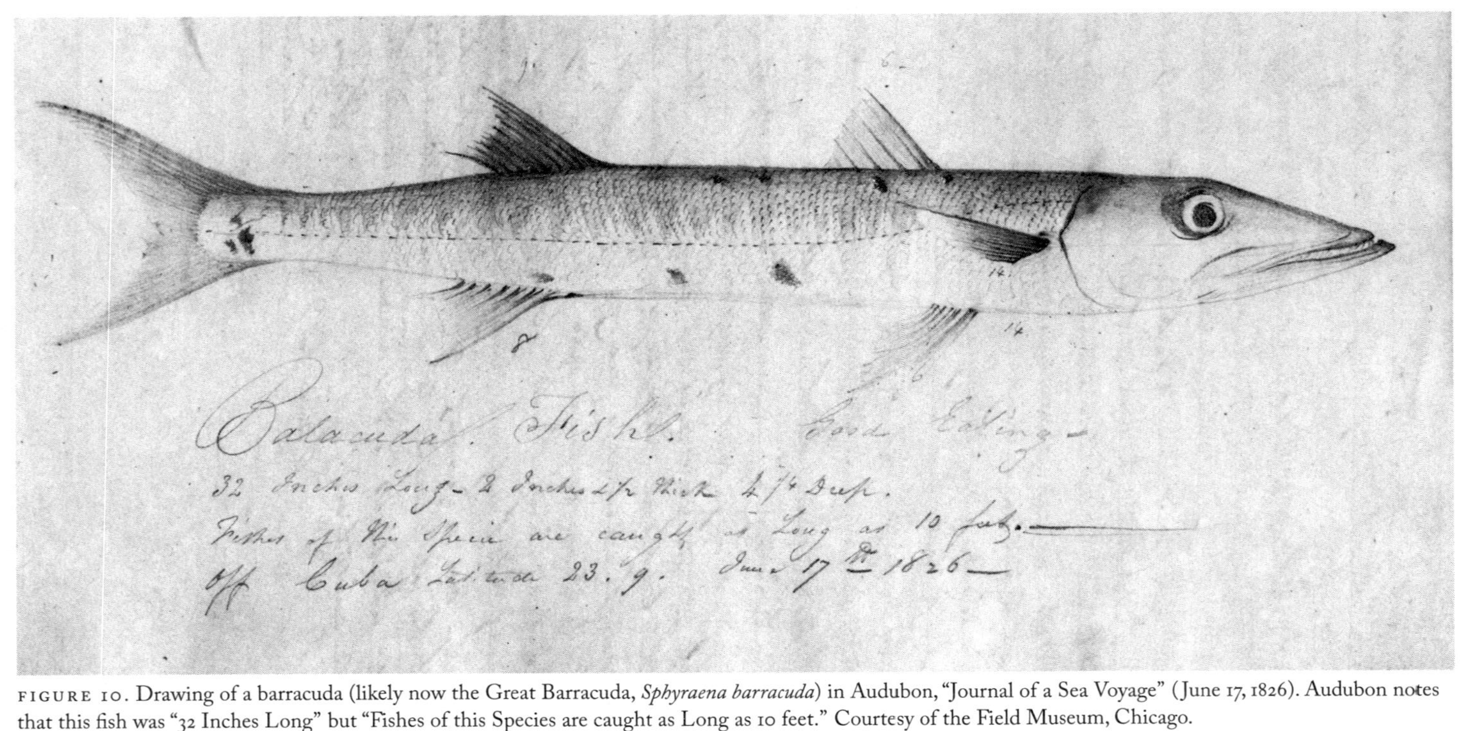

FIGURE 10. Drawing of a barracuda (likely now the Great Barracuda, *Sphyraena barracuda*) in Audubon, "Journal of a Sea Voyage" (June 17, 1826). Audubon notes that this fish was "32 Inches Long" but "Fishes of this Species are caught as Long as 10 feet." Courtesy of the Field Museum, Chicago.

about ¾ of an Inch, Both were furnish[d] with single raws of divided conical teeth about ½ Inch in length—Just so parted as to admit those of the upper Jaw between each of those of the Lower—the fish might [weigh] about 200 = the eyes were small proportionnally speaking, and the fish having a breathing apperture above of Course had no Gills. Porpoises move in Large company, and generally during Spring and Early summer close by pairs—coming on top to breath and playfully exibit themselves about Vessels—I have seen a parcel of them Leap, perpendicularly about 20 feet and fall with a heavy dash on the sea = Our Capt[e] told us that small boats had been sometimes sunk by one of these Fishes falling into it in one of these frisks =[6]

Whilst I am engaged with the finny Tribe, I may as well tell you that one morning when moving gently 2 Miles per hour, the Capt[e] Call[d] me to shew me some pretty Fishes Just Caught from our Cabin windows = these measured about 3 Inches, thin & broad of Shape and very quick through the watter; we had a pin hook and with this caught 370 in about 2 hours, they were sweet food = they are named Generally *Rudder Fish* [fig. 11] and allways Keep in the Lee side of the Rudder as it affords a strong Eddy to support them and enable them to follow the Vessel in that situation when going doubly fast—When the Sea become Calm they disperse themselves about the sides and bow and then will not

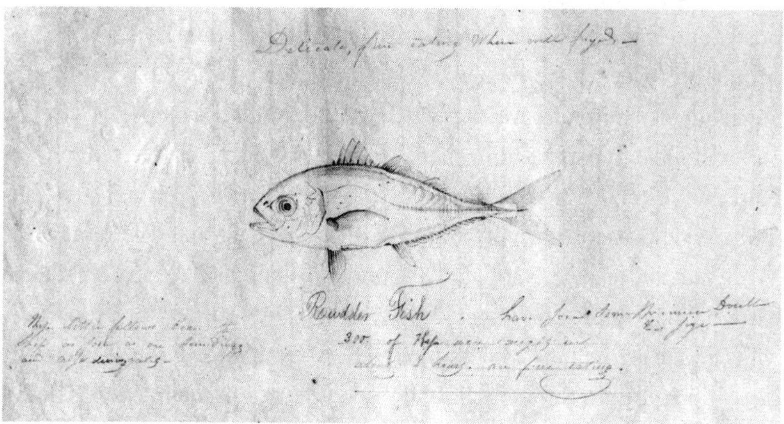

FIGURE 11. Drawing of a rudderfish (perhaps a juvenile Banded Rudderfish, *Seriola zonata*) in Audubon, "Journal of a Sea Voyage" (June 1826). "These little fellows leave the Ship as soon as our Soundings [i.e., when the ship approaches shallow water] and also during gales," Audubon notes. "300 of these were caught in about 2 hours. are fine eating." Courtesy of the Field Museum, Chicago.

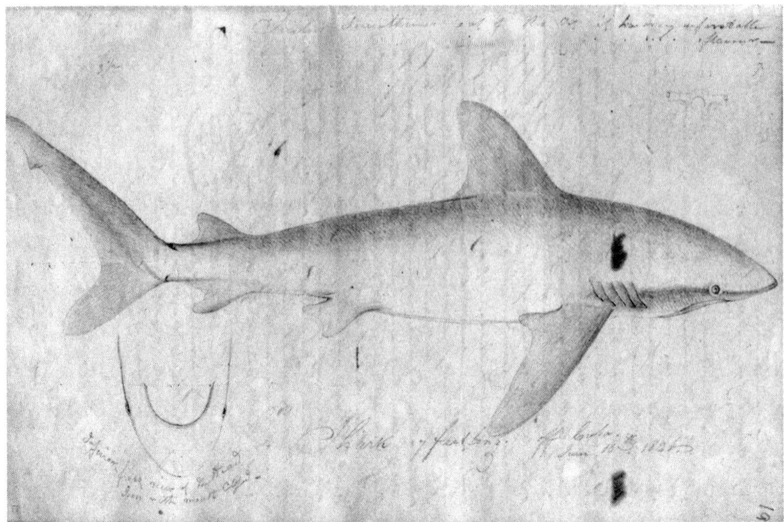

FIGURE 12. Drawing of a "Shark 7 feet long" caught off the coast of Cuba (likely the sandbar shark, *Carcharhinus plumbeus*) in Audubon, "Journal of a Sea Voyage" (Junc 18, 1826). Note the small sketch of a hammerhead shark head at the upper right. Courtesy of the Field Museum, Chicago.

bite—the least breese bring the all into a Compact body astern [again] when they seaze the baited Hook the Instant it reaches the watters—by this time we have caught and eat about 500 =[7]

We also have caught 2 Sharks [fig. 12] one a female about 7 feet that had 10 young alive and able to swim well—one of them was thrown over board and made off as if accustomed to take care of himself for some time = however it is to be remarked that these Fishes being Viviparous consequently never Leave the Mother unless fully formed—of Course I Concluded that the young here spoken of had never Left the Dam being yet fasten[ed] to the Womb by the feeding conduit = an other Was Cut in 2 and the head half swam off out of our Sight—the remainder Were cut to pieces as well as the parent for bait for Dolphins that are extremely partial to that meat[8]

The weather being Calm and pleasant, I felt anxious to have a view of the Ship from off her and Cap[e] Hatch politely took me in the Yawl and had it row[d] all around the Delos, this was a sight I had not enjoyed for nearly 20 years and was much pleased with—afterwards having occasion to go out to try the bearings of the Current I again accompanied him and Bathed in the sea not without however feeling some fears =

to try the bearings of the Current we took an Iron Pot fastened to a line of 120 fathom and Made a Log Board out of a Barrel's head laden on one edge to sink it perpendicularly on its edge and tried the velocity of the Current with it fixed to a Line by the help of a second Glass, whilst our Iron Pot sunk at the end of our line acted as an Anchor—[9]

I must now change for a Moment my theme and speak of Birds awhile—Mother Carey's Chickens (Procellaria's) came about us and I longed to have at least one in my possession—I had wachted [*sic*] their Evolutions; their gentle patting of the Sea, when on the wing with their legs hanging and webbs expanded; saw them take large and long ranges in search of food and returning still for the bits of fat thrown overboard and for them intended, I had often looked at different figures given by Scientific Men, but all this could not diminish for a moment the long wished for pleasure of possessing one in Natura Fideli: I loaded a piece and drop[d] the first one that came after, along Side, and the captain again, desirous of pleasing, went for it =

I Made 2 Drawings of it, it proved a female with eggs, numerous, but not larger than grains of fine powder, inducing one to think that these Birds must either breed, earlier, or much latter than any others in our Southern Latitude—I would be inclined to think that the specimen I Inspected had not laid this season, although I am full satisfied that it was an old Bird—[10]

During Many Weeks following this Date I Discovered that Many flew *Mated* side by Side and Occasionally particularly in Calm pleasant Weather Caressed each other as Ducks are Known to do—

about this time we saw a small Vessel with all sails set toward us, we were becalmed and the unknown had a light Breese, it approach[d] gradually, suspicions were intertained that it might be a Pirate as we that same day had undoutedly heard reports of Cannons from the very course she was coming; we were well manned tolerably armed and yet uneasiness was perceivable on every face more or less—yet we were all bent on resistance Knowing well that such Gentry, gave no quarters, to Purses at least = night arrived, a Small Squally breese struck us and off we moved were ought of sight in a Short time and resumed the mirth and good Mien that had existed amongst us.[11] Two Days afterwards a Brig that had been in our Wake Came near us, was hailed and found to be the Gleaner of Portland commanded by an acquaintance of our commander and Bound also to Liverpool, this Vessel had left the City of N. Orleans 5 days before us—we kept Close together and the next day Cap[e] Hatch and Myself Boarded her and were kindly received; after a Short stay, her Cap[e] called Jellerson came with us and remained the day[12]—I Opened My Drawings and show[d] a few of them, M[r] Swift was anxious to see some and I wanted to Examine in what state they kept—the weather being dry and Clear, I feared Nothing—it was agreed that Both Vessels should keep Company untill through the Gulph Stream for security sake against *Pirates* =[13]

So fine has the weather been so far that all belonging to the Cabin have constantly slept on Deck over which an Owning [*sic*] has been extended to keep the heat of the Sun and Dampness of the atmosphere at Night from us—

when full one hundred Leagues at sea a female Rice Bunting came a Board and remain[d] with us one night and part of a day—a Warbler also came but remained only a few minutes an[d] made for the Land we had left—it moved whilst on Board with great activity and Sprightliness, the Bunting to the Contrary was exausted, panted, and I have no doubt died of Inanition—[14]

Many Sooty Terns were in sight during several days I saw One Frigate Pelican high in air, and could only Judge it to be such through the help of the Telescope. flocks of unknown Birds were also about the Ship, during a whole day, they Swam well and prefered the watter to the air, They resembled Large Phalaropes but could not be certain =[15]

a Small alligator that I had purchased for 1 Dollar at New Orleans Died at the end of 9 Days, through My want of Knowledge that Salt watter was poisonous to him—in 2 days he Swelled to nearly double his Natural Size, breathed hard and died—[16]

in Latitude 24. 27[ds] a Green Heron came on Board and remained untill frightened by me, then flew toward the Brig Gleaner, it did not appear in the least fatigued;[17]

The Cap[e] of the Gleaner told me that on a preceeding Voyage from Europe to N. Orleans when about 50 leagues from the Balize a full Grown *Hooping Crane* came on board his vessel during the night passing over the length of his Deck close over his head, over that of the helm's man and fell in his Yawl. and that the Next Morning the Bird was found there completly Exausted, when every one [on] Board Supposed that it had pass[d] on—a Cage was made for it, it refused food and lingered a few days when it died—when pluck[d] was found sound and free from any wound, and in good Case—a very singular case in Birds of this Kind, that are inured to extensive Journies and of Course liable to spend much time without assistance of food—[18]

I have not written since the 27th for reasons as natural as Can be; I had scarce any new Incidents to relate—Now, however that it is the 4th of June and that at 12 'o' clock I found Myself a few Miles South of the Line for the 2[d] time in my Life, I feel rather an Inclination—thinking daily and I might say allmost Constantly of my Wife of my family, and Hopes all in *the Breese* (which by the bye is quite Contrary) My time goes on Dully Lying on the Deck on my Matress, on a hard pressed bale of Cotton, having no one scarcely to talk to, only a few Books and but Indiferent fare to engage one even to raise from that situation to feed myself = but to the purpose—I am really south of the Line—What Ideas it conveys to me, of my Birth, of the Expectations of My younger days, well &[c] &[c]—[19]

[. . .]

I have now been at sea 3 Sundays and yet have not made the Shore of Cuba and scarcely doubling the Florida Cape—but it is not worth while repining—

I have seen since my last date a Large *Sword Fish* but only saw it—2 Ganets, killed a *Great footed* Hawk This Bird [after] having alighted several times on our Yards, Made a Dash at a Warbler, feeding on the Flies about the Vessel, Seized it and Eat it in our Sight *on the Wing* Much Like a Missisippy Kite Devouring the Red Throated Lizards—Caught a live a Non Descript Warblers [*sic*]—which I named the *Cape Florida Songsters*: saw 2 Frigate Pelicans at a great hight and a Large Spicies of Petrel entirely unknown to me—We had a severe Squall (as I call[d] it) and plenty of Dull times with all—read Byron's poems The Corsair &[c] &[c]—&[c] &[c]—and Now—I will Shut My Book—[20]

[. . .]

JUNE AT SEA, 1826

[. . .] having come into the company of a Brigg Bound to Havanna from Liverpool, called the Howard Cap^e Joseph Birney, I wrote to thee, Mr R. Currell & E. Coste to give thee again an account of our Slow movements. it was the 16th Instant and I Hoped that my Letter might reach thee in Two weeks—[21]

We have been in sight of Cuba [figs. 13, 14] these last 4 days—the heat excessive = I saw 3 Beautifull White headed Pigeons or Doves flying about our Ship, but after severall rounds they Shaped their Course towards the Floridas and disapeared—The Dolphins we cacth [*sic*] here are Suspected Poisonous and assertain if they are so or not, a Piece is Boiled along with a Dollar untill quite cooked when if the Piece of Silver coin is not Tarnished either black or Green, the Fish is good and safe eating; I found Bathing in Sea Watter extremely refreshing and therefore enjoy this Luxury every night before Lying down on my Mattress. we have had in sight and allmost in Company 4 or 5 sails of Vessel for several days—[22]

[. . .]

AT SEA JUNE 20TH 1826 OFF FLORIDA COAST.

The Birds that at diferent times during my Passage Thus far towards England, that I had taken for a Specie of Large Phaleropes, were about

FIGURE 13. Drawing of the "[northwest] End of the Island of Cuba. Ship Delos June 15th at 5 P.M. by sea," in Audubon, "Journal of a Sea Voyage." Audubon notes that he drew "the Bearings and distances of the principal head Lands" at a distance of twenty miles. Courtesy of the Field Museum, Chicago.

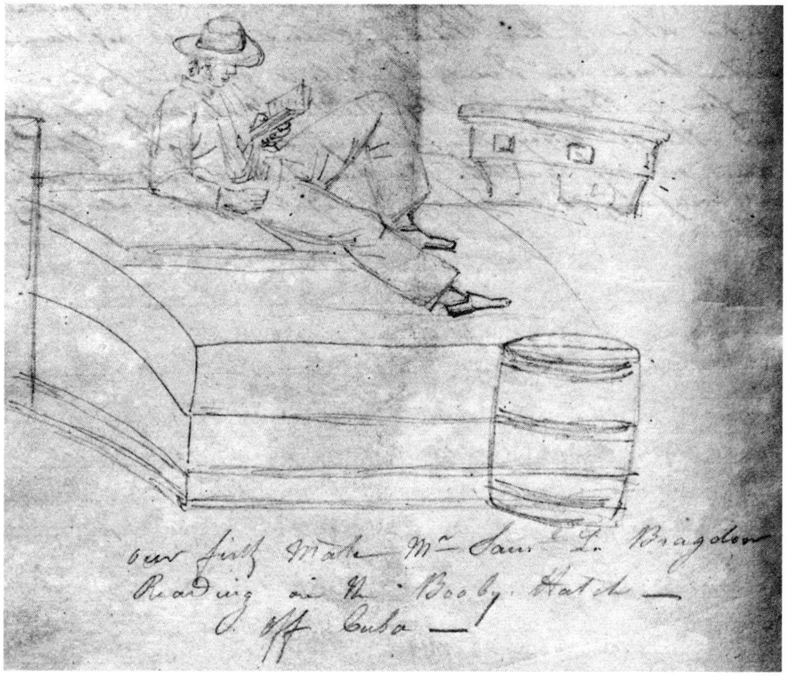

FIGURE 14. Drawing of "our first Mate M[r] Sam[l] L. Bragdon Reading on the Booby Hatch—off Cuba—," June 1826. Courtesy of the Field Museum, Chicago.

[our] vessel in great Numbers, and our Mate was so fortunate as to kill four at one Shot that were pick[d] up by the Yawl at my Request = I was surprised and pleased at finding them belonging to the Genus *Procellarias* or Petrel, made a Sketch as usual Size of Life and Preserved the Skins of all of them.[23]

These Birds skim very low over the Sea in Search of the Bunches of Floating sea Weed that abound over this Gulph, flapping their Winds [*sic*] 6 or 7 times in quick Succession and their sailing an equal Intermediate length of time say 3 or 4 Seconds with great apparent ease, Carrying their tail much Spread and Long wings Squarely angular with their body. = Raising & falling with such beautifull ease to motions of the Waves that one might Suppose they receive a Special power to that Effect from the Element below them on approaching a Bunch of Weeds they raise their Wings Obliquely, Deep their legs & feet, run apparently on the watter, and rest at last on the sea where they swim with all the ease of the Genus Anas, Dive freely, at times several feet in Pursuit of the Fishes that at their approach of the Weeds leave for safety and seize them with great agility as well as Voraciousness—4 or 5 and sometimes from 15 to 20 will then alight on and about one Bunch of Weed and during their Stay about it, Diving, Flutering and swiming all in a heap present quite agreable groups—during this Period Many Gulls of different Kinds are hovering over and about the same Spot, Vociferating their anger & Disappointment at not being quite so well able to furnish themselves with the delicate fare = No sooner have all the fishes being taken or chased, that all the Birds, Raise, Diffuse, and extend their flight in search of more =[24]

I heard no sound Issuing from them although many came within 20 paces of us, consequently, I Suppose Them endowed with excellent quick power of Sight, as at the Very Moment that one Individual, lighted Many Imediately made for the Spot and reach[d] it in an Instant.

[. . .]

CAPES OF FLORIDA JUNE 22[D] 1826

Whilst sailing under a gentle Breese Last [night] the Bird Outlined on this Sheet Commonly called by Seamen *Nody*. [fig. 15] alighted on the boom of the Vessel and a few Minutes afterwards was caught by the mate. It then Issued a rough Cry not unlike that of a young Common Crow when taken from the Nest. It bit severely and with quickly renewed Movements of the Bill, which when it missed the objects in view Snapp[d] Like that of our Larger fly Catchers:

I found it one of the same Specie that hovered over the sea Weeds in company with the Large Petrels.—& that I thought then had the whole head White: having Kept it alive during the whole night when I took it in hand to Draw it, it was Dull Looking and silent. I know nothing of this Bird more than what Our Sailors say, that it is a Nody and frequently alights about Vessels in this Latitude and particularly in the neighbourhood of the Florida Keys: the Bird was in Beautifull Plumage but poor. The Gullet was of great Extension, the Punch Was empty the heart Large for the Bird, but the Leaver was uncommonly so: =[25]

a Short time before the Capture of the above Bird a Vessel of War a Ship that We all supposed to be a south American Republican [or

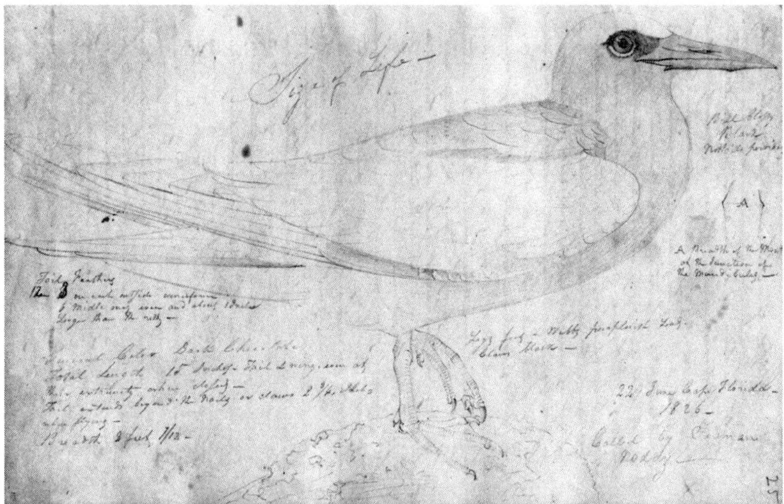

FIGURE 15. "Size of Life" drawing of a seabird "Called by Seaman Noddy" (now the brown noddy) in Audubon, "Journal of a Sea Voyage" (June 22, 1826, Cape Florida). Audubon noted that the birds "General Color" was "Dark Chocolate" and measured total length, claws, and breadth, adding several relative alignments and colors of parts to inform future drawings. Courtesy of the Field Museum, Chicago.

Columbian] came between us and the Thalia, their distance from us about 1½ Mile, [a Stern] fired a Gun, & detained her for Some time, the reasons probable to us were the Ships Passenger's being Spaniards & Spanish property the Cargo. however this morning Both Vessels were in View, making diferent routes, the Man of War deigned Not come to us and none on Board were much vexed at this mark of Iñatation.—[26]

This day was calm, after My Drawing finished, I Caught 4 Dolphins; how much I have gaized on these Beautifull Creatures, watching Their last moments of Life, changing their hue in Twenty Varieties of richest arrangements of Tints, from Burnished Gold to Silver Bright; Mixed with touches of ultramarine Blues[27] spots, red, & bronse, & Green—Shivering[28] & quivering to death on our hard Broiling Deck. and yet I felt but a few Moments before a peculiar Share of Pleasure in seizing them with a Sharp Hook allured by false profession—

Two More Nody's were Shot by our Mate this day, they resembled in all particulars the Specimens I have drawn. We saw about 20.—

We at Last Entered the Atlantic Ocean this Morning 23^{d} with a propitious Breese—the Land Birds have left us and, I—I Leave My

Beloved America, My Wife Children and acquaintances—the purpose of this Voyage is to Visit Not only England but all Europe with the [Intention] of Publishing My Work of the Birds of America; If not sadly disapointed, My return to these happy Shores will be the brightest Birth day I Shall have ever enjoyed: Oh America, Wife Children and acquaintances Farewell!

[. . .]

JULY 9TH 1826, AT SEA

[. . .]

Our 4th of July was passed Near the Grand Banks, how diferently from My Last, and how diferently from any that I can recollect ever having spent—The weather was Thick foggy and as Dull as myself, Not a sound of rejoicing did reach my ear, Not once did I hear the sublime "Hail Columbia happy Land" No Nothing—perhaps nothing could have so forcibly awakened me from My Dosing situation than the Like of a Pleasure so powerfully felt by me when at Home—it was then that I suddenly arose from my Lethargy and remarked the reality of My absence and present situation. The day past as I conceive One spent by a General who has Lost a Great advantage over an Ennemy, I complained of myself, I attributed all my disapointment to my want of foresight, but I complained to No one *else* I felt Sorrowfull in the extreme as if America had Lost much this day—My Compagnon passengers Lay strewed about the Deck and on the Cotton Bales, basking like Crocodiles during all the Intervals granted to the Sun to peep at them through the Smoacky heaziness that accompanied us—yet the Breese was strong, the Waves moved Magestically and thousands of Large Petrells displayed their elegant aerial Movements to Me—how much I envied their power of Flights to enable me to be here, there and all over the Globe comparatively Speaking in a Moment—throwing themselves Edge ways against the Breese as if a well sharpen[d] arrow just with the Strength and grace of One Sprung from the Bow of an Appollon[29]

I had remarked a regular Increase in the number of these Petrels ever since the capes of Florida, but here they were so numerous & for part of a Day flew in Such succession toward the West & South West that I

Concluded they were Migrating to some well Known Shore to deposit their Eggs or perhaps Leading their Young—these very seldom alighted, they were full the side of a common Gull and as they flew they shewed in quick Alternativeness The whole upper or under parts of their body—sometimes skimming Low, at other forming Imense curves, then Dashing along the deep troughs of the Sea, going round our Vessel (allways out of Gun Shot reach) as if She had been at Anchor—their Lower parts are White, a broad white patch on the rump, the head apparently all White, & the upper parts of the Body, & Wings above, sooty Brown—I would conceive that one of these petrels fly over as Much Distance in one hour as the Little black petrels in our Wake do in 12—[30]

since We have left the Neighbourhood of the Banks these Bird[s] have gradually disapeared, and Now in Latitude 44.53—I see none—Our sailors and Captain speak of them as Companions in storms as much as the Little relatives The Mother Carey's Chickens—

As sudenly as if We had Just Turned the summit of a Mountain Deviding a Country south of the Equator from Iceland, the Weather Altered in the present Latitude & Longitude My Light Summer Clothing, Was Not Suficient, Indeed a Cloth Coat felt Light &Scanty, and the Dews that fell during the Nights rendered the Deck were I allways slept too damp now to be comfortable = this however of Two evils I prefer[d] for I could not withstand the More desagreable Odor of the Cabin, Where Now, the Captain, Officers & M[r] Swift eat their Meals Daily =

setting during the day as I am Now, with my poor Book in My Lap on a Parcel of Coiled Cables Near the helm's Man, (who by the Bye Gazes at Me as Much as he Looks at his Compass) I Spend Nearly all My Time, part of it reading; thoughtlessly leaning over the railing, Looking on the many braking Waves that urges us on, and again thinking of America as the sun to our eyes toward her reposing place declines I am forced To Make a better choice of Situation and perhaps Will go and Lie on the Starboard Side of the Long Boat, where Our Cook, ready at trying to Please will talk to me untill wearied of this from the Spot I remove again = Nights gradually bring on the *Wish to repose in Sleep* when after a few Stories told, each gradually leaves The Spot and goes and lays down, either in his Hamock, his Birth [*sic*]. or the Harder Chicken Coop, that Line both Side of our Compagnion Way—

here the days have Increased astonishingly at Nine o'clock I Can easily read Large print, the Day opens at 2, and 25 Minutes after 4 Phoebus enlivens the Globe and promises a fair prosperous sixteen hours—

Our unconncerned, Happy Mariners, get to their daily Labor at 6 of the Morn and chearly spend the day, Improving the Appearance of All about our Ship, rendering her the More secure this While—their Joviality, their Industry, their Witticisms, would enable probably any other than A Friend far away from his Friends to pass the time away—

I have told you that I sat frequently on a parcel of Coiled Cables, but you are still Ignorant, that since I Left New Orleans I have sheared My Beard but once—that It now profusely expands from each ear out, and from out My Chin and Neck around like a Crowd of Stifen[d] Bristles which along with the Tawny Acquired hue of My Skin since On Board of this floating Prison renders Me as unlike the Daughter of Titian as Satan is to God—[31]

We had for several days a stiff propitious Brease that Wafted us over the Briny deep full Nine Miles per hour, this was congenial to My Wishes, but not to my feelings; the Vessel felt the Motion before me and Chifted My Body too soon or unwarly; Caused me Violent head aches far more distresfull than any sea sick feeling ever experienced—during that Period I found food Highly season[d] and spirituous Liquors of great benefit—

here for [the] 3[[d]] or 4th time I read of Thomson's the 4 seasons, and I believe enjoyed them better than ever—when I came to his Castle of Indolence, I felt the all powerfull extent of his Jenius operating on Me as a Cathartic swallowed when well aware that My Body was not in a fit condition (through situation) to be benefited by it—[32]

as we drew Nearer the Shores of the far famed Spot, even the Clouds seem[d] to prefer a diference of Consistancy and Shapes; No Longer did the Vivifying Orb, settle with her globular shape all fiery [beyond] the deep, it Shewed, dull, pale, sickly, and as if sorry that *through diferences that for ever must exist* Its light refulgent was not to be extended over the Globe untill the Omnipotent God had granted to each of all its Portions that real sense of Freedom now only better felt in the Western Hemisphere = here foggs suceeded foggs; the Englishmen on Board pronounced it, *Clear weather of England*, but I Named it the Blasting atmosphere of Comfort—

I would continue now but the dampness is So powerfull although The Sun Still Stracks through the haze, that my Paper is Damp and receives the Ink quite too freely—Dear Friend Adieu—

Amongst the Inmates composing our amount of Live Stock we had A Large Hen; This Bird [was] quite familiar and allowed the privileges of the Decks; She had been Hatch[d] on Board at New Orleans, and our Cook who Claimed her as private property was much attached to her as well as our Mates; One Morning She imprudently flew over Board when running about 3 Miles per hour.

The Yawl was Imediately Lowered four Men rowed her swiftly from us towards the floating Bird that anxiously Look[d] at her place of [nativ] abode untill picked up out of the Sea—her return on Board appeared to please every one and I was much gratified to discover that Such Kind Treatment was used towards a Bird; it assured me that all exertions possible would be made to save the lives of any of our Seamen Should They fall over Board = Our Hen however ended her Life most distressfully, a few weeks after this narrow escape, She again Made over the sides and the Vessel moving at 9 Knots the Sea High and rough with squally weather the captain thought it Imprudent to risk his men for the Bird and we lost Sight of her in a few Moments—

We had our Long Boat as usual Lashed fast to the Deck but Instead of being filled with Lumber &[c] as is usually the Case it now contained Three Passengers, all Bound to Europe to visit their Friends with Intention of returning the same Autumn to America—One named Vowles had several Books which he politely offered me—he blowed sweetly on the Flute and was a Man superior to his Apparent situation = We had a Taylor also, this personnage was called a Deck Passenger, but the fact is that full Two Thirds of his Time was spent sleeping on the Windlass = this man however Like All others in the World was usefull in his way, he work[d] when ever Called on and would with much good will, put a Button, or a patch on anyone's Clothing—his name was *Crow* he Lived on Biscuit and raw Bacon the whole Voyage—

At Noon one beautifull day We discovered Two sails a head of our

Ship and our Captain renewed his exertions to overtake them, the Masts were freshly greased, all our sails brought to a Nice bearing, the helms men ordered to be wary and exact and at the brake of day next We were Just between them—We had [not] however the comtemplated [*sic*] pleasure of Speaking to them; I discovered that as soon as the Breese became lighter, they gained away from us and Vice versa—

We now saw no Fish except now & then a School of Porpoises; and I frequently longed for one of the hundreds of Dolphins that we had Caught in the Gulph of Mexico—[33]

Some Wales [*sic*] were seen by the Sailors, but I saw nothing of them—

I frequently sat during this Tedious Voyage, watching our Captain at his Work, I do not remember having seen many more Industrious, and apt at doing almost every thing that he needed himself = he was a good and Nice Carpenter, Turner, Cooper, Black & white Smith, excellent Taylor &[c] I saw Making a pair of Pantaloons of fine Cloth with all the Neatness that a City Brother of the Cross Legged faculty could have used = he made a handsome patent swif [*sic*] for his Wife—he could also platt Straws in all sorts of ways and Made excellent bearded Fish Hooks out of Common Needles, at this very Moment he is employed at Finishing a handsome smoothing plane for his own use, manufactured out of a Piece of Beech Wood that probably grew on the Banks of the Ohio, as I perceive it had belong[d] to some part of a Flat Boat, and brought on Board here to be used for fuel—I thought him an excellent sailor, the More squally it blew, the Gayer he generally would be—and frequently during Such times, when drenched to The Skin he would laugh and say "Who would not sell a handsome plantation and go to Sea."[34]

I became anxious to understand the means of Assertaining the latitude on Land and also to find the true rising of the Sun whilst travelling in the unhihabited [*sic*] parts of America, this he shew[d] Me with pleasure and I Calculate our Latitude & Longitude from this time—

I found it necessary to employ all my time as much as possible therefore, I frequently went about the Deck, a pencil in hand viewing the diferent Attitudes of the Sailors at Work and Made Many Sketches [figs. 14, 16, 17]—They frequently caused a general laugh and they passed agreably a moment—

FIGURE 16. Drawing of the second mate, William Hobart (left), Captain Joseph Hatch (middle), and the carpenter (right) making powder flasks on deck, in Audubon, "Journal of a Sea Voyage" (July 1826). Courtesy of the Field Museum, Chicago.

Our Mates exibited a Kindness toward me that I would not suffer to remain unoticed, under any consideration = They were all alertness at meeting all my Wishes, indeed I often felt vexed that they Should exert themselves as much, when as I was quite able to help myself; yet frequently before I was aware of it, Should I walk either to the bow or Stern, I would find My Mattrass, Books &c all carefully removed into My *Bunk*. The 1st Mate was Named S. L. Bragdon. from Wells [fig. 14]. The 2d Wam Hobart from Kennebunk [fig. 16]—[35]

Now I expect that you will ask what sort of a Machine my *Bunk* was—the question would be natural enough and before you Make it,

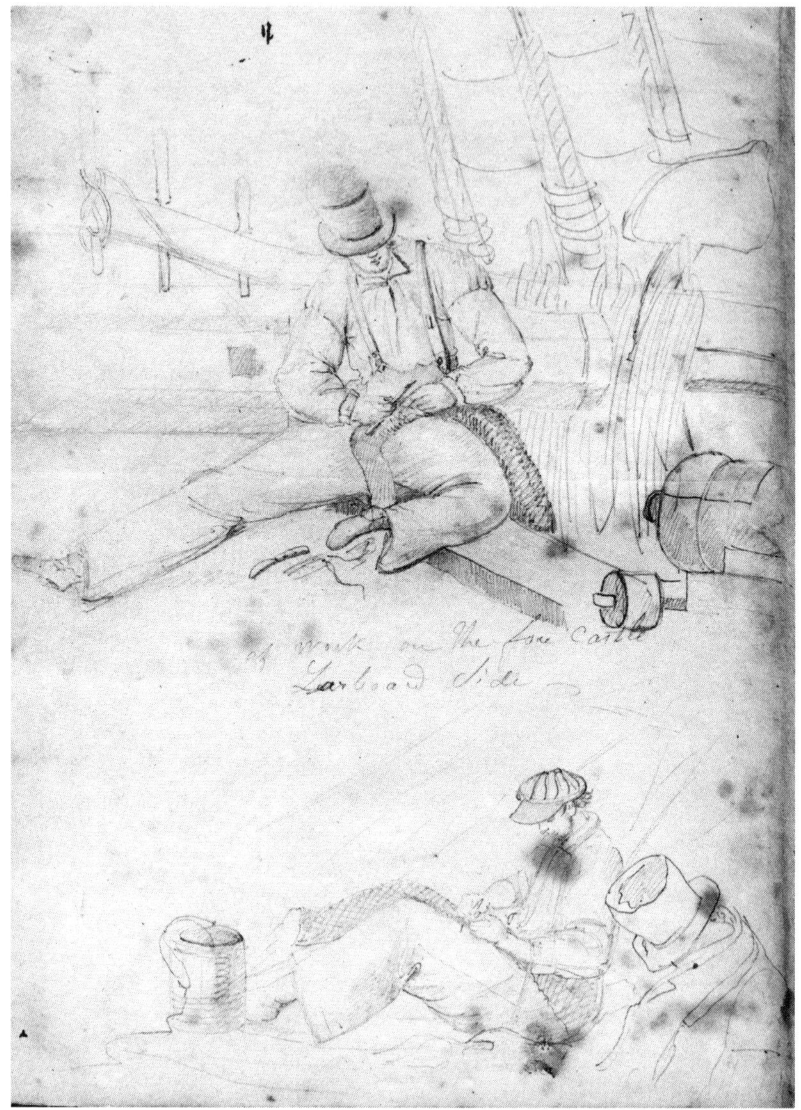

FIGURE 17. Drawing of sailors "at work on the fore Castle Larboard [port] Side," perhaps knitting for personal use or making rope fenders or chafe gear, in Audubon, "Journal of a Sea Voyage" (July 1826). Courtesy of the Field Museum, Chicago.

Like our Mates I will try to surprise you = Imagine (and that I Know you can easily do) a flat Box without a lid measuring 6½ feet by 3 in breadth[d] and 9 Inches deep made of White Pine—again Imagine 2 pieces of the same wood raising from the center of each end about 2½ feet, notched at their Tops to receive a light pole length ways, over Which a paire of my

Sheets sawed [*sic*] together is fixed and covers the whole, representing an elongated Tent wherein My Matrass, Pillows, Coat, Shoes Books &c &c are snugly fitted, free from the rays of the Sun, and Nearly so from the watter during rain—This is What the Sailors Call My Bunk and so I Shall Call it Myself—

Every Sailor or every set of Sailors have a Deity at Sea on whom they call more or less frequently for fair Wind as the Case may require; during our long stay in the Gulph of Mexico, from Our Cape to the Cook (or as by Courtesy I will call him *the Stuart*) this relation of Eolus was called on many times every day; it was a Saint of great renown, one whom I believed by the Bye *has Stranded* as many poor Devils as any other saint or saintess ever did, he was hailed St Anthony—the prayers of all our Crew, those of our Cape, of our Stuart, Nay even those of Mr Swift and Mine proved unavailing, Not a breath of fair wind would he Entice his Master to send us, Indeed I became so disgusted with the personnage at last, that I propose one Morning when Nature seemed all a Sleep and our Vessel Was so becalmed that a feather dropd from our Mast's head would scarce have deviated in its easy fall to the Deck, To Abandon this renowned, fattened Saint and Call on One More in need of our regards; the proposition was unanimously Accepted and Saint Mark Appointed as Chief Director of the Breeses Intented and much longed for to Carry our Vessel to the Shores of England—[36]

Will you believe it—Yes you will as it is I that writes it—St Mark Came to our Calling under an Easy Gait; the Delos Moved 3 Miles per hour; All on Board begged of him to come nearer us and in 3 days he helpd us on full 400 miles:

[. . .]

We spoke to the Brigg Albion bound to Quebec, with many passengers but only balasted;—[37]

The Little petrils had Left us for 2 days, I thought that probably the Cold weather had drove them away; I was satisfied that several in our Wake had followed us ever since the Gulph of Mexico—of Course the sudden diference of the Weather must have been seriously felt by them; or perhaps do they not near the European Coats [*sic*] More =[38]

I had a beautifull View of a Whale about 500 yards from the Vessel; When we first perceived it; the Watter thrown throu his Valve had the

Appearance of a Small thick Cloud in the hOrison [*sic*], When near us It dove and exibited its Tail in appearance about 12 or 14 feet Wide =[39]

Never do I recollect having felt the Weather so cold in July Wrapt up in our Cloaks We felt Chills and the drissl rain

[. . .]

AT SEA JULY 15TH 1826[40]

The same dull, Cold, damp weather, still prevails; Still the Wind is Northwest and propitious as can be—On a Passage like this how much a Man May find to think upon—I am pretty sure that few memorable events of My Life (if memorable I may dare Call them or any of them) have not be recalled to Memory, Weighed, disaranged and Improved (in thoughts only not in action unfortuneally) untill the whole of my Life has been with scrutiny surveyed and all the Lines, Land Marks, Beacons, stranding places, &c &c all fairly and unfairly construed have been brought present to my Eye sight and bodily feelings—Yes I have had time enough, I assure thee to consult on all points and there can exist no doubt that had I being fortunate enough When ever I have erred (and I have no doubt I erred enough) had [I had] such an equal Opportunity to think before I acted I would have committed but few errors and probably never a Sin—

[. . .]

The Mate's Cabin Still further on My right—several Mice are running about the floor picking their scanty fare = The Cocroaches, began to Issue from their daily retreats; my bottom is sore from sitting on the Mate's hard Chest, I Look at the sea through the Two Windows, and Shut the Book—Why? because the Last object on which My eyes rested was the Captain's Hammock swinging so imediately over My Bunk that it reminded me Most painfully of the Many hurried Times I have been Obliged to put My Nostrils between My Thum and Index for safe Keeping from Winds neither from the South West nor Norwest but from . . .—Ah My Dear what strange incidents happen at Sea—[41]

A Whale! a Whale! run Mr Audubon There's a Whale close along side—the Pen, the Book, were abandoned The Mice frightened, I ran up and Lo! There rolled most Magestically The wonder of the Oceans—It was of Immense Magnitude; its dark auburn body fully overgrew the Vessel in size: One Might have thought it was the God of the Seas beconing [*sic*] us to the Shores of Europe—I saw it and therefore believed its Existence—[42]

Yesterday night ended the 9th Sunday spent at sea—The Weather as usual, but the breese very light—each person anxious to reach the Shore conceived a diference in the appearance of the watter—Indeed I once thought and said that I smelt the Putrid sea weeds on the Shore, several who had not as sensible noses thought it probable—during the afternoon all the Noses were up and pointed towards Clear Cape (which might have been with more propriety named Foggy) when suddenly our Captain smelt something new, it had become stronger gradually ever since the Morning as the Imagined Land Smell had made its Escape from the Sloche Barrel Lashed to the Camhouse and when the real cause was assertained (which now required scarce a moment) a horse [*sic*] laugh was raised for a while when a good Share of dejection shewed on all the visages and turned nearly all the Company's Noses Blue—we had many whales near us during the day and an immense number of Porpoises; our Captain who prefers their flesh to The Best of Veal, beef or Mutton said he would freely give 5$ for one; but our Harpoon was now broken, and although several were fastened for a while to the Grains—these proved too light, and the fishes regularly after a few bounces made their Escape, probably to go and die in misery = Two European Hawks were seen, and also 2 Curlews. This gave me some Hopes that we might see the desired object Shortly—[43]

how uncomfortable the motions of a Vessel are to a man unused to that, when writing as I am now all crank sided with one half of my Bottom wearing fast, whilt the other invain [*sic*] is seeking for support—this is not all, one as I said before unused to this desagreable movement may now and then slide off his seat and go and throw down a person peaceably reading three feet off; (I wish I could have said three yards but our Cabin is hardly that wide and as I sit imediatly in the center of the base line it could not beso [*sic*].) this person might conceive it an intended insult, indeed might say so, words might arise and perhaps blows might fall where after much trouble and hard labour on both side, to hold fast to attack and defend, an other heavy roll of the sea might come and force each adversary to seek diferent ways a retreat = Many persons Speak lightly of Leaving America to go and Visit Europe; Many indeed when return[d], who have not found Europe what they wished, speak lightly of the whole = I cannot touch the subject so superficially—I spoke for many Years of this my present Voyage; allways dreaded it, before I undertook it, and now that after being, swung about, rolled, heaved, bruised and shifted probably a round half Million of Times within the first 60 days of a Voyage that I calocated [*sic*] (Moderately speaking) to last full 15 Months, have I not good substantial reasons to think of it prudently as I go, and to try *when I return home* again to speak of it *rationnally*?

Just as the word *rationnally* (which by the bye means much more than many rationnaly conceive) our second Mate entered the Cabin and repeated the Two last words of the man at the Helm at the same time that he called M[r] Bragdon, (whom you recollect is the 1st Mate,) saying *Seven Bell.*—had it not been for this hapenning at *this* very Moment I probably would have forgotten to tell you that we had a Bell on Board—It is not the *sad Curfew or Couvre feu*:, it is the sounding Instrument of Joy to each man at the helm as it is the sorrowfull token to the sleeping one in the forecastle that he must raise, go to the relief and gaze on the Sails within half an hour and the compass for full 2 hours—Yes we have a Bell, it sounds either 4 Sharp Strokes, or 4 times Twice, at four in the morning, or at 12 the meridian—

[. . .][44]

All these things I would have omitted probably (had not the 2[d] Mate entered the cabin so *à point*) as I would have omitted many other Incidents less alarming had I not written at the very moment they took Place (an advise I would regularly give to any person anxious to Employ his Time as much as I am by writting down all *he Sees, all he thinks*, or all—yes out with it: *All he does*—)

[. . .]

A few Minutes before 12; during a Dark squally night when our Vessel was running swiftly. Close to the wind in the Warmer latitudes of the Gulph of Mexico; The Man at the Helm cried out "sail oh"! "close to windward". I Jumped from my Bunk where I had been thinking of thee

My Dearest Friend and—Stared Towards the Spot like a Wild Man; the Captain had Leaped to the Deck from below in an anstant.—the Vessel was small—(it was a schooner running full before the Wind) and the thoughts of a Pirate approaching to Board us fill[d] all My Veins with fear and apprehension—all was silent—all dreadfull suspence—when the thundering Voice of our Commandant reach my Ears and I have no doubt those of every one on Board with "strack the Bell there" This was done—when all of a Sudden the Little stranger hall[d] to and passed so Close to our Stern than [*sic*] an Active man, might have Leaped from one Vessel to another = had our Bell struck one Minute latter, The Schooner would have struck our Heavy Strong broad side and sunk in an Instant—moving as fast as Both Ships then did, We had Just time enough to gather from the Breese a few heavy Vociferations from the Captain of the unknown to to [*sic*] the Man at his helm to whom he promised a good *Whaling* and in a few Moments we were far apart and thanking God that Matters thus So happily ended.

[. . .]

Our Captain is again Turning; we have a Brigg in sight and not very far—but we have not the Land in sight: no! and God Knows when we will have it—[45]

My Time is really dull not a Book on Board that I have not read Twice since here (I mean on Board this Ship) and I believe Twice before—thought as I said yesterday of Every Thing I can well remember throu the Mist of Times and feel as Dull as ever = I movd from the Deck here; from here to the deck; lay There a little, and down here longer: it is all a Like; dull uncomfortable; nay: was it uncomfortable only, I do not believe I would Complain, but it is all Iddle time I spend here; all dreary Iddle time: the most misirable. pitifull. sinfull way of Spending even One moment—

[. . .]

Now Where the Devil are you running To Audubon?—running—why—Towards the shores of that England that Gave Birth to a Milton!! to a Shakespeare!!—to a Driden—that raised West: that Enable Thomson to prove his Merits = that Called Goldsmith by a well deserved name—where Johnson flourish[d]—that gazed on the pencil of Hogarth!

with admiration—Laughed with Smollet—Might have Cried with Young—Was delighted of *Late* with Scott and shed Tears for her Byron—[46]

Oh England! renowned Isle! how Shall I Enter thee? good God? what have I pronounced?—I am fit to enter her dominions at all? My Heart swells—The Bird seazed when sitting on her Nest could not be more terrified—I Look up: Yes, for Mercy I Look up; and Yet, how much I dread!—how far I would thus have gone, When Cap[e] Hatch call[d] out and said the Brigg Homer was Close to us—The preliminary questions of "Brig Oh! and Ship I![")][47] where returned—When from whence came you? &[c] &[c] had being all Interchanged with a few Hundreds of &[c] besides, I reach the rail way and saw the Brigg *Homer* 26 days Less from New Orleans than We are—(a mere *Moment* in the Life of Man and scarce an Attom in eternal Calculations) *She looked well* although her sails were patched *With Russia Duck* to save Duty on Importation[48]

[. . .]

AT SEA JULY 18TH 1826

The Sun, now, is shining clear, over Ireland: That land was seen at 3 o'clock this morning by our sailor at the helm and our Mate with a stentorial voice announced us the News = I cannot conceive why I felt noparticular [*sic*] pleasure, not even a diference of sensation from my feelings of Yesterday or the day previous or three weeks ago:—what can be the Reason? when I have landed in France, or America, I allways bounced with Joy—now I look indeferently on the shore, although it looks well—Indeed I feel mortified that I can scarce write, for the want of better spirits—

My Dear Friend, oh it is Thee That concerns me; it is our Dear Children that fill all my thoughts; the Immense Ocean that devides us and the times that must be spent far from Thee . . . I Cannot write—oh may God prepare you and Bless You All!—

I have come again in the Cabin, we have had Irish *Fishermen* along side (I would call them Beggars but as they are Much like me, *brothers in blood* I would be shocked to say so, although they acted *Through a Cur-*

rent of Actual Misfortune) as if *they* had been [Conceived][49] and form[d] of Inferior Materials to *Men Americans*—

[. . .]

I am approaching very fast the Shores of England—indeed Wales is abreast of our Ship, and we can plainly distinguish the Hedges that devide the fields of Grain = but what nakedness the Country exibits scarce a patch of Timber to be seen—our fine Forests of Pines, of Oaks, of heavy Walnut Trees, of magnific Magnolias, of Hickories, or ash, or Sugar trees; are represented here by a dimin[utive] growth named *Furze*—

Come, come, no criticizing, I have not seen the country, I have not visited any of the Noble's castle's nor any of their renowned parks—no. I never was in England, except when I turned *page over page* with a pleasure, that I Hope I may feel again. The animating Natural, Thomson! or the inticing Scot!—well then, I will look on, and think a while: =

ST. GEORGE'S CHANNEL. THURSDAY 20TH JULY 1826

[. . .]

We passed yesterday morning *The Tuscar* a Handsome light house, on a naked rock—this morning we saw *Holy Head* and now we are not exceeding 25 Miles from *Liverpool*—I feel no pleasure My Dearest Friend; no, and was it not for *thy* sake and, the sake of *our children*. as God Almighty, was the maker of The Sun—I would readily. ah! and most willingly: embark *to morrow* to reach America's Shores and—ho my Dearest Friend—[50]

The pilot Boat that came to us This morning contained several Men—all dress[d] in blue, with Overcoats of *Oiled Linen* all *good Hearty*, Healthy *Men*—but rather too much Shaped Like their boat That undoubtedly was very clumsy, and a miserable sailor compared to our New York—Psha—I will hold my pen and—go on Deck to see if it rains still

Now, it does not rain and I may safely say (without being Jocose) that the sight, now in sight, is truly beautifull 56 Vessels with spreaden sails are in view on our Lea—and mountains after mountains fainting in the orison are on our right—Lucy. I have now cast my eyes on the *Land of England* = from the Bow, it is plainly distinguishable—My Dull thoughts have all abandoned me; My Heart is elated—I see The Dear Country that gave thee Birth and I *Love it* because!! *I Love Thee*!!!—

Notes

1. Nathaniel Wells Pope was a physician in St. Francisville, Louisiana, and Audubon's clerk and hunting companion during his Kentucky days; Richard Rhodes, *John James Audubon: The Making of an American* (New York: Knopf, 2004), 232. The *Red River* (150 tons) was built for "Captain Kimble" of New Orleans in 1825 by Whitney & Stone, a steamboat yard in Marietta, Ohio; Martin R. Andrews, ed., *History of Marietta and Washington County and Representative Citizens* (Chicago: Biographical Publishing Company, 1902), 285. On Diedrich Holl ("D. Hall") of St. Francisville, see Daniel Patterson, ed., *John James Audubon's Journal of 1826: The Voyage to* The Birds of America (Lincoln: University of Nebraska Press, 2011), 3n1; Carolyn E. DeLatte, *Lucy Audubon: A Biography*, updated ed. (1982; Baton Rouge: Louisiana State University Press, 2008), 161; 1820 US Census for St Francisville, Feliciana, Louisiana (Page: 46; NARA Roll: M33_31; Image: 47). The 1820 census also lists a resident of the Parish of New Orleans and slaveowner named John Holiday (Census Place: Orleans, Louisiana; Page: 120; NARA Roll: M33_32; Image: 134). Joseph Hatch Jr. (1798–1856), a recurring figure in Audubon's "Journal of a Sea Voyage," was a captain based in Kennebunkport, Maine. Dates derived from Ancestry.com; "Maine, Nathan Hale Cemetery Collection, 1780–1980," FamilySearch.org (Augusta: Maine State Library, 2020). Little information about the *Delos* is available; Maria Audubon told Francis Hobart Herrick that the ship capsized "on the Grand Banks of Newfoundland in the summer of 1831" (Herrick, *Audubon the Naturalist: A History of His Life and Times*, 2nd ed., 2 vols. [1938; New York: Dover, 1968], 1:348n1). This is confirmed by David Remich, *History of Kennebunk from Its Earliest Settlements to 1890* (Portland, ME: Lakeside Press, 1911): "The ship Delos, Charles Williams master, of and for this port [i.e., Kennebunk] from Liverpool, sprung a leak while scudding in severe gale, in longitude 45, September 16, 1831. . . . In a sinking condition, with eight feet of water in her hold, it was found necessary, on the eighteenth, to abandon her. Fortunately a bark, which proved to be the Frances Mary, from Ireland for Quebec, was in sight and answered their signal of distress, taking on board the officers and the crew, who were landed at Quebec on the eleventh of October. The Delos was partly loaded with salt and copper; a quantity of specie and a few hundred weight of copper were saved. The ship was insured and the cargo partially insured in Boston" (391).

2. The French ornithologist Charles-Lucien Bonaparte was the second Prince of Canino and Musignano (1803–1857) and a nephew of Napoleon I. James Randall Currell (ca. 1778–1839) was a New Orleans merchant.

3. The *Hercules* was jointly owned by Thomas Woodhouse Bakewell, Lucy's brother, and her brothers-in-law Nicholas Berthoud and Alexander Gordon, the latter based in Liverpool. The *Hercules* returned from New Orleans to Kentucky a year later and in December 1828 was lost "by the perils" of the Ohio River, whereupon Berthoud sued Gordon's company for restitution of his interest. The case reached the Supreme Court of the Louisiana, which affirmed a district court's judgment in favor of Berthoud; *Berthoud v. Gordon, Forstall & Co.*, June 1834; Thomas Curry, *Cases Argued and Determined in the Supreme Court of the State of Louisiana* (St. Paul, MN: West, 1912), 8:267–70.

4. Audubon's "dolphin" fish is more commonly known today as the mahi-mahi, dorado, or dolphinfish (*Coryphaena hippurus*). See more in "A Long Calm at Sea" and fig. 20. The "grain" is a fish-spear or harpoon with prongs.

5. Audubon's "Ballocuda" here is likely the great barracuda (*Sphyraena barracuda*), the most widespread species of barracuda, which has inky splotches on the belly and flanks (see fig. 10).

6. Audubon's "porpoise" is a species of ocean dolphin, the mammal, perhaps the common bottlenose dolphin (*Tursiops truncatus*). Mariners and naturalists did occasionally catch and eat these animals, and it was common to refer to porpoises and dolphins, the small toothed whales, collectively as porpoises. It was also common among both mariners and naturalists in the 1820s to refer to whales of any size colloquially—and even taxonomically for some—as fish, even though, as Audubon alludes ("of Course, had no Gills"), whales were by that time well known to be warm-blooded mammals. See D. Graham Burnett, *Trying Leviathan* (Princeton, NJ: Princeton University Press, 2007), 136–44. Bob stays are ropes or chains holding a ship's bowsprit downward to the stem. "Scutle fish," or cuttlefish, meant squid here. Squid are common food for toothed whales of all sizes; Audubon's "punch" (paunch) is a reference to the stomach.

7. Audubon's "Rudder Fish" were perhaps a school of juvenile banded rudderfish (*Seriola zonata*), common to the Gulf of Mexico year-round.

8. From the description and sketch (fig. 12), Audubon's sharks here were likely sandbar sharks (*Carcharhinus plumbeus*), a global species that is today classified as Vulnerable and decreasing (IUCN 2009). David Ebert, personal communication, June 11, 2020.

9. The captain's interest and strategy in trying to track the current is notable, since this particular passage with no wind from New Orleans out into the open North Atlantic turned out to be an exceptionally long one. The Florida Current, which runs toward the east between Florida and Cuba, and then to the north to form the Gulf Stream, is a true highway, but there are eddies and countercurrents in the Gulf, which, adding to the lack of wind, might have slowed down the *Delos* even further.

10. "Mother Carey's Chickens" was a sailor nickname for storm-petrels (family *Hydrobatidae* and *Oceanitidae*). See "Wilson's Petrel," plate 20, and fig. 31. "Scientific men" seems to be a reference to Alexander Wilson. With "Natura Fidelis" ("faithful nature"), Audubon was showing off his Latin.

11. Audubon and the crew's concern about pirates was warranted. The threat in this region was only recently on the decline, due to the US Navy sending seventeen vessels to the Caribbean in 1823 to try to control piracy. The Straits of Florida was a known merchant ship highway, and the Florida Keys, Bahamas, and Caribbean islands provided shelter and quick access to this homebound route. Benjamin Labaree et al., *America and the Sea: A Maritime History* (Mystic, CT: Mystic Seaport, 1998), 324. See also "Death of a Pirate."

12. The *Phenix Gazette* (Washington, DC) of November 27 announced the availability for sale of the cargo of the brig *Gleaner*, Jellerson, master (8,000 bushels coarse salt, 200 sacks fine salt, 600 bushels corn), and advertised the ship's capacity as 3,300 barrels ("a good vessel and will take freight to any port").

13. John Swift from St. Francisville, son of Benjamin Swift and featured in one of Audubon's pencil drawings in the original manuscript (not included here), was headed to Dublin to meet his parents. A happy-go-lucky fellow, he had brought eleven gallons of whiskey on board with him, which he shared freely with "all hands" (as Audubon notes in a later entry, July 18, 1826, not included in this volume).

14. The "Rice Bunting" appears as the "Rice Bird" in Havell 54; it is now known as the bobolink (*Dolichonyx oryzivorus*). Audubon knew of several species of warblers; it is not uncommon even today for small land birds to land on ships, either, as he writes, in distress or

for an opportune break from migration. The shortest distance between Florida and Cuba is less than a hundred statute miles.

15. For more on the sooty tern, now *Onychoprion fuscatus* (plate 4; Havell 235), see "The Sooty Tern." The bird in Audubon's "Frigate Pelican" (plate 3; Havell 271) was also known in the nineteenth century as the man-o-war bird and the sky-hawk and is now called the magnificent frigatebird (*Fregata magnificens*); see "The Frigate Pelican."

16. One of Audubon's first published essays was "Observations of the Natural History of the Alligator," *Edinburgh New Philosophical Journal* 2 (1826–1827): 270–80, which he read and wrote during his subsequent stay in Edinburgh. In the paper, he doesn't mention this event or what he learned about the alligator and salt water.

17. Audubon's "Green Heron" (Havell 333) is now *Butorides virescens*. For historical and current systematics debate, see Cornell Lab of Ornithology, *Birds of the World*, birdsoftheworld.org.

18. Audubon's secondhand "Hooping Crane" might have been the whooping crane (*Grus americana*) or the sandhill crane (*Antigone canadensis*), both of which he painted (Havel 226, 261), but at the time there was some confusion about juveniles and the difference in species. He painted the sandhill crane while alive, in captivity in his backyard in Boston, 1832–1833; the bird was gathered by Captain Clark of the US Navy on a voyage from Florida to Boston; Susanne M. Low, *A Guide to Audubon's* Birds of America, 2nd ed. (1988; New Haven, CT: William Reese Co. and Donald A. Heald, 2002), 144. As of 2019, the whooping crane is classified as Endangered, with fewer than 250 mature adults, but their population seems to be increasing; the sandhill crane, as of 2016, is of Least Concern and also has an increasing population (IUCN).

19. Audubon's "Line" here refers to the Tropic of Cancer (~23.5° N latitude, north of the coast of Cuba).

20. This "Sword Fish" might have been the broadbill swordfish (*Xiphias gladius*), but few sailors, or even naturalists, in the nineteenth century differentiated between swordfish, marlin, and sailfish at sea. Audubon's "gannets" here are likely the "Booby Gannet" (Havell 207), or more commonly today the brown booby (now *Sula leucogaster*). Audubon's "Great-footed Hawk" (Havell 16) is known today as the peregrine falcon (*Falco peregrinus*). Lord Byron's *The Corsair* was a popular tale in verse, published in 1814, focused on the pirate Conrad and his ill-fated but noble attempt to free the women in the harem of the Pacha Seyd.

21. Captain Birney later made headlines in an unfortunate way, when he and his crew were swept off the deck of the Admiralty packet *The Star*; see *Reports of the Commissioners Appointed to Inquire into the Laws and Regulations Regarding Pilotage* (London, 1832), 7:296. Tensions between Britain and Cuba, which was under Spanish rule, were at an all-time high, since British naval officers suspected the Cubans of carrying on with the slave trade. The 1826 census of Cuba revealed a slave population of 287,000. A manifest for the brig *Howard*, arriving November 20, 1826, in the port of New Orleans from "Rum Key" (Rum Cay, Bahamas) lists J. Bonney [Birney] as master (www.immigrantships.net/v4/1800v4/howard18261120.html). "E. Coste" was an unidentified Louisiana resident, not to be confused with Napoleon Coste (see notes to "The Florida Keys").

22. Audubon painted the White-headed Pigeon (Havell 177), now the white-crowned pigeon (*Patagioenas leucocephala*), in April 1832, at Indian Key, Florida, just after the birds had arrived from Cuba, and it seems certain that the memory of having seen them leaving Cuba in 1826 influenced his later representation, both in the drawing and the text he wrote for *Ornithological Biography*. While these birds are flying back to Florida to procure food for their young,

Audubon, by contrast, is leaving the New World and his family behind to pursue his dreams. The white-crowned pigeon, found only in the Caribbean and the coast of southern Florida, is classified as Near Threatened (IUCN, 2004). For the widespread popular belief that a silver dollar or, more commonly, a silver spoon will turn jet-black when poison is present, see, for example, R. Montgomery Martin, *History of the British Colonies* (London: Cochrane, 1835), 5:197.

23. This June 20 entry comes from a page torn out of the original manuscript, which was located by Alice Ford and is given here from the facsimile she provided; see *The 1826 Journal of John James Audubon* (Norman: University of Oklahoma Press, 1967), 35. The petrels were Audubon's "Dusky Petrels" (Havell 299), now known as Audubon's shearwaters (*Puffinus lherminieri*). Audubon retold the story of this capture at sea in his biography of the bird in *OB* 3 (1835), 620–21.

24. "Audubon's "Floating sea Weed" is Sargassum, a floating brown algae that Benjamin Franklin referred to as "gulf weed." Sargassum (*Sargassum spp.*) includes several species and serves as habitat, egg deposit, and food source for a range of invertebrates, fish, and seabirds. Benjamin Franklin, "A Letter . . . to Mr. Alphonsus le Roy," *Transactions of the American Philosophical Society* 2 (1786): 294–329; Jeff Schell, personal communication, June 14, 2020. *Anas* is the genus created by Linnaeus containing the "dabbling" or surface-feeding ducks (teals, mallards, pintails, etc.).

25. Audubon's "Nody" or "Noddy Tern" (Havell 275) is now known as the brown noddy (*Anous stolidus*). He painted his noddy in the Florida Keys in 1832, on "Noddy Key," which is probably now Bush Key (where brown noddies still breed, the only current rookery close to the US mainland), and he also drew a detailed sketch while aboard the *Delos* (see fig. 15).

26. According to a passage missing from the Field Museum journal but retained in the fragmentary copy of the journal written by a different hand and now held by the Beinecke Library (p. 15), this was the *Thalia* from Philadelphia, captained by John Butler, traveling from Havana to Minorca. Butler seems to have been a kind of navigational expert on Latin American waters; see his comment on the entrance of the Rio de la Plata in Thomas Arnold, *The American Practical Lunarian and Seaman's Guide* (Philadelphia, August 1822), 523n. "Iñatation" for "inattention" might have been a joke directed at the Spanish ship.

27. "Blues" was inkblotted in the manuscript.

28. Smudged in manuscript; here restored for clarity.

29. Apollo received a golden bow and arrows from his father, Zeus.

30. No petrels known seem to match this exact description; possible candidates include Cory's or greater shearwaters and white-capped petrels.

31. Titian's 1545 well-known portrait of his (milky-skinned) daughter Lavinia Vecellio is at the Museo di Capodimonte, Naples. A variety of other works by Titian were suspected of showing Lavinia, too, and Audubon—who wants to make a joke about his "satanic" tan—could also have been thinking of a 1560–1565 Titian portrait of a young woman in Gemäldegalerie Dresden, mentioned in travel accounts as early as 1806; see, for example, J. G. Lemaistre, *Travels after the Peace of Amiens through Parts of France, Italy, Switzerland, Germany*, 3 vols. (London: J. Johnson, 1806), 2:404. An 1815 engraving by James Heath, showing a girl also thought to be Lavinia holding a small casket, circulated widely (the original, featuring that young woman with a fruit platter, is in the Gemäldegalerie Berlin). Audubon's quip that the ship is a prison recalls, maybe accidentally, Samuel Johnson's famous remark, cited by Boswell: "No man will be a sailor who has contrivance enough to get himself into a

jail; for being in a ship is being in a jail, with the chance of being drowned." James Boswell, *The Journal of a Tour to the Hebrides* (Philadelphia: John F. Watson, 1810), 117.

32. James Thomson (1700–1748), Scottish poet, was the author of the perennially popular poem *The Seasons* (1726–1730), which inspired sentimental nature worship, and *The Castle of Indolence* (1748).

33. Audubon was using "Porpoises" as synonymous with ocean dolphins, the small toothed whales. "Dolphins" refers to the *fish* now called mahi-mahi, as it does earlier in this journal and in "A Long Calm at Sea."

34. Audubon was so impressed by this swift, a wooden cross from which yarn is wound off, that he provided an annotated illustration in his journal (not included in this volume).

35. Sam Bragdon, from Wells, Maine, was promoted to captain the next year; the ship news shows him in charge of the *Delos*, arriving from Liverpool in Boston on August 20, 1827 (*Zion's Herald*, August 29, 1827, 139). One reading of this scene is that the joke is on Audubon, in that sailors are often eager to clean loose gear off the deck, for order and safety.

36. "Stuart" is "steward," the crew member charged with tending to the officer's cabin, including serving food, cleaning, etc., a race-occupation regularly disparaged aboard American ships in the nineteenth century. See Margaret Creighton, *Rites and Passages: The Experience of American Whaling, 1830–1870* (Cambridge: Cambridge University Press, 1995), 185–87. Predictably, Audubon in his journal describes the steward of the *Delos*, a Black man, in explicitly racist terms. St. Anthony of Padua is often considered the patron saint of sailors (especially in Spain, France, and Italy); his replacement, St. Mark, is known as the patron saint of Venice (in which capacity he also appears as the helper of Venetian soldiers).

37. "Balasted" means that the *Albion* was empty of commercial cargo, sailing only with iron or stone ballast for stability.

38. The "Little petrils" here seem to be storm-petrels.

39. Experienced whalemen could tell the species of whale from the character of the blow from the spout hole, or "valve," as Audubon calls it; a few species of large whale exhale a small, thick cloud, and some whale species have tail flukes that can span fourteen feet, such as a blue or sei whale. The sperm whale is known for displaying its tail before a deep dive, and it is also the only large whale with just one spout hole, but Audubon was presumably not close enough to see that here.

40. Though dated Saturday, July 15, 1826, this entry appears to cover several days, since Audubon notes later that "yesterday's" entry was written on a Sunday.

41. Audubon was joking here about the smell of the captain's flatulence: foul winds from astern.

42. A reference to St. John going into Jesus's empty tomb: "and he saw and believed" (John 20:8). Audubon's elation at seeing a large whale is notable, as so many mariners and passengers in the nineteenth century viewed whales more in economic terms or as monstrous, not with the joy and wonder of twentieth- and twenty-first-century whale watchers.

43. Cape Clear is off the southwest coast of Ireland. The "Camhouse," or more commonly camboose or caboose, was a galley built on the upper deck of a ship, and the "Sloche [slush] Barrel" often held used fat from cooking, kept for greasing the masts and for other uses. It was common for mariners in the nineteenth century to harpoon and capture dolphins for fresh food. If he had a particular species in mind, the "European Hawk" was perhaps what is now the Eurasian sparrowhawk (*Accipiter nisus*). See the review "Hewitson's British Oology,"

in *The Analyst: A Quarterly Journal of Science, Literature, Natural History, and Fine Arts* 5 (London: Simpkin, Marshall, & Co., 1836): 76. His "2 Curlews" here might have been Eurasian curlews (*Numenius arquata*) or whimbrels (*Numenius phaeopus*).

44. The omitted passage is a coarse, racist anecdote about the steward's flannel shirt sticking out of his pants, "like the sun setting in our western prairies."

45. Brigs, schooners, and other types of sailing ship are differentiated by number of masts and types of sails.

46. Audubon parades his British culture credentials, listing writers (among them, John Dryden, James Thomson, Dr. Johnson, and Tobias Smollett) and artists (painter and engraver William Hogarth and the Pennsylvania-born painter Benjamin West, who settled in London in 1763). It is not clear what Audubon meant by the "well deserved name" the English had given to novelist and poet Oliver Goldsmith, but Horace Walpole called him an "inspired idiot," in reference to the curious combination of literary achievement, hack writing, and dissolute lifestyle he displayed. Edward Young (1683–1765) was celebrated for his didactic poem on death, *Night Thoughts* (1742–1745). Byron's poetry was in Audubon's baggage, and his admiration for the Scottish novelist Sir Walter Scott is well known; he would later devote an ecstatic passage in this journal to him, imploring him to come to the United States and describe its grandeur "for future ages" before it was gone for good (December 12, 1826). After several abortive attempts to meet Scott, he finally got his chance on January 22, 1827. Scott found Audubon "handsome and interesting," with "simplicity" as his dominant characteristic. Maria R. Audubon, ed., *Audubon and His Journals* (New York: Charles Scribner's Sons, 1897), 1:206n1.

47. "Brig Ho! And Ship Hi!" Note how Audubon's native French, with its silent *h*, interferes with his spelling.

48. The *Homer* gained some notoriety in 1838 when it was used during the Trail of Tears to ship Seminole prisoners from Fort Moultrie to New Orleans and then on to Arkansas. Seminole leader Ee-mat-la, or King Phillip, died during the passage up the Mississippi. Charles H. Coe, *Red Patriots: The Story of the Seminoles* (Cincinnati: Editor, 1898), 119. "Russia[n] Duck" is white linen canvas.

49. Inkblotted in Audubon's manuscript but restored here for clarity.

50. Tuskar Rock is a group of rocks 6.8 miles off the southeast coast of County Wexford, Ireland. The lighthouse began operating in June 1815. Holyhead is a town in Wales and a port serving Ireland.

II

Ornithological Biography (1831–1839)

On June 20, 1838, Robert Havell pulled the first print of the 435th and final plate of Audubon's *The Birds of America.* Audubon's gigantic undertaking ended with a whimper—the last engraving featured two western birds Audubon had never seen himself, chunky little American dippers, perched on two cliffs overlooking a stylized waterfall (Havell, who had never seen a western landscape either, just invented one for the occasion). But Audubon wasn't done yet. Since 1831, he had been hard at work on his *Ornithological Biography*, producing a steady stream of essays about birds, their appearance, behavior, and feeding habits, that were meant to accompany the plates. The fifth and last installment of *Ornithological Biography* would take another year to be complete.

With each new volume released by Adam & Charles Black in Edinburgh, Audubon's confidence as a writer grew. But the basic format of the essays had been in place from the beginning of the project, and Audubon adhered to it through all five volumes. The typical Audubon bird essay opens with information about a bird's habitat. After asking that the reader accompany him in spirit, Audubon offers a personal account of how and when he captured the bird in question so that he could draw it for the reader's benefit. Then follow detailed observations about habits (flight patterns, migration, courtship, song, breeding behavior) and morphology (size, color, plumage). Not all of the essays are equally detailed; his own interests and different levels of exposure to a bird in the field determined the degree of attention he would devote to a species.

The science in Audubon's essays was strictly optional; as he announced in the introduction to the first volume, readers could skip the more technical parts. For the least ornithologically savvy, he had stuck entertaining frontier stories in between the bird essays, a treat especially for his European readers. He called these narratives "delineations of American scenery and manners,"[1] short episodes, of sometimes questionable authenticity, about life in the woods or along the coast and at sea. Yet, despite his now well-developed writerly and artistic ambitions, Audubon, in his own estimation, was first and foremost a scientist, a term that, coincidentally, was coined at just around that time by William Whewell in Cambridge.[2] Consequently, in volumes 4 and 5 of *Ornithological Biography*, Audubon offered no more narrative entertainments and, in an effort to establish his bona fides as a naturalist, doubled down on the science, adding detailed anatomical reports for each bird, complete with exact measurements (which he transferred from his journals) and results from the dissection of his specimens.

Audubon called his bird essays "biographies" to indicate the care and attention he had bestowed on each species in his avian universe. The essays about waterbirds collected in this anthology are united by Audubon's deep admiration not only for the birds that survive in this often treacherous environment but also for the men who, unlike Audubon, make their living on the water. Audubon was reluctant to share credit, especially when it came to his gifted background painters Joseph Mason, Maria Martin, and George Lehman,[3] but he rarely forgot to tell us who his captains were. Whether they take him through the Florida Keys or to Labrador, they are, to Audubon, the epitome of expertise, to the extent that his prose positively begins to dance when he watches a Florida wrecker, one of the salvage ships ubiquitous in the Keys ("how trim, how clean-rigged, and how well manned!"), make its perilous way among the reefs: "There, in that narrow passage, well known to her commander, she rolls, tumbles, and dances, like a giddy thing, her copper sheathing now gleaming, and again disappearing under the waves." Throughout his life, Audubon's perspective on sea travel remained very much that of a landlubber, shocked at the unpredictability of the weather at sea, where birds seem to live so effortlessly, gliding easily over, or riding on, the ocean's "proud waves" ("A Long Calm at Sea"). A storm at sea is a sublime sight but it is also, especially for a seasickness-prone traveler like Audubon, a physical experience. "The waters drifted like snow; the tough mangroves hid their tops amid their roots, and the loud roaring of the waves driven among them blended with the howl of the tempest," he writes in "The Florida Keys (Part Two)." The waves, in such a storm, became like ferocious whips lashing into the defenseless traveler: "It was not rain that fell; the masses of water flew in a horizontal direction, and where a part of my body was exposed, I felt as if a smart blow had been given me on it." While Audubon and, it seems, the rest of nature, too, cower before a big storm, the frigatebird remains unimpressed. Its resilience tops that of the sailors: "as the angry blasts curl the waves, the thunder mutters afar; all nature is involved in gloom, and all is in confusion, save only the Man-of-war Bird, who gallantly meets the gale" ("The Frigate Pelican"). During the roughest winds, the Wandering Shearwater (as Audubon calls the great shearwater) may be seen skimming along "the troughs of the waves on extended wings in large curves." Note Audubon's use of the word "trough," a nautical term indicating a hollow between two wave crests in the sea, which suggests that he has learned a thing or two from spending so much time with the sailors.

"Split the Lark," Emily Dickinson would quip a few decades later, "and you'll find the music."[4] The idea is that you won't: the wonder of birds does not reside in their anatomy. Audubon would have disagreed. From admiring a shearwater skimming above unruly waters Audubon can shift effortlessly to opening the stomach of a fine specimen he has caught ("I found fishes, portions of crabs, sea-weeds, and oily substances"). The lengthy appendix to the final volume of *Ornithological Biography* elevates Dickinson's lark-splitting to the level of fine art. Audubon here supplies the missing anatomical descriptions for birds represented in volumes 1–3; no longer sidelined by chatty episodes, they appear massed together, an endless gallery of death. For these anatomical epilogues, not for the faint of heart, came festooned with drawings, produced by Audubon's Scottish editor William MacGillivray (1796–1852), of lungs, tracheae, and looping intestinal tracts. We have omitted

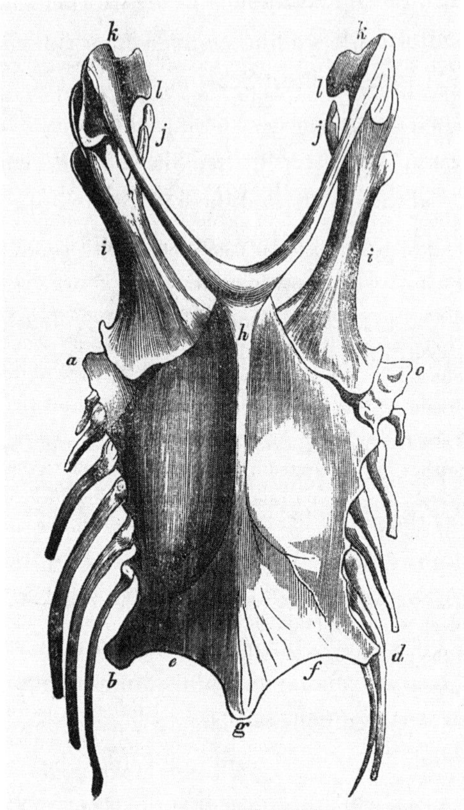

FIGURE 18. William MacGillivray, sternum of American white pelican. Woodcut from Audubon, *Ornithological Biography*, vol. 4 (1838). Courtesy of Williams College.

these anatomical postscripts in our edition (except in "Black-footed Albatross"); a representative example of such an anatomical illustration appears as figure 18 (see also figs. 26 and 27).

Audubon not only routinely split his larks, he ate them too, sometimes with pleasing results (Wilson's plover was "delicious eating," he felt), while on other occasions his stomach rebelled (gannet was "so bad that, . . . it ought to be rejected"). In Audubon's case, getting to know his birds from the inside out, or, when he ingested them, from the outside in, does not diminish his appreciation; it enhances it: "see the powerful fisher, on well-spread pinions, and high over the water, glide silently along, surveying each swelling wave below." Even though, he freely admits, such admiration might last only until that moment when you see that powerful gannet plunging downward to the water again, "intent on filling its empty stomach," snatching a fish from the water, "its beloved element," and swallowing it whole.

It appears that, in Audubon's world, living things are defined mostly by their stomachs. His episode "Cod-Fishing" turns that concept into a metaphor of sinister proportions. When Audubon takes us into the bowels of a cod-processing vessel anchored off the coast of Labrador, we witness a giant, industrial-strength stomach at work. What Audubon performed one bird at a time is here carried out by several men working in concert like the organs of a massive body: "One begins with breaking off the head of the fish, a slight pull of the hand and a gash with the knife effecting this in a moment. He slits up its belly, with one hand pushes it aside to his neighbour, then throws overboard the head, and begins to doctor another." If one suspects the verb "doctor" to be slightly ironical, subsequent steps in the process confirm the impression. These hands don't heal, they divide: "The next man tears out the entrails, separates the liver, which he throws into a cask, and casts the rest overboard. A third person dexterously passes his knife beneath the vertebræ of the fish, separates them from the flesh, heaves the latter through the hatchway, and the former into the water." Audubon's description captures the inevitable waste generated during the process ("throws overboard", "casts . . . overboard," "heaves . . . into the water"), which leads to the ship drifting in an expanding pool of offal, while the gutted remains of each fish are salted, packed, and readied for export—and further digestion, one might add, this time by thousands of human stomachs in the Mediterranean or elsewhere.[5] The inherent destructiveness of this operation was already evident at the time Audubon paid his visit. Cod-fishing off the Labrador coast was the result of the overfishing inshore in Newfoundland, where the bays had gradually been emptied of fish. By the end of the century, the Labrador offshore fishery was in decline, too.[6] Like Audubon's bird essays, this episode does not release us into a place of comfortable complacency. But there is a difference: Labrador birds like the gannet eat to survive and feed their young, while human voraciousness has long exceeded the parameters of the simple motto ("use, don't waste") espoused by James Fenimore Cooper's fictional frontiersman Natty Bumppo, a literary character Audubon admired and on whom he, at times, modeled himself.[7]

Audubon's bird essays were so polished, so unabashedly literary, that they drew the unrestrained ire of British naturalist Charles Waterton (1782–1865), who, in a volley of attacks, doubted that Audubon could have been their sole author—a scurrilous charge when one remembers that Audubon had, at least in this one instance, freely acknowledged the assistance of a collaborator, thanking William MacGillivray for "completing the scientific details, and smoothing down the asperities" of his prose (*OB* 1 [1831], xix).[8] The few surviving autographs reveal the extent of MacGillivray's influence: He fixed Audubon's intuitive spelling and clipped his wings when he had flown too high or descended too low (if an ornithological metaphor of the kind Audubon liked to use himself is permitted). By channeling the syntactic torrents Audubon had unleashed into shorter sentences and substituting readily relatable phrases for some of Audubon's more eccentric word choices (for example, "as birds generally do" for "the generality of other birds"), he made Audubon's prose accessible to a broader audience.[9] Drawing on specimens at the Edinburgh University Natural History Museum, MacGillivray also composed the anatomical descriptions and drew the accompanying sketches, as Audubon also disclosed (*OB* 4 [1838], xxiii–xxiv). Lucy joined the team as a copyist, though she likely contributed more than secretarial work. Audubon never publicly acknowledged her "dawn-to-dusk" labor on *Ornithological Biography*.[10]

There is no doubt that some of the "swiftness of thought" that had made Audubon's journal-writing so remarkable has disappeared from these essays.[11] If the journals were Audubon "raw," these essays give us Audubon "cooked," to evoke a distinction made by Scott Russell Sanders.[12] In addition, Audubon had learned, and borrowed, from his predecessors and contemporaries, French ornithologists such as the Comte de Buffon, François Levaillant, or René Primevère Lesson (see notes to "Black Skimmer").[13] His bird biographies would have been unthinkable without the essays in Alexander Wilson's *American Ornithology* (1808–1814). Yet the immense synthetic effort that went into Audubon's writing, the determination with which he fused anatomical detail, journal notes, accounts by other observers, and insights gleaned from previous writers into near-seamless narratives, made *Ornithological Biography* an unparalleled resource for other scientists, including Charles Darwin (as discussed in the introduction to this volume). Certainly, Audubon's science was not error-free; even friends like Charles-Lucien Bonaparte suspected that he would, on occasion, misrepresent evidence or even invent stories.[14] It is worth remembering here that, throughout his life, Audubon was a salesman as well as a naturalist, operating without the institutional support and the network of connections commanded by that constant thorn in Audubon's flesh, George Ord (1781–1866), vice president and then president of the Academy of Natural Sciences in Philadelphia. Nevertheless, Audubon created an abiding model for field ornithology today. One of the great pleasures as we were working on this volume was to hear biologists praise and confirm Audubon's sharp observations especially of bird behavior.

Audubon reused the essays in *Ornithological Biography* for the so-called Royal Octavo edition of *The Birds of America* (1840–1844), pairing each installment with a lithograph based on the corresponding plate from the double elephant folio. Small modifications in the text reflect the more democratic appeal of this affordable edition of *The Birds of America*. An example in our edition is found in "The Fish Hawk, or Osprey," which opens with Audubon's funny remark that this bird, so much more powerful than the "Kingfisher," should really be called the "*Imperial Fisher*"—were that name not inappropriate in the context of a republic. In the more egalitarian Royal Octavo, produced and printed in the United States of America, this flippant joke seemed out of place. Audubon deleted the passage.

Notes

1. This is how Audubon identified these essays on the title page of *Ornithological Biography* when the first volume appeared in 1835. When Francis Hobart Herrick collected Audubon's episodes in a separate volume in 1926, he changed "manners" to the more nationalistic "character": *Delineations of American Scenery and Character*, with an introduction by Herrick (New York: G. A. Baker, 1926).

2. See William Whewell, "Review of *On the Connexion of the Physical Sciences*," *Quarterly Review* 51 (1834): 54–68; Susannah Gibson, *The Spirit of Inquiry: How One Extraordinary Society Shaped Modern Science* (Oxford: Oxford University Press, 2019), 75–76.

3. Shirley Streshinsky, *Audubon: Life and Art in the American Wilderness* (New York: Villard, 1993), 201.

4. Emily Dickinson, #861, *The Complete Poems of Emily Dickinson*, ed. Thomas H. Johnson (Boston: Little, Brown, & Co., 1955), 412.

5. On the Mediterranean as the "most demanding cod market," see Mark Kurlansky, *Cod: A Biography of a Fish That Changed the World* (New York: Penguin, 1998), 104–5.

6. "19th Century Cod Fisheries," Newfoundland and Labrador Heritage, https://www.heritage.nf.ca/articles/economy/19th-century-cod.php (accessed January 14, 2021).

7. Christoph Irmscher, *The Poetics of Natural History*, rev. ed. (New Brunswick, NJ: Rutgers University Press, 2019), 225–27.

8. On the Waterton-Audubon feud, see John Chalmers, *Audubon in Edinburgh and His Scottish Associates* (Edinburgh: National Museums of Scotland/Royal College of Surgeons, 2003), 136–42.

9. On MacGillivray's editing, see Irmscher, *Poetics*, 209–20. A general evaluation of the Audubon-MacGillivray collaboration is offered by Chalmers, *Audubon in Edinburgh*, 146–57. MacGillivray believed (pre-DNA) that species could be distinguished by the structure of their innards; see Roberta J. M. Olson, "Audubon's Innovations and the Traditions of Ornithological Illustration: Some Things Old, Some Things Borrowed, but Most Things New," in Olson, *Audubon's Aviary: The Original Watercolors for* The Birds of America (New York: New-York Historical Society/Rizzoli, 2012), 40–101, 96.

10. See Carolyn E. DeLatte, *Lucy Audubon: A Biography*, updated ed. (1982; Baton Rouge: Louisiana State University Press, 2008), 219.

11. See the headnote to "Journal of a Sea Voyage" in this volume.

12. Scott Russell Sanders, introduction to *Audubon Reader: The Best Writings of John James Audubon*, ed. Sanders (Bloomington: Indiana University Press, 1986), 1–17.

13. On Audubon's familiarity with French ornithology (though focused mostly on the illustrations), see Linda Dugan Partridge, "By the Book: Audubon and the Tradition of Ornithological Illustration," *Huntington Library Quarterly* 59, nos. 2–3 (1998): 269–301, as well as Olson, "Audubon's Innovations," esp. 41-48.

14. See Patricia Stroud, *The Emperor of Nature: Charles-Lucien Bonaparte and His World* (Philadelphia: University of Pennsylvania Press, 2000), 118–19. For a reckoning with Audubon's ornithological missteps, see Matthew R. Halley, "Audubon's Bird of Washington: Unravelling the Fraud That Launched *The Birds of America*," *Bulletin of the British Ornithologists' Club* 140, no. 2 (2020): 110–141. But these charges against Audubon are not new; see, for example, Peter Matthiessen on Audubon's "uneven reputation," in *Wildlife in America* (New York: Viking, 1959), 118–19, 133.

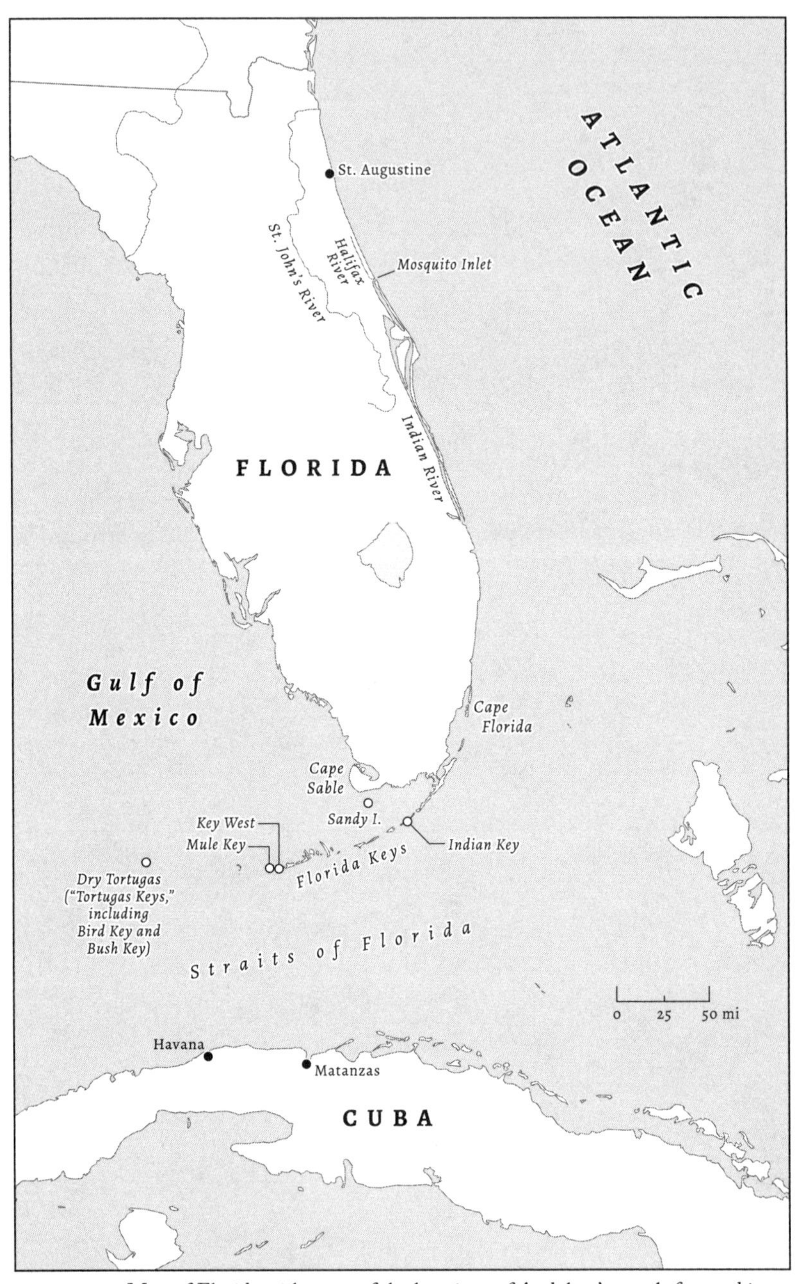

FIGURE 19. Map of Florida with some of the locations of Audubon's travels featured in *Ornithological Biography*. Erin Greb Cartography.

Southern Waters

A LONG CALM AT SEA

ON the 17th of May 1826, I left New Orleans on board the ship Delos, commanded by JOSEPH HATCH, Esq. of Kennebunk, bound for Liverpool. The steamer Hercules, which towed the ship, left us several miles outside the Balize, about ten hours after our departure; but there was not a breath of wind, the waters were smoother than the prairies of the Oppelousas, and notwithstanding our great display of canvass, we lay, like a dead whale, floating at the mercy of the currents. The weather was uncommonly fair, and the heat excessive; and in this helpless state we continued for many days. About the end of a week we had lost sight of the Balize, although I was assured by the commander, that all this while the ship had rarely answered the helm. The sailors whistled for wind, and raised their hands in all directions, anxious as they were to feel some motion in the air; but all to no purpose; it was a dead calm, and we concluded that Æolus had agreed with Neptune to detain us, until our patience should be fairly tried, or our sport exhausted; for sport we certainly had, both on board and around the ship. I doubt if I can better contribute to your amusement at present, than by giving you a short account of the occurrences that took place, during this sleepy fit of the being on whom we depended for our progress toward merry England.[1]

Vast numbers of beautiful dolphins [fig. 20] glided by the side of the vessel, glancing like burnished gold through the day, and gleaming like meteors by night. The captain and his mates were expert at alluring them with baited hooks, and not less so at piercing them with a five-pronged instrument, which they called grains; and I was delighted with the sport, because it afforded me an opportunity of observing and noting some of the habits of this beautiful fish, as well as several other kinds.[2]

FIGURE 20. Drawing of a "dolphin" (now more often known as the mahi-mahi, *Coryphaena hippurus*), in Audubon, "Journal of a Sea Voyage" (May 28, 1826). Courtesy of the Field Museum, Chicago.

On being hooked, the Dolphin flounces vigorously, shoots off with great impetuosity to the very end of the line, when, being suddenly checked, it often rises perpendicularly several feet out of the water, shakes itself violently in the air, gets disentangled, and thus escapes. But when well secured, it is held in play for a while by the experienced fisher, soon becomes exhausted, and is hauled on board. Some persons prefer pulling them in at once, but they seldom succeed, as the force with which the fish shakes itself on being raised out of the water, is generally sufficient to enable it to extricate itself. Dolphins move in shoals, varying from four or five to twenty or more, hunting in packs in the waters, as wolves pursue their prey on land. The object of their pursuit is generally the Flying-fish, now and then the Bonita; and when nothing better can be had, they will follow the little Rudder-fish, and seize it immediately under the stern of the ship. The Flying-fishes, after having escaped for a while by dint of their great velocity, but on being again approached by the Dolphin, emerge from the waters, and spreading their broad wing-like fins, sail through the air and disperse in all directions, like a covey of timid partridges before the rapacious falcon. Some pursue a direct course, others diverge on either side; but in a short time they all drop into their natural element. While they are travelling in the air, their keen and hungry pursuer, like a greyhound, follows in their wake, and performing a succession of leaps, many feet in extent, rapidly gains upon the quarry, which is often seized just as it falls into the sea.[3]

Dolphins manifest a very remarkable sympathy with each other. The moment one of them is hooked or grained, those in company make up to it, and remain around until the unfortunate fish is pulled on board, when they generally move off together, seldom biting at any thing thrown out to them. This, however, is the case only with the larger individuals, which keep apart from the young, in the same manner as is observed in several species of birds; for when the smaller Dolphins are in large shoals, they all remain under the bows of a ship, and bite in succession at any sort of line, as if determined to see what has become of their lost companions, in consequence of which they are often all caught.

You must not suppose that the Dolphin is without its enemies. Who, in this world, man or fish, has not enough of them? Often it conceives itself on the very eve of swallowing a fish, which, after all, is nothing but a piece of lead, with a few feathers fastened to it, to make it look like a flying-fish, when it is seized and severed in two by the insidious Balacouda, which I have once seen to carry off by means of its sharp teeth, the better part of a Dolphin that was hooked, and already hoisted to the surface of the water.[4]

The Dolphins caught in the Gulf of Mexico during this calm were suspected to be poisonous; and to ascertain whether this was really the case, our cook, who was an African Negro, never boiled or fried one without placing beside it a dollar. If the silver was not tarnished by the time the Dolphin was ready for the table, the fish was presented to the passengers, with an assurance that it was perfectly good. But as not a single individual of the hundred that we caught had the property of converting silver into copper, I suspect that our African sage was no magician.

One morning, that of the 22d of June, the weather sultry, I was surprised, on getting out of my hammock, which was slung on deck, to find the water all around swarming with Dolphins, which were sporting in great glee. The sailors assured me that this was a certain "token of wind," and, as they watched the movement of the fishes, added, "aye, and of a fair breeze too." I caught several Dolphins in the course of an hour, after which scarcely any remained about the ship. Not a breath of air came to our relief all that day, no, nor even the next. The sailors were in despair, and I would probably have become despondent also, had not my spirits been excited by finding a very large Dolphin on my hook. When I had hauled it on board, I found it to be the largest I had ever caught. It was a magnificent creature. See how it quivers in the agonies of death! Its tail flaps the hard deck, producing a sound like the rapid roll of a drum. How beautiful the changes of its colours! Now it is blue, now green, silvery, golden, and burnished copper; now it presents a blaze of all the hues of the rainbow intermingled; but, alack! It is dead, and the play of its colours is no longer seen. It has settled into the deep calm that has paralyzed the energies of the blustering winds, and smoothed down the proud waves of the ocean.[5]

The best bait for the Dolphin is a long stripe of shark's flesh. I think it generally prefers this to the semblance of a flying-fish, which indeed it does not often seize unless when the ship is under weigh, and it is made to rise to the surface. There are times, however, when hunger and the absence of their usual food, will induce the Dolphins to dash at any sort of bait; and I have seen some caught by means of a piece of white linen fastened to a hook. Their appetite is as keen as that of the Vulture, and whenever a good opportunity occurs, they gorge themselves to such a degree that they become an easy prey to their enemies the Balacouda and the Bottle-nosed Porpoise. One that had been grained while lazily swimming immediately under the stern of our ship, was found to have its stomach completely crammed with flying-fish, all regularly disposed side by side, with their tails downwards,—by which I mean to say that the Dolphin always *swallows its prey tail foremost*. They looked in fact like so many salted herrings packed in a box, and were to the number of twenty-two, each six or seven inches in length.[6]

The usual length of the Dolphins caught in the Gulf of Mexico is about three feet, and I saw none that exceeded four feet two inches. The weight of one of the latter size was only eighteen pounds; for this fish is extremely narrow in proportion to its length, although rather deep in its form. When just caught, the upper fin, which reaches from the forehead to within a short distance of the tail, is of a fine dark blue. The upper part of the body in its whole length is azure, and the lower parts are of a golden hue, mottled irregularly with deep blue spots. It seems that they at times enter very shallow water, as in the course of my last voyage along the Florida coast, some were caught in a seine, along with their kinsman the "Cavalier," of which I shall speak elsewhere.[7]

The flesh of the Dolphin is rather firm, very white, and lies in flakes when cooked. The first caught are generally eaten with great pleasure, but when served many days in succession, they become insipid. It is not, as an article of food, equal to the Balacouda, which is perhaps as good as any fish caught in the waters of the Gulf of Mexico.

Notes

1. "A Long Calm at Sea" was first published in *OB* 3 (1835), 491–94. For more on Hatch and the *Delos*, see note to "Journal of a Sea Voyage," April 26. "La Balize," from "la balise" or "marker buoy," was a fort village at the mouth of the Mississippi River Delta that represented the primary entry for pilots and a point at which to transfer cargo to or from New Orleans. The little village and fort were often moved in the 1700s and 1800s, and abandoned entirely by the mid-nineteenth century, due to the natural movement of the Mississippi and to hurricanes, replaced by Pilottown (Plaquemines Parish, Louisiana) farther upriver.

2. Audubon's "dolphin" fish is more commonly known today as the mahi-mahi, dorado, or dolphinfish (*Coryphaena hippurus*). (A second, rarer and smaller species, the pompano dolphinfish, *Coryphaena equiselis*, doesn't match Audubon's drawing.) The dolphinfish population remains stable today and is classified of Least Concern, although it remains prized by sailors and recreational and commercial fishermen for food (IUCN, 2010). The behaviors Audubon described in his journal while aboard the *Delos* and in this biography match current observations, such as preying on flying fish and staying by a boat after an "unfortunate one" has been captured.

3. Audubon's fish here in the Gulf of Mexico and Straits of Florida are the "Flying-fish," several species of which inhabit these offshore waters, perhaps the most common being the Atlantic flyingfish (*Cheilopogon melanurus*); the "Bonita," now more commonly bonito, a close relative of the tuna, of which there are several species, such as the Atlantic bonito (*Sarda sarda*), found throughout the Gulf of Mexico and along the North American East Coast; and the "Rudder-fish," perhaps the banded rudderfish (*Seriola zonata*), common to this area (see fig. 11).

4. The "Balacouda," now more commonly spelled barracuda, is here likely the great barracuda (*Sphyraena barracuda*). See fig. 10.

5. The loss of the brilliant colors of a dolphinfish as it dies has been a common motif in sea literature, found in poetry such as William Falconer's *The Shipwreck* (1762). Descriptions of this fading color were so prevalent that Richard Henry Dana Jr. wrote that he felt let down when he saw it himself, because it had been overplayed, in *Two Years before the Mast* (New York: Harper & Bros., 1840), 24.

6. The "Bottle-nosed Porpoise" is now the bottlenose dolphin, *Tursiops truncatus*.

7. The identity of the "Cavalier" is uncertain, as is the reference to the discussion of that fish "elsewhere" in Audubon's work. It is possible that Audubon misheard the term "Cavalla," a vernacular term for the crevalle jack (*Caranx hippos*) or a similar species of jack fish.

THE FLORIDA KEYS

As the Marion neared the inlet called "Indian Key," which is situated on the eastern coast of the peninsula of Florida, my heart swelled with uncontrollable delight. Our vessel once over the coral reef that every where stretches along the shore like a great wall, reared by an army of giants, we found ourselves in safe anchoring ground, within a few furlongs of the land. The next moment saw the oars of a boat propelling us towards the shore, and in brief time we stood on the desired beach. With what delightful feelings did we gaze on the objects around us!—the gorgeous flowers, the singular and beautiful plants, the luxuriant trees. The balmy air which we breathed filled us with animation, so pure and salubrious did it seem to be. The birds which we saw were almost all new to us; their lovely forms appeared to be arrayed in more brilliant apparel than I had ever before seen, and as they gambolled in happy playfulness among the bushes, or glided over the light green waters, we longed to form a more intimate acquaintance with them.[1]

Students of nature spend little time in introductions, especially when they present themselves to persons who feel an interest in their pursuits. This was the case with Mr THRUSTON, the Deputy Collector of the island, who shook us all heartily by the hand, and in a trice had a boat manned at our service. Accompanied by him, his pilot and fishermen, off we went, and after a short pull landed on a large key. Few minutes had elapsed, when shot after shot might be heard, and down came whirling through the air the objects of our desire. One thrust himself into the tangled groves that covered all but the beautiful coral beach that in a continued line bordered the island, while others gazed on the glowing and diversified hues of the curious inhabitants of the deep. I saw one of my party rush into the limpid element, to seize on a crab, that with claws extended upwards, awaited his approach, as if determined not to give way. A loud voice called him back to the land, for sharks are as abundant

FIGURE 21. A determined crab. Robert Havell Jr. after John James Audubon, "Cayenne Tern" (royal tern), 1835 (detail). Aquatint engraving. *The Birds of America*, plate 273. Courtesy of the Lilly Library. At the feet of the tern, Audubon painted what is likely a stylized spider crab, perhaps *Maguimithrax spinosissimus*, which is common on the shores of Florida. In *Ornithological Biography* (3 [1835], 509), Audubon wrote that he added it to the painting because of its "singularly bright red colour, which, when the animal is boiled, changes to pale yellow," although that color change is dubious to modern ecologists (Darryl Felder and Gustav Paulay, personal communication, August 11, 2020).

along these shores as pebbles, and the hungry prowlers could not have got a more savoury dinner.[2]

The pilot, besides being a first-rate shot, possessed a most intimate acquaintance with the country. He had been a "conch-diver," and no matter what number of fathoms measured the distance between the surface of the water and its craggy bottom, to seek for curious shells in their retreat seemed to him more pastime than toil. Not a Cormorant or Pelican, a Flamingo, an Ibis, or Heron, had ever in his days formed its nest without his having marked the spot; and as to the Keys to which the Doves are wont to resort, he was better acquainted with them than many fops are with the contents of their pockets. In a word, he positively knew every channel that led to these islands, and every cranny along their shores. For years his employment had been to hunt those singular animals called Sea Cows or Manatees, and he had conquered hundreds of them, "merely," as he said, because the flesh and hide bring "a fair price," at Havannah. He never went anywhere to land without "Long Tom," which proved indeed to be a wonderful gun, and which made smart havoc when charged with "groceries," a term by which he designated the large shot which he used. In like manner, he never paddled his light canoe without having by his side the trusty javelin, with which he unerringly transfixed such fishes as he thought fit either for market or for his own use. In attacking turtles, netting, or overturning them, I doubt if his equal ever lived on the Florida coast. No sooner was he made acquainted with my errand, than he freely offered his best services, and from that moment until I left Key West he was seldom out of my hearing.[3]

While the young gentlemen who accompanied us were engaged in procuring plants, shells, and small birds, he tapped me on the shoulder, and with a smile said to me, "Come along, I'll shew you something better worth your while." To the boat we betook ourselves, with the Captain and only a pair of tars, for more he said would not answer. The yawl for a while was urged at a great rate, but as we approached a point, the oars were taken in, and the pilot alone skulling, desired us to make ready, for in a few minutes we should have "rare sport." As we advanced, the more slowly did we move, and the most profound silence was maintained, until suddenly coming almost in contact with a thick shrubbery of mangroves, we beheld, right before us, a multitude of pelicans. A discharge of artillery seldom produced more effect;—the dead, the dying, and the wounded, fell from the trees upon the water, while those unscathed flew screaming through the air in terror and dismay. "There," said he, "did not I tell you so; is it not rare sport?" The birds, one after another, were lodged under the gunwales, when the pilot desired the Captain to order the lads to pull away. Within about half a mile we reached the extremity of the key. "Pull away," cried the pilot, "never mind them on the wing, for those black rascals don't mind a little firing—now, boys, lay her close under the nests." And there we were, with four hundred cormorants' nests over our heads. The birds were sitting, and when we fired, the number that dropped as if dead and plunged into the water was such, that I thought by some unaccountable means or other we had killed the whole colony. You would have smiled at the loud laugh and curious gestures of the pilot. "Gentlemen," said he, "almost a blank shot!" And so it was, for, on following the birds as one after another peeped up from the water, we found only a few unable to take to wing. "Now," said the pilot, "had you waited until *I had spoken* to the black villains, you might have killed a score or more of them." On inspection, we found that our shots had lodged in the tough dry twigs of which these birds form their nests, and that we had lost the more favourable opportunity of hitting them, by not waiting until they rose. "Never mind," said the pilot, "if you wish it, you may load the *Lady of the Green Mantle** with them in less than a week. Stand still, my lads; and now, gentlemen, in ten minutes you and I will bring down a score of them." And so we did. As we rounded the island, a beautiful bird of the species called Peale's Egret, came up and was shot. We now landed, took in the rest of our party, and returned to Indian Key, where we arrived three hours before sunset.[4]

The sailors and other individuals to whom my name and pursuits had become known, carried our birds to the pilot's house. His good wife had a room ready for me to draw in, and my assistant might have been seen busily engaged in skinning, while GEORGE LEHMAN was making a sketch of the lovely isle.[5]

Time is ever precious to the student of nature. I placed several birds in their natural attitudes, and began to outline them. A dance had been prepared also, and no sooner was the sun lost to our eye, than males and females, including our captain and others from the vessel, were seen advancing gaily towards the house in full apparel. The birds were skinned, the sketch was on paper, and I told my young men to amuse themselves. As to myself, I could not join in the merriment, for, full of the remembrance of you, reader, and of the patrons of my work both in America and in Europe, I went on "grinding"—not on an organ, like the Lady of Bras d'Or, but on paper, to the finishing, not merely of my outlines, but of my notes respecting the objects seen this day.[6]

The room adjoining that in which I worked, was soon filled. Two miserable fiddlers screwed their screeching silken strings—not an inch of catgut graced their instruments; and the bouncing of brave lads and fair lasses shook the premises to the foundation. One with a slip came down heavily on the floor, and the burst of laughter that followed echoed over the isle. Diluted claret was handed round to cool the ladies, while a beverage of more potent energies warmed their partners. After supper our captain returned to the Marion, and I, with my young men, slept in light swinging hammocks under the eaves of the piazza.

*The name given by the wreckers and smugglers to the Marion. [Audubon's footnote]

It was the end of April, when the nights were short and the days therefore long. Anxious to turn every moment to account, we were on board MR THRUSTON's boat at three next morning. Pursuing our way through the deep and tortuous channels that every where traverse the immense muddy soap-like flats that stretch from the outward Keys to the Main, we proceeded on our voyage of discovery. Here and there we met with great beds of floating sea-weeds, which shewed us that Turtles were abundant there, these masses being the refuse of their feeding. On talking to MR THRUSTON of the nature of these muddy flats, he mentioned that he had once been lost amongst their narrow channels for several days and nights, when in pursuit of some smugglers' boat, the owners of which were better acquainted with the place than the men who were along with him. Although in full sight of several of the Keys, as well as of the mainland, he was unable to reach either, until a heavy gale raised the water, when he sailed directly over the flats, and returned home almost exhausted with fatigue and hunger. His present pilot often alluded to the circumstance afterwards, ending with a great laugh, and asserting that had he "been there, the rascals would not have escaped."

Coming under a Key on which multitudes of Frigate Pelicans had begun to form their nests, we shot a good number of them, and observed their habits. The boastings of our pilot were here confirmed by the exploits which he performed with his long gun, and on several occasions he brought down a bird from a height of fully a hundred yards. The poor birds, unaware of the range of our artillery, sailed calmly along, so that it was not difficult for "Long Tom," or rather for his owner, to furnish us with as many as we required. The day was spent in this manner, and towards night we returned, laden with booty, to the hospitable home of the pilot.[7]

The next morning was delightful. The gentle sea-breeze glided over the flowery isle, the horizon was clear, and all was silent save the long breakers that rushed over the distant reefs. As we were proceeding towards some Keys, seldom visited by men, the sun rose from the bosom of the waters with a burst of glory that flashed on my soul the idea of that power which called into existence so magnificent an object. The moon, thin and pale, as if ashamed to shew her feeble light, concealed herself in the dim west. The surface of the waters shone in its tremulous smoothness, and the deep blue of the clear heavens was pure as the world that lies beyond them. The Heron heavily flew towards the land, like the glutton retiring at day-break, with well-lined paunch, from the house of some wealthy patron of good cheer. The Night Heron and the Owl, fearful of day, with hurried flight sought safety in the recesses of the deepest swamps; while the Gulls and Terns, ever cheerful, gambolled over the water, exulting in the prospect of abundance. I also exulted in hope, my whole frame seemed to expand; and our sturdy crew shewed, by their merry faces, that nature had charms for them too. How much of beauty and joy is lost to them who never view the rising sun, and of whose waking existence the best half is nocturnal!

Twenty miles our men had to row before we reached "Sandy Island," and as on its level shores we all leaped, we plainly saw the southernmost cape of the Floridas. The flocks of birds that covered the shelly beaches, and those hovering over head, so astonished us that we could for a while scarcely believe our eyes. The first volley procured a supply of food sufficient for two days' consumption. Such tales, you have already been told, are well enough at a distance from the place to which they refer; but you will doubtless be still more surprised when I tell you that our first fire among a crowd of the Great Godwits laid prostrate sixty-five of these

FIGURE 22. Florida key. Robert Havell Jr. after John James Audubon, "Booby Gannet" (brown booby), 1834. Aquatint engraving. *The Birds of America*, plate 207. The background, painted by George Lehman, shows a detail view of Indian Key. Note the masthead on the right of the island, a lookout for passing traffic and shipwrecks. Courtesy of the Lilly Library.

birds. Rose-coloured Curlews stalked gracefully beneath the mangroves; Purple Herons rose at almost every step we took, and each cactus supported the nest of a White Ibis. The air was darkened by whistling wings, while, on the waters, floated Gallinules and other interesting birds. We formed a kind of shed with sticks and grass, the sailor cook commenced his labours, and ere long we supplied the deficiencies of our fatigued frames. The business of the day over, we secured ourselves from insects by means of mosquito-nets, and were lulled to rest by the cacklings of the beautiful Purple Gallinules![8]

In the morning we arose from our sandy beds, and——

Notes

1. The two "Florida Keys" episodes were first published, separately, in *OB* 2 (1834), 312–316, 345–49. On the US revenue cutter *Marion* (1825), 79 feet long with six cannon, see Donald L. Canney, *U.S. Coast Guard Revenue Cutters, 1790–1935* (Annapolis: Naval Institute Press, 1995), 12. The captain was Robert Day, acting on the orders of the Collector of the Port of Charleston, James H. Pringle; the pilot was First Lieutenant Napoleon Coste (1809–1885), later commander of the revenue cutter *Campbell* and a frequent supplier of bird skins to Audubon. He had joined the US Revenue Service in 1830 after working as a Key West pilot. The function of revenue cutters at that time was to patrol the coastline to prevent arms smuggling, the slave trade, and piracy. They protected shipping and settlers in the Keys, in addition at times to supporting the US Navy. In 1838, Lieutenant Coste assumed command of the *Campbell* (see also notes to "Common Gannet"). Indian Key was a central location for wreckers in the region in the 1830s, including homes, docks, and a warehouse.

2. Alfred Thruston was a US customs inspector for Indian Key. See Peter Force, *National Calendar for 1830* (Washington, DC: Peter Force, 1830), 154. The pilot was James Egan, who arrived in Indian Key from the Bahamas around 1830 and opened the first boardinghouse there in 1832.

3. They were likely hunting for the queen conch *Strombus gigas.*

4. "The Lady of the Green Mantle" is an allusion to a mysterious lady in Sir Walter Scott's 1824 novel *Redgauntlet,* whom the main character later marries. Audubon's "Peale's Egret," the white morph of his purple heron/reddish egret (Havell 256), is now known most commonly as the reddish egret (*Egretta rufescens*). Audubon's friend Charles-Lucien Bonaparte thought it was a separate species (Bonaparte, *American Ornithology* [Philadelphia: Carey and Lea, 1833], 4:96), while Audubon thought it the juvenile phase, rather than a morph (*OB* 3 [1835], 411–12.)

5. The "pilot's house" was Mr. Egan's boardinghouse in Key West. George Lehman (ca. 1800–1870) was a Swiss-born landscape artist, engraver, and lithographer, who in 1824 immigrated to the United States with his family; he provided many backgrounds for Audubon and may also have painted the lesser yellowlegs, known then as the yellow shank (Havell 288). Audubon and Lehman first met in 1824; Audubon hired him in 1829. Lehman had accompanied Audubon to Charleston in October 1831 and then on to Florida in November 1831. Lehman's

sketch of Indian Key provides the background for Audubon's brown booby (Booby Gannet; Havell 207, detail fig. 22).

6. "The Lady of Bras d'Or" was an inside reference to Sophia Jones, Audubon's pretentious hostess during his 1833 visit to Bradore (Bras d'Or), Labrador, who described a wonderful instrument to him that turned out to be a hand-organ or hurdy-gurdy; see Audubon's episode "The Squatters of Labrador," *OB* 2 (1834), 158.

7. On the "Frigate Pelican," or magnificent frigatebird, see, in this volume, "The Frigate Pelican" and plate 3.

8. "Sandy Island," or Sandy Key, is one of a couple islets in the region with "Sandy" in the name (see fig. 19). Audubon's "Great Marbled Godwit" (Havell 238) is now referred to as simply the marbled godwit (*Limosa fedoa*). His "Rose-coloured Curlew" was perhaps a rare vagrant in Florida, a bird he also painted as his scarlet ibis (Havell 397), now *Eudocimus ruber*. Audubon's "Purple Heron" (Havell 256) is now called the reddish egret (*Egretta rufescens*), red morph. He refers to the white morph of this species as "Peale's Egret" earlier in this episode, n. 4.

THE FLORIDA KEYS (PART 2)

I LEFT you abruptly, perhaps uncivilly, reader, at the dawn of day, on Sandy Island, which lies just six miles from the extreme point of South Florida. I did so because I was amazed at the appearance of things around me, which in fact looked so different then from what they seemed at night, that it took some minutes' reflection to account for the change. When we laid ourselves down in the sand to sleep, the waters almost bathed our feet; when we opened our eyes in the morning, they were at an immense distance. Our boat lay on her side, looking not unlike a whale reposing on a mud-bank. The birds in myriads were probing their exposed pasture-ground. There great flocks of Ibises fed apart from equally large collections of Godwits, and thousands of Herons gracefully paced along, ever and anon thrusting their javelin bills into the body of some unfortunate fish confined in a small pool of water. Of Fish-Crows I could not estimate the number, but from the havoc they made among the crabs, I conjecture that these animals must have been scarce by the time of next ebb. Frigate Pelicans chased the Jager, which himself had just robbed a poor Gull of its prize, and all the Gallinules ran with spread wings from the mud-banks to the thickets of the island, so timorous had they become when they perceived us.[1]

Surrounded as we were by so many objects that allured us, not one could we yet attain, so dangerous would it have been to venture on the mud; and our pilot having assured us that nothing could be lost by waiting, spoke of our eating, and on this hint told us that he would take us to a part of the island where "our breakfast would be abundant although uncooked." Off we went, some of the sailors carrying baskets, others large tin pans and wooden vessels, such as they use for eating their meals in. Entering a thicket of about an acre in extent, we found on every bush several nests of the Ibis, each containing three large and beautiful eggs, and all hands fell to gathering. The birds gave way to us, and ere long we had a heap of eggs that promised delicious food. Nor did we stand long in expectation, for, kindling a fire, we soon prepared, in one way or other, enough to satisfy the cravings of our hungry maws. Breakfast ended, the pilot looking at the gorgeous sunrise, said, "Gentlemen, prepare yourselves for fun, the tide is acoming."

Over these enormous mud-flats, a foot or two of water is quite sufficient to drive all the birds ashore, even the tallest Heron or Flamingo, and the tide seems to flow at once over the whole expanse. Each of us provided with a gun, posted himself behind a bush, and no sooner had the water forced the winged creatures to approach the shore, than the work of destruction commenced. When it at length ceased, the collected mass of birds of different kinds looked not unlike a small haycock. Who could not with a little industry have helped himself to a few of their skins? Why, reader, surely no one as fond of these things as I am. Every one assisted in this, and even the sailors themselves tried their hand at the work.

Our pilot, good man, told us he was no hand at such occupations, and would go after something else. So taking Long Tom and his fishing-tackle, he marched off quietly along the shores. About an hour afterwards we saw him returning, when he looked quite exhausted, and on our inquiring the cause said, "There is a dew-fish yonder and a few balacoudas, but I am not able to bring them, or even to haul them here; please send the sailors after them." The fishes were accordingly brought, and as I had never seen a dew-fish, I examined it closely, and took an outline of its form, which some days hence you may perhaps see. It exceeded a hundred pounds in weight, and afforded excellent eating. The balacouda is also a good fish, but at times a dangerous one, for, according to the pilot, on more than one occasion "some of these gentry" had followed him when waist-deep in the water, in pursuit of a more valuable prize, until in self-defence he had to spear them, fearing that "the gentlemen" might at one dart cut off his legs, or some other nice bit, with which he was unwilling to part.[2]

Having filled our cask from a fine well long since dug in the sand of Cape Sable, either by Seminole Indians or pirates, no matter which, we left Sandy Isle about full tide, and proceeded homewards, giving a call here and there at different keys, with the view of procuring rare birds, and also their nests and eggs. We had twenty miles to go "as the birds fly," but the tortuosity of the channels rendered our course fully a third longer. The sun was descending fast, when a black cloud suddenly obscured the majestic orb. Our sails swelled by a breeze, that was scarcely felt by us, and the pilot, requesting us to sit on the weather gunwale, told us that we were "going to get it." One sail was hauled in and secured, and the other was reefed although the wind had not increased. A low murmuring noise was heard, and across the cloud that now rolled along in tumultuous masses, shot vivid flashes of lightning. Our experienced guide steered directly across a flat towards the nearest land. The sailors passed their quids from one cheek to the other, and our pilot having covered himself with his oil-jacket, we followed his example. "Blow, sweet breeze," cried he at the tiller, and "we'll reach land before the blast overtakes us, for, gentlemen, it is a furious cloud yon."

A furious cloud indeed was the one which now, like an eagle on outstretched wings, approached so swiftly, that one might have deemed it in haste to destroy us. We were not more than a cable's length from the shore, when, with imperative voice, the pilot calmly said to us, "Sit quite still, Gentlemen, for I should not like to lose you overboard just now; the boat can't upset, my word for that, if you will but sit still—here we have it!"

Reader, persons who have never witnessed a hurricane, such as not unfrequently desolates the sultry climates of the south, can scarcely form an idea of their terrific grandeur. One would think that, not content with laying waste all on land, it must needs sweep the waters of the shallows quite dry, to quench its thirst. No respite for an instant does it afford to the objects within the reach of its furious current. Like the scythe of the destroying angel, it cuts every thing by the roots, as it were with the careless ease of the experienced mower. Each of its revolving sweeps collects a heap that might be likened to the full sheaf which the husbandman flings by his side. On it goes with a wildness and fury that are indescribable; and when at last its frightful blasts have ceased, Nature, weeping and disconsolate, is left bereaved of her beauteous offspring. In some instances, even a full century is required, before, with all her powerful energies, she can repair her loss. The planter has not only lost his mansion, his crops, and his flocks, but he has to clear his lands anew, covered and entangled as they are with the trunks and branches of trees that are every where strewn. The bark overtaken by the storm, is cast on the lee-shore, and if any are left to witness the fatal results, they are the "wreckers" alone, who, with inward delight, gaze upon the melancholy spectacle.

Our light bark shivered like a leaf the instant the blast reached her sides. We thought she had gone over; but the next instant she was on the shore. And now in contemplation of the sublime and awful storm, I gazed around me. The waters drifted like snow; the tough mangroves hid their tops amid their roots, and the loud roaring of the waves driven among them blended with the howl of the tempest. It was not rain that fell; the masses of water flew in a horizontal direction, and where a part of my body was exposed, I felt as if a smart blow had been given me on it. But enough!—in half an hour it was over. The pure blue sky once more embellished the heavens, and although it was now quite night, we considered our situation a good one.

The crew and some of the party spent the night in the boat. The pilot, myself, and one of my assistants took to the heart of the mangroves, and having found high land, we made a fire as well as we could, spread a tarpauling, and fixing our insect bars over us, soon forgot in sleep the horrors that had surrounded us.[3]

Next day, the Marion proceeded on her cruize, and in a few more days, having anchored in another safe harbour, we visited other Keys, of which I will, with your leave, give you a short account.

The Deputy-Collector of Indian Isle gave me the use of his pilot for a few weeks, and I was the more gratified by this, that besides knowing him to be a good man and a perfect sailor, I was now convinced that he possessed a great knowledge of the habits of birds, and could without loss of time lead me to their haunts. We were a hundred miles or so farther to the south. Gay May like a playful babe gambolled on the bosom of his mother nature, and every thing was replete with life and joy. The pilot had spoken to me of some birds, which I was very desirous of obtaining. One morning, therefore, we went in two boats to some distant isle, where they were said to breed. Our difficulties in reaching that Key might to some seem more imaginary than real, were I faithfully to describe them. Suffice it for me to tell you that after hauling our boats and pushing them with our hands, for upwards of nine miles, over the flats, we at last reached the deep channel that usually surrounds each of the mangrove islands. We were much exhausted by the labour and excessive heat, but we were now floating on deep water, and by resting a short while under the shade of some mangroves, we were soon refreshed by the breeze that gently blew from the Gulf. We further repaired our strength by taking some food; and I may as well tell you here, that during all the time I spent in that portion of the Floridas, my party restricted themselves to fish and soaked biscuit, while our only and constant beverage was water and mollasses. I found that in these warm latitudes, exposed as we constantly were to alternate heat and moisture, ardent spirits and more substantial food would prove dangerous to us. The officers, and those persons who from time to time kindly accompanied us, adopted the same regimen, and not an individual of us had ever to complain of so much as a headach [*sic*].

But we were under the mangroves—at a great distance on one of the flats, the Heron which I have named *Ardea occidentalis* was seen moving majestically in great numbers. The tide rose and drove them away, and as they came towards us, to alight and rest for a time on the tallest trees, we shot as many as I wished. I also took under my charge several of their young alive.[4]

At another time we visited the "Mule Keys." There the prospect was in many respects dismal in the extreme. As I followed their shores, I saw bales of cotton floating in all the coves, while spars of every description lay on the beach, and far off on the reefs I could see the last remains of a lost ship, her dismantled hulk. Several schooners were around her; they were wreckers. I turned me from the sight with a heavy heart. Indeed, as I slowly proceeded, I dreaded to meet the floating or cast ashore bodies of some of the unfortunate crew. Our visit to the Mule Keys was in no way profitable, for besides meeting with but a few birds in two or three instances, I was, whilst swimming in the deep channel of a mangrove isle, much nearer a large shark than I wish ever to be again.

"The service" requiring all the attention, prudence and activity of Captain DAY and his gallant officers, another cruize took place, of which you will find some account in the sequel; and while I rest a little on the deck of the Lady of the Green Mantle, let me offer my humble thanks to the Being who has allowed me the pleasure of thus relating to you, kind reader, a small part of my adventures.[5]

Notes

1. Audubon's jager here is now known as the pomarine jaeger (Havell 253, *Stercorarius pomarinus*); see also note to "Journal of a Collecting Voyage," August 17.

2. The "dew-fish" was probably a reference to the Atlantic goliath grouper (*Epinephelus itajara*), a gargantuan species that can reach upward of seven hundred pounds and is now considered Vulnerable by the IUCN (2016).

3. "Insect bars" are mosquito nets.

4. Audubon's "Great White Heron," *Ardea occidentalis* (Havell 281), turns out to be a subspecies of the great blue heron, *Ardea herodias* (Havell 211).

5. The "sequel" here is likely the episode "The Turtlers" in this volume.

THE BROWN PELICAN

THE Brown Pelican [plate 1], which is one of the most interesting of our American birds, is a constant resident in the Floridas, where it resorts to the Keys and the salt-water inlets, but never enters fresh-water streams, as the White Pelican is wont to do. It is rarely seen farther eastward than Cape Hatteras, but is found to the south far beyond the limits of the United States. Within the recollection of persons still living, its numbers have been considerably reduced, so much indeed that in the inner Bay of Charleston, where twenty or thirty years ago it was quite abundant, very few individuals are now seen, and these chiefly during a continuance of tempestuous weather. There is a naked bar, a few miles distant from the mainland, between Charleston and the mouth of the Santee, on which my friend JOHN BACHMAN some years ago saw a great number of these birds, of which he procured several; but at the present day, few are known to breed farther east than the salt-water inlets running parallel to the coast of Florida, forty or fifty miles south of St Augustine, where I for the first time met with this Pelican in considerable numbers.[1]

My friend JOHN BULLOW, Esq. took me in his barge to visit the Halifax, which is a large inlet, and on which we soon reached an island where the Brown Pelicans had bred for a number of years, but where, to my great disappointment, none were then to be seen. The next morning, being ten or twelve miles farther down the stream, we entered another inlet, where I saw several dozens of these birds perched on the mangroves, and apparently sound asleep. I shot at them from a very short distance, and with my first barrel brought two to the water, but although many of them still remained looking at us, I could not send the contents of my second barrel to them, as the shot had unluckily been introduced into it before the powder. They all flew off one after another, and still worse, as the servants approached those which had fallen upon the water, they also flew away.[2]

On arriving at the Keys of Florida, on board the Marion Revenue Cutter, I found the Pelicans pretty numerous. They became more abundant the farther south we proceeded, and I procured specimens at different places, but nowhere so many as at Key West. There you would see them flying within pistol-shot of the wharfs, the boys frequently trying to knock them down with stones, although I believe they rarely succeed in their efforts. The Marion lay at anchor several days at a short distance from this island, and close to another. Scarcely an hour of daylight passed without our having Pelicans around us, all engaged at their ordinary occupations, some fishing, some slumbering as it were on the bosom of the ocean, or on the branches of the mangroves. This place and all around for about forty miles, seemed to be favourite resorts of these birds; and as I had excellent opportunities of observing their habits, I consider myself qualified to present you with some account of them.

The flight of the Brown Pelican, though to appearance heavy, is remarkably well sustained, that bird being able not only to remain many hours at a time on wing, but also to mount to a great height in the air to perform its beautiful evolutions. Their ordinary manner of proceeding, either when single or in flocks, is by easy flappings and sailings alternating at distances of from twenty to thirty yards, when they glide along with great speed. They move in an undulated line, passing at one time high, at another low, over the water or land, for they do not deviate from their course on coming upon a key or a point of land. When the waves run high, you may see them "troughing," as the sailors say, or directing their course along the hollows. While on wing they draw in their head between their shoulders, stretch out their broad webbed feet to their whole extent, and proceed in perfect silence.

When the weather is calm, and a flood of light and heat is poured down upon nature by the genial sun, they are often, especially during the love season, seen rising in broad circles, flock after flock, until they attain a height of perhaps a mile, when they gracefully glide on constantly expanded wings, and course round each other, for an hour or more at a time, after which, in curious zigzags, and with remarkable velocity, they descend towards their beloved element, and settle on the water, on large sand-bars or on mangroves. It is interesting beyond description to observe flocks of Brown Pelicans thus going through their aërial evolutions.

Now, Reader, look at those birds standing on their strong column-like legs, on that burning sand-bar. How dexterously do they wield that great bill of theirs, as they trim their plumage! Now along each broad quill it passes, drawing it out and displaying its elasticity; and now with necks stretched to their full length, and heads elevated, they direct its point in search of the insects that are concealed along their necks and breasts. Now they droop their wings for a while, or stretch them alternately to their full extent; some slowly lie down on the sand, others remain standing, quietly draw their head over their broad shoulders, raise one of their feet, and placing their bill on their back, compose themselves to rest. There let them repose in peace. Had they alighted on the waters, you might have seen them, like a fleet at anchor, riding on the ever-rolling billows as unconcernedly as if on shore. Had they perched on yon mangroves, they would have laid themselves flat on the branches, or spread their wings to the sun or the breeze, as Vultures are wont to do.

But see, the tide is advancing; the billows chase each other towards the shores; the mullets joyful and keen leap along the surface, as they fill the bays with their multitudes. The slumbers of the Pelicans are over; the drowsy birds shake their heads, stretch open their mandibles and pouch by way of yawning, expand their ample wings, and simultaneously soar away. Look at them as they fly over the bay; listen to the sound of the splash they make as they drive their open bills, like a pock-net, into the sea, to scoop up their prey; mark how they follow that shoal of porpoises, and snatch up the frightened fishes that strive to escape from them. Down they go, again and again. What voracious creatures they are!

The Brown Pelicans are as well aware of the time of each return of the tide, as the most watchful pilots. Though but a short time before they have been sound asleep, yet without bell or other warning, they suddenly open their eyelids, and all leave their roosts, the instant when the waters, which have themselves reposed for a while, resume their motion. The Pelicans possess a knowledge beyond this, and in a degree much surpassing that of man with reference to the same subject: they can judge with certainty of the changes of weather. Should you see them fishing all together, in retired bays, be assured, that a storm will burst forth that day; but if they pursue their finny prey far out at sea, the weather will be fine, and you also may launch your bark and go to the fishing. Indeed, most sea-birds possess the same kind of knowledge, as I have assured myself by repeated observation, in a degree corresponding to their necessities; and the best of all prognosticators of the weather, are the Wild Goose, the Gannet, the Lestris, and the Pelican.[3]

This species procures its food on wing, and in a manner quite different from that of the White Pelican. A flock will leave their resting place, proceed over the waters in search of fish, and when a shoal is perceived, separate at once, when each, from an elevation of from fifteen to twenty-five feet, plunges in an oblique and somewhat winding direction, spreading to the full stretch its lower mandible and pouch, as it reaches the water, and suddenly scoops up the object of its pursuit, immersing the head and neck, and sometimes the body, for an instant. It immediately swallows its prey, rises on wing, dashes on another fish, seizes and devours it, and thus continues, sometimes plunging eight or ten times in a few minutes, and always with unerring aim. When gorged, it rests on the water for a while, but if it has a brood, or a mate sitting on her eggs, it flies off at once towards them, no matter how heavily laden it may be. The generally received idea that Pelicans keep fish or water in their pouch, to convey them to their young, is quite erroneous. The water which enters the pouch when it is immersed, is immediately forced out between the partially closed mandibles, and the fish, unless larger than those on which they usually feed, is instantly swallowed, to be afterwards disgorged for the benefit of the young, either partially macerated, or whole, according to the age and size of the latter. Of all this I have satisfied myself, when within less than twenty yards of the birds as they were fishing; and I never saw them fly without the pouch being closely contracted towards the lower mandible. Indeed, although I now much regret that I did not make the experiment when I had the means of doing so, I doubt very much if a Pelican could fly at all with its burden so much out of trim, as a sailor would say.

They at times follow the porpoise, when that animal is in pursuit of prey, and as the fishes rise from the deep water towards the surface, come in cunningly for their share, falling upon the frightened shoal, and seizing one or more, which they instantly gobble up. But one of the most curious traits of the Pelican is, that it acts unwittingly as a sort of purveyor to the Gulls just as the Porpoise acts towards itself. The Black-headed Gull of WILSON, which is abundant along the coast of the Floridas in spring and summer, watches the motions of the Pelicans. The latter having plunged after a shoal of small fishes, of which it has caught a number at a time, in letting off the water from amongst them, sometimes allows a few to escape; but the Gull at that instant alights on the bill of the Pelican, or on its head, and seizes the fry at the moment they were perhaps congratulating themselves on their escape. This every body on board the Marion observed as well as myself, while that vessel was at anchor in the beautiful harbour of Key West, so that it is not again necessary for me to lay before you a certificate with numerous signatures. To me such sights were always highly interesting, and I doubt if in the course of my endeavours to amuse you, I ever felt greater pleasure than I do at this moment, when, with my journal at my side, and the Gulls and Pelicans in my mind's eye as distinctly as I could wish, I ponder on the faculties which Nature has bestowed on animals which we merely consider as possessed of instinct. How little do we yet know of the operations of the Divine Power! On the occasions just mentioned, the Pelicans did not manifest the least anger towards the Gulls. It is said that the Frigate Pelican or Man-of-war Bird, forces the Brown Pelican to disgorge its food, but of this I never saw an instance; nor do I believe it to be the case, considering the great strength and powerful bill of the Pelican compared with those of the other bird. Indeed, if I had been told that when the Frigate Bird assails the Pelican, the latter opens its large pouch and swallows it entire, I might as soon have believed the one story as the other. But of this more anon, when we come to the habits of the bird in question.[4]

On the ground this species is by no means so active, for it walks heavily, and when running, which it now and then does while in play, or during courtship, it looks extremely awkward, as it then stretches out its neck, partially extends its wings, and reels so that one might imagine it ready to fall at each step. If approached when wounded and on the water, it swims off with speed, and when overtaken, it suddenly turns about, opens its large bill, snaps it violently several times in succession, causing it to emit a smart noise in the manner of owls, strikes at you, and bites very severely. While I was at Mr BULLOW's, his Negro hunter waded after one whose wing had been broken. The Pelican could not be seized without danger, and I was surprised to see the hunter draw his butcher's knife, strike the long blade through the open pouch of the bird, hook it, as it were, by the lower mandible, and at one jerk swing it up into the air with extreme dexterity, after which he broke its neck and dragged it ashore.[5]

The pouch measures from six to ten inches in depth, according to the age of the bird after the first moult. The superb male whose portrait is before you, and which was selected from among a great number, had it about the last mentioned size, and capable of holding a gallon of water, were the mandibles kept horizontal. This membrane is dried and used for keeping snuff, gunpowder and shot. When fresh it may be extended so as to become quite thin and transparent, like a bladder.

This Pelican seldom seizes fish that are longer than its bill, and the size of those on which it ordinarily feeds is much smaller. Indeed, several which I examined, had in the stomach upwards of a hundred fishes, which were only from two to three inches in length. That organ is long, slender, and rather fleshy. In some I found a great number of live blue-coloured worms, measuring two and a half inches in length, and about the thickness of a crow-quill. The gut is about the size of a swan's quill, and from ten to twelve feet in length, according to the age of the individual.

At all periods the Brown Pelican keeps in flocks, seldom amounting to more than fifty or sixty individuals of both sexes, and of different ages. At the approach of the pairing time, or about the middle of April, the old males and females separate from the rest, and remove to the inner keys or to large estuaries, well furnished with mangroves of goodly size. The young birds, which are much more numerous, remain along the shores of the open sea, unless during heavy gales.

Now let us watch the full grown birds. Some skirmishes have taken place, and the stronger males, by dint of loud snappings of their bill, some hard tugs of the neck and head, and some heavy beats with their wings, have driven away the weaker, which content themselves with less prized belles. The females, although quiet and gentle on ordinary occasions, are more courageous than the males, who, however, are assiduous in their attentions, assist in forming the nest, feed their mates while sitting, and even share the labour of incubation with them. Now see the mated birds, like the citizens of a newly laid out town in some part of our western country, breaking the dry sticks from the trees, and conveying them in their bills to yon mangrove isle. You see they place all their mansions on the south-west side, as if to enjoy the benefit of all the heat of that sultry climate. Myriads of mosquitoes buzz around them, and alight on the naked parts of their body, but this seems to give them no concern. Stick after stick is laid, one crossing another, until a strong platform is constructed. Now roots and withered plants are brought, with which a basin is formed for the eggs. Not a nest, you observe, is placed very low; the birds prefer the tops of the mangroves, although they do not care how many nests are on one tree, or how near the trees are to each other. The eggs, of which there are never more than three, are rather elliptical, and average three inches and one-eighth in length, by two inches and one-eighth in their greatest breadth. The shell is thick and rather rough, of a pure white colour, with a few faint streaks of a rosy tint, and blotches of a very pale hue, from the centre towards the crown of the egg.

The young are at first covered with cream-coloured down, and have the bill and feet disproportionately large. They are fed with great care, and so abundantly, that the refuse of their food, putrid and disgusting, lies in great quantities round them; but neither young nor old regard this, however offensive it may be to you. As the former grow the latter bring larger fish to them. At first the food is dropped in a well macerated state into their extended throats; afterwards the fish is given to them entire; and finally the parent birds merely place it on the edge of the nest. The young increase in size at a surprising rate. When half fledged they seem a mere mass of fat, their partially indurated bill has acquired considerable length, their wings droop by their sides, and they would be utterly unable to walk. The Vultures at this period often fall upon them and devour them in the absence of their parents. The Indians also carry them off in considerable numbers; and farther eastward, on the Halifax river, for instance, the Negroes kill all they can find, to make gombo soup of them during winter. The crows, less powerful, but quite as cunning, suck the eggs; and many a young one which has accidentally fallen from the nest, is sure to be picked up by some quadruped, or devoured by the Shark or Balacouda. When extensive depredations have thus been made, the birds abandon their breeding places, and do not return to them. The Pelicans in fact are, year after year, retiring from the vicinity of man, and although they afford but very unsavoury food at any period of their lives, will yet be hunted beyond the range of civilization, just as our best of all game, the Wild Turkey, is now, until to meet with them the student of nature will have to sail round Terra del Fuego, while he may be obliged to travel to the Rocky Mountains before he find the other bird. Should you approach a settlement of the Pelicans and fire a few shots at them, they all abandon the place, and leave their eggs or young entirely at your disposal.

At all seasons, the Negroes of the plantations on the eastern coast of the Floridas lie in wait for the Pelicans. There, observe that fellow, who, with rusty musket, containing a tremendous charge of heavy shot, is concealed among the palmettoes, on the brink of a kind of embankment formed by the shelly sand. Now comes a flock of Pelicans, forcing their way against the breeze, unaware of the danger into which they rush, for there, a few yards apart, several Negroes crouch in readiness to fire; and let me tell you, good shots they are. Now a blast forces the birds along the shore; off goes the first gun, and down comes a Pelican; shot succeeds shot; and now the Negroes run up to gather the spoil. They skin the birds like so many racoons, cut off the head, wings and feet; and should you come this way next year, you may find these remains bleached in the sun. Towards night, the sable hunters carry off their booty, marching along in Indian file, and filling the air with their extemporaneous songs. At home they perhaps salt, or perhaps smoke them; but in whatever way the Pelicans are prepared, they are esteemed good food by the sons of Africa.

The Brown Pelican is a strong and tough bird, although not so weighty as the white species. Its flesh is, in my opinion, always impure. It seems never satisfied with food, and it mutes so profusely, that not a spot of verdure can be seen on the originally glossy and deep-coloured mangroves on which it nestles; and I must say that, much as I admire it in some respects, I should be sorry to keep it near me as a pet.

During winter, when the mullets, a favourite fish with the Brown Pelican, as it is with me, retires into deeper water, these birds advance farther to seaward, and may be seen over all parts of the Gulf of Mexico, and between the Florida Reefs and the opposite isles, especially during fine weather. They are very sensible to cold, and in this respect are tender birds. Now and then, at this season, they are seen on Lake Borgne and over Lake Pontchartrain, but never on the Mississippi beyond the rise of the tides, the space higher up being abandoned to the White Pelican. The keenness of their sight is probably equal to that of any hawk, and their hearing is also very acute. They are extremely silent birds, but when excited they utter a loud and rough grunt, which is far from musical. The young take two years to attain maturity. Several persons in the Floridas assured me that the Brown Pelicans breed at all seasons of the year; but as I observed nothing to countenance such an idea, I would give it as my opinion that they raise only one brood in the season.

Their bodies are greatly inflated by large air-cells; their bones, though strong, are very light; and they are tough to kill.

The Mangrove

THE species of Mangrove represented in the plate is very abundant along the coast of Florida and on almost all the Keys, excepting the Tortugas. Those islands which are named Wet Keys are entirely formed of Mangroves, which raising their crooked and slender stems from a bed of mud, continue to increase until their roots and pendent branches afford shelter to the accumulating debris, when the earth is gradually raised above the surface of the water. No sooner has this taken place than the Mangroves in the central part of the island begin to decay, and in the course of time there is only an outer fringe or fence of trees, while the interior becomes overgrown with grass and low bushes. Meantime the Mangroves extend towards the sea, their hanging branches taking root wherever they come in contact with the bottom, and their seeds also springing up. I am at a loss for an object with which to compare these trees, in order to afford you an idea of them; yet if you will figure to yourself a tree reversed, and standing on its summit, you may obtain a tolerable notion of their figure and mode of growth. The stem, roots and branches are very tough and stubborn, and in some places the trees are so intertwined that a person might find it as easy to crawl over them as to make his way between them. They are evergreen, and their tops afford a place of resort to various species of birds at all seasons, while their roots and submersed branches give shelter to numberless testaceous mollusca and small fishes. The species represented is rarely observed on the coast of Florida of a greater height than twenty-five or thirty feet, and its average height is not above fifteen feet. The Land Mangrove, of which I have seen only a few, the finest of which were on Key West, is a tall tree, much larger and better shaped than the other, with narrower leaves and shorter fruits.[6]

Notes

1. Audubon's "The Brown Pelican" was first published in *OB* 3 (1835), 376–86. For *The Birds of America* he painted an adult brown pelican (now *Pelecanus occidentalis*) on a red mangrove, *Rhizophora mangle* (plate 1; Havell 251), apparently from a specimen killed in the Florida Keys in April or May 1832. He also, likely from a juvenile collected in 1821, painted a second image (Havell 421). Audubon described this species as already in decline by the 1830s, perhaps due to overhunting. By the mid-twentieth century, the brown pelican was on the brink of extinction, in large part due to the use of pesticides. When it was named Louisiana's state bird in 1966, no pelicans actually bred in the state, and it was officially designated a US Endangered Species in 1970. Yet as of 2009, brown pelicans have been removed from the endangered species list throughout their entire range. Despite mortality following the BP–Deepwater Horizon Gulf oil spill of 2010, modern populations remain healthy and the brown pelican ranges along the entire West Coast, around the Gulf of Mexico, and as far north as Delaware on the East Coast (Least Concern, IUCN, 2018).

The naturalist John Bachman (1790–1874) was Audubon's most important collaborator. Bachman was born in Rhinebeck, NY, ordained as a Lutheran minister in 1814, and served for sixty years as pastor of St. John's Lutheran Church, Charleston, SC. His wife, Harriet, bore fourteen children, five of whom did not survive infancy. Her sister, Maria Martin (1796–1863), supplied many paintings of plants Audubon used as backgrounds; she became Bachman's second wife in 1847. John Woodhouse Audubon married Bachman's daughter Maria, and Victor Gifford Audubon married her sister Eliza; both women, within eight months, succumbed to tuberculosis. The text for Audubon's last work, *The Viviparous Quadrupeds of North America* (1845–1848), was mostly Bachman's creation. The American white pelican, a species that he also wrote of extensively and compared in a separate biography (Havell 311; *OB* 4 [1838], 88–102, fig. 18), is now *Pelecanus erythrorhynchos*.

2. John Joachim Bulow (1807–1836), educated in France, had inherited Bulow (formerly Savannah) Plantation in Charleston County, SC, as well as a 2,200-acre sugar plantation (with 197 enslaved men, women, and children documented in the 1830 census) in Bulowville, Florida (burned by people of the Seminole tribe in 1836 and now a historic state park).

3. Audubon's "Lestris" here is his "Arctic Yager," *Lestris parasiticus* (Havell 267), which is now known as the long-tailed jaeger (*Stercorarius longicaudus*); see detail, fig. 36.

4. Wilson's account of the "Black-headed Gull," now the laughing gull (*Leucophaeus atricilla*), is in his *American Ornithology*, vol. 9 (Philadelphia: Bradford and Inskeep, 1814), 89–93. Audubon's version of the "Black-headed/Laughing Gull" appears in Havell 314. For more regarding the magnificent frigatebird stealing food from the brown pelican, see "The Frigate Pelican."

5. This "Negro hunter" might have been an enslaved person. "Black codes" in many states restricted access to firearms even for free Blacks, although there were exceptions for hunting in the presence of a white person or guarding a master's plantation, or for Blacks carrying a license from a justice of the peace. In 1831 Florida canceled all licenses for free Blacks; a complete gun ban for enslaved people followed in 1840. See Steve Ekwall, "The Racist Origins of US Gun Control," https://www.sedgwickcounty.org/media/29093/the-racist-origins-of-us-gun-control.pdf.

6. Audubon painted the brown pelican (Havell 251) with the red mangrove (*Rhizophora mangle*), and this description was published with that bird biography in *OB* 3 (1835), 386. His "Land Mangrove" could be one of three species of mangrove trees in the region that are less tolerant to saltwater, but perhaps Audubon is referring to the buttonwood mangrove (*Conocarpus erectus*), which can grow to fifty feet or more, with indeed a fuller shape, narrower leaves, and smaller berries. In addition to the ecological function Audubon writes of here, mangrove forests provide essential habitat for larger organisms like sharks and manatees, act as storm barriers for coastal human communities, and store more carbon than terrestrial woodlands.

THE TURTLERS

THE Tortugas are a group of islands lying about eighty miles from Key West, and the last of those that seem to defend the peninsula of the Floridas. They consist of five or six extremely low uninhabitable banks formed of shelly sand, and are resorted to principally by that class of men called Wreckers and Turtlers. Between these islands are deep channels, which, although extremely intricate, are well known to those adventurers, as well as to the commanders of the revenue cutters, whose duties call them to that dangerous coast. The great coral reef or wall lies about eight miles from these inhospitable isles, in the direction of the Gulf, and on it many an ignorant or careless navigator has suffered shipwreck. The whole ground around them is densely covered with corals, sea-fans, and other productions of the deep, amid which crawl innumerable testaceous animals, while shoals of curious and beautiful fishes fill the limpid waters above them. Turtles of different species resort to these banks, to deposit their eggs in the burning sand, and clouds of sea-fowl arrive every spring for the same purpose. These are followed by persons called "Eggers," who, when their cargoes are completed, sail to distant markets, to exchange their ill-gotten ware for a portion of that gold, on the acquisition of which all men seem bent.[1]

The Marion having occasion to visit the Tortugas, I gladly embraced the opportunity of seeing those celebrated islets. A few hours before sunset the joyful cry of "land" announced our approach to them, but as the breeze was fresh, and the pilot was well acquainted with all the windings of the channels, we held on, and dropped anchor before twilight. If you have never seen the sun setting in those latitudes, I would recommend to you to make a voyage for the purpose, for I much doubt, if, in any other portion of the world, the departure of the orb of day is accompanied with such gorgeous appearances. Look at the great red disk, increased to triple its ordinary dimensions! Now it has partially sunk beneath the distant line of waters, and with its still remaining half irradiates the whole heavens with a flood of golden light, purpling the far off clouds that hover over the western horizon. A blaze of refulgent glory streams through the portals of the west, and the masses of vapour assume the semblance of mountains of molten gold. But the sun has now disappeared, and from the east slowly advances the grey curtain which night draws over the world.

The Night-hawk is flapping its noiseless wings in the gentle sea-breeze; the Terns, safely landed, have settled on their nests; the Frigate Pelicans are seen wending their way to distant mangroves; and the Brown Gannet, in search of a resting-place, has perched on the yard of the vessel. Slowly advancing landward, their heads alone above the water, are observed the heavily-laden Turtles, anxious to deposit their eggs in the well-known sands. On the surface of the gently rippling stream, I dimly see their broad forms, as they toil along, while at intervals may be heard their hurried breathings, indicative of suspicion and fear. The moon with her silvery light now illumines the scene, and the Turtle having landed, slowly and laboriously drags her heavy body over the sand, her "flappers" being better adapted for motion in the water than on shore. Up the slope, however, she works her way, and see how industriously she removes the sand beneath her, casting it out on either side. Layer after layer she deposits her eggs, arranging them in the most careful manner, and, with her hind-paddles, brings the sand over them. The business is accomplished, the spot is covered over, and, with a joyful heart, the Turtle swiftly retires toward the shore, and launches into the deep.[2]

But the Tortugas are not the only breeding places of the Turtles; these animals, on the contrary, frequent many other keys, as well as various parts of the coast of the mainland. There are four different species, which are known by the names of the *Green* Turtle, the *Hawk-billed* Turtle, the *Loggerhead* Turtle, and the *Trunk* Turtle. The first is considered the best as an article of food, in which capacity it is well known to most epicures. It approaches the shores, and enters the bays, inlets and rivers, early in the month of April, after having spent the winter in the deep waters. It deposits its eggs in convenient places, at two different times in May, and once again in June. The first deposit is the largest, and the last the least, the total quantity being at an average about two hundred and forty. The Hawk-billed Turtle, whose shell is so valuable as an article of commerce, being used for various purposes in the arts, is the next with respect to the quality of its flesh. It resorts to the outer keys only, where it deposits its eggs in two sets, first in July, and again in August, although it "crawls" the beaches of these keys much earlier in the season, as if to look for a safe place. The average number of its eggs is about three hundred. The Loggerhead visits the Tortugas in April, and lays from that period until late in June three sets of eggs, each set averaging a hundred and seventy. The Trunk Turtle, which is sometimes of an enormous size, and which has a pouch like a pelican, reaches the shores latest. The shell and flesh are so soft that one may push his finger into them, almost as into a lump of butter. This species is therefore considered as the least valuable, and indeed is seldom eaten, unless by the Indians, who, ever alert when the turtle season commences, first carry off the eggs, and afterwards catch the Turtles themselves. The average number of eggs which it lays in the season, in two sets, may be three hundred and fifty.[3]

The Loggerhead and the Trunk Turtles are the least cautious in choosing the places in which to deposit their eggs, whereas the two other species select the wildest and most secluded spots. The Green Turtle resorts either to the shores of the Main, between Cape Sable and Cape Florida, or enters Indian, Halifax, and other large rivers or inlets, from which it makes its retreat as speedily as possible, and betakes itself to the open sea. Great numbers, however, are killed by the Turtlers and Indians, as well as by various species of carnivorous animals, as cougars, lynxes, bears and wolves. The Hawk-billed, which is still more wary, and is always the most difficult to surprise, keeps to the sea islands. All the species employ nearly the same method in depositing their eggs in the sand, and as I have several times observed them in the act, I am enabled to present you with circumstantial account of it.

On first nearing the shores, and mostly on fine calm moonlight nights, the Turtle raises her head above the water, being still distant thirty or forty yards from the beach, looks around her, and attentively examines the objects on the shore. Should she observe nothing likely to disturb her intended operations, she emits a loud hissing sound, by which such of her many enemies as are unaccustomed to it, are startled, and so are apt to remove to another place, although unseen by her. Should she hear any noise, or perceive indications of danger, she instantly sinks and goes off to a considerable distance; but should every thing be quiet, she advances slowly towards the beach, crawls over it, her head raised to the full stretch of her neck, and when she has reached a place fitted for her purpose, she gazes all round in silence. Finding "all well," she proceeds to form a hole in the sand, which she effects by removing it from *under* her body with her *hind* flappers, scooping it out with so much dexterity that the sides seldom if ever fall in. The sand is raised alternately with each flapper, as with a large ladle, until it has accumulated behind her, when supporting herself with her head and fore part on the ground fronting her body, she with a spring from each flapper, sends the sand around her, scattering it to the distance of several feet. In this manner the hole is dug to the depth of eighteen inches or sometimes more than two feet. This labour I have seen performed in the short period of nine minutes. The eggs are then dropped one by one, and disposed in regular layers, to the number of a hundred and fifty, or sometimes nearly two hundred. The whole time spent in this part of the operation may be about twenty minutes. She now scrapes the loose sand back over the eggs, and so levels and smooths the surface, that few persons on seeing the spot could imagine any thing had been done to it. This accomplished to her mind, she retreats to the water with all possible dispatch, leaving the hatching of the eggs to the heat of the sand. When a turtle, a logger-head for example, is in the act of dropping her eggs, she will not move although one should go up to her, or even seat himself on her back, for it seems that at this moment she finds it necessary to proceed at all events, and is unable to intermit her labour. The moment it is finished, however, off she starts; nor would it then be possible for one, unless he were as strong as a Hercules, to turn her over and secure her.

To upset a turtle on the shore, one is obliged to fall on his knees, and, placing his shoulder behind her forearm, gradually raise her up by pushing with great force, and then with a jerk throw her over. Sometimes it requires the united strength of several men to accomplish this; and, if the turtle should be of very great size, as often happens on that coast, even hand-spikes are employed [fig. 23]. Some turtlers are so daring as to swim up to them while lying asleep on the surface of the water, and turn them over in their own element, when, however, a boat must be at hand to enable them to secure their prize. Few turtles can bite beyond the reach of their fore legs, and few, when once turned over, can, without assistance, regain their natural position; but, notwithstanding this, their flappers are generally secured by ropes so as to render their escape impossible.

Persons who search for turtles' eggs are provided with a light stiff cane or a gun-rod, with which they go along the shores, probing the sand near the tracks of the animals, which, however, cannot always be seen, on account of the winds and heavy rains, that often obliterate them. The nests are discovered not only by men, but also by beasts of

FIGURE 23. Men turning over turtles on a beach of the Florida Keys in the way Audubon described. From J. B. Holder, "Along the Florida Reef, First Paper," *Harper's New Monthly Magazine* 42, no. 249 (February 1871): 358. Courtesy of Harpers, Williams College.

prey, and the eggs are collected, or destroyed on the spot in great numbers, as on certain parts of the shores hundreds of turtles are known to deposit their eggs within the space of a mile. They form a new hole each time they lay, and the second is generally dug near the first, as if the animal were quite unconscious of what had befallen it. It will readily be understood that the numerous eggs seen in a turtle on cutting it up could not be all laid the same season. The whole number deposited by an individual in one summer may amount to four hundred, whereas if the animal is caught on or near her nest, as I have witnessed, the remaining eggs, all small, without shells, and as it were threaded like so many large beads, exceed three thousand. In an instance where I found that number, the turtle weighed nearly four hundred pounds. The young, soon after being hatched, and when yet scarcely larger than a dollar, scratch their way through their sandy covering, and immediately betake themselves to the water.

The food of the Green Turtle consists chiefly of marine plants, more especially the Grasswrack (*Zostera marina*), which they cut near the roots to procure the most tender and succulent parts. Their feeding grounds, as I have elsewhere said, are easily discovered by floating masses of these plants on the flats, or along the shores to which they resort. The Hawk-billed species feeds on sea-weeds, crabs, various kinds of shellfish, and fishes; the Loggerhead mostly on the fish of conch-shells of large size, which they are enabled, by means of their powerful beak, to crush to pieces with apparently as much ease as a man cracks a walnut. One which was brought on board the Marion, and placed near the fluke of one of her anchors, made a deep indentation in that hammered piece of iron that quite surprised me. The Trunk Turtle feeds on mollusca, fish, crustacea, sea urchins, and various marine plants.[4]

All the species move through the water with surprising speed; but the Green and Hawk-billed in particular, remind you, by their celerity and the ease of their motions, of the progress of a bird in the air. It is therefore no easy matter to strike one with a spear, and yet this is often done by an accomplished turtler.

While at Key West and other islands on the coast, where I made the observations here presented to you, I chanced to have need to purchase some turtles, to feed my friends on board the Lady of the Green Mantle—not my friends her gallant officers, or the brave tars who formed her crew, for all of them had already been satiated with turtle soup, but my friends the Herons, of which I had a goodly number alive in coops, intending to carry them to JOHN BACHMAN of Charleston, and other persons for whom I ever feel a sincere regard. So I went to a "crawl," accompanied by Dr BENJAMIN STROBEL, to inquire about prices, when, to my surprise, I found that the smaller the turtles, above ten pounds weight, the dearer they were, and that I could have purchased one of the loggerhead kind that weighed more than seven hundred pounds, for little more money than another of only thirty pounds. While I gazed on the large one, I thought of the soups the contents of its shell would have furnished for a "Lord Mayor's dinner," of the numerous eggs which its swollen body contained, and of the curious carriage which might be made of its shell,—a car in which Venus herself might sail over the Caribbean sea, provided her tender doves lent their aid in drawing the divinity, and provided no shark or hurricane came to upset it. The turtler assured me that although the "great monster" was in fact better meat than any other of a less size, there was no disposing of it, unless indeed it had been in his power to have sent it to some very distant market. I would willingly have purchased it, but I knew that if killed, its flesh could not keep much longer than a day, and on that account I bought eight or ten small ones, which "my friends" really relished exceedingly, and which served to support them for a long time.[5]

Turtles such as I have spoken of, are caught in various ways on the coasts of the Floridas, or in estuaries and rivers. Some turtlers are in the habit of setting great nets across the entrance of streams, so as to answer the purpose either at the flow or at the ebb of the waters. These nets are formed of very large meshes, into which the turtles partially enter, when, the more they attempt to extricate themselves, the more they get entangled. Others harpoon them in the usual manner; but in my estimation no method is equal to that employed by Mr EGAN, the Pilot of Indian Isle.[6]

That extraordinary turtler had an iron instrument, which he called a *peg*, and which at each end had a point not unlike what nail-makers call a brad, it being four-cornered but flattish, and of a shape somewhat resembling the beak of an Ivory-billed Woodpecker, together with a neck and shoulder. Between the two shoulders of this instrument a fine tough line, fifty or more fathoms in length, was fastened by one end being passed through a hole in the centre of the peg, and the line itself was carefully coiled up and placed in a convenient part of the canoe. One extremity of this peg enters a sheath of iron that loosely attaches it to a long wooden spear, until a turtle has been pierced through the shell by the other extremity. He of the canoe paddles away as silently as possible whenever he spies a turtle basking on the water, until he gets within a distance of ten or twelve yards, when he throws the spear so as to hit the animal about the place which an entomologist would choose, were it a large insect, for pinning it to a piece of cork. As soon as the turtle is struck, the wooden handle separates from the peg, in consequence of the looseness of its attachment. The smart of the wound urges on the animal as if distracted, and it appears that the longer the peg remains in its shell, the more firmly fastened it is, so great a pressure is exercised upon it by the shell of the turtle, which being suffered to run like a whale, soon becomes fatigued, and is secured by hauling in the line with great care. In this manner, as the Pilot informed me, eight hundred Green Turtles were caught by one man in twelve months.

Each turtler has his *crawl*, which is a square wooden building or pen, formed of logs, which are so far separated as to allow the tide to pass freely through, and stand erect in the mud. The turtles are placed in this inclosure, fed and kept there until sold. If the animals thus confined have not laid their eggs previous to their seizure, they drop them in the water, so that they are lost. The price of Green Turtles, when I was at Key West, was from four to six cents per pound.

The loves of the turtles are conducted in a most extraordinary manner; but as the recital of them must prove out of place here, I shall pass them over. There is, however, a circumstance relating to their habits, which I cannot omit, although I have it not from my own ocular evidence, but from report. When I was in the Floridas, several of the turtlers assured me, that any turtle taken from the depositing ground, and carried on the deck of a vessel several hundred miles, would, if then let loose, certainly be met with at the same spot, either immediately after, or in the following breeding season. Should this prove true, and it certainly may, how much will be enhanced the belief of the student in the uniformity and solidity of Nature's arrangements, when he finds that the turtle, like a migratory bird, returns to the same locality, with perhaps a delight similar to that experienced by the traveller, who, after visiting distant countries, once more returns to the bosom of his cherished family.[7]

Notes

1. "The Turtlers" was first published in *OB* 2 (1834), 370–76. Audubon's "Tortugas," named in 1513 by Juan Ponce de León for the preponderance of sea turtles encountered in surrounding waters, are now known as the Dry Tortugas National Park—a network of seven small islands nearly seventy miles from Key West. The "dry" refers to lack of freshwater for drinking. The "great coral reef or wall" is now the Tortugas Bank. The Dry Tortugas would also be the setting for James Fenimore Cooper's *Jack Tier; or, The Florida Reef* (1848).

2. Audubon's "Night-hawk" here was likely his "Night Hawk" (Havell 147), now either the common nighthawk (*Chordeiles minor*) or the similar Antillean nighthawk, recognized only later (*C. gundlachii*). His "Brown Gannet," "Booby Gannet" elsewhere (Havell 207), is now the brown booby (*Sula leucogaster*).

3. The green turtle (*Chelonia mydas*) is now considered globally Endangered by the IUCN (2004), due first to indigenous subsistence hunting and then to over three centuries of colonial commercial hunting around the Caribbean, with methods and markets as described by Audubon. See Shakira Crawford, *The Last Turtlemen of the Caribbean* (Chapel Hill: University of North Carolina Press, 2020), 15–35. The hawksbill turtle (*Eretmochelys imbricata*) is listed as Critically Endangered by the IUCN, at least as of 2008. The loggerhead turtle

(*Caretta caretta*) is considered globally Vulnerable (IUCN, 2015). Audubon's "Trunk Turtle," now more commonly called the leatherback (*Dermochelys coriacea*), is Vulnerable (IUCN, 2013). Weighing up to two thousand pounds, leatherbacks are the largest of modern sea turtle species.

4. Audubon's "Grasswrack" (*Zostera marina*) is a species of aquatic plant known as sea wrack or common eelgrass.

5. The Charleston-born Benjamin Strobel, a physician and editor of the *Key West Gazette* from 1829 to 1832, had trained at the Medical College of South Carolina and learned his natural history from Bachman. He recorded his experiences with Audubon (who was in Key West from May 4–21, 1832) in an article for the *Key West Gazette* (May 23, 1832), as well as one of his (anonymously published) "Sketches of Florida," published in the *Charleston Mercury* (February 3, 1836). See E. A. Hammond, "Dr. Strobel's Account of John J. Audubon," *Auk* 80, no. 4 (October 1963): 462–66. The Audubon House, a museum in Key West, sits on the property formerly owned by Dr. Strobel.

6. "Mr. Egan" is James Egan; see "The Florida Keys." With the focus on catching females on the beach, and then the use of nets, the decimation of sea turtles throughout the Caribbean had been well underway for a century before Audubon's observations, although the establishment of kraals in Key West began significantly only in the early 1800s, in part because vessels like the *Marion* cleared away competition from Bahamian fishermen. Canning turtle meat and soup began in the 1850s, supplying a distant luxury market that Audubon recognizes with "The Lord Mayor's dinner." The killing and holding of turtles (mostly imported by the 1900s) for meat and shell and then tourism, continued in the Florida Keys region into the 1970s, was eventually shut down by the Endangered Species Act and the long-depressed supply. See Callum Roberts, *The Unnatural History of the Sea* (Washington, DC: Island Press, 2007), 62–67; Frederick True, "The Turtle and Terrapin Fisheries," in *The Fisheries and Fisheries Industries of the United States*, ed. George Brown Goode, sec. V, vol. 2 (Washington, DC: Government Printing Office, 1887), 496–98; David S. Lee, "The Key West Turtle Kraals Museum—But a Short Step Back in Time," *Bulletin of the Chicago Herpetological Society* 47, no. 7 (2012): 81–88.

7. Over a century later, in the 1950s, turtle conservationist and biologist Archie Carr, in *The Windward Road* (New York: Knopf, 1956), explored similar evidence regarding the open-ocean homing ability of green turtles, in part citing evidence related to the escape from kraals of turtles that had been branded by Caribbean hunters and could thus be individually recognized and tracked.

BLACK SKIMMER OR RAZOR-BILLED SHEARWATER

THIS bird [plate 2], one of the most singularly endowed by nature, is a constant resident on all the sandy and marshy shores of our more southern States, from South Carolina to the Sabine River, and doubtless also in Texas, where I found it quite abundant in the beginning of spring. At this season parties of Black Skimmers extend their movements eastward as far as the sands of Long Island, beyond which however I have not seen them. Indeed in Massachusetts and Maine this bird is known only to such navigators as have observed it in the southern and tropical regions.[1]

To study its habits therefore, the naturalist must seek the extensive sand-bars, estuaries, and mouths of the rivers of our Southern States, and enter the sinuous bayous intersecting the broad marshes along their coasts. There, during the warm sunshine of the winter days, you will see thousands of Skimmers, covered as it were with their gloomy mantles, peaceably lying beside each other, and so crowded together as to present to your eye the appearance of an immense black pall accidentally spread on the sand. Such times are their hours of rest, and I believe of sleep, as, although partially diurnal, and perfectly able to discern danger by day, they rarely feed then, unless the weather be cloudy. On the same sands, yet apart from them, equal numbers of our common Black-headed Gulls may be seen enjoying the same comfort in security. Indeed the Skimmers are rarely at such times found on sand or gravel banks which are not separated from the neighbouring shores by some broad and deep piece of water. I think I can safely venture to say that in such places, and at the periods mentioned, I have seen not fewer than ten thousand of these birds in a single flock. Should you now attempt to approach them, you will find that as soon as you have reached within twice the range of your long duck-gun, the crowded Skimmers simultaneously rise on their feet, and watch all your movements. If you advance nearer, the whole flock suddenly taking to wing, fill the air with their harsh cries, and soon reaching a considerable height, range widely around, until, your patience being exhausted, you abandon the place. When thus taking to wing in countless multitudes, the snowy white of their under parts gladdens your eye, but anon, when they all veer through the air, the black of their long wings and upper parts produces a remarkable contrast to the blue sky above. Their aerial evolutions on such occasions are peculiar and pleasing, as they at times appear to be intent on removing to a great distance, then suddenly round to, and once more pass almost over you, flying so close together as to appear like a black cloud, first ascending, and then rushing down like a torrent. Should they see that you are retiring, they wheel a few times close over the ground, and when assured that there is no longer any danger, they alight pell-mell, with wings extended upwards, but presently closed, and once more huddling together they lie down on the ground, to remain until forced off by the tide. When the Skimmers repose on the shores of the mainland during high-water, they seldom continue long on the same spot, as if they felt doubtful of security; and a person watching them at such times might suppose that they were engaged in searching for food.[2]

No sooner has the dusk of evening arrived than the Skimmers begin to disperse, rise from their place of rest singly, in pairs, or in parties from three or four to eight or ten, apparently according to the degree of hunger they feel, and proceed in different directions along parts of the shores previously known to them, sometimes going up tide-rivers to a considerable distance. They spend the whole night on wing, searching diligently for food. Of this I had ample and satisfactory proof when ascending the St John's River in East Florida, in the United States' Schooner the Spark. The hoarse cries of the Skimmers never ceased more than an hour, so that I could easily know whether they were passing upwards or downwards in the dark. And this happened too when I was at least a hundred miles from the mouth of the river.[3]

Being aware, previously to my several visits to the peninsula of the Floridas and other parts of our southern coasts where the Razor-bills are abundant, of the observations made on this species by M. LESSON, I paid all imaginable attention to them, always aided with an excellent glass, in order to find whether or not they fed on bivalve shell-fish found in the shallows of sand-bars and other places at low water; but not in one single instance did I see any such occurrence, and in regard to this matter I agree with WILSON in asserting that, while with us, these birds do not feed on shell-fish. M. LESSON's words are as follows:—"Quoique le Bec-en-ciseaux semble défavorisé par la forme de son bec, nous acquîmes la preuve qu'il savait s'en servir avec avantage et avec la plus grande adresse. Les plages sablonneuses de Penco sont, en effect, remplies de *mactres*, coquilles bivalves, que la marée descendante laisse presque à sec dans des petites mares; le Bec-en-ciseaux, très au fait de cet phénomène, se place auprès de ces mollusques, attend que leur valve s'entr'ouvre un peu et profite aussitôt de ce movement en enforçant la lame inférieure et tranchante de son bec entre les valves qui se referment. L'oiseau enlève alors la coquille, la frappe sur la grève, coupe le ligament du mollusque et peut ensuite avaler celui-ci sans obstacle. Plusieurs fois nous avons été témoins de cet instinct très perfectionné."*[4]

While watching the movements of the Black Skimmer as it was searching for food, sometimes a full hour before it was dark, I have seen it pass its lower mandible at an angle of about 45 degrees into the water, whilst its *moveable* upper mandible was elevated a little above the surface. In this manner, with wings raised and extended, it ploughed as it were, the element in which its quarry lay to the extent of several yards at a time, rising and falling alternately, and that as frequently as it thought it necessary for securing its food when in sight of it; for I am certain that these birds never immerse their lower mandible until they have observed the object of their pursuit, for which reason their eyes are constantly directed downwards like those of Terns and Gannets. I have at times stood nearly an hour by the side of a small pond of salt water having a communication with the sea or a bay, while these birds would pass within a very few yards of me, then apparently quite regardless of my presence, and proceed fishing in the manner above described. Although silent at the commencement of their pursuit, they become noisy as the darkness draws on, and then give out their usual call notes, which resemble the syllables *hurk, hurk*, twice or thrice repeated at short intervals, as if to induce some of their companions to follow in their wake. I have seen a few of these birds glide in this manner in search of prey over a long salt-marsh bayou, or inlet, following the whole of its sinuosities, now and then lower themselves to the water, pass their bill along the surface, and on seizing a prawn or a small fish, instantly rise, munch and swallow it on wing. While at Galveston Island, and in the company of my generous

* "Although the black skimmer [razor-billed shearwater] would seem to be disadvantaged by the shape of its beak, we discovered that it used its beak advantageously and with the utmost dexterity. The sandy beaches of Penco are, in effect, full of [Arctic] surf clams, bivalves, which the receding tide leaves nearly entirely exposed in small intertidal pools; the black skimmer, being very aware of this phenomenon, positions itself near these mollusks, waits for their valves to open slightly, and takes advantage of this movement by forcing the sharp-edged lower mandible of its beak between the valves, which close back up. The bird then lifts up the shell, strikes it against the shore, and cuts the ligament of the mollusk, which it can then swallow without difficulty. We witnessed this highly perfected instinct numerous times." [Eds. translation]

friend EDWARD HARRIS and my son, I observed three Black Skimmers, which having noticed a Night Heron passing over them, at once rose in the air, gave chase to it, and continued their pursuit for several hundred yards, as if intent on overtaking it. Their cries during this chase differed from their usual notes, and resembled the barkings of a very small dog.[5]

The flight of the Black Skimmer is perhaps more elegant than that of any water bird with which I am acquainted. The great length of its narrow wings, its partially elongated forked tail, its thin body and extremely compressed bill, all appear contrived to assure it that buoyancy of motion which one cannot but admire when he sees it on wing. It is able to maintain itself against the heaviest gale; and I believe no instance has been recorded of any bird of this species having been forced inland by the most violent storm. But, to observe the aërial movements of the Skimmer to the best advantage, you must visit its haunts in the love season. Several males, excited by the ardour of their desires, are seen pursuing a yet unmated female. The coy one, shooting aslant to either side, dashes along with marvellous speed, flying hither and thither, upwards, downwards, in all directions. Her suitors strive to overtake her; they emit their love-cries with vehemence; you are gladdened by their softly and tenderly enunciated *ha, ha*, or the *hack, hack, cae, cae*, of the last in the chase. Like the female they all perform the most curious zigzags, as they follow in close pursuit, and as each beau at length passes her in succession, he extends his wings for an instant, and in a manner struts by her side. Sometimes a flock is seen to leave a sand-bar, and fly off in a direct course, each individual apparently intent on distancing his companions; and then their mingling cries of *ha, ha, hack, hack, cae, cae*, fill the air. I once saw one of these birds fly round a whole flock that had alighted, keeping at the height of about twenty yards, but now and then tumbling as if its wings had suddenly failed, and again almost upsetting, in the manner of the Tumbler Pigeon.[6]

On the 5th of May 1837, I was much surprised to find a large flock of Skimmers alighted and apparently asleep, on a dry grassy part of the interior of Galveston Island in Texas, while I was watching some marsh hawks that were breeding in the neighbourhood. On returning to the shore, however, I found that the tide was much higher than usual, in consequence of a recent severe gale, and had covered all the sand banks on which I had at other times observed them resting by day.

The instinct or sagacity which enables the Razor-bills, after being scattered in all directions in quest of food during a long night, often at great distances from each other, to congregate again towards morning, previously to their alighting on a spot to rest, has appeared to me truly wonderful; and I have been tempted to believe that the place of rendezvous had been agreed upon the evening before. They have a great enmity towards Crows and Turkey Buzzards when at their breeding ground, and on the first appearance of these marauders, some dozens of Skimmers at once give chase to them, rarely desisting until quite out of sight.

Although parties of these birds remove from the south to betake themselves to the eastern shores, and breed there, they seldom arrive at Great Egg Harbour before the middle of May, or deposit their eggs until a month after, or about the period when, in the Floridas and on the coast of Georgia and South Carolina, the young are hatched. To these latter sections of the country we will return, Reader, to observe their actions at this interesting period. Were I to speak of the vast numbers that congregate for the purpose of breeding, some of my readers might receive the account with as little favour as they have accorded to that which I have given of the wild pigeons; and therefore I will present you with a statement by my friend the Rev. JOHN BACHMAN, which he has inserted in my journal. "These birds are very abundant, and breed in great numbers on the sea islands at Bull's Bay. Probably twenty thousand nests were seen at a time. The sailors collected an enormous number of their eggs. The birds screamed all the while, and whenever a Pelican or Turkey Buzzard passed near, they assailed it by hundreds, pouncing on the back of the latter, that came to rob them of their eggs, and pursued them fairly out of sight. They had laid on the dry sand, and the following morning we observed many fresh-laid eggs, when some had been removed the previous afternoon." Then, Reader, judge of the deafening angry cries of such a multitude, and see them all over your head begging for mercy as it were, and earnestly urging you and your cruel sailors to retire and leave them in the peaceful charge of their young, or to settle on their lovely rounded eggs, should it rain or feel chilly.

The Skimmer forms no other nest than a slight hollow in the sand. The eggs, I believe, are always three, and measure an inch and three quarters in length, an inch and three-eighths in breadth. As if to be assimilated to the colours of the birds themselves, they have a pure white ground, largely patched or blotched with black or very dark umber, with here and there a large spot of a light purplish tint. They are as good to eat as those of most Gulls, but inferior to the eggs of Plovers and other birds of that tribe. The young are clumsy, much of the same colour as the sand on which they lie, and are not able to fly until about six weeks, when you now perceive their resemblance to their parents. They are fed at first by the regurgitation of the finely macerated contents of the gullets of the old birds, and ultimately pick up the shrimps, prawns, small crabs, and fishes dropped before them. As soon as they are able to walk about, they cluster together in the manner of the young of the Common Gannet, and it is really marvellous how the parents can distinguish them individually on such occasions. This bird walks in the manner of the Terns, with short steps, and the tail slightly elevated. When gorged and fatigued, both old and young birds are wont to lie flat on the sand, and extend their bills before them; and when thus reposing in fancied security, may sometimes be slaughtered in great numbers by the single discharge of a gun. When shot at while on wing, and brought to the water, they merely float, and are easily secured. If the sportsman is desirous of obtaining more, he may easily do so, as others pass in full clamour close over the wounded bird.

Notes

1. First published in *OB* 4 (1838), 203–11. Audubon's "Black Skimmer/Razor-billed Shearwater" (plate 2; Havell 323) is now more commonly known only as the black skimmer (*Rynchops niger*). The black skimmer is considered a species of Least Concern, although its global population is decreasing (IUCN, 2008). Audubon likely painted his black skimmer in Florida. As he explains, these birds can be found throughout the eastern coastal United States and around the coastal Gulf of Mexico; although there were historical and modern records of their breeding as far north as the Massachusetts coast, this was presumably no longer the case by the 1830s due to egg hunters. See M. Gochfeld, J. Burger, and K. L. Lefevre, "Black Skimmer," v. 1.0 (2020), birdsoftheworld.org.

2. Audubon's observation of a flock of ten thousand black skimmers is notable. Along the northern coast of the Gulf of Mexico, nearly a dozen colonies had over a thousand breeding pairs in 1976, but Gochfel, Burger, and Lefevre found no flocks the size of Audubon's observation (2020).

3. The *USS Spark* was a 50-ton navy gunboat commanded by William Piercy. Acquired in Baltimore in 1831, it patrolled the lower East Coast for smugglers. Audubon's trip on the *Spark* was abruptly ended when a sailor accidentally shot himself. See Richard Rhodes, *John James Audubon: The Making of an American* (New York: Knopf, 2004), 361–62.

4. Translation by the editors and Bryan Donaldson, personal communication, June 10, 2020. Several small corrections have been made here to match the original French passage by René Primevère Lesson (1794–1849), who was a French naturalist and surgeon and trained at the Naval Medical School at Rochefort (where Audubon's early attempt at a naval career had foundered). See Lesson, *Manuel d'ornithologie ou Description des pincipales espèces d'oiseaux* (Paris: Roret, 1828), 2:385–86. Penco is in Chile.

5. Audubon's "Night Heron" (Havell 236) is now more commonly the black-crowned night-heron (*Nycticorax nycticorax*). Edward Harris (1799–1863) was a New Jersey farmer and ornithologist and one of Audubon's major supporters. He accompanied Audubon on his 1843 expedition up the Missouri River. Audubon named Harris's hawk and Harris's sparrow after him.

6. "Tumbler Pigeons" are specialized breeds of common pigeons, rock pigeons (*Columba livia*), bred to literally tumble backward.

DEATH OF A PIRATE

IN the calm of a fine moonlight night, as I was admiring the beauty of the clear heavens, and the broad glare of light that glanced from the trembling surface of the waters around, the officer on watch came up and entered into conversation with me. He had been a turtler in other years, and a great hunter to boot, and although of humble birth and pretensions, energy and talent, aided by education, had raised him to a higher station. Such a man could not fail to be an agreeable companion, and we talked on various subjects, principally, you may be sure, birds and other natural productions. He told me he once had a disagreeable adventure, when looking out for game, in a certain cove on the shores of the Gulf of Mexico; and, on my expressing a desire to hear it, he willingly related to me the following particulars, which I give you, not perhaps precisely in his own words, but as nearly so as I can remember.[1]

"Towards evening, one quiet summer day, I chanced to be paddling along a sandy shore, which I thought well fitted for my repose, being covered with tall grass, and as the sun was not many degrees above the horizon, I felt anxious to pitch my mosquito bar or net, and spend the night in this wilderness. The bellowing notes of thousands of bull-frogs in a neighbouring swamp might lull me to rest, and I looked upon the flocks of blackbirds that were assembling as sure companions in this secluded retreat.

I proceeded up a little stream, to insure the safety of my canoe from any sudden storm, when, as I gladly advanced, a beautiful yawl came unexpectedly in view. Surprised at such a sight in a part of the country then scarcely known, I felt a sudden check in the circulation of my blood. My paddle dropped from my hands, and fearfully indeed, as I picked it up, did I look towards the unknown boat. On reaching it, I saw its sides marked with stains of blood, and looking with anxiety over the gunwale, I perceived to my horror, two human bodies covered with gore. Pirates or hostile Indians I was persuaded had perpetrated the foul deed, and my alarm naturally increased; my heart fluttered, stopped, and heaved with unusual tremors, and I looked towards the setting sun in consternation and despair. How long my reveries lasted I cannot tell; I can only recollect that I was roused from them by the distant groans of one apparently in mortal agony. I felt as if refreshed by the cold perspiration that oozed from every pore, and I reflected that though alone, I was well armed, and might hope for the protection of the Almighty.

Humanity whispered to me that, if not surprised and disabled, I might render assistance to some sufferer, or even be the means of saving a useful life. Buoyed up by this thought, I urged my canoe on shore, and seizing it by the bow, pulled it at one spring high among the grass.

The groans of the unfortunate person fell heavy on my ear, as I cocked and reprimed my gun, and I felt determined to shoot the first that should rise from the grass. As I cautiously proceeded, a hand was raised over the weeds, and waved in the air in the most supplicating manner. I levelled my gun about a foot below it, when the next moment, the head and breast of a man covered with blood were convulsively raised, and a faint hoarse voice asked me for mercy and help! A death-like silence followed his fall to the ground. I surveyed every object around with eyes intent, and ears impressible by the slightest sound, for my situation that moment I thought as critical as any I had ever been in. The croakings of the frogs, and the last blackbirds alighting on their roosts, were the only sounds or sights; and I now proceeded towards the object of my mingled alarm and commiseration.

Alas! the poor being who lay prostrate at my feet, was so weakened by loss of blood, that I had nothing to fear from him. My first impulse was to run back to the water, and having done so, I returned with my cap filled to the brim. I felt at his heart, washed his face and breast, and rubbed his temples with the contents of a phial, which I kept about me as an antidote for the bites of snakes. His features, seamed by the ravages of time, looked frightful and disgusting; but he had been a powerful man, as the breadth of his chest plainly shewed. He groaned in the most appalling manner, as his breath struggled through the mass of blood that seemed to fill his throat. His dress plainly disclosed his occupation:—a large pistol he had thrust into his bosom, a naked cutlass lay near him on the ground, a red silk handkerchief was bound over his projecting brows, and over a pair of loose trowsers he wore fisherman's boots. He was, in short, a pirate [fig. 24].[2]

My exertions were not in vain, for as I continued to bathe his temples, he revived, his pulse resumed some strength, and I began to hope that he might perhaps survive the deep wounds which he had received. Darkness, deep darkness, now enveloped us. I spoke of making a fire. 'Oh! for mercy's sake,' he exclaimed, 'don't.' Knowing, however, that under existing circumstances it was expedient for me to do so, I left him, went to his boat, and brought the rudder, the benches, and the oars, which

FIGURE 24. Pirates at sea. Frontispiece of pirates murdering officers, in *Mutiny and Murder: Confession of Charles Gibbs . . . annexed, is a solemn Address to Youth* (1831), the story of a violent American pirate who was eventually hanged for his role in a mutiny on a ship out of New Orleans (here represented by a stylized small boat). Courtesy of Williams College.

with my hatchet I soon splintered. I then struck a light, and presently stood in the glare of a blazing fire. The pirate seemed struggling between terror and gratitude for my assistance; he desired me several times in half English and Spanish to put out the flames, but after I had given him a draught of strong spirits, he at length became more composed. I tried to staunch the blood that flowed from the deep gashes in his shoulders and side. I expressed my regret that I had no food about me, but when I spoke of eating he sullenly waved his head.

My situation was one of the most extraordinary that I have ever been placed in. I naturally turned my talk towards religious subjects, but, alas, the dying man hardly believed in the existence of a God. 'Friend,' said he, 'for friend you seem to be, I never studied the ways of Him of whom you talk. I am an outlaw, perhaps you will say a wretch,—I have been for many years a Pirate. The instructions of my parents were of no avail to me, for I have always believed that I was born to be a most cruel man. I now lie here, about to die in the weeds, because I long ago refused to listen to their many admonitions. Do not shudder when I tell you—these now useless hands murdered the mother whom they had embraced. I feel that I have deserved the pangs of the wretched death that hovers over me; and I am thankful that one of my kind will alone witness my last gaspings.'

A fond but feeble hope that I might save his life, and perhaps assist in procuring his pardon, induced me to speak to him on the subject. 'It is all in vain, friend—I have no objection to die—I am glad that the villains who wounded me were not my conquerors—I want no pardon from *any one*—Give me some water, and let me die alone.'

With the hope that I might learn from his conversation something that might lead to the capture of his guilty associates, I returned from the creek with another capful of water, nearly the whole of which I managed to introduce into his parched mouth, and begged him, for the sake of his future peace, to disclose his history to me. 'It is impossible,' said he, 'there will not be time; the beatings of my heart tell me so. Long before day, these sinewy limbs will be motionless. Nay, there will hardly be a drop of blood in my body; and that blood will only serve to make the grass grow. My wounds are mortal, and I must and will die without what you call confession.'

The moon rose in the east. The majesty of her placid beauty impressed me with reverence. I pointed towards her, and asked the Pirate if he could not recognise God's features there. 'Friend, I see what you are driving at,' was his answer,—'you, like the rest of our enemies, feel the desire of murdering us all.—Well—be it so—to die is after all nothing more than a jest; and were it not for the pain, no one, in my opinion, need care a jot about it. But, as you really have befriended me, I will tell you all that is proper.'

Hoping his mind might take a useful turn, I again bathed his temples and washed his lips with spirits. His sunk eyes seemed to dart fire at mine—a heavy and deep sigh swelled his chest and struggled through his blood-choked throat, and he asked me to raise him for a little. I did so, when he addressed me somewhat as follows, for, as I have told you, his speech was a mixture of Spanish, French and English, forming a jargon, the like of which I had never heard before, and which I am utterly unable to imitate. However I shall give you the substance of his declaration.

'First tell me, how many bodies you found in the boat, and what sort of dresses they had on.' I mentioned their number, and described their apparel. 'That's right,' said he, 'they are the bodies of the scoundrels who followed me in that infernal Yankee barge. Bold rascals they were, for when they found the water too shallow for their craft, they took to it and waded after me. All my companions had been shot, and to lighten my own boat I flung them overboard; but as I lost time in this, the two ruffians caught hold of my gunwale, and struck on my head and body in such a manner, that after I had disabled and killed them both in the boat, I was scarce able to move. The other villains carried off our schooner and one of our boats, and perhaps ere now have hung all my companions whom they did not kill at the time. I have commanded my beautiful vessel many years, captured many ships, and sent many rascals to the devil. I always hated the Yankees, and only regret that I have not killed more of them.—I sailed from Matanzas.—I have often been in concert with others. I have money without counting, but it is buried where it will never be found, and it would be useless to tell you of it.' His throat filled with blood, his voice failed, the cold hand of death was laid on his brow, feebly and hurriedly he muttered, 'I am a dying man, farewell!'

Alas! It is painful to see death in any shape; in this it was horrible, for there was no hope. The rattling of his throat announced the moment of dissolution, and already did the body fall on my arms with a weight that was insupportable. I laid him on the ground. A mass of dark blood poured from his mouth; then came a frightful groan, the last breathing of that foul spirit; and what now lay at my feet in the wild desert?—a mangled mass of clay!

The remainder of that night was passed in no enviable mood; but my feelings cannot be described. At dawn I dug a hole with the paddle of my canoe, rolled the body into it, and covered it. On reaching the boat I found several buzzards feeding on the bodies, which I in vain attempted to drag to the shore. I therefore covered them with mud and weeds, and launching my canoe, paddled from the cove with a secret joy for my escape, overshaded with the gloom of mingled dread and abhorrence."

Notes

1. "Death of a Pirate" was first printed in *OB* 2 (1834), 185–89.

2. As stated in the notes to "Journal of a Sea Voyage," piracy had only recently been on the wane in the Florida Straits, mostly due to patrols by US Navy vessels actively looking to protect merchant travel beginning in the early 1820s. No sources have been identified for this polished story. Captain Charles Johnson had published the exceptionally popular *A General History of the Robberies and Murders of the Most Notorious Pyrates* a century earlier, in 1724, and Audubon was reading Byron's *The Corsair* while aboard the *Delos*, but while the details of buried treasure, pistols, and red silk kerchief sound clichéd today, this is still a half century before Robert Louis Stevenson's *Treasure Island* (1883), the novel that seems to have had the most lasting impact on our perceptions of piracy under sail. See David Cordingly, *Under the Black Flag: The Romance and the Reality of Life among the Pirates* (London: Harcourt Brace, 1995), 3–7. Audubon's "Death of a Pirate" has some intriguing parallels to a popular pamphlet published only a couple years earlier titled *Mutiny and Murder: Confession of Charles Gibbs* (Providence: Israel Smith, 1831), a brutal and moralizing narrative of a pirate who preyed on American ships in the Straits of Florida, buried treasure, and was eventually hung, having murdered, he claimed in his statement of repentance, some four hundred people during his blood-soaked career (see fig. 24).

THE FRIGATE PELICAN

PREVIOUS to my visit to the Florida Keys, I had seen but few Frigate Birds [plate 3], and those only at some distance, while I was on the Gulf of Mexico, so that I could merely recognise them by their mode of flight. On approaching Indian Key, however, I observed several of them, and as

I proceeded farther south, their numbers rapidly increased; but on the Tortugas very few were observed. This bird rarely travels farther eastward than the Bay of Charleston in South Carolina, although it is abundant at all seasons from Cape Florida to Cape Sable, the two extreme points of the peninsula. How far south it may be found I cannot tell.[1]

The Frigate Pelicans may be said to be as gregarious as our Vultures: You see them in small or large flocks, according to circumstances. Like our Vultures, they spend the greater part of the day on wing, searching for food; and like them also, when gorged or roosting, they collect in large flocks, either to fan themselves or to sleep close together. They are equally lazy, tyrannical, and rapacious, domineering over birds weaker than themselves, and devouring the young of every species, whenever an opportunity offers, in the absence of the parents; in a word, they are most truly Marine Vultures.

About the middle of May, a period which to me appeared very late for birds found in so warm a climate as that of the Florida Keys, the Frigate Pelicans assemble in flocks of from fifty to five hundred pairs or more. They are seen flying at a great height over the islands on which they have bred many previous seasons, courting for hours together; after which they return towards the mangroves, alight on them, and at once begin to repair the old nests or construct new ones. They pillage each other's nests of their materials, and make excursions for more to the nearest keys. They break the dry twigs of trees with ease, passing swiftly on wing, and snapping them off by a single grasp of their powerful bill. It is indeed a beautiful sight to see them when thus occupied, especially when several are so engaged, passing and repassing with the swiftness of thought over the trees whose tops are blasted; their purpose appears as if accomplished by magic. I know only two other birds that perform the same action: one of them is the Forked-tailed Hawk, the other our swift or Chimney Swallow; but neither of them is so expert as the Frigate Pelican. It sometimes happens that this bird accidentally drops a stick while travelling towards its nest, when, if this should happen over the water, it plunges after it and seizes it with its bill before it has reached the waves.[2]

The nests are usually placed on the south side of the keys, and on such trees as hang over the water, some low, others high, several in a single tree, or only one, according to the size of the mangrove, but in some cases lining the whole side of the island. They are composed of sticks crossing each other to the height of about two inches, and are flattish but not very large. When the birds are incubating, their long wings and tail are seen extending beyond the nest for more than a foot. The eggs are two or three, more frequently the latter number, measure two inches and seven-eighths in length, two in breadth, being thus of a rather elongated form, and have a thick smooth shell, of a greenish-white colour, frequently soiled by the filth of the nests. The young are covered with yellowish-white down, and look at first as if they had no feet. They are fed by regurgitation, but grow tardily, and do not leave the nest until they are able to follow their parents on wing.[3]

At that period the plumage of the young females is marbled with grey and brown, with the exception of the head and the lower parts, which are white. The tail is about half the length it attains at the first moult, and is brownish-black, as are the primaries. After the first change of plumage, the wings become longer, and their flight is almost as elegant and firm as that of older birds.

The second spring plumage of this sex is brownish-black on the upper parts, that colour extending over the head and around the neck in irregular patches of brown, continued in a sharp angle towards the breast, but separated on its sides by the white that ascends on either side of the neck towards the head. The lower tail-coverts are brownish-black, as are the lower parts of the belly and flanks; the shoulders alone remaining as at first. The tail and wings are perfect.

The third spring, the upper parts of the head and neck are of a purer brownish-black, which extends down to the extremity of the angle, as are the feathers of the belly and the lower tail-coverts, the dark colour reaching now to within five inches of the angle on the breast. The white of the intermediate space has become much purer; here and there light tints of bronze appear; the feet, which at first were dull yellow, have become of a rich reddish-orange, and the bill is pale blue. The bird is now capable of breeding, although its full plumage is not obtained until the next moult, when the colours become glossy above, and the white of the breast pure.

The changes which the males undergo are less remarkable. They are at first, when fully fledged, entirely of the colour seen on the upper parts of the young females; and the tint is merely improved afterwards, becoming of a deeper brownish-black, and acquiring purer reflections of green, purple and bronze, which in certain lights are seen on every part of the head, neck and body, and in very old males on the wings and tail. They also commence breeding the third spring. But I now return to the habits of this interesting bird.[4]

The Frigate Pelican is possessed of a power of flight which I conceive superior to that of perhaps any other bird. However swiftly the Cayenne Tern, the smaller Gulls or the Jager move on wing, it seems a matter of mere sport to it to overtake any of them. The Goshawk, the Peregrine, and the Gyr Falcon, which I conceive to be the swiftest of our hawks, are obliged to pursue their victim, should it be a Green-winged Teal or Passenger Pigeon, at times for half a mile, at the highest pitch of their speed, before they can secure them. The bird of which I speak comes from on high with the velocity of a meteor, and on nearing the object of its pursuit, which its keen eye has spied while fishing at a distance, darts on either side to cut off all retreat, and with open bill forces it to drop or disgorge the fish which it has just caught. See him now! Yonder, over the waves leaps the brilliant dolphin, as he pursues the flying-fishes, which he expects to seize the moment they drop into the water. The Frigate Bird, who has marked them, closes his wings, dives toward them, and now ascending, holds one of the tiny things across his bill. Already fifty yards above the sea, he spies a porpoise in full chase, launches towards the spot, and in passing seizes the mullet that had escaped from its dreaded foe; but now, having obtained a fish too large for his gullet, he rises, munching it all the while, as if bound for the skies. Three or four of his own tribe have watched him and observed his success. They shoot towards him on broadly extended pinions, rise in wide circles, smoothly, yet as swiftly as himself. They are now all at the same height, and each as it overtakes him, lashes him with its wings, and tugs at his prey. See! one has fairly robbed him, but before he can secure the contested fish it drops. One of the other birds has caught it, but he is pursued by all. From bill to bill, and through the air, rapidly falls the fish, until it drops quite dead on the waters, and sinks into the deep. Whatever disappointment the hungry birds feel, they seem to deserve it all.[5]

Sights like these you may every day see, if you take ship and sail for the Florida Keys. I have more to tell you, however, and of things that to me were equally pleasing. While standing in the cool veranda of Major GLASSEL of the United States army, at Key West, I observed a Frigate Pelican that had forced a Cayenne Tern, yet in sight, to drop a fish, which the broad-winged warrior had seized as it fell. This fish was rather large for the Tern, and might probably be about eight inches in length. The Frigate Pelican mounted with it across his bill about a hundred yards, and then tossing it up caught it as it fell, but not in the proper manner. He therefore dropped it, but before it had fallen many yards, caught it again. Still it was not in a good position, the weight of the head, it seemed, having prevented the bird from seizing it by that part. A second time the fish was thrown upwards, and now at last was received in a convenient manner, that is, with its head downwards, and immediately swallowed.[6]

When the morning light gladdens the face of nature, and while the warblers are yet waiting in silence the first rays of the sun, whose appearance they will hail with songs of joy, the Frigate Bird, on extended pinions, sails from his roosting place. Slowly and gently, with retracted neck he glides, as if desirous of quietly trying the renovated strength of his wings. Toward the vast deep he moves, rising apace, and before any other bird views the bright orb emerging from the waters. Pure is the azure of the heavens, and rich the deep green of the smooth sea below; there is every prospect of the finest weather; and now the glad bird shakes his pinions; and far up into the air, far beyond the reach of man's unaided eye, he soars in his quiet but rapid flight. There he floats in the pure air, but thither can fancy alone follow him. Would that I could accompany him! But now I see him again, with half-closed wings, gently falling towards the sea. He pauses a while, and again dives through the air. Thrice, four times, has he gradually approached the surface of the ocean; now he shakes his pinions as violently as the swordsman whirls his claymore; all is right; and he sweeps away, shooting to this side and that, in search of prey.

Mid-day has arrived, and threatening clouds obscure the horizon; the breeze, ere felt, ruffles the waters around; a thick mist advances over the deep; the sky darkens, and as the angry blasts curl the waves, the thunder mutters afar; all nature is involved in gloom, and all is in confusion, save only the Man-of-war Bird, who gallantly meets the gale. If he cannot force his way against the storm, he keeps his ground, balancing himself like a hawk watching his prey beneath; but now the tempest rages, and rising obliquely, he shoots away, and ere long surmounts the tumultuous clouds, entering a region calm and serene, where he floats secure until the world below has resumed its tranquillity.

I have frequently observed the Frigate Bird scratch its head with its feet while on wing; and this happening one day, when the bird fell through the air, as it is accustomed to do at such times, until it came within shot, I killed it when almost over my head, and immediately picked it up. I had been for years anxious to know what might be the use of the pectinated claws of birds; and on examining both its feet with a glass, I found the racks crammed with insects, such as occur on the bird's head, and especially around the ears. I also observed that the pectinated claws of birds of this species were much longer, flatter, and more comb-like than those of any other species with which I am acquainted. I now therefore feel convinced, that, however useful this instrument may be on other occasions, it is certainly employed in cleansing parts of the skin of birds which cannot be reached by the bill.

At times these birds may be seen chasing and jostling each other as if engaged in a frolic, after which they bear away on extended wings, and fly in a direct course until out of sight. But although their flight is easy and powerful, in a degree not surpassed by any other bird, they move with great difficulty on the ground. They can rise, however, from a sandbar, no matter how low and level it may be. At such times, as well as when sitting on the water, which it occasionally does, the bird raises its wings almost perpendicularly, spreads its tail half erect, and at the first flap of the former, and simultaneous stroke of the latter, on the ground or the water, bounces away. Its feet, however, are of little service beyond what I have mentioned, and the supporting of its body when it has alighted on a branch, on which it rarely stands very erect, although it moves sideways on it, as Parrots sometimes do. It never dives, its bill in form resembling that of the Cormorants, which also never plunge from on wing in pursuit of fish, and only dip into the water when dropping from a perch or a rock to escape danger, as the Anhingas and some other birds are also accustomed to do.

When the Frigate Pelican is in want of a dead fish, a crab, or any floating garbage suited to its appetite, it approaches the water in the manner of Gulls, holding its wings high, and beating them until the bill has performed its duty, which being accomplished, the bird immediately rises in the air and devours its prey.

These birds see well at night, although they never go to sea excepting by day. At various times I have accidentally sailed by mangrove keys on which hundreds were roosted, and apparently sound asleep, when, on my firing a gun for the purpose of starting whatever birds might be there, they would all take to wing and sail as beautifully as during day, returning to the trees as the boats proceeded. They are by no means shy; indeed they seem unaware of danger from a gun, and rarely all go off when a party is shooting at them, until a considerable number has been obtained. The only difficulty I experienced in procuring them was on account of the height to which they so soon rose on leaving the trees; but we had excellent guns, and our worthy pilot's "Long Tom" distinguished itself above the rest. At one place, where we found many hundreds of them, they sailed for nearly half an hour over our heads, and about thirty were shot, some of them at a remarkable height, when we could hear the shot strike them, and when, as they fell to the water, the sound of their great wings whirling through the air resembled that produced by a sail flapping during a calm. When shot at and touched ever so slightly, they disgorge their food in the manner of Vultures, Gulls and some Terns; and if they have fallen and are approached, they continue to vomit the contents of their stomach, which at times are extremely putrid and nauseous. When seized, they evince little disposition to defend themselves, although ever so slightly wounded, but struggle and beat themselves until killed. Should you, however, place your fingers within their open bill, you might not withdraw them scatheless.

They are extremely silent, and the only note which I heard them utter was a rough croaking one. They devour the young of the Brown Pelican when quite small, as well as those of other birds whose nests are flat and exposed during the absence of the parent birds; but their own young suffer in the same manner from the still more voracious Turkey Buzzard. The notion that the Frigate Bird forces the Pelicans and Boobies to disgorge their prey is erroneous. The Pelican, if attacked or pursued by this bird, could alight on the water or elsewhere, and by one stroke of its sharp and powerful bill destroy the rash aggressor. The Booby would in all probability thrust its strong and pointed bill against the assailant with equal success. The Cayenne Tern, and other species of that genus, as well as several small Gulls, all abundant on the Florida coasts, are its purveyors, and them it forces to disgorge or drop their prey. Those of the deep are the dolphins, porpoises, and occasionally the sharks. Their sight is wonderfully keen, and they now and then come down from a great height to pick up a dead fish only a few inches long floating on the water. Their flesh is tough, dark, and, as food, unfit for any other person than one in a state of starvation.

I have given a figure of a very beautiful old male in spring plumage, which was selected from a great number of all ages. I have also represented the feet of an individual between two and three years old, on account of the richness of their colour at that age, whereas in the adult males they are quite black.

Notes

1. First published in *OB* 3 (1835), 495–503. The magnificent frigatebird is the only frigatebird of five global species found in North American waters. The species is of Least Concern, and its population is increasing (IUCN, 2018).

2. Audubon's "Forked-tailed Hawk" appears to be his "Swallow-tailed Hawk" (Havell 72), now more commonly the swallow-tailed kite (*Elanoides forficatus*). The "swift or Chimney Swallow" is now more commonly the chimney swift (*Chaetura pelagica*).

3. Later observers have reported similar resident abundance in the region, but among ornithologists there has been some debate as to the veracity of Audubon's account that frigatebirds regularly nested in the Florida Keys in the early 1800s. Nesting has occurred in the region since the 1960s, however. Ornithologists agree today that magnificent frigatebirds lay only one egg. Henry M. Stevenson and Bruce H. Anderson, *The Birdlife of Florida* (Gainesville: University Press of Florida, 1994), 50–51.

4. In the anatomical appendix to his biography of the "Frigate Pelican," not included here, Audubon wrote briefly about the orange "gular sac," but the fact that he didn't write about the distinctive bright red gular pouch of the adult male, inflated during breeding, suggests he never witnessed this sight or behavior himself.

5. Audubon's "Cayenne Tern" is now known as the royal tern, *Thalasseus maximus* (Havell 273). Audubon's "Jager/Yager" is today more commonly spelled jaeger, of which three species are found on the US East Coast; Audubon painted and wrote of them all. Part of the magnificent frigatebird's extraordinary ability to soar and dive in flight comes from their having the lowest wing-loading of any bird on earth, meaning they have an enormous wingspan (up to 8 feet) with an exceptionally light body (less than 3.5 pounds); see Chris Elphick, John B.

Dunning Jr., and David Allen Sibley, *The Sibley Guide to Bird Life & Behavior* (2001), 167. Walt Whitman was also thrilled by the frigatebird's flight: "thou art all wings," he wrote in "To the Man-of-War Bird" (1881–1882). See Whitman, *The Sea Is a Continual Miracle*, ed. Jeffrey Yang (Hanover, NH: University Press of New England, 2017), 198. The "brilliant dolphin" here, as earlier, is a fish, the mahi-mahi (*Coryphaena hippurus*); see notes to "A Long Calm at Sea" and fig. 20. The "robbery" of other birds—scaring them to drop their fish—is known today as kleptoparasitism.

6. James M. Glassel died at sea on the *Seaman*, November 3, 1838.

THE SOOTY TERN

EARLY in the afternoon of the 9th of May 1832, I was standing on the deck of the United States' revenue-cutter the Marion. The weather was very beautiful, although hot, and a favourable breeze wafted us onwards in our course. Captain ROBERT DAY, who stood near me, on looking toward the south-west, ordered some person to be sent to the top to watch the appearance of land. A young lad was instantly seen ascending the rigging, and not many minutes after he had attained his post, we heard from him the cry of "land." It was the low keys of the Tortugas, toward which we had been steering. No change was made in the course of the "Lady of the Green Mantle," who glided along as if aware of the knowledge possessed by her commander. Now the light-house lantern appeared, like a bright gem glittering in the rays of the sun. Presently the masts and flags of several wreckers shewed us that they were anchored in the small but safe harbour. We sailed on, and our active pilot, who was also the first lieutenant of the Marion, pointed out to me a small island which he said was at this season the resort of thousands of birds, which he described by calling them "Black and White Sea Swallows," [plate 4] and again another islet, equally well stocked with another kind of Sea Swallow, which he added were called Noddies [fig. 15], because they frequently alighted on the yards of vessels at night, and slept there. He assured me that both species were on their respective breeding-grounds by millions, that the eggs of the first lay on the sand under bushes, at intervals of about a foot, while the nests of the last were placed as thickly on the bushes of their own chosen island. "Before we cast anchor," he added, "you will see them rise in swarms like those of bees when disturbed in their hive, and their cries will deafen you."[1]

You may easily imagine how anxious I was to realize the picture; I expressed a wish to be landed on the island; but the kind officer replied, "My good Sir, you will soon be tired of their incessant noise and numbers, and will enjoy the procuring of Boobies much better." After various tacks, we made our way through the curious and extremely dangerous channels leading to the small harbour, where we anchored. As the chain grated the ear, I saw a cloud-like mass arise over the "Bird Key," from which we were only a few hundred yards distant; and in a few minutes the yawl was carrying myself and my assistant ashore. On landing, I felt for a moment as if the birds would raise me from the ground, so thick were they all round, and so quick the motion of their wings. Their cries were indeed deafening, yet not more than half of them took to wing on our arrival, those which rose being chiefly male birds, as we afterwards ascertained. We ran across the naked beach, and as we entered the thick cover before us, and spread in different directions, we might at every step have caught a sitting bird, or one scrambling through the bushes to escape from us. Some of the sailors, who had more than once been there before, had provided themselves with sticks, with which they knocked down the birds as they flew thick around and over them. In less than half an hour, more than a hundred Terns lay dead in a heap, and a number of baskets were filled to the brim with eggs. We then returned on board, and declined disturbing the rest any more that night. My assistant, Mr H. WARD, of London, skinned upwards of fifty specimens, aided by Captain DAY's servant. The sailors told me that the birds were excellent eating, but on this point I cannot say much in corroboration of their opinion, although I can safely recommend the eggs, for I considered them delicious, in whatever way cooked, and during our stay at the Tortugas we never passed a day without providing ourselves with a good quantity of them.[2]

The next morning Mr WARD told me that great numbers of the Terns left their island at two o'clock, flew off towards the sea, and returned a little before day, or about four o'clock. This I afterwards observed to be regularly the case, unless there happened to blow a gale, a proof that this species sees as well during the night as by day, when they also go to sea in search of food for themselves and their young. In this respect they differ from the *Sterna stolida*, which, when overtaken at sea by darkness, even when land is only a few miles distant, alight on the water, and frequently on the yards of vessels, where if undisturbed they sleep until the return of day. It is from this circumstance that they have obtained the name of Noddy, to which in fact they are much better entitled than the present species, which has also been so named, but of which I never observed any to alight on a vessel in which I was for thirty-five days in the Gulf of Mexico, at a time when that bird was as abundant during the day as the other species, of which many were caught at my desire by the sailors.[3]

The present species rarely alights on the water, where it seems incommoded by its long tail; but the other, the *Sterna stolida* which, in the shape of its tail, and in some of its habits, shews an affinity to the Petrels, not only frequently alights on the sea, but swims about on floating patches of the Gulf Weed, seizing on the small fry and little crabs that are found among the branches of that plant, or immediately beneath them.

I have often thought, since I became acquainted with the habits of the bird which here occupies our attention, that it differs materially from all the other species of the same genus that occur on our coasts. The *Sterna fuliginosa* never dives headlong and perpendicularly as the smaller species are wont to do, such as *St. Hirundo*, *St. arctica*, *St. minuta*, *St. Dougallii*, or *St. nigra*, but passes over its prey in a curved line, and picks it up. Its action I cannot better compare to that of any other bird than the Night Hawk, while plunging over its female. I have often observed this Tern follow and hover in the wake of a porpoise, while the latter was pursuing its prey, and at the instant when by a sudden dash it frightens and drives toward the surface the fry around it, the Tern as suddenly passes over the spot, and picks up a small fish or two.[4]

Nor is the flight of this Tern characterized by the buoyancy and undecidedness, if I may so speak, of the other species mentioned above, it being as firm and steady as that of the Cayenne Tern, excepting during the movements performed in procuring its food. Like some of the smaller gulls, this bird not unfrequently hovers close to the water to pick up floating objects, such as small bits of fat pork and greasy substances thrown overboard purposely for making the experiment. It is not improbable that the habits peculiar to this species, the Noddy, and one or two others, of which I shall have occasion to speak elsewhere, may tend to induce systematic writers to place them in a new "subgenus."

There is a circumstance connected with the habits of the two species of which I now more particularly speak, which, although perhaps somewhat out of place, I cannot refrain from introducing here. It is that the *Sterna stolida always forms a nest on trees or bushes*, on which that bird alights with as much ease as a Crow or Thrush; whereas the *Sterna fuliginosa* never forms a nest of any sort, but deposits its eggs in a slight cavity which it scoops in the sand under the trees. But, reader, let us return to the Bird Key.

Early the next morning I was put on shore, and remained there until I had completed my observations on the Terns. I paid no attention to their lamentable cries, which were the less piercing that on this occasion I did not molest them in the least. Having seated myself on the shelly sand, which here formed the only soil, I remained almost motionless for several hours, in consequence of which the birds alighted about me, at the distance of only a few yards, so that I could plainly see with what efforts and pains the younger females deposited their eggs. Their bill was open, and their pantings indicated their distress, but after the egg had been expelled, they immediately walked off in an awkward manner, until they reached a place where they could arise without striking the branches of the bushes near them, when they flew away. Here and there, in numerous places within twenty yards of me, females, having their complement of eggs, alighted, and quietly commenced the labour of incubation. Now and then a male bird also settled close by, and immediately disgorged a small fish within the reach of the female. After some curious reciprocal nods of their heads, which were doubtless intended as marks of affection, the caterer would fly off. Several individuals, which had not commenced laying their eggs, I saw scratch the sand with their feet, in the manner of the common fowl, while searching for food. In the course of this operation, they frequently seated themselves in the shallow basin to try how it fitted their form, or find out what was still wanted to ensure their comfort. Not the least semblance of a quarrel did I observe between any two of these interesting creatures; indeed, they all appeared as if happy members of a single family; and as if to gratify my utmost wishes, a few of them went through the process of courtship in my presence. The male birds frequently threw their heads over their back as it were, in the manner of several species of gulls; they also swelled out their throats, walked round the females, and ended by uttering a soft puffing sound as they caressed them. Then the pair for a moment or two walked round each other, and at length rose on wing and soon disappeared. Such is one of the many sights it has been my good fortune to witness, and by each of them have I been deeply impressed with a sense of the pervading power of the Deity.

The Sooty Tern always lays three eggs as its full number, and in no instance, among thousands of the nests which were on the Bird Key, did I find one more when the female was sitting close. I was desirous of ascertaining whether the male and the female incubate alternately; but this I was unable to do, as the birds frequently left their eggs for half an hour or even three quarters at a time, but rarely longer. This circumstance, together with the very slight difference in size and colour between the sexes, was the cause of my failure.

It was curious to observe their actions whenever a large party landed on the island. All those not engaged in incubation would immediately rise in the air and scream aloud; those on the ground would then join them as quickly as they could, and the whole forming a vast mass, with a broad extended front, would as it were charge us, pass over for fifty yards or so, then suddenly wheel round, and again renew their attack. This they would repeat six or eight times in succession. When the sailors, at our desire, all shouted as loud as they could, the phalanx would for an instant become perfectly silent, as if to gather but meaning; but the next moment, like a huge wave breaking on the beach, it would rush forward with deafening noise.

When wounded and seized by the hand, this bird bites severely, and utters a plaintive cry differing from its usual note, which is loud and shrill, resembling the syllables *oo-ee, oo-ee*. Their nests are all scooped near the roots or stems of the bushes, and under the shade of their boughs, in many places within a few inches of each other. There is less difference between their eggs, than is commonly seen in those of water birds, both with respect to size and colouring. They generally measure two inches and one-eighth, by one and a-half, have a smooth shell, with the ground of a pale cream colour, sparingly marked with various tints of lightish umber, and still lighter marks of purple, which appear as if within the shell. The Lieutenant, N. LACOSTE, Esq. informed me that shortly after the young are hatched, they ramble pell-mell over the island, to meet their parents, and be fed by them; that these birds have been known to collect there for the purpose of breeding, since the oldest wreckers on that coast can recollect; and that they usually arrive in May, and remain until the beginning of August, when they retire southward to spend the winter months. I could not however obtain a sufficiently accurate description of the different states of plumage which they go through, so as to enable me to describe them in the manner I should wish to do. All that I can say is, that before they take their departure, the young are greyish-brown above, dull white beneath, and have the tail very short.[5]

At Bird Key we found a party of Spanish Eggers from Havannah. They had already laid in a cargo of about eight tons of the eggs of this Tern and the Noddy. On asking them how many they supposed they had, they answered that they never counted them, even while selling them, but disposed of them at seventy-five cents per gallon; and that one turn to market sometimes produced upwards of two hundred dollars, while it took only a week to sail backwards and forwards and collect their cargo. Some eggers, who now and then come from Key West, sell their eggs at twelve and a half cents the dozen; but wherever these eggs are carried, they must soon be disposed of and eaten, for they become putrid in a few weeks.

On referring to my journals once more, I find the following remarks with reference to the Sooty Tern. It would appear that at some period not very remote, the Noddy, *Sterna stolida*, must have had it in contemplation to appropriate to itself its neighbour's domains; as on examination of this island, several thousand nests of that bird were found built on the tops of the bushes, although no birds of the species were about them. It is therefore probable that if such an attempt was made by them, they were defeated and forced to confine themselves to the neighbouring island, where they breed by themselves, although it is only a few miles distant. That such interferences and conflicts now and then occur among different species of birds, has often been observed by other persons, and in several instances by myself, particularly among Herons. In these cases, right or wrong, the stronger party never fails to dislodge the weaker, and keep possession of the disputed ground.

Notes

1. First published in *OB* 3 (1835), 263–69. Audubon painted these "Black and White Sea Swallows," now *Onychoprion fuscatus* (plate 4; Havell 235), on the visit that he described to the Dry Tortugas, Florida Keys, in May 1832. As late as the 1950s, these birds numbered over a hundred thousand on the Keys. Today the population is down to thousands, although within the protection of the National Park Service. The species is classified as Least Concern globally (IUCN, 2018), but sooty tern colonies in the Dry Tortugas and throughout the tropics face various anthropogenic threats today, such as sea level rise and habitat loss. See Elizabeth A. Schreiber, et al., "Sooty Tern," v. 1.0 (2020), birdsoftheworld.org; Joanna Burger, *Birdlife of the Gulf of Mexico* (College Station: Texas A & M Press, 2018), 3–4. The "Noddy" is Audubon's "Noddy Tern," now the brown noddy; see fig. 15. The first lieutenant of the *Marion* was Napoleon Coste (see notes to first "Florida Keys" essay).

2. Henry Ward, English taxidermist, accompanied Audubon to the United States in 1831 and helped him mount specimens during and after his 1831/1832 excursion to Florida. At the instigation of John Bachman, Ward was hired by the Charleston Museum, then owned by the Charleston Literary and Philosophical Society, so that he could support himself while preparing bird skins. Taking money and specimens with him and leaving unpaid debts behind, Ward absconded to England in 1833, where he peddled mutilated bird skins to collectors.

3. The "thirty-five days in the Gulf of Mexico" refer to Audubon's 1826 transatlantic voyage aboard the *Delos*; see "Journal of a Sea Voyage" in this volume.

4. Audubon's *Sterna Hirundo* is his "Great/Common Tern" (Havell 309), now common tern; *St. arctica* is the Arctic tern, now *Sterna paradisaea* (Havell 250); *St. minuta* is his "Lesser Tern" (Havell 319), now least tern (*Sternula antillarum*); *St. Dougallii* is the roseate tern (Havell 240); and *St. nigra* is the "Black Tern" (Havell 280), now *Chlidonias niger*.

5. "Lieutenant, N. Lacoste" is surely Napoleon Coste (see notes to first "Florida Keys" essay).

THE WRECKERS OF FLORIDA

LONG before I reached the lovely islets that border the south-eastern shores of the Floridas, the accounts I had heard of "The Wreckers" [fig. 25] had deeply prejudiced me against them. Often had I been informed of the cruel and cowardly methods which it was alleged they employed to allure vessels of all nations to the dreaded reefs, that they might plunder their cargoes, and rob their crews and passengers of their effects. I therefore could have little desire to meet with such men under any circumstances, much less to become liable to receive their aid; and

FIGURE 25. Florida Keys wrecker on his boat, tiller in hand. "A rough specimen of humanity," as depicted in a story of a ship aground at the Dry Tortugas; "Wrecking on the Florida Keys," *Harpers New Monthly Magazine* 18, no. 107 (April 1859): 577. Courtesy of Williams College.

with the name of Wreckers, there were associated in my mind ideas of piratical depredation, barbarous usage, and even murder.[1]

One fair afternoon, while I was standing on the polished deck of the United States' revenue cutter the Marion, a sail hove in sight, bearing in an opposite course, and "close-hauled" to the wind. The gentle rake of her masts, as she rocked to and fro in the breeze, brought to my mind the wavings of the reeds on the fertile banks of the Mississippi. By-and-by the vessel altering her course, approached us. The Marion, like a sea-bird, with extended wings, swept through the waters, gently inclining to either side, while the unknown vessel leaped as it were from wave to wave, like the dolphin in eager pursuit of his prey. In a short time, we were gliding side by side, and the commander of the strange schooner saluted our captain, who promptly returned the compliment. What a beautiful vessel! we all thought; how trim, how clean-rigged, and how well manned! She swims like a duck; and now with a broad sheer, off she makes for the reefs, a few miles under our lee. There, in that narrow passage, well known to her commander, she rolls, tumbles, and dances, like a giddy thing, her copper sheathing now gleaming, and again disappearing under the waves. But the passage is thrid,[2] and now, hauling on the wind, she resumes her former course, and gradually recedes from the view. Reader, it was a Florida Wrecker!

When at the Tortugas, I paid a visit to several vessels of this kind, in company with my excellent friend ROBERT DAY, Esq. We had observed the regularity and quickness of the men then employed at their arduous tasks, and as we approached the largest schooner, I admired her form so well adapted to her occupation, her great breadth of beam, her light draught, the correctness of her water-line, the neatness of her painted sides, the smoothness of her well-greased masts, and the beauty of her rigging. We were welcomed on board with all the frankness of our native tars. Silence and order prevailed on her decks. The commander and the second officer led us into a spacious cabin, well lighted, and furnished with every convenience for fifteen or more passengers. The former brought me his collection of marine shells, and whenever I pointed to one that I had not seen before, offered it with so much kindness, that I found it necessary to be careful in expressing my admiration of any particular shell. He had also many eggs of rare birds, which were all handed over to me, with an assurance that before the month should expire, a new set could easily be procured, "for," said he, "we have much idle time on the reefs at this season." Dinner was served, and we partook of their fare, which consisted of fish, fowl, and other materials. These rovers, who were both from "down east," were stout active men, cleanly and smart in their attire. In a short time, we were all extremely social and merry. They thought my visit to the Tortugas, in quest of birds, was rather "a curious fancy;" but, notwithstanding, they expressed their pleasure while looking at some of my drawings, and offered their services in procuring specimens. Expeditions far and near were proposed, and on settling that one of them was to take place on the morrow, we parted friends.[3]

Early next morning, several of these kind men accompanied me to a small key called Booby Island, about ten miles distant from the lighthouse. Their boats were well manned, and rowed with long and steady strokes, such as whalers and men-of-war's men are wont to draw. The captain sang, and at times, by way of frolic, ran a race with our own beautiful bark. The Booby Isle was soon reached, and our sport there was equal to any we had elsewhere. They were capital shots, had excellent guns, and knew more about boobies and noddies than nine-tenths of the best naturalists in the world. But what will you say when I tell you that the Florida Wreckers are excellent at a deer hunt, and that at certain seasons, "when business is slack," they are wont to land on some extensive key, and in a few hours procure a supply of delicious venison.[4]

Some days afterwards, the same party took me on an expedition in quest of sea-shells. There we were all in the water at times to the waist, and now and then much deeper. Now they would dip, like ducks, and on emerging would hold up a beautiful shell. This occupation they seemed to enjoy above all others.

The duties of the Marion having been performed, intimation of our intended departure reached the Wreckers. An invitation was sent to me to go and see them on board their vessels, which I accepted. Their object on this occasion was to present me with some superb corals, shells, live turtles of the Hawk-billed species, and a great quantity of eggs. Not a "pecayon" would they receive in return, but putting some letters in my hands, requested me to "be so good as put them in the mail at Charleston," adding that they were for their wives "down east." So anxious did they appear to be to do all they could for me, that they proposed to sail before the Marion, and meet her under weigh, to give me some birds that were rare on the coast, and of which they knew the haunts. Circumstances connected with "the service" prevented this, however; and with sincere regret, and a good portion of friendship, I bade these excellent fellows adieu. How different, thought I, is often the knowledge of things acquired by personal observation, from that obtained by report![5]

Notes

1. First published in *OB* 3 (1835), 158–63. Wreckers salvaged ships that had wrecked in the shallow reef system for a percentage of the ship and cargo they rescued. Initially in the hands of Bahamian turtlers and fishermen, wrecking soon became the Keys' chief industry. In 1826, Congress created a new judicial district court in Key West to rein in a profession that was

often (and without evidence) known for its ruthlessness. Audubon met these men at the height of the industry. As ships switched to steam engines and lighthouses offered navigational help, the industry declined. See John Viele, *The Florida Keys: The Wreckers* (Sarasota: Pineapple Press, 2001), 3:xi–xiv, 52.

2. "Thrid" means "threaded" here; in use by other writers in the nineteenth century and earlier.

3. "Rovers" from "down east" references the fact that many wreckers were fishermen from New England who had come to the Keys to fish or work as wreckers.

4. "Booby Island" is probably the former North Key, which had disappeared by the 1870s. "Boobies and noddies" are the brown booby (*Sula leucogaster*), which Audubon also knew as the "Brown Gannet" or his "Booby Gannet" (Havell 207), and the brown noddy (*Anous stolidus*; see fig. 15).

5. On the hawksbill turtle, see notes to "The Turtlers." At the end of this episode as printed in *Ornithological Biography*, but not included here, Audubon quoted an equally romantic account of the Florida wreckers from Benjamin Strobel, which ends with a ballad, "The Wrecker's Song."

AMERICAN FLAMINGO

ON the 7th of May 1832, while sailing from Indian Key, one of the numerous islets that skirt the south-eastern coast of the Peninsula of Florida, I for the first time saw a flock of Flamingoes [plate 5]. It was on the afternoon of one of those sultry days which, in that portion of the country, exhibit towards evening the most glorious effulgence that can be conceived. The sun, now far advanced toward the horizon, still shone with full splendour, the ocean around glittered in its quiet beauty, and the light fleecy clouds that here and there spotted the heavens, seemed flakes of snow margined with gold. Our bark was propelled almost as if by magic, for scarcely was a ripple raised by her bows as we moved in silence. Far away to seaward we spied a flock of Flamingoes advancing in "Indian line," with well-spread wings, outstretched necks, and long legs directed backwards. Ah! Reader, could you but know the emotions that then agitated my breast! I thought I had now reached the height of all my expectations, for my voyage to the Floridas was undertaken in a great measure for the purpose of studying these lovely birds in their own beautiful islands. I followed them with my eyes, watching as it were every beat of their wings; and as they were rapidly advancing towards us, Captain DAY, who was aware of my anxiety to procure some, had every man stowed away out of sight and our gunners in readiness. The pilot, Mr EGAN, proposed to offer the first taste of his "groceries" to the leader of the band. As I have more than once told you, he was a first-rate shot, and had already killed many Flamingoes. The birds were now, as I thought, within a hundred and fifty yards; when suddenly, to our extreme disappointment, their chief veered away, and was of course followed by the rest. Mr EGAN, however, assured us that they would fly round the Key, and alight not far from us, in less than ten minutes, which in fact they did, although to me these minutes seemed almost hours. "Now they come," said the pilot, "keep low." This we did; but, alas! the Flamingoes were all, as I suppose, very old and experienced birds, with the exception of one, for on turning round the lower end of the Key, they spied our boat again, sailed away without flapping their wings, and alighted about four hundred yards from us, and upwards of one hundred from the shore, on a "soap flat" of vast extent, where neither boat nor man could approach them. I however watched their motions until dusk, when we reluctantly left the spot and advanced toward Indian Key. Mr LOGAN then told me that these birds habitually returned to their feeding-grounds toward evening, that they fed during the greater part of the night, and were much more nocturnal in their habits than any of the Heron tribe.[1]

When I reached Key West, my first inquiries, addressed to Dr BENJAMIN STROBEL, had reference to the Flamingoes, and I felt gratified by learning that he had killed a good number of them, and that he would assist us in procuring some. As on that Key they are fond of resorting to the shallow ponds formerly kept there as reservoirs of water, for the purpose of making salt, we visited them at different times, but always without success; and, although I saw a great number of them in the course of my stay in that country, I cannot even at this moment boast of having had the satisfaction of shooting a single individual.

A very few of these birds have been known to proceed eastward of the Floridas beyond Charleston in South Carolina, and some have been procured there within eight or ten years back. None have ever been observed about the mouths of the Mississippi; and to my great surprise I did not meet with any in the course of my voyage to the Texas, where, indeed, I was assured they had never been seen, at least as far as Galveston Island. The western coast of Florida, and some portions of that of Alabama, in the neighbourhood of Pensacola, are the parts to which they mostly resort; but they are said to be there always extremely shy, and can be procured only by waylaying them in the vicinity of their feeding-grounds toward evening, when, on one occasion, Dr STROBEL shot several in the course of a few hours. Dr LEITNER also procured some in the course of his botanical excursions along the western coast of the Floridas, where he was at last murdered by some party of Seminole Indians, at the time of our last disastrous war with those children of the desert.[2]

Flamingoes, as I am informed, are abundant on the Island of Cuba, more especially on the southern side of some of its shores, and where many islets at some distance from the mainland afford them ample protection. In their flight they resemble Ibises, and they usually move in lines, with the neck and legs fully extended, alternately flapping their wings for twenty or thirty yards and sailing over a like space. Before alighting they generally sail round the place for several minutes, when their glowing tints become most conspicuous. They very rarely alight on the shore itself, unless, as I am told, during the breeding season, but usually in the water, and on shallow banks, whether of mud or of sand, from which however they often wade to the shores. Their walk is stately

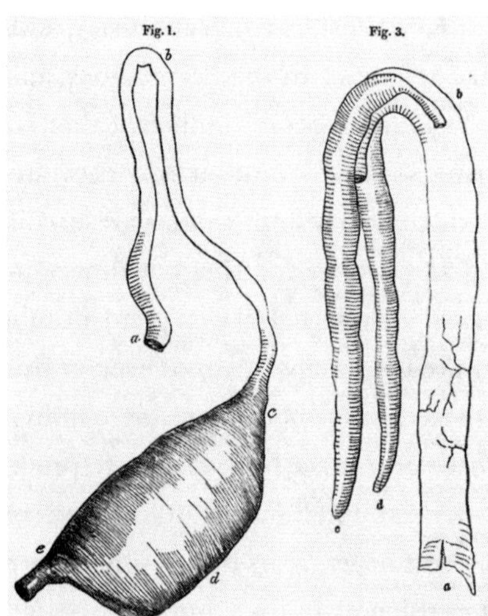

FIGURE 26. William MacGillivray, digestive system of a female American flamingo. Woodcut from Audubon, *Ornithological Biography*, vol. 5 (1839).

and slow, and their cautiousness extreme, so that it is very difficult to approach them, as their great height enables them to see and watch the movements of their various enemies at a distance. When travelling over the water, they rarely fly at a greater height than eight or ten feet; but when passing over the land, no matter how short the distance may be, they, as well as Ibises and Herons, advance at a considerable elevation. I well remember that on one occasion, when near Key West, I saw one of them flying directly towards a small hummock of mangroves, to which I was near, and towards which I made, in full expectation of having a fine shot. When the bird came within a hundred and twenty yards, it rose obliquely, and when directly over my head, was almost as far off. I fired, but with no other effect than that of altering its course, and inducing it to rise still higher. It continued to fly at this elevation until nearly half a mile off, when it sailed downwards, and resumed its wonted low flight.[3]

Notes

1. First published in *OB* 5 (1839), 255–64. Audubon's "American Flamingo" (plate 5; Havell 431) is *Phoenicopterus ruber* (some call this the greater American flamingo, a subspecies: *ruber ruber*), the only flamingo species native to the Caribbean Sea. As Audubon writes here, he observed flamingos in 1832 in the Florida Keys but couldn't acquire any, so he had to wait to paint them until 1838, when he received specimens from the US while he was in London; Susanne M. Low, *A Guide to Audubon's* Birds of America, 2nd ed. (1988; New Haven, CT: William Reese Co. and Donald A. Heald, 2002), 226. Despite breeding site disruptions in the past, the American flamingo is a species of Least Concern, and populations have been on the rise since the 1990s (IUCN, 2018), but they appear only as occasional visitors along the Gulf and Atlantic Coast in the twenty-first century, nesting in the Bahamas, Cuba, and elsewhere. Modern ornithologists have also observed them feeding nocturnally outside of breeding season. See Chris Elphick, John B. Dunning Jr., and David Allen Sibley, *The Sibley Guide to Bird Life & Behavior* (2001), 187–89; J. del Hoyo, P. F. D. Boesman, and E. F. J. Garcia, "American Flamingo," v. 1.0 (2020), birdsoftheworld.org. Captain Benjamin Logan of Mobile, Alabama, was an avid amateur naturalist.

2. Edward Frederick Leitner (1812–1838), German botanist and graduate of the Medical College of South Carolina, died on January 15, 1838, after being wounded in a confrontation with members of the Seminole tribe at Jupiter Inlet, Florida. Audubon credited the eminent Leitner multiple times, also in his *The Quadrupeds of North America* (1851–1854). See George E. Gifford, "Edward Frederick Leitner (1812–1838), Physician-Botanist," *Bulletin of the History of Medicine* 46, no. 6 (November–December 1972): 568–90. For more on Audubon and the Seminole people, see notes to "St John's River in Florida" in this volume.

3. Audubon's drawing of the flamingo is based on specimens sent to him from Cuba by Jean Chartrand in or around 1838, after repeated requests made to John Bachman had failed; see Audubon to John Bachman, April 14, 1838, in *John James Audubon, Writings and Drawings*, ed. Christoph Irmscher (New York: Library of America, 1999), 848–51. Chartrand was born on

the Millefleurs Plantation in Saint-Domingue (Haiti) ca. 1787, two years after Audubon was born nearby, and was whisked out during the rebellion in 1791 when his mother was killed. Chartrand inherited the coffee (later, sugar) plantation El Labirintero in Cuba.

WILSON'S PLOVER

READER, imagine yourself standing motionless on some of the sandy shores between South Carolina and the extremity of Florida, waiting with impatience for the return of day;—or, if you dislike the idea, imagine me there. The air is warm and pleasant, the smooth sea reflects the feeble glimmerings of the fading stars, the sound of living thing is not heard; nature, universal nature, is at rest. And here am I, inhaling the grateful sea-air, with eyes intent on the dim distance. See the bright blaze that issues from the verge of the waters! And now the sun himself appears, and all is life, or seems to be; for as the influence of the Divinity is to the universe, so is that of the sun to the things of this world. Far away beyond that treacherous reef, floats a gallant bark, that seems slumbering on the bosom of the waters like a silvery sea-bird. Gentle breezes now creep over the ocean, and ruffle its surface into tiny wavelets. The ship glides along, the fishes leap with joy, and on my ear comes the well known note of the bird which bears the name of one whom every ornithologist must honour. Long have I known the bird myself, and yet desirous of knowing it better, I have returned to this beach many successive seasons for the purpose of observing its ways, examining its nest, marking the care with which it rears its young, and the attachment which it manifests to its mate. Well, let the scene vanish! and let me present you with the results of my observations.[1]

Wilson's Plover! [See plate 6.] I love the name because of the respect I bear towards him to whose memory the bird has been dedicated. How pleasing, I have thought, it would have been to me, to have met with him on such an excursion, and, after having procured a few of his own birds, to have listened to him as he would speak of a thousand interesting facts connected with his favourite science and my ever-pleasing pursuits. How delightful to have talked, among other things, of the probable use of the *double claws* which I have found attached to the toes of the species which goes by his name, and which are also seen in other groups of

PLATE 1. Robert Havell Jr. after John James Audubon, "Brown Pelican," 1835. Aquatint engraving. *The Birds of America*, plate 251. Courtesy of the Lilly Library.

PLATE 2. Robert Havell Jr. after John James Audubon, "Black Skimmer or Shearwater" (black skimmer), 1836. Aquatint engraving. *The Birds of America*, plate 323. Courtesy of the Lilly Library.

PLATE 3. Robert Havell Jr. after John James Audubon, "Frigate Pelican" (magnificent frigatebird), 1835. Aquatint engraving. *The Birds of America*, plate 271. Courtesy of the Lilly Library.

PLATE 4. Robert Havell Jr. after John James Audubon, "Sooty Tern," 1834. Aquatint engraving. *The Birds of America*, plate 235. Courtesy of the Lilly Library.

PLATE 5. Robert Havell Jr. after John James Audubon, "American Flamingo," 1838. Aquatint engraving. *The Birds of America*, plate 431. Courtesy of the Lilly Library.

PLATE 6. Robert Havell Jr. after John James Audubon, "Wilson's Plover," 1834. Aquatint engraving. *The Birds of America*, plate 209. Courtesy of the Lilly Library.

PLATE 7. Robert Havell Jr. after John James Audubon, "American oyster-catcher" (American oystercatcher), 1834. Aquatint engraving. *The Birds of America*, plate 223. Courtesy of the Lilly Library.

PLATE 8. Robert Havell Jr. after John James Audubon, "Fish Hawk, or Osprey" (osprey), n.d. (1827–1830). Aquatint engraving. *The Birds of America*, plate 81. Courtesy of the Lilly Library.

PLATE 9. Robert Havell Jr. after John James Audubon, "Little Auk" (little guillemot, dovekie), 1836. Aquatint engraving. *The Birds of America*, plate 339. Courtesy of the Lilly Library.

PLATE 10. Robert Havell Jr. after John James Audubon, "Long-billed Curlew," 1834. Aquatint engraving. *The Birds of America*, plate 231. Courtesy of the Lilly Library.

PLATE 11. Robert Havell Jr. after John James Audubon, "Dusky Albatros" (perhaps light-mantled or sooty albatross), 1838. Aquatint engraving. *The Birds of America*, plate 407. Courtesy of the Lilly Library.

PLATE 12. Robert Havell Jr. after John James Audubon, "Gannet" (northern gannet), 1836. Aquatint engraving. *The Birds of America*, plate 326. Courtesy of the Lilly Library.

PLATE 13. Robert Havell Jr. after John James Audubon, "Foolish Guillemot" (common murre), 1834. Aquatint engraving. *The Birds of America*, plate 218. Courtesy of the Lilly Library.

PLATE 14. Robert Havell Jr. after John James Audubon, "Black Backed Gull" (great black-backed gull), 1835. Aquatint engraving. *The Birds of America*, plate 241. Courtesy of the Lilly Library.

PLATE 15. Robert Havell Jr. after John James Audubon, "Wandering Shearwater" (great shearwater), 1835. Aquatint engraving. *The Birds of America*, plate 283. Courtesy of the Lilly Library.

PLATE 16. Robert Havell Jr. after John James Audubon, "Razor-billed Auk" (razorbill), 1834. Aquatint engraving. *The Birds of America*, plate 214. Courtesy of the Lilly Library.

PLATE 17. Robert Havell Jr. after John James Audubon, "Common Cormorant" (great cormorant), 1835. Aquatint engraving. *The Birds of America*, plate 266. Courtesy of the Lilly Library.

PLATE 18. Robert Havell Jr. after John James Audubon, "Puffin" (Atlantic puffin), 1834. Aquatint engraving. *The Birds of America*, plate 213. Courtesy of the Lilly Library.

PLATE 19. Robert Havell Jr. after John James Audubon, "Great Auk," 1836. Aquatint engraving. *The Birds of America*, plate 341. Courtesy of the Lilly Library.

PLATE 20. Robert Havell Jr. after John James Audubon, "Wilson's Petrel" (Wilson's storm-petrel), 1835. Aquatint engraving. *The Birds of America*, plate 270. Courtesy of the Lilly Library.

shore and sea birds. Perhaps he might have informed me why the claws of some birds are pectinated on one toe and not on the rest, and why that toe itself is so cut. But alas! WILSON was with me only a few times, and then *nothing* worthy of his attention was procured.[2]

This interesting species, which always looks to me as if in form a miniature copy of the Black-bellied Plover, is a constant resident in the southern districts of the Union. There it breeds, and there too it spends the winter. Many individuals, no doubt, move farther south, but great numbers are at all times to be met with from Carolina to the mouths of the Mississippi, and in all these places I have found it the whole year round. Some go as far to the eastward as Long Island in the State of New York, where, however, they are considered as rarities; but beyond this, none, I believe, are seen along our eastern shores. This circumstance has seemed the more surprising to me, that its relative the Piping Plover proceeds as far as the Magdeleine Islands; and that the latter bird should also breed in the Carolinas a month earlier than Wilson's Plover ever does, seems to me not less astonishing.[3]

Wilson's Plover begins to lay its eggs about the time when the young of the Piping Plover are running after their parents. Twenty or thirty yards from the uppermost beat of the waves, on the first of June, or some day not distant from it, the female may be seen scratching a small cavity in the shelly sand, in which she deposits four eggs, placing them carefully with the broad end outermost. The eggs, which measure an inch and a quarter by seven and a half eighths, are of a dull cream colour, sparingly sprinkled all over with dots of pale purple and spots of dark brown. The eggs vary somewhat in size, and in their ground colour, but less than those of many other species of the genus. The young follow their parents as soon as they are hatched, and the latter employ every artifice common to birds of this family, to entice their enemies to follow them and thus save their offspring.[4]

The flight of this species is rapid, elegant, and protracted. While travelling from one sand-beach or island to another, they fly low over the land or water, emitting a fine clear soft note. Now and then, when after the breeding season they form into flocks of twenty or thirty, they perform various evolutions in the air, cutting backwards and forwards, as if inspecting the spot on which they wish to alight, and then suddenly descend, sometimes on the sea-beach, and sometimes on the more elevated sands at a little distance from it. They do not run so nimbly as the Piping Plovers, nor are they nearly so shy. I have in fact frequently walked up so as to be within ten yards or so of them. They seldom mix with other species, and they shew a decided preference to solitary uninhabited spots.

Their food consists principally of small marine insects, minute shellfish, and sandworms, with which they mix particles of sand. Towards autumn they become almost silent, and being then very plump, afford delicious eating. They feed fully as much by night as by day, and the large eyes of this as of other species of the genus, seem to fit them for nocturnal searchings.

The young birds assemble together, and spend the winter months apart from the old ones, which are easily recognised by their lighter tints. While in the Floridas, near St Augustine, in the months of December and January, I found this species much more abundant than any other; and there were few of the Keys that had a sandy beach, or a rocky shore, on which one or more pairs were not observed.

Notes

1. First published in *OB* 3 (1835), 73–76. Wilson's Plover, now *Charadrius wilsonia* (plate 6; Havell 209), was painted perhaps in Florida in 1832; Susanne M. Low, *A Guide to Audubon's* Birds of America, 2nd ed. (1988; New Haven, CT: William Reese Co. and Donald A. Heald, 2002), 126. Despite current population declines and a shrinking range along the coasts of the United States due to loss of habitat and human disturbance, this is still considered a global species of Least Concern (IUCN, 2016).

2. The species is named after Alexander Wilson, to whom Audubon effusively tips his hat, although in other bird essays he disputes Wilson's explanations of bird behaviors and distribution; see, e.g., his essay "Wilson's Petrel" and the Introduction to this volume. Wilson recorded the type specimen in 1813 in Cape May, New Jersey, where the bird was and still is a rare visitor.

3. Audubon painted the "Black-bellied Plover" (Havell 334), now *Pluvialis squatarola*, and the "Piping Plover" (Havell 220), now *Charadrius melodus*. Wilson's plover's breeding and wintering range (in the southern states of the US to the Mississippi) is still similar to what Audubon's describes, and the species also lives and breeds around the coasts of the Gulf of Mexico and Baja California. The "Magdeleine" Islands, as Audubon most often spelled them in *Ornithological Biography*, are now more commonly spelled as "Magdalen" (see figs. 33 and 35). In the Labrador journal as published by Lucy Audubon, they were the "Magdalene" Islands.

4. Wilson's plovers use a broken-wing display, both stationary and moving, which is common to plovers and other birds to try to appear vulnerable and lure predators away from their young.

ST JOHN'S RIVER IN FLORIDA

Soon after landing at St Augustine, in East Florida, I formed acquaintance with Dr SIMMONS, Dr POCHER, Judge SMITH, the Misses JOHNSON, and other individuals, my intercourse with whom was as agreeable as beneficial to me. Lieutenant CONSTANTINE SMITH, of the United States army, I found of a congenial spirit, as was the case with my amiable, but since deceased friend, Dr BELL of Dublin. Among the planters who extended their hospitality to me, I must particularly mention General HERNANDEZ, and my esteemed friend JOHN BULOW, Esq. To all these estimable individuals I offer my sincere thanks.[1]

While in this part of the peninsula, I followed my usual avocations, although with little success, it being then winter. I had letters from the Secretaries of the Navy and Treasury of the United States, to the commanding officers of vessels of war of the revenue service, directing them to afford me any assistance in their power; and the schooner Spark having come to St Augustine, on her way to the St John's River, I presented my credentials to her commander Lieutenant PIERCY, who readily and with politeness, received me and my assistants on board. We soon after set sail, with a fair breeze. The strict attention to duty on board even this small vessel of war, afforded matter of surprise to me. Every thing went on with the regularity of a chronometer: orders were given, answered to, and accomplished, before they ceased to vibrate on the ear. The neatness of the crew equalled the cleanliness of the white planks of the deck; the sails were in perfect condition; and, built as the Spark was, for swift sailing, on she went gambolling from wave to wave.[2]

I thought that, while thus sailing, no feeling but that of pleasure could exist in our breasts; but, alas! how fleeting are our enjoyments. When we were almost at the entrance of the river, the wind changed, the sky became clouded, and, before many minutes had elapsed, the little bark was lying to "like a duck," as her commander expressed himself. It blew a hurricane:—let it blow, reader. At the break of day we were again at anchor within the bar of St Augustine.

Our next attempt was successful. Not many hours after we had crossed the bar, we perceived the star-like glimmer of the light in the great lantern at the entrance of the St John's River. This was before daylight; and, as the crossing of the sand-banks or bars, which occur at the mouths of all the streams of this peninsula is difficult, and can be accomplished only when the tide is up, one of the guns was fired as a signal for the government pilot. The good man, it seemed, was unwilling to leave his couch, but a second gun brought him in his canoe alongside. The depth of the channel was barely sufficient. My eyes, however, were not directed towards the waters, but on high, where flew some thousands of snowy Pelicans, which had fled affrighted from their resting grounds. How beautifully they performed their broad gyrations, and how matchless, after a while, was the marshalling of their files, as they flew past us![3]

On the tide we proceeded apace. Myriads of Cormorants covered the face of the waters, and over it Fish-Crows innumerable were already arriving from their distant roosts. We landed at one place to search for the birds whose charming melodies had engaged our attention, and here and there some young Eagles we shot, to add to our store of fresh provisions! The river did not seem to me equal in beauty to the fair Ohio; the shores were in many places low and swampy, to the great delight of the numberless Herons that moved along in gracefulness, and the grim alligators that swam in sluggish sullenness. In going up a bayou, we caught a great number of the young of the latter for the purpose of making experiments upon them.

After sailing a considerable way, during which our commander and officers took the soundings, as well as the angles and bearings of every nook and crook of the sinuous stream, we anchored one evening at a distance of fully one hundred miles from the mouth of the river. The weather, although it was the 12th of February, was quite warm, the thermometer on board standing at 75°, and on shore at 90°. The fog was so thick that neither of the shores could be seen, and yet the river was not a mile in breadth. The "blind mosquitoes" covered every object, even in the cabin, and so wonderfully abundant were these tormentors, that they more than once fairly extinguished the candles whilst I was writing my journal, which I closed in despair, crushing between the leaves more than a hundred of the little wretches. Bad as they are, however, these blind mosquitoes do not bite. As if purposely to render our situation doubly uncomfortable, there was an establishment for jerking beef, on the nearer shores to the windward of our vessel, from which the breeze came laden with no sweet odours.

In the morning when I arose, the country was still covered with thick fogs, so that although I could plainly hear the notes of the birds on shore, not an object could I see beyond the bowsprit, and the air was as close and sultry as on the previous evening. Guided by the scent of the jerkers' works, we went on shore, where we found the vegetation already far advanced. The blossoms of the jessamine, ever pleasing, lay steeped in dew; the humming bee was collecting her winter's store from the snowy flowers of the native orange; and the little warblers frisked along the twigs of the smilax. Now, amid the tall pines of the forest, the sun's rays began to force their way, and as the dense mists dissolved in the atmosphere, the bright luminary at length shone forth. We explored the woods around, guided by some friendly live-oakers who had pitched their camp in the vicinity. After a while the Spark again displayed her sails, and as she silently glided along, we spied a Seminole Indian approaching us in his canoe. The poor dejected son of the woods, endowed with talents of the highest order, although rarely acknowledged by the proud usurpers of his native soil, has spent the night in fishing, and the morning in procuring the superb-feathered game of the swampy thickets; and with both he comes to offer them for our acceptance. Alas! thou fallen one, descendant of an ancient line of freeborn hunters, would that I could restore to thee thy birthright, thy natural independence, the generous feelings that were once fostered in thy brave bosom. But the irrevocable deed is done, and I can merely admire the perfect symmetry of his frame, as he dexterously throws on our deck the trouts and turkeys which he has captured. He receives a recompense, and without smile or bow, or acknowledgement of any kind, off he starts with the speed of an arrow from his own bow.[4]

Alligators were extremely abundant, and the heads of the fishes which they had snapped off lay floating around on the dark waters. A rifle bullet was now and then sent through the eye of one of the largest, which, with a tremendous splash of its tail, expired. One morning we saw a monstrous fellow lying on the shore. I was desirous of obtaining him to make an accurate drawing of his head, and, accompanied by my assistant and two of the sailors, proceeded cautiously towards him. When within a few yards, one of us fired and sent through his side an ounce ball, which tore open a hole large enough to receive a man's hand. He slowly raised his head, bent himself upwards, opened his huge jaws, swung his tail to and fro, rose on his legs, blew in a frightful manner, and fell to the earth. My assistant leaped on shore, and, contrary to my injunctions, caught hold of the animal's tail, when the alligator, awakening from its trance, with a last effort crawled slowly towards the water, and plunged heavily into it. Had he thought of once flourishing his tremendous weapon there might have been an end of his assailant's life, but he fortunately went in peace to his grave, where we left him, as the water was too deep. The same morning, another of equal size was observed swimming directly for the bows of our vessel, attracted by the gentle rippling of the water there. One of the officers, who had watched him, fired and scattered his brain through the air, when he tumbled and rolled at a fearful rate, blowing all the while most furiously. The river was bloody for yards around, but although the monster passed close by the vessel, we could not secure him, and after a while he sunk to the bottom.

Early one morning I hired a boat and two men, with the view of returning to St Augustine by a short cut. Our baggage being placed on board, I bade adieu to the officers, and off we started. About four in the afternoon we arrived at the short cut, forty miles distant from our point of departure, and where we had expected to procure a waggon, but were disappointed. So we laid our things on the bank, and, leaving one of my assistants to look after them, I set out, accompanied by the other, and my Newfoundland dog.[5] We had eighteen miles to go; and as the sun was only two hours high, we struck off at a good rate. Presently we entered a pine barren. The country was as level as a floor; our path, although narrow, was well beaten, having been used by the Seminole Indians for ages, and the weather was calm and beautiful. Now and then a rivulet occurred, from which we quenched our thirst, while the magnolias and other flowering plants on its banks relieved the dull uniformity of the woods. When the path separated into two branches, both seemingly leading the same way, I would follow one, while my companion took the other, and unless we met again in a short time, one of us would go across the intervening forest.

The sun went down behind a cloud, and the south-east breeze that sprung up at this moment, sounded dolefully among the tall pines. Along the eastern horizon lay a bed of black vapour, which gradually rose, and soon covered the heavens. The air felt hot and oppressive, and we knew that a tempest was approaching. Plato was now our guide, the white spots on his skin being the only objects that we could discern amid the darkness, and as if aware of his utility in this respect, he kept a short way before us on the trail. Had we imagined ourselves more than a few miles from the town, we would have made a camp, and remained under its shelter for the night; but conceiving that the distance could not be great, we resolved to trudge along.

Large drops began to fall from the murky mass overhead; thick, impenetrable darkness surrounded us, and to my dismay, the dog refused to proceed. Groping with my hands on the ground, I discovered that several trails branched out at the spot where he lay down; and when I had selected one, he went on. Vivid flashes of lightning streamed across the heavens, the wind increased to a gale, and the rain poured down upon us like a torrent. The water soon rose on the level ground so as almost to cover our feet, and we slowly advanced, fronting the tempest. Here and there a tall pine on fire presented a magnificent spectacle, illumining the trees around it, and surrounded with a halo of dim light, abruptly bordered with the deep black of the night. At one time we passed through a tangled thicket of low trees, at another crossed a stream flushed by the heavy rain, and again proceeded over the open barrens.

How long we thus, half-lost, groped our way, is more than I can tell you; but at length the tempest passed over, and suddenly the clear sky became spangled with stars. Soon after we smelt the salt-marshes, and walking directly towards them, like pointers advancing on a covey of partridges, we at last to our great joy descried the light of the beacon near St Augustine. My dog began to run briskly around, having met with ground on which he had hunted before, and taking a direct course, led us to the great causeway that crosses the marshes at the back of the town. We refreshed ourselves with the produce of the first orange tree that we met with, and in half an hour more arrived at our hotel. Drenched with rain, steaming with perspiration, and covered to the knees with mud, you may imagine what figures we cut in the eyes of the good people whom we found snugly enjoying themselves in the sitting room. Next morning, Major GATES, who had received me with much kindness, sent a waggon with mules and two trusty soldiers for my companion and luggage.[6]

Notes

1. "St John's River in Florida" was first published in *OB* 2 (1834), 291–95. Dr. William Hayne Simmons (1784–1870), a native of Charleston, was a physician and plantation owner in East Florida, who, in concert with John Lee Williams of Pensacola, selected Tallahassee as Florida's new territorial capital. He was the author of *Notices of East: With an Account of the Nation of Seminole Indians by a Recent Traveler in the Province* (1822). Joseph Lee Smith (1776–1846) was a colonel in the army of the United States in the war of 1812 and a Florida territorial judge. José Mariano (or Joseph Marion) Hernández (1788–1857) was the first delegate from the Florida Territory and the first Hispanic American to serve in the United States Congress.

2. The St. Johns River, the longest that is entirely in the state of Florida, flows 310 miles northward from Blue Cypress Lake toward Jacksonville, near which it joins the Atlantic. A variety of ecosystems characterize the river, including swamps around its headwaters, clear-water springs in its middle stretch, and estuaries toward the sea.

3. Audubon's "snowy Pelicans" were surely American white pelicans, *Pelecanus erythrorhynchos* (Havell 311).

4. Live oak (*Quercus spp.*), with its long, curved limbs, was used in the construction of ships (especially for bow stems and knees); live oakers, often with the use of enslaved labor, built camps and trail systems in the woods, usually near convenient landing places (live oak, because of its weight, could not be floated downstream). By 1832, at the time of this encounter (Audubon wrote this for publication about a year later), the Seminole tribe was still a recently established community, formed from First Contact tribes who had survived Spanish war and disease, Maskókî (Creek) peoples who have moved to Florida, and runaway Blacks. The Spanish had ceded Floridian lands to the US in 1821. The Seminole mounted one of the fiercest, most successful Native American resistance campaigns of the nineteenth century, known as the three Seminole Wars (1814–1818, 1835–1842, 1856–1858), though, by that point, like all Native Americans in the southeast, they were cheated and coerced to move off their lands by a range of policies and violence enabled by Andrew Jackson's 1830 Indian Removal Act. Audubon's deeply ingrained racial prejudice is evident in stereotypical phrases such as "children of the desert" (in "American Flamingo"). His observations on the plight of Native American peoples, writ large, continued to appear in his writings as he traveled around the country, although the descriptions remained tinged with his belief in white superiority, as evidenced in 1843 when he traveled up the Missouri River into the Dakotas, seeing the ravages of smallpox and starvation among Native American tribes; see *John James Audubon, Writings and Drawings*, ed. Christoph Irmscher (New York: Library of America, 1999), 640–44. Earlier, in 1837, he witnessed a forced removal march of Maskókî peoples as he traveled through Alabama, expressing genuine recognition of the cruelty of their treatment, but still in terms of an artistic vision: "their future and latter days Must be Spent in the deepest of Sorrows . . . a Picture as I hope I never will again witness in reality" (Audubon to John Bach-

man, February 24, 1837, in *Writings*, 840). See Seminole Tribe of Florida, "History: Indian Resistance and Removal" (accessed 2020), www.semtribe.com/STOF/history/introduction; Richard White, "Indian Removal Policy," in *The Native Americans: An Illustrated History* (Atlanta: Turner, 1993), 293–99, 319; Michelle C. Neely, *Against Sustainability* (New York: Fordham University Press, 2020), 85–103. In 1833 Audubon was particularly harsh in his description of the people of the Mi'kmaq First Nation (Labrador journal, August 15, 1833); see also the introduction and coda to this volume.

5. Audubon's beloved Newfoundland dog Plato, "a well-trained and most sagacious animal" ("The Great White Heron," *OB* 3 [1835], 542).

6. William Gates (1788–1868), a veteran of the War of 1812, was the brevet major in charge of Fort Marion in St. Augustine from 1829 to 1832 (his second tour). He arrested Seminole leader Osceola, or Asi-yahola, in October 1837 at Fort Marion. After serving in the war with Mexico and the Civil War, he retired in 1867 as a brigadier general.

Mid-Atlantic Waters

THE AMERICAN OYSTER-CATCHER

OUR Oyster-Catcher has a very extensive range [plate 7]. It spends the winter along the coast from Maryland to the Gulf of Mexico, and being then abundant on the shores of the Floridas, may be considered a constant resident in the United States. At the approach of spring, it removes toward the Middle States, where, as well as in North Carolina, it breeds. It seems scarcer between Long Island and Portland in Maine, where you again see it, and whence it occurs all the way to Labrador, in which country I found that several were breeding in the month of July. Unless in winter, when these birds assemble in parties of twenty-five or thirty individuals, they are seldom met with in greater numbers than from one to four pairs, with their families, which appear to remain with the parent birds until the following spring. It is never found inland, nor even far up our largest rivers, but is fond of remaining at all times on the sandy beaches and rocky shores of our salt-water bays or marshes. In Labrador, I met with it farther from the open sea than in any other part, yet always near salt-water. I have never met with any other species on the coasts of North America.[1]

Shy, vigilant, and ever on the alert, the Oyster-Catcher walks with a certain appearance of dignity, greatly enhanced by its handsome plumage and remarkable bill. If you stop to watch it, that instant it sounds a loud shrill note of alarm; and should you advance farther towards it, when it has neither nest nor young, off it flies quite out of sight. Few birds, indeed, are more difficult to be approached, and the only means of studying its habits I found to be the use of an excellent telescope, with which I could trace its motions when at the distance of a quarter of a mile, and pursuing its avocations without apprehension of danger. In this manner I have seen it probe the sand to the full length of its bill, knock off limpets from the rocks on the coast of Labrador, using its weapon sideways and insinuating it between the rock and the shell like a chisel, seize the bodies of gaping oysters on what are called in the Southern States and the Floridas "Racoon oyster beds," and at other times take up a "razor-handle" or solen, and lash it against the sands until the shell was broken and the contents swallowed. Now and then they seem to suck the sea-urchins, driving in the mouth, and introducing their bill by the aperture, without breaking the shell; again they are seen wading up to their bodies from one place to another, seizing on shrimps and other Crustacea, and even swimming for a few yards, should this be necessary to enable them to remove from one bank to another without flying. Small crabs, fiddlers, and sea-worms, are also caught by it, the shells of which in a broken state I have found in its gizzard in greater or less quantity. Frequently, while on wet sea-beaches, it pats the sand, to force out the insects; and in one instance I saw an individual run from the water to the dry sand, with a small flounder in its bill, which it afterwards devoured.

This bird forms no regular nest, but is contented with scratching the dry sand above high-water mark, so as to form a slight hollow, in which it deposits its eggs. On the coast of Labrador, and in the Bay of Fundy, it lays its eggs on the bare rock. When the eggs are on sand, it seldom sits on them during the heat of the sun; but in Labrador, it was found sitting as closely as any other bird. Here, then, is another instance of the extraordinary difference of habit in the same bird under different circumstances. It struck me so much that had I not procured a specimen in Labrador, and another in our Middle Districts, during the breeding season, and found them on the closest examination to be the same, I should perhaps have thought the birds different. Everywhere, however, I observed that this bird is fond of places covered with broken shells and drifted sea-weeds or grasses, as a place of security for its eggs, and where, in fact, it is no very easy matter to discover them. The eggs are two or three, measure two inches and one-eighth in length, by an inch and a half in breadth, and are of the form of those of a common hen. They are of a pale cream colour, spotted with irregular marks of brownish-black, and others of a paler tint, pretty equally dispersed all over. The birds, even when not sitting on them, are so very anxious about them, that on the least appearance of an enemy, they scream out loudly, and if you approach the nest, fly over and around you, although always at a considerable distance. When you meet with the young, which run as soon as they are hatched, the old birds manifest the greatest anxiety. They run before you, or fly around you, with great swiftness, and emit peculiar notes, which at once induce their little ones to squat among the sand and broken shells, where, on account of their dull greyish-colour, it is very difficult to see them unless you pass within a foot or two of them, when they run off emitting a plaintive note, which renders the parents doubly angry. Their shape is now almost round, and the streaks of their back and rump, as well as the curved points of their bills, might induce you to believe them to be any thing but the young of an Oyster-Catcher. I have caught some, which I thought were more than a month old, and yet were unable to fly, although full feathered. They appeared weakened by their fatness, and were overtaken by running after them on the sands. There were no parent birds near or in sight of them; yet I much doubt if they procured their own food at this period, and have more reason to believe that, like some other species of birds, they were visited and supplied with food at particular hours of the day or of the night, as is the case with Herons and Ibises, for the Oyster-Catcher is scarcely nocturnal.

By the beginning of October these birds return to the south. I saw them at Labrador until the 11th of August, but cannot say at what period they leave that country. When wounded while wading or on the shore, they make for the water, on which they float buoyantly and move with ease.

The flight of the American Oyster-Catcher is powerful, swift, elegant at times, and greatly protracted. While they are on wing, their beauties are as effectually displayed as those of the Ivory-billed Woodpecker of our woods, the colours of which are somewhat similar. The transparent white of their wings contrasts with their jetty tips, and is enriched by the coral hue of the bill, while the beautiful white of their lower parts has a very pleasing effect. Their loud cries, too, of *wheep, wheep, wheeop*, which sound in your ears, are quite different from any you have heard; and as they perform their various evolutions, all charming in themselves, you cannot, if unacquainted with the bird, refrain from asking what it is? Now wheeling with wonderful impetuosity, they pass within a hundred yards of you, and suddenly checking their flight return, not low over the waters as before, but high in the air. Again, they form their ranks in a broad front, and again, as if suddenly alarmed by the report of a distant gun, they close pell-mell, and dip towards the sands or the waters. Shoot one at such a moment, and you may expect to kill another; but as this is done, the wary birds, as if suddenly become aware of your intentions, form themselves into a straggling line, and before a minute has elapsed, far beyond reach, and fading on the view, are the remaining Oyster-Catchers.

The gullet of this species is capable of being considerably distended. When your finger is introduced into it, it passes with ease into a sort of crop, where the food is apparently prepared before entering the gizzard, which is rather muscular. How this bird disposes of the hard particles of shells, pebbles, and other matters, with which its food is mixed, is beyond my comprehension, and one which I gladly leave for your solution. Their flesh is dark, tough, and unfit for eating, unless in cases of extreme necessity.

The females and young are dark olive-brown above, like the males, but of a browner shade. I have represented a male bird. I have never met with the European Oyster-Catcher, *Hæmatopus Ostralegus*, in any part of the United States, and, although I cannot of course aver that it does not occur there, I believe that the American or Mantled Oyster-Catcher has been confounded with it by WILSON and others. Indeed, the figure given by WILSON resembles that of the European bird, but his description of the female and young almost agrees with the present species, the dimensions also being nearly the same.[2]

Notes

1. First published in *OB* 3 (1835), 181–85. Audubon painted his "American/Pied Oyster-Catcher," now known as the American oystercatcher, *Haematopus palliatus* (plate 7; Havell 223), along the Louisiana coast in June 1821. Hunted close to extinction in the nineteenth century, the American oystercatcher rebounded after the Migratory Bird Treaty Act in 1918. Though in many states recovery has been slow, the American oystercatcher is now considered a species of Least Concern (IUCN, 2016), while *H. ostralegus*, the Eurasian oystercatcher, is Near Threatened with its population decreasing globally (IUCN, 2019). The latter is native to Europe and parts of Asia and Africa. Once known as the "sea pie," the oystercatcher received its current name when Mark Catesby observed its feeding habits: "On these Banks of Oysters do these Birds principally, if not altogether, subsist; Nature having not only formed their

bills suitable to the work, but armed the feet and legs for a defence against the sharp edges of the Oysters." Catesby, *The Natural History of Carolina, Florida, and the Bahamas Islands* (London: author, 1731), 1:85.

2. Audubon's "European Oyster-Catcher" is now the Eurasian oystercatcher (*Haematopus ostralegus*), also known as the common pied oystercatcher. Regarding Wilson's depiction of the oystercatchers, see Alexander Wilson, *American Ornithology*, vol. 8 (Philadelphia: Bradford and Inskeep, 1814), plate 1, 15–18.

THE FISH HAWK, OR OSPREY

COMPARING the great size of this bird, its formidable character, its powerful and protracted flight, and the dexterity with which, although a land bird, it procures its prey from the waters of the ocean, with the very inferior powers of the bird named the Kingsfisher, I should be tempted to search for a more appropriate appellation than that of Fish Hawk, and, were I not a member of a republic, might fancy that of *Imperial Fisher* more applicable to it.[1]

The habits of this famed bird differ so materially from those of almost all others of its genus, that an accurate description of them cannot fail to be highly interesting to the student of nature.

The Fish Hawk [plate 8] may be looked upon as having more of a social disposition than most other Hawks. Indeed, with the exception of the Swallow-tailed Hawk (*Falco furcatus*), I know none so gregarious in its habits. It migrates in numbers, both during spring, when it shews itself along our Atlantic shores, lakes, and rivers, and during autumn, when it retires to warmer climes. At these seasons, it appears in flocks of eight or ten individuals, following the windings of our shores in loose bodies, advancing in easy sailings or flappings, crossing each other in their gyrations. During the period of their stay in the United States, many pairs are seen nestling, rearing their young, and seeking their food, within so short a distance of each other, that while following the margins of our eastern shores, a Fish Hawk or a nest belonging to the species, may be met with at every short interval.[2]

The Fish Hawk may be said to be of a mild disposition. Not only do these birds live in perfect harmony together, but they even allow other birds of very different character to approach so near to them as to build their nests of the very materials of which the outer parts of their own are constructed. I have never observed a Fish Hawk chasing any other bird whatever. So pacific and timorous is it, that, rather than encounter a foe but little more powerful than itself, it abandons its prey to the White-headed Eagle, which, next to man, is its greatest enemy. It never forces its young from the nest, as some other Hawks do, but, on the contrary, is seen to feed them even when they have begun to procure food for themselves.

Notwithstanding all these facts, a most erroneous idea prevails among our fishermen, and the farmers along our coasts, that the Fish Hawk's nest is the best *scare-crow* they can have in the vicinity of their houses or grounds. As these good people affirm, no Hawk will attempt to commit depredations on their poultry, so long as the Fish Hawk remains in the country. But the absence of most birds of prey from those parts at the time when the Fish Hawk is on our coast, arises simply from the necessity of retiring to the more sequestered parts of the interior for the purpose of rearing their young in security, and the circumstance of their visiting the coasts chiefly at the period when myriads of water-fowl resort to our estuaries at the approach of winter, leaving the shores and salt-marshes at the return of spring, when the Fish Hawk arrives. However, as this notion has a tendency to protect the latter bird, it may be so far useful, the fisherman always interposing when he sees a person bent upon the destruction of his favourite bird.

The Fish Hawk differs from all birds of prey in another important particular, which is, that it never attempts to secure its prey in the air, although its rapidity of flight might induce an observer to suppose it perfectly able to do so. I have spent weeks on the Gulf of Mexico, where these birds are numerous, and have observed them sailing and plunging into the water, at a time when numerous shoals of flying-fish were emerging from the sea to evade the pursuit of the dolphins. Yet the Fish Hawk never attempted to pursue any of them while above the surface, but would plunge after one of them or a bonita-fish, after they had resumed their usual mode of swimming near the surface.

The motions of the Fish Hawk in the air are graceful, and as majestic as those of the Eagle. It rises with ease to a great height by extensive circlings, performed apparently by mere inclinations of the wings and tail. It dives at times to some distance with the wings partially closed, and resumes its sailing, as if these plunges were made for amusement only. Its wings are extended at right angles to the body, and when thus flying it is easily distinguishable from all other Hawks by the eye of an observer accustomed to note the flight of birds. Whilst in search of food, it flies with easy flappings at a moderate height above the water, and with an apparent listlessness, although in reality it is keenly observing the objects beneath. No sooner does it spy a fish suited to its taste, than it checks its course with a sudden shake of its wings and tail, which gives it the appearance of being poised in the air for a moment, after which it plunges headlong with great rapidity into the water, to secure its prey, or continue its flight, if disappointed by having observed the fish sink deeper.

When it plunges into the water in pursuit of a fish, it sometimes proceeds deep enough to disappear for an instant. The surge caused by its descent is so great as to make the spot around it present the appearance of a mass of foam. On rising with its prey, it is seen holding it in the manner represented in the Plate. It mounts a few yards into the air, shakes the water from its plumage, squeezes the fish with its talons, and immediately proceeds towards its nest, to feed its young, or to a tree, to devour the fruit of its industry in peace. When it has satisfied its hunger, it does not, like other Hawks, stay perched until hunger again urges it forth, but usually sails about at a great height over the neighbouring waters.

The Fish Hawk has a great attachment to the tree to which it carries its prey, and will not abandon it, unless frequently disturbed, or shot at whilst feeding there. It shews the same attachment to the tree on which it has built its first nest, and returns to it year after year.

This species arrives on the southern coasts of the United States early in the month of February, and proceeds eastward as the season advances. In the Middle Districts, the fishermen hail its appearance with joy, as it is the harbinger of various species of fish which resort to the Atlantic coasts, or ascend the numerous rivers. It arrives in the Middle States about the beginning of April, and returns southward at the first appearance of frost. I have occasionally seen a few of these birds on the muddy lakes of Louisiana, in the neighbourhood of New Orleans, during the winter months; but they appeared emaciated, and were probably unable to follow their natural inclinations, and proceed farther south.

As soon as the females make their appearance, which happens eight or ten days after the arrival of the males, the love-season commences, and soon after, incubation takes place. The loves of these birds are conducted in a different way from those of the other Falcons. The males are seen playing through the air amongst themselves, chasing each other in sport, or sailing by the side or after the female which they have selected, uttering cries of joy and exultation, alighting on the branches of the tree on which their last year's nest is yet seen remaining, and doubtless congratulating each other on finding their home again. Their caresses are mutual. They begin to augment their habitation, or to repair the injuries which it may have sustained during the winter, and are seen sailing together towards the shores, to collect the drifted sea-weeds with which they line the nest anew. They alight on the beach, search for the driest and largest weeds, collect a mass of them, clench them in their talons, and fly towards their nest with the materials dangling beneath. They both alight and labour together. In a fortnight the nest is complete, and the female deposits her eggs, which are three or four in number, of a broadly oval form, yellowish-white, densely covered with large irregular spots of reddish-brown.

The nest is generally placed in a large tree in the immediate vicinity of the water, whether along the seashore, on the margins of the inland lakes, or by some large river. It is, however, sometimes to be seen in the interior of a wood, a mile or more from the water. I have concluded that, in the latter case, it was on account of frequent disturbance, or attempts at destruction, that the birds had removed from their usual haunt. The nest is very large, sometimes measuring fully four feet across, and is composed of a quantity of materials sufficient to render its depth equal to its diameter. Large sticks, mixed with sea-weeds, tufts of strong grass, and other materials, form its exterior, while the interior is composed of sea-weeds and finer grasses. I have not observed that any particular species of tree is preferred by the Fish Hawk. It places its nest in the forks of an oak or a pine with equal pleasure. But I have observed that the tree chosen is usually of considerable size, and not unfrequently a decayed one. I dare not, however, affirm that the juices of the plants which compose the nest, ever become so detrimental to the growth of a tree as ultimately to kill it. In a few instances, I have seen the Fish Crow and the Purple Grakle raising their families in nests built by them among the outer sticks of the Fish Hawk's nest.

The male assists in incubation, during the continuance of which the one bird supplies the other with food, although each in turn goes in quest of some for itself. At such times the male bird is now and then observed rising to an immense height in the air, over the spot where his mate is seated. This he does by ascending almost in a direct line, by means of continued flappings, meeting the breeze with his white breast, and occasionally uttering a cackling kind of note, by which the bystander is enabled to follow him in his progress. When the Fish Hawk has attained its utmost elevation, which is sometimes such that the eye can no longer perceive him, he utters a loud shriek, and dives smoothly on half-extended wings towards his nest. But before he readies it, he is seen to expand his wings and tail, and in this manner he glides towards his beloved female, in a beautifully curved line. The female partially raises herself from her eggs, emits a low cry, resumes her former posture, and her delighted partner flies off to the sea, to seek a favourite fish for her whom he loves.

The young are at length hatched. The parents become more and more attached to them, as they grow up. Abundance of food is procured to favour their development. So truly parental becomes the attachment of the old birds, that an attempt to rob them of those dear fruits of their love, generally proves more dangerous than profitable. Should it be made, the old birds defend their brood with great courage and perseverance, and even sometimes, with extended claws and bill, come in contact with the assailant, who is glad to make his escape with a sound skin.

The young are fed until fully fledged, and often after they have left the nest, which they do apparently with great reluctance. I have seen some as large as the parents, filling the nest, and easily distinguished by the white margins of their upper plumage, which may be seen with a good glass at a considerable distance. So much fish is at times carried to the nest, that a quantity of it falls to the ground, and is left there to putrify around the foot of the tree. Only one brood is raised each season.

The Fish Hawk seldom alights on the ground, and when it does so, walks with difficulty, and in an extremely awkward manner. The only occasions on which it is necessary for them to alight, are when they collect materials for the purpose of repairing their nest at the approach of autumn, or for building a new one, or repairing the old, in spring.

I have found this bird in various parts of the interior of the United States, but always in the immediate neighbourhood of rivers or lakes. When I first removed to Louisville in Kentucky, several pairs were in the habit of raising their brood annually on a piece of ground immediately opposite the foot of the Falls of the Ohio in the State of Indiana. The ground belonged to the venerable General CLARK, and I was several times invited by him to visit the spot. Increasing population, however, has driven off the birds, and few are now seen on the Ohio, unless during their migrations to and from Lake Erie, where I have met with them.[3]

I have observed many of these birds at the approach of winter, sailing over the lakes near the Mississippi, where they feed on the fish which the Wood Ibis kills, the Hawks themselves being unable to discover them whilst alive in the muddy water with which these lakes are filled. There the Ibises wade among the water in immense flocks, and so trample the bottom as to convert the lakes into filthy puddles, in which the fishes are unable to respire with ease. They rise to the surface, and are instantly killed by the Ibises. The whole surface is sometimes covered in this manner with dead fish, so that not only are the Ibises plentifully supplied, but Vultures, Eagles and Fish Hawks, come to participate in the spoil. Except in such places, and on such occasions, I have not observed the Fish Hawk to eat of any other prey than that which it had procured by plunging headlong into the water after it.

I have frequently heard it asserted that the Fish Hawk is sometimes drawn under the water and drowned, when it has attempted to seize a fish which is too strong for it, and that some of these birds have been found sticking by their talons to the back of Sturgeons and other large fishes. But, as nothing of this kind ever came under my observation, I am unable to corroborate these reports. The roosting place of this bird is generally on the top-branches of the tree on which its nest is placed, or of one close to it.

Fish Hawks are very plentiful on the coast of New Jersey, near Great Egg Harbour, where I have seen upwards of fifty of their nests in the course of a day's walk, and where I have shot several in the course of a morning. When wounded, they defend themselves in the manner usually exhibited by Hawks, erecting the feathers of the head, and trying to strike with their powerful talons and bill, whilst they remain prostrate on their back.

The largest fish which I have seen this bird take out of the water, was a Weak Fish, such as is represented in the plate, but sufficiently large to weigh more than five pounds. The bird carried it into the air with difficulty, and dropped it, on hearing the report of a shot fired at it.

The Weak Fish

THE Weak Fish makes its appearance along our eastern shores about the middle of April, and remains until autumn. It is caught in the seine, and sold in our markets, being a delicate well-flavoured fish. It seldom attains any remarkable size. It is particularly plentiful about Great Egg Harbour, in New Jersey.[4]

Notes

1. First published in published in *OB* 1 (1831), 415–21. Audubon painted his "Fish Hawk, or Osprey," now osprey, *Pandion haliaetus* (plate 8; Havell 81), with a weakfish (*Cynoscion regalis*), after observing and killing a bird along the coast of New Jersey in 1829. Osprey are now considered a species of Least Concern, with their populations increasing perhaps even beyond the numbers in Audubon's time, despite steep population declines due to pesticide pollution in the 1950s–1970s (IUCN, 2019).

2. Audubon's "Swallow-tailed Hawk" (Havell 72) is now the American swallow-tailed kite (*Elanoides forficatus*).

3. General George Rogers Clark (1752–1818), frontier military leader in the American Revolution and Indian commissioner. In 1779, Clark captured Fort Sackville at Vincennes, Indiana, from the British. Clark, the older brother of William Clark (of Lewis and Clark), lived in Clarksville, in a two-room cabin overlooking the Falls of the Ohio, until 1809, when he suffered a stroke and moved to Locust Grove, eight miles from Louisville, Kentucky.

4. The weakfish (*Cynoscion regalis*) is known as an excellent table fish and can reach, despite Audubon's assertion, a length of up to three feet and weight of eighteen pounds. As a result of overfishing, populations are now depleted beyond a sustainable point and considered Endangered (IUCN, 2019).

LITTLE GUILLEMOT

THIS interesting little bird sometimes makes its appearance on our eastern coasts during very cold and stormy weather. It does not proceed much farther southward than the shores of New Jersey, where it is of very rare occurrence. Now and then some are caught in a state of exhaustion, as I have known to be the case especially in Passamaquody Bay near Eastport in Maine, and in the vicinity of Boston and Salem in Massachusetts.[1]

In the course of my voyages across the Atlantic, I have often observed the Little Guillemots [plate 9] in small groups, rising and flying to short distances at the approach of the ship, or diving close to the bow and reappearing a little way behind. Now with expanded wings they would flutter and run as it were on the surface of the deep; again, they would seem to be busily engaged in procuring food, which consisted apparently of shrimps, other crustacea, and particles of sea-weeds, all of which I have found in their stomach. I have often thought how easy it would be to catch these tiny wanderers of the ocean with nets thrown expertly from the bow of a boat, for they manifest very little apprehension of danger from the proximity of one, insomuch that I have seen several killed with the oars. Those which were caught alive and placed on the deck, would at first rest a few minutes with their bodies flat, then rise upright and run about briskly, or attempt to fly off, which they sometimes accomplished, when they happened to go in a straight course the whole length of the ship so as to rise easily over the bulwarks. On effecting their escape they would alight on the water and immediately disappear.

During my visit to Labrador and Newfoundland I met with none of these birds, although the cod-fishers assured me that they frequently breed there. I am informed by Dr TOWNSEND that this species is found near the mouth of the Columbia River.[2]

Notes

1. First published in *OB* 4 (1838), 304–9. Audubon's painting of the "Little Auk/Little Guillemot" (plate 9; Havell 339), known today as the dovekie, *Alle alle*, shows a male bird in breeding plumage on a rock and a female in winter plumage in the water with what appears

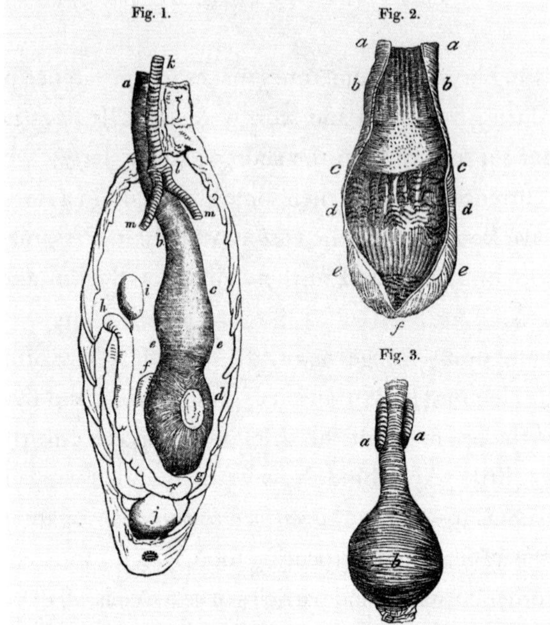

FIGURE 27. William MacGillivray, digestive system of the little guillemot (dovekie). Woodcut from Audubon, *Ornithological Biography*, vol. 4 (1838). This illustration in the anatomical appendix to the "Little Guillemot" biography came with an uncharacteristically thorough and sarcastic correction of a previous representation, which Audubon and MacGillivray rejected as based on the misguided idea that there was nothing for birds to eat in the Arctic: "the many compilers, . . . who have pressed it into their service, may, in their future editions, with propriety leave it out, and supply its place with something equally ingenious" (*OB* 4 [1838], 308–9). Courtesy of Williams College.

to be a stylized caridean shrimp (infraorder *Caridea*) in its beak (Sammy DeGrave, personal communication, July 26, 2020). Audubon apparently did *not* see dovekies during his Labrador travels. Today, dovekies are of Least Concern and are the most abundant type of auk in the North Atlantic, although their population size seems to be declining. Twenty-first-century ornithologists record a range no farther south than Long Island in the winter, perhaps due to warming temperatures. No dovekies live in the Pacific. Dovekies specialize in eating copepods, amphipods, krill, and small fish.

2. John Kirk Townsend (1809–1851) was a Philadelphia-born physician, taxidermist, and ornithologist, who, along with Thomas Nuttall (see notes to "The Long-Billed Curlew"), accompanied Nathaniel Wyeth's 1834–1835 expedition to the Pacific. The skins of western birds Townsend brought home from his expedition belonged to the Academy of Natural Sciences, which had sponsored the expedition, but thanks to his friend Edward Harris and other supporters, Audubon was able to acquire ninety-three duplicates: "Cheap as dirt, too. . . . Such

beauties! Such rarities! Such novelties!" Audubon to John Bachman, October 23, 1836, in *The Letters of John James Audubon, 1826–40*, ed. Howard Corning (1930; New York: Kraus Reprint, 1969), 2:135–36.

THE LONG-BILLED CURLEW

THE Long-billed Curlew [plate 10] is a constant resident in the southern districts of the United States, whereas the other species are only autumnal and winter visitors. It is well known by the inhabitants of Charleston that it breeds on the islands on the coast of South Carolina; and my friend the Reverend JOHN BACHMAN has been at their breeding grounds. That some individuals go far north to breed, is possible enough, but we have no authentic account of such an occurrence, although many *suppositions* have been recorded. All that I have to say on this subject is, that the bird in question is quite unknown in the Magdeleine Islands, where, notwithstanding the assertions of the fishermen, they acknowledged that they had mistaken Godwits for Curlews. In Newfoundland, I met with a well-informed English gentleman, who had resided in that island upwards of twenty years, and described the Common Curlew of Europe with accuracy, but who assured me that he had observed only two species of Curlew there, one about the size of the Whimbrel—the *Numenius hudsonicus*, the other smaller—the *N. borealis*, and that only in August and the beginning of September, when they spend a few days in that country, feed on berries, and then retire southward. Mr JONES of Labrador, and his brother-in-law, who is a Scotch gentleman, a scholar, and a sportsman, gave me the same account. None of my party observed an individual of the species in the course of our three months' stay in the country, although we saw great numbers of the true Esquimaux Curlew, *N. borealis*. Yet I would not have you to suppose that I do not give credit to the reports of some travellers, who have said that the Long-billed Curlew is found in the fur countries during summer. This may be true enough; but none of the great northern travellers, such as RICHARDSON, ROSS, PARRY, or FRANKLIN, have asserted this as a fact. Therefore if the bird of which I speak has been seen far north, it was in all probability a few stragglers that had perhaps been enticed to follow some other species. I am well aware of the propensity it has to ramble, as I have shot some in Missouri, Indiana, Kentucky, Arkansas, and Mississippi; but the birds thus obtained were rare in those districts, where the species only appears at remote periods; and in every instance of the kind I have found the individuals much less shy than usual, and apparently more perplexed than frightened by the sight of man.[1]

Until my learned friend, Prince CHARLES BONAPARTE, corrected the errors which had been made respecting the Curlews of North America, hardly one of these birds was known from another by any naturalist, American or European. To WILSON, however, is due the merit of having first published an account of the Long-billed Curlew as a species distinct from the Common Curlew of Europe.[2]

This bird is the largest of the genus found in North America. The great length of its bill is of itself sufficient to distinguish it from every other. The bill, however, in all the species, differs greatly, according to the age of the individual, and in the present Curlew I have seen it in some birds nearly three inches shorter than in others, although all were full grown. In many of its habits, the Long-billed Curlew is closely allied to the smaller species of Ibis; its flight and manner of feeding are similar, and it has the same number of eggs. Unlike the Ibis, however, which always breeds on trees, and forms a large nest, the Curlew breeds on the ground, forming a scanty receptacle for its eggs; yet, according to my friend BACHMAN, the latter, like the former, places its nests "so close together, that it is almost impossible for a man to walk between them, without injuring the eggs."

The Long-billed Curlew spends the day in the sea-marshes, from which it returns at the approach of night, to the sandy beaches of the sea-shores, where it rests until dawn. As the sun sinks beneath the horizon, the Curlews rise from their feeding-grounds in small parties, seldom exceeding fifteen or twenty, and more usually composed of only five or six individuals. The flocks enlarge, however, as they proceed, and in the course of an hour or so the number of birds that collect in the place selected for their nightly retreat, sometimes amounts to several thousands. As it was my good fortune to witness their departures and arrivals, in the company of my friend BACHMAN, I will here describe them.

Accompanied by several friends, I left Charleston one beautiful morning, the 10th of November 1831, with a view to visit Cole's Island, about twenty miles distant. Our crew was good, and although our pilot knew but little of the cuttings in and out of the numerous inlets and channels in our way, we reached the island about noon. After shooting various birds, examining the island, and depositing our provisions in a small summer habitation then untenanted, we separated; some of the servants went off to fish, others to gather oysters, and the gunners placed themselves in readiness for the arrival of the Curlews. The sun at length sunk beneath the water-line that here formed the horizon; and we saw the birds making their first appearance. They were in small parties of two, three, or five, and by no means shy. These seemed to be the birds which we had observed near the salt-marshes, as we were on our way. As the twilight became darker the number of Curlews increased, and the flocks approached in quicker succession, until they appeared to form a continuous procession, moving not in lines, one after another, but in an extended mass, and with considerable regularity, at a height of not more than thirty yards, the individuals being a few feet apart. Not a single note or cry was heard as they advanced. They moved for ten or more yards with regular flappings, and then sailed for a few seconds, as is invariably the mode of flight of this species, their long bills and legs stretched out to their full extent. They flew directly towards their place of rest, called the "Bird Banks," and were seen to alight without performing any of the evolutions which they exhibit when at their feeding-places, for they had not been disturbed that season. But when we followed them to the Bird Banks, which are sandy islands of small extent, the moment they saw us land the congregated flocks, probably amounting to several thousand individuals all standing close together, rose at once, performed a few evolutions in perfect silence, and re-alighted as if with one accord on the extreme margins of the sand-bank close to tremendous breakers. It was now dark, and we left the place, although some flocks were still arriving. The next morning we returned a little before day; but again as we landed, they all rose a few yards in the air, separated into numerous parties, and dispersing in various directions, flew off towards their feeding-grounds, keeping low over the waters, until they reached the shores, when they ascended to the height of about a hundred yards, and soon disappeared.[3]

Now, Reader, allow me to say a few words respecting our lodgings.

Fish, fowl, and oysters had been procured in abundance; and besides these delicacies, we had taken with us from Charleston some steaks of beef, and a sufficiency of good beverage. But we had no cook, save your humble servant. A blazing fire warmed and lighted our only apartment. The oysters and fish were thrown on the hot embers; the steaks we stuck on sticks in front of them; and ere long every one felt perfectly contented. It is true we had forgotten to bring salt with us; but I soon proved to my merry companions that hunters can find a good substitute in their powder-flasks. Our salt on this occasion was gunpowder, as it has been with me many a time; and to our keen appetites, the steaks thus salted were quite as savoury as any of us ever found the best cooked at home. Our fingers and mouths, no doubt, bore marks of the "villanous salt-petre," or rather of the charcoal with which it was mixed, for plates or forks we had none; but this only increased our mirth. Supper over, we spread out our blankets on the log floor, extended ourselves on them with our feet towards the fire, and our arms under our heads for pillows. I need not tell you how soundly we slept.

The Long-billed Curlews are in general easily shot, but take a good charge. So long as life remains in them, they skulk off among the thickest plants, remaining perfectly silent. Should they fall on the water, they swim towards the shore. The birds that may have been in company with a wounded one fly off uttering a few loud whistling notes. In this respect, the species differs from all the others, which commonly remain and fly about you. When on land, they are extremely wary; and unless the plants are high, and you can conceal yourself from them, it is very difficult to get near enough. Some one of the flock, acting as sentinel, raises his wings, as if about to fly, and sounds a note of alarm, on which they all raise their wings, close them again, give over feeding, and watch all your motions. At times a single step made by you beyond a certain distance is quite enough to raise them, and the moment it takes place, they all scream and fly off. You need not follow the flock. The best mode of shooting them is to watch their course for several evenings in succession; for after having chosen a resting place, they are sure to return to it by the same route, until greatly annoyed.

The food of the Long-billed Curlews consists principally of the small crabs called fiddlers, which they seize by running after them, or by pulling them out of their burrows. They probe the wet sand to the full length of their bill, in quest of sea-worms and other animals. They are also fond of small salt-water shell-fish, insects, and worms of any kind; but I have never seen them searching for berries on elevated lands, as the Esquimaux Curlews are wont to do. Their flesh is by no means so delicate as that of the species just mentioned, for it has usually a fishy taste, and is rarely tender, although many persons consider it good. They are sold at all seasons in the markets of Charleston, at about twenty-five cents the pair.

Rambling birds of this species are sometimes seen as far as the neighbourhood of Boston; for my learned friend THOMAS NUTTALL says in his Manual, that "they get so remarkably fat, at times, as to burst the skin in falling to the ground, and are then superior in flavour to almost any other game bird of the season. In the market of Boston, they are seen as early as the 8th of August." I found them rather rare in East Florida in winter and spring. They were there seen either on large savannahs, or along the sea shore, mixed with marbled Godwits, Tell-tales, and other species.[4]

Notes

1. First published in *OB* 3 (1835), 240–45. Audubon's "Long-billed Curlew," now *Numenius americanus* (plate 10; Havell 231), features a background view of Charleston, South Carolina, painted by George Lehman. The long-billed curlew is listed as a species of Least Concern, but populations are decreasing and numbers along the US East Coast are far lower than they were historically (IUCN, 2016; birdsoftheworld.org, 2020). Current ornithologists agree with Audubon's observations in that the long-billed curlew does not spend much time along the North American coast anywhere north of the Carolinas, knowing now that their primary breeding area is inland in the northwest, in regions such as Utah, Wyoming, and southern Saskatchewan; they are not now known to summer and breed off the coast of South Carolina as Audubon had heard. *Numenius hudsonicus* is a reference to Audubon's "Hudsonian Curlew/ Great Esquimaux Curlew" (Havell 237), now known as the whimbrel (*Numenius phaeopus*). *Numenius borealis* refers to the "Esquimaux Curlew" (Havell 208), now the Eskimo curlew, which is critically endangered today. "Numenius" is derived from the Greek *noumenia* or "new moon," a reference to the bird's curved bill. Captain William Randall Jones (1790–18??) was master of the sealing station at Bradore (Bras d'Or) Bay, Quebec, when Audubon stopped there at the end of July 1833 (see Audubon's episode "The Squatters of Labrador," *OB* 2 [1834], 154–59). His brother-in-law was Samuel Robertson (1795–1839), whose sealing station was at Sparr Point (now La Tabatière, Quebec). Robertson and Jones had both married daughters of Louis Chevalier, owner of a fishing station and trading post up the Esquimaux River (Labrador journal, July 23 and 26, 1833). Sir John Richardson (1787–1865) was a Scottish naval surgeon, explorer, and naturalist who participated in the first two over-

land expeditions to the Canadian Arctic coast of Sir John Franklin (1786–1847) and wrote *Fauna Boreali-Americana; or, The Zoology of the Northern Parts of British America* (1831). Arctic explorer Sir John Ross (1777–1856) located the north magnetic pole, and Sir William Edward Parry (1790–1855) came closest to discovering the fabled Northwest Passage.

2. Audubon's references on curlews are to Charles-Lucien Bonaparte, *The Genera of North American Birds, and a Synopsis of the Species Found within the Territory of the United States* (New York: J. Seymour, 1828), 314–15; and Alexander Wilson, *American Ornithology*, vol. 8, (Philadelphia: Bradford and Inskeep, 1814), 23.

3. The "servants" here were almost certainly enslaved people.

4. Thomas Nuttall (1786–1859) was an English botanist and zoologist. He resigned a position as curator of the botanic garden and lecturer in natural history at Harvard to botanize and collect in the American West, sailing on the return voyage to Boston with Richard Henry Dana Jr., who wrote of him in *Two Years before the Mast* (1840). From 1836 to 1841, Nuttall worked at the Academy of Natural Sciences in Philadelphia before returning home to England. Audubon's quotation is from Nuttall's *Manual of the Ornithology of the United States and Canada: The Water Birds* (Boston: Hillard, Gray, and Company, 1834), 96.

Western Waters

BLACK-FOOTED ALBATROSS

FOR a specimen of this Albatross, I am indebted to Dr TOWNSEND, who procured it on the 25th December 1834, on the Pacific Ocean, in lat. 30° 44', N. long. 146°. It is clearly distinct from the other two described in this work, namely the Dusky and the Yellow-nosed; but I have received no information respecting its habits. Not finding any of the meagre notices or descriptions to which I can refer to agree with this bird, I have taken the liberty of giving it a name, being well assured that, should it prove to have been described, some person will kindly correct my mistake.[1]

DIOMEDEA NIGRIPES

Male.

Bill longer than the head, nearly straight, stout, compressed. Upper mandible with its dorsal outline straight and declinate until near the middle, when it becomes a little concave, and along the unguis curves in the third of a circle, the ridge convex, very broad and convex at the base, with its basal margin curved in the third of a circle, the ridge separated in its whole length by a groove, margined below by a prominent line, from the sides, which are prominently convex, the edges sharp, the unguis decurved, strong, acute, with the sides a little convex. Nostrils sub-basal, prominent, tubular, having a horny sheath. Lower mandible with the angle narrow, reaching to the tip, and having at its extremity a slender horny interposed process; the outline of the crura gently ascending, slightly convex, toward the end a little concave, at the tip deflected, the sides ascending and considerably convex, but at the base concave, the edges sharp and inflexed, the tip compressed, its upper edges decurved.

Head rather large, ovate, anteriorly compressed; neck of moderate length; body full. Feet rather short, stoutish; tibia bare for an inch and ten-twelfths, reticulated all round with very small convex scales; tarsus rather slender, covered all round with small roundish convex scales; toes three, long, slender, for half their length covered above with transverse series of flat scales, in the rest of their extent scutellate; the second ten-twelfths of an inch shorter than the middle, which is scarcely longer than the outer. Claws rather small, slender, slightly arched, rather compressed, somewhat obtuse.

Plumage full, soft and blended. Wings very long and very narrow, the humerus and cubitus being extremely elongated; the first primary longest, the rest rapidly diminishing; secondaries extremely short. Tail of twelve rounded feathers, extremely short, rounded, the lateral feathers one inch shorter than the middle.

Bill dusky, the greater part of the lower mandible, and the middle of the upper, tinged with yellowish-brown. Feet and claws black. The fore part of the head, cheeks and throat light dusky-grey, the capistral feathers nearly white, as is a small patch at the posterior angle of the eye; the upper part of the head, the hind neck, and all the upper parts, including the wings and tail, are of a sooty brown tinged with grey, as are the lower surface of the wings and the axillaries. The lower parts are of a dull grey tint, deeper on the fore parts and sides of the neck.

Length to end of tail 36 inches; bill along the ridge 5, along the edge of lower mandible 5; wing from flexure 21; tail 3; bare part of tibia 1 10/12; tarsus 3 10/12; inner toe 1 10/12, its claw 6/12; middle toe 4 5/12, its claw 8/12; outer toe 4 7/12, its claw 6/12.

The three Albatrosses described in this volume may very easily be distinguished by the form of the bill, independently of all other characters. Thus:

Diomedea nigripes has the bill much thicker, or less compressed than the other two species; its ridge very broad and convex at the base, its basal outline being semicircular and two inches in extent, so that its sides behind overlap and obliterate the sutural space behind the nostrils.

Diomedea chlororhynchos has the bill much compressed, its ridge convex in its whole length, but with its basal outline, although semicircular, only half an inch in extent, so that between its margins and those of the sides of the bill there is behind the eye a space nearly a quarter of an inch in breadth.

Diomedea fusca [plate 11] has the bill as much compressed as that of *D. chlororhynchos*; but its ridge, in place of being convex, is carinate, and instead of having its base semicircular, as in the other two species, has it running up on the forehead into a very acute angle.

Many other differences might be pointed out, but these will suffice to distinguish the species. It may be remarked, that such descriptions are absolutely necessary to render the species of this genus intelligible; for at present it seems impossible to form any correct idea from the notices given in books; and if descriptions are not sufficient to enable one to refer an object to its species, of what use can they be?

Note

1. First published in *OB* 5 (1839), 327–29. Audubon's "Black-footed Albatross," now *Phoebastria nigripes*, was a bird he described and was the first to name as the type species, but he did not paint the bird. Black-footed albatrosses are considered Near Threatened, mostly due to fisheries entanglements and hooks (IUCN, 2018). Small compared to other albatrosses, the black-footed are still visitors to open water off the Oregon coast today. The other two albatross species that Audubon described in the anatomical section of "Black-footed Albatross," the only such section we've included in this volume, are (1) *Diomedea chlororhynchos*, his yellow-nosed albatross, which had been previously identified ("well known," he wrote in his short biography; *OB* 5 [1839], 326–27). But his description of the yellow on the lower mandible and the gray on the head suggests less the modern Atlantic or Indian yellow-nosed albatross than the Buller's or gray-headed (all now *Thalassarche spp.*), none of which are found anywhere near the Oregon coast today—although some yellow-nosed vagrants have been recorded in the North Atlantic and Caribbean; and (2) *Diomedea fusca*, his "Dusky/Brown Albatross," which he also made the subject of a separate biography and *did* paint (plate 11; Havell 407; *OB* 5 [1839], 116–17), known today, perhaps, as the sooty albatross (*Phoebetria fusca*) or the light-mantled albatross (*P. palpebrata*). Neither the sooty nor the light-mantled has yellow feet, however, and there are no records of either anywhere near the coast of Oregon—they are Southern Ocean seabirds—so proper identification is a mystery, which seems ironic in light of Audubon's comment at the end of this short "Black-footed Albatross" biography. These descriptions were also based on skins sent to him from Townsend (see notes to "Little Guillemot"). Perhaps these latter two albatross species (and the "Gigantic Fulmar") were extremely rare vagrants from half the globe away, on some singular storm or feeding event? Or, more likely, did Townsend get these skins from elsewhere, perhaps from a Southern Ocean naturalist-mariner, or collect them himself on his homeward journey around Cape Horn? For some insight, consult Frank L. Burns and Witmer Stone, "Townsend's Sooty Albatross," *Auk* 51, no. 2 (April 1934): 225–26. Although some of the skins Audubon bought from Townsend are still in the collections of the Philadelphia Academy of Natural Sciences, these skins are not among them (Nate Rice, manager of the Ornithology Collection, and Robert Peck, Curator and Fellow, Academy of Natural Sciences at Drexel University, personal communications, July 24 and 30, 2020) or, as far as the editors have been able to determine, at other institutions.

GIGANTIC FULMAR

A SPECIMEN of the Gigantic Fulmar, shot at some distance from the mouth of the Columbia River, has been sent to me by Dr TOWNSEND, along with those of the other species of the same genus described in this volume, and which it resembles in form and proportions. The great size of this bird gives it at first sight the appearance of an Albatross. It is described as frequent in the southern seas, gliding silently over the surface of the waters, and subsisting on carcasses of cetacea, seals, birds, and other animal matter; the sailors distinguishing them by the name of "Mother Carey's Geese."[1]

Notes

1. Audubon's note on the "Gigantic Fulmar," which he called *Procellaria gigantea* and did not paint, was first printed in *OB* 5 (1839), 330–31. Modern ornithologists explain that the southern giant petrel (*Macronectes giganteus*) or the northern giant petrel (*M. halli*), both with a wingspan of over six feet, rarely range north of even 20°S, although there are two records of a *Macronectes sp.* in the waters of France and Hawaii. Perhaps Townsend killed an exceptionally rare vagrant and this has not been recognized by modern ornithologists (see notes to "The Little Guillemot")? See Derek Onley and Paul Scofield, *Albatrosses, Petrels & Shearwaters of the World* (2007), 143; C. Carboneras, F. Jutglar, and G. M. Kirwan, "Southern Giant-Petrel," v. 1.0 (2020), birdsoftheworld.org. In the anatomical section of this biography, Audubon cited Shaw's *General Zoology* (1825), which explains in words quite similar to those that Audubon/MacGillivray used. Shaw wrote, "Frequent in the Southern Seas," where the birds fly "close to the surface of the water, but without appearing to move [their wings]," and "their food appears to consist principally of fish, but they will nevertheless feed upon the dead carcases of seals, birds, &c. The sailors call them by the name of Mother Cary's Geese." George Shaw and J. F. Stephens, *General Zoology; or, Systematic Natural History: Birds*, vol. 13, part 1 (London: J. and A. Arch, et al., 1825), 237–38. Both southern and northern giant petrels are of Least Concern today (IUCN, 2018).

New England and Atlantic Canada

THE BAY OF FUNDY

IT was in the month of May that I sailed in the United States' Revenue Cutter the Swiftsure, engaged in a cruize in the Bay of Fundy. Our sails were quickly unfurled, and spread out to the breeze. The vessel seemed to fly over the surface of the liquid element, as the sun rose in full splendour, while the clouds that floated here and there formed, with their glowing hues, a rich contrast with the pure azure of the heavens above us. We approached apace the island of Grand Manan, of which the stupendous cliffs gradually emerged from the deep with the majestic boldness of her noblest native chief. Soon our bark passed beneath its craggy head, covered with trees, which, on account of the height, seemed scarcely larger than shrubs. The prudent Raven spread her pinions, launched from the cliff, and flew away before us; the Golden Eagle soaring aloft, moved majestically along in wide circles; the Guillemots sat on their eggs upon the shelvy precipices, or plunging into the water, dived, and rose again at a great distance; the Broad-breasted Eider Duck covered her eggs among the grassy tufts; on a naked rock the seal lazily basked, its sleek sides glistening in the sunshine; while shoals of porpoises were swiftly gliding through the waters around us, shewing by their gambols that, although doomed to the deep, their life was not devoid of pleasure. Far away stood the bold shores of Nova Scotia, gradually fading in the distance, of which the grey tints beautifully relieved the wing-like sails of many a fishing bark.[1]

Cape after cape, forming eddies and counter currents far too terrific to be described by a landsman, we passed in succession, until we reached a deep cove, near the shores of White Head Island, which is divided from Grand Manan by a narrow strait, where we anchored secure from every blast that could blow. In a short time we found ourselves under the roof of Captain FRANKLAND, the sole owner of the isle, of which the surface contains about fifteen hundred acres. He received us all with politeness, and gave us permission to seek out its treasures, which we immediately set about doing, for I was anxious to study the habits of certain Gulls that breed there in great numbers. As Captain COOLEDGE, our worthy commander, had assured me, we found them on their nests on almost every *tree* of a wood that covered several acres. What a treat, reader, was it to find birds of this kind lodged on fir trees, and sitting comfortably on their eggs! Their loud cackling notes led us to their place of resort, and ere long we had satisfactorily observed their habits, and collected as many of themselves and their eggs as we considered sufficient. In our walks we noticed a rat, the only quadruped found in the island, and observed abundance of gooseberries, currants, rasps, strawberries, and huckleberries. Seating ourselves on the summit of the rocks, in view of the vast Atlantic, we spread out our stores, and refreshed ourselves with our simple fare.[2]

Now we followed the objects of our pursuit through the tangled woods, now carefully picked our steps over the spongy grounds. The air was filled with the melodious concerts of birds, and all nature seemed to smile in quiet enjoyment. We wandered about until the setting sun warned us to depart, when, returning to the house of the proprietor, we sat down to an excellent repast, and amused ourselves with relating anecdotes and forming arrangements for the morrow. Our Captain complimented us on our success, when we reached the Swiftsure, and in due time we betook ourselves to our hammocks.

The next morning, a strange sail appearing in the distance, preparations were instantly made to pay her commander a visit. The signal-staff of White Head Island displayed the British flag, while Captain FRANKLAND and his men stood on the shore, and as we gave our sails to the wind, three hearty cheers filled the air, and were instantly responded to by us. The vessel was soon approached, but all was found right with her, and squaring our yards, onward we sped, cheerily bounding over the gay billows, until our Captain sent us ashore at Eastport.

At another time my party was received on board the Revenue Cutter's tender the Fancy,—a charming name for so beautiful a craft. We set sail towards evening. The cackling of the "old wives" that covered the bay filled me with delight, and thousands of Gulls and Cormorants seemed as if anxious to pilot us into Head Harbour Bay, where we anchored for the night. Leaping on the rugged shore, we made our way to the lighthouse, where we found Mr SNELLING, a good and honest Englishman from Devonshire. His family consisted of three wild looking lasses, beautiful, like the most finished productions of nature. In his lighthouse, snugly ensconced, he spent his days in peaceful forgetfulness of the world, subsisting principally on the fish of the bay.[3]

When day broke, how delightful was it to see fair Nature open her graceful eyelids, and present herself arrayed in all that was richest and purest before her Creator. Ah, reader, how indelibly are such moments engraved on my soul! with what ardour have I at such times gazed around me, full of the desire of being enabled to comprehend all that I saw! How often have I longed to converse with the feathered inhabitants of the forest, all of which seemed then intent on offering up their thanks to the object of my own admiration! But the wish could not be gratified, although I now feel satisfied that I have enjoyed as much of the wonders and beauties of nature as it was proper for me to enjoy. The delightful trills of the Winter Wren rolled through the underwood, the red squirrel smacked time with his chops, the loud notes of the Robin sounded clearly from the tops of the trees, the rosy Grosbeak nipped the tender blossoms of the maples, and high over head the Loons passed in pairs, rapidly wending their way toward far distant shores. Would that I could have followed in their wake![4]

The hour of our departure had come; and, as we sailed up the bay, our pilot, who had been fishing for cod, was taken on board. A few of his fish were roasted on a plank before the embers, and formed the principal part of our breakfast. The breeze was light, and it was not until after noon that we arrived at Point Lepreaux Harbour, where every one, making choice of his course, went in search of curiosities and provender.[5]

Now, reader, the little harbour in which, if you wish it, we shall suppose we still are, is renowned for a circumstance which I feel much inclined to endeavour to explain to you. Several species of Ducks, that in myriads cover the waters of the Bay of Fundy, are at times destroyed in this particular spot in a very singular manner. When July has come, all the water-birds that are no longer capable of reproducing, remain like so many forlorn bachelors and old maids, to renew their plumage along the shores. At the period when these poor birds are unfit for flight, troops of Indians make their appearance in light bark-canoes, paddled by their squaws and papooses. They form their flotilla into an extended curve, and drive before them the birds, not in silence, but with simultaneous horrific yells, at the same time beating the surface of the water with long poles and paddles. Terrified by the noise, the birds swim a long way before them, endeavouring to escape with all their might. The tide is high, every cove is filled; and into the one where we now are, thousands of Ducks are seen entering. The Indians have ceased to shout, and the canoes advance side by side. Time passes on, the tide swiftly recedes as it rose, and there are the birds left on the beach. See with what pleasure each wild inhabitant of the forest seizes his stick, the squaws and younglings following with similar weapons! Look at them rushing on their prey, falling on the disabled birds, and smashing them with their cudgels, until all are destroyed! In this manner upwards of five hundred wild fowls have often been procured in a few hours.

Three pleasant days were spent about Point Lepreaux, when the Fancy spread her wings to the breeze. In one harbour we fished for shells, with a capital dredge, and in another searched along the shore for eggs. The Passamaquody chief is seen gliding swiftly over the deep in his fragile bark. He has observed a porpoise breathing. Watch him, for now he is close upon the unsuspecting dolphin. He rises erect, aims his musket; smoke rises curling from the pan, and rushes from the iron tube, when soon after the report comes on the ear;—meantime the porpoise has suddenly turned back downwards;—it is dead. The body weighs a hundred pounds or more, but this to the tough-fibred son of the woods is nothing; he reaches it with his muscular arms, and at a single jerk, while with his legs he dexterously steadies the canoe, he throws it lengthwise at his feet. Amidst the highest waves of the Bay of Fundy, these feats are performed by the Indians during the whole of the season when the porpoises resort thither.[6]

You have often no doubt heard of the extraordinary tides of this bay; so had I, but, like others, I was loth to believe that the reports were strictly true. So I went to the pretty town of Windsor [fig. 28], in Nova Scotia, to judge for myself. But let us leave the Fancy for a while, and

FIGURE 28. View of Minas Bay from the town of Windsor, Nova Scotia, engraved from a drawing by William Henry Bartlett in *Canadian Scenery Illustrated*, vol. 2 (London: George Virtue, 1842), 112. Courtesy of Williams College.

fancy ourselves at Windsor. Late one day in August, my companions and I were seated on the grassy and elevated bank of the river, about eighty feet or so above its bed, which was almost dry, and extended for nine miles below like a sandy wilderness. Many vessels lay on the high banks, taking in their lading of gypsum. We thought the appearance very singular, but we were too late to watch the tide that evening. Next morning we resumed our station, and soon perceived the water flowing towards us, and rising with a rapidity of which we had previously seen no example. We planted along the steep declivity of the bank a number of sticks, each three feet long, the base of one being placed on a level with the top of that below it, and when about half flow the tide reached their tops, one after another, rising three feet in ten minutes, or eighteen in the hour; and, at high water, the surface was sixty-five feet above the bed of the river! On looking for the vessels which we had seen the preceding evening, we were told that most of them had gone with the night tide.[7]

But now we are again on board the Fancy; Mr CLAREDGE stands near the pilot, who sits next to the man at the helm. On we move swiftly, for the breeze has freshened; many islands we pass in succession; the wind increases to a gale; with reefed sails we dash along, and now rapidly pass a heavily laden sloop gallantly running across our course with undiminished sail; when suddenly we see her upset. Staves and spars are floating around, and presently we observe three men scrambling up her sides, and seating themselves on the keel, where they make signals of distress to us. By this time we have run to a great distance; but CLAREDGE, cool and prudent, as every seaman ought to be, has already issued his orders to the helmsman and crew, and now near the wind we gradually approach the sufferers. A line is thrown to them, and next moment we are alongside the vessel. A fisher's boat, too, has noticed the disaster; and, with long strokes of her oars, advances, now rising on the curling wave, and now sinking out of sight. By our mutual efforts the men are brought on board, and the sloop is slowly towed into a safe harbour. In an hour after my party was safely landed at Eastport, where, on looking over the waters, and observing the dense masses of vapour that veiled the shores, we congratulated ourselves at having escaped from the Bay of Fundy.[8]

Notes

1. "The Bay of Fundy" was first published in *OB* 2 (1834), 484–89. The 110-ton US revenue cutter *Swiftsure* (1825), schooner-rigged, was renamed *Crawford* on December 31, 1839, and would have been assigned about four officers, fifteen sailors, and four cannon. The ship was sold on April 1, 1839; Donald L. Canney, *U.S. Coast Guard Revenue Cutters, 1790–1935* (Annapolis: Naval Institute Press, 1995), 12–13. The crew included Captain Uriah Coolidge (ca. 1781–1838), who had been assigned to the Passamaquoddy Customs District, as well as First Lieutenant John Whitcomb and Second Lieutenant Thomas Stoddard. Audubon, his son John Woodhouse, and Audubon's assistant George Shattuck (see notes to "Common Gannet") boarded the *Swiftsure* in Eastport, Maine, on May 22, 1833, and returned May 26, 1833. See Peter Logan, *Audubon: America's Greatest Naturalist and His Voyage of Discovery to Labrador* (San Francisco: Ashbryn Press, 2016), 565n232, 568n5. Although the "Broad-breasted Eider Duck" seems not to have been a common name in regular, published usage, this was likely Audubon's "Eider Duck" or common eider (Havell 246), *Somateria mollissima*, which he encountered often during his Labrador expedition. Audubon's "porpoises" here might have been harbor porpoises (*Phocoena phocoena*), as opposed to the ocean dolphins he encountered on his 1826 voyage in the Florida Keys; see notes to "Journal of a Sea Voyage."

2. William Frankland, born in Whitby, Yorkshire, was both the "governor" and the sole inhabitant of the roughly 1,525-acre White Head Island, Bay of Fundy. Audubon provides an extensive description of this curious nesting habit of the gulls—acquired, as Frankland informed him, because his family and egg hunters "annoyed" the birds—in his biography of the herring gull (*OB* 3 [1835], 588–89). While tree-nesting is well known for Bonaparte's gull (*Chroicocephalus philadelphia*), some observers have confirmed Audubon's experience but without attaching special significance to it. See R. M. Strong, "On the Habits and Behavior of the Herring Gull, *Larus Argentatus Pont.* (Concluded)," *Auk* 31, no. 2 (April 1914): 194–95.

3. The *Fancy* was commanded by Captain Joseph H. Claridge (Logan, *Audubon*, 97). Head Harbour Bay is on the northern tip of Campobello Island, in southwestern New Brunswick, at the entrance to Passamaquoddy Bay.

4. Audubon's "rosy Grosbeak" is probably the rose breasted grosbeak, *Pheucticus ludovicianus* (Havell 127).

5. "Point Lepreaux Harbour" is Point Lepreau, New Brunswick, at the eastern limit of Maces Bay (see fig. 33).

6. The trip to Point Lepreau lasted from May 9 to 14, 1833. Similar to Audubon but with more experience, Manly Hardy later wrote in great detail of the skill of Penobscot and Passamaquoddy men hunting porpoise with a gun in small sailing canoes in the 1860s; see "Hunting the Porpoise," *Field and Stream* 9, no. 2 (June 1904): 109–12. The Passamaquoddy also hunted larger whales into the early twentieth century, such as killer whales and finbacks. The Passamaquoddy and Penobscot tribes, since the 1980s, have managed to get some of their ancestral land and waters returned to them.

7. The Bay of Fundy has the greatest tidal range in the world. The tide is particularly extreme near Minas Basin and Windsor on the Nova Scotia side, which has a known tidal range of up to fifty-three feet (not quite the nearly sixty-five feet Audubon suggests here). The energy produced by the tides stirs up nutrients from the floor of the ocean, providing an abundant food supply for birds and fish.

8. Writing to his wife, Lucy, on the afternoon of his return to Eastport, Audubon praised the crew of the *Fancy*: "depend upon it the Yankees are the Lads for the Ocean"; May 14, 1833, in *The Letters of John James Audubon, 1826–40*, ed. Howard Corning (1930; New York: Kraus Reprint, 1969), 1:220.

COMMON GANNET

ON the morning of the 14th of June 1833, the white sails of the Ripley were spread before a propitious breeze, and onward she might be seen gaily wending her way toward the shores of Labrador. We had well explored the Magdeleine Islands, and were anxious to visit the Great Gannet Rock, where, according to our pilot, the birds from which it derives its name bred. For several days I had observed numerous files proceeding northward, and marked their mode of flight while thus travelling. As our bark dashed through the heaving billows, my anxiety to reach the desired spot increased. At length, about ten o'clock, we discerned at a distance a white speck, which our pilot assured us was the celebrated rock of our wishes [fig. 29]. After a while I could distinctly see its top from the deck, and thought that it was still covered with snow several feet deep. As we approached it, I imagined that the atmosphere around was filled with flakes, but on my turning to the pilot, who smiled at my simplicity, I was assured that nothing was in sight but the Gannets [plate 12] and their island home. I rubbed my eyes, took up my glass, and saw that the strange dimness of the air before us was caused by the innu-

FIGURE 29. Gannet Rock. Robert Havell Jr. after John James Audubon, "Gannet" (northern gannet), 1836 (detail). Aquatint engraving. *The Birds of America*, plate 326. Courtesy of the Lilly Library.

merable birds, whose white bodies and black-tipped pinions produced a blended tint of light-grey. When we had advanced to within half a mile, this magnificent veil of floating Gannets was easily seen, now shooting upwards, as if intent on reaching the sky, then descending as if to join the feathered masses below, and again diverging toward either side and sweeping over the surface of the ocean. The Ripley now partially furled her sails, and lay to, when all on board were eager to scale the abrupt sides of the mountain isle, and satisfy their curiosity.[1]

Judge, Reader, of our disappointment. The weather, which hitherto had been beautiful, suddenly changed, and we were assailed by a fearful storm. However, the whale-boat was hoisted over, and manned by four sturdy "down-easters," along with THOMAS LINCOLN and my son. I remained on board the Ripley, and commenced my distant observations, which I shall relate in due time.[2]

An hour has elapsed; the boat, which had been hid from our sight, is now in view; the waves run high, and all around looks dismal. See what exertions the rowers make; it blows a hurricane, and each successive billow seems destined to overwhelm their fragile bark. My anxiety is intense, as you may imagine; in the midst of my friends and the crew I watch every movement of the boat, now balanced on the very crest of a rolling and foaming wave, now sunk far into the deep trough. We see how eagerly yet calmly they pull. My son stands erect, steering with a long oar, and LINCOLN is bailing the water which is gaining on him, for the spray ever and anon dashes over the bow. But they draw near, a rope is thrown and caught, the whale-boat is hauled close under our lee-board; in a moment more all are safe on deck, the helm round, the schooner to, and away under bare poles she scuds toward Labrador.

THOMAS LINCOLN and my son were much exhausted, and the sailors required a double allowance of grog. A quantity of eggs of various kinds, and several birds, had been procured, for wherever sufficient room for a gannet's nest was not afforded on the rock, one or two Guillemots occupied the spot, and on the ledges below the Kittiwakes lay thick like snow-flakes. The discharging of their guns produced no other effect than to cause the birds killed or severely wounded to fall into the water, for the cries of the countless multitudes drowned every other noise. The party had their clothes smeared with the nauseous excrements of hundreds of gannets and other birds, which in shooting off from their nests caused numerous eggs to fall, of which some were procured entire. The confusion on and around the rock was represented as baffling all description; and as we gazed on the mass now gradually fading on our sight, we all judged it well worth the while to cross the ocean to see such a sight. But yet it was in some measure a painful sight to me, for I had not been able to land on this great breeding place, of which, however, I here present a description given by our pilot Mr GODWIN.[3]

"The top of the main rock is a quarter of a mile wide, from north to south, but narrower in the other direction. Its elevation is estimated at about four hundred feet. It stands in Lat. 47° 52'. The surf beats its base with great violence, unless after a long calm, and it is extremely difficult to land upon it, and still more so to ascend to the top or platform. The only point on which a boat may be landed lies on the south side, and the moment the boat strikes it must be hauled dry on the rocks. The whole surface of the upper platform is closely covered with nests, placed about two feet asunder, and in such regular order that a person may see between the lines, which run north and south, as if looking along the furrows of a deeply ploughed field. The Labrador fishermen and others who annually visit this extraordinary resort of the Gannets, for the purpose of procuring their flesh to bait their cod-fish hooks, ascend armed with heavy short clubs, in parties of eight, ten, or more, and at once begin their work of destruction. At sight of these unwelcome intruders, the affrighted birds rise on wing with a noise like thunder, and fly off in such a hurried and confused manner as to impede each other's progress, by which thousands are forced downwards, and accumulate into a bank many feet high; the men beating and killing them with their clubs until fatigued, or satisfied with the number they have slain." Here Mr GODWIN assured us that he had visited the Gannet Rock ten seasons in succession, for the purpose just mentioned, and added, that on one of these occasions, "six men had destroyed five hundred and forty Gannets in about an hour, after which the party rested a while, and until most of the living birds had left their immediate neighbourhood, for all around them, beyond the distance of about a hundred yards, thousands of Gannets were yet sitting on their nests, and the air was filled with multitudes of others. The dead birds are now roughly skinned, and the flesh of the breast cut up in pieces of different sizes, which will keep good for bait about a fortnight or three weeks. So great is the destruction of these birds for the purpose mentioned, that the quantity of their flesh so procured supplies with bait upwards of forty boats, which lie fishing close to the Island of Brion each season. By the 20th of May the rock is covered with birds on their nests and eggs, and about a month afterwards the young are hatched. The earth is scratched by the birds for a few inches deep, and the edges surrounded by sea-weeds and other rubbish, to the height of eight or ten inches, tolerably well matted together. Each female Gannet lays a single egg, which is pure white, but not larger than a good-sized hen's egg. When the young are hatched, they are bluish-black, and for a fortnight or more their skin is not unlike that of the common dog-fish. They gradually become downy and white, and when five or six weeks old look like great lumps of carded wool."[4]

I was well pleased with this plain statement of our pilot, as I had with my glass observed the regularity of the lines of nests, and seen many of the birds digging the earth with their strong bills, while hundreds of them were carrying quantities of that long sea-weed called Eel-grass, which they seem to bring from towards the Magdeleine Islands. While the Ripley lay to near the rock, thousands of the Gannets constantly flew over our heads; and although I shot at and brought several to the water, neither the reports nor the sight of their dead companions seemed to make any impression on them.

On weighing several of the Gannets brought on board, I found them to average rather more than seven pounds; but Mr GODWIN assured me that when the young birds are almost ready to fly, they weigh eight and sometimes nine pounds. This I afterwards ascertained to be true, and I account for the difference exhibited at this period by the young birds, by the great profusion of food with which their parents supply them, regardless in a great measure of their own wants. The Pilot further told me that the stench on the summit of the rock was insupportable, covered as it is during the breeding season, and after the first visits of the fishermen, with the remains of carcasses of old and young birds, broken and rotten eggs, excrements, and multitudes of fishes. He added that the Gannets, although cowardly birds, at times stand and await the approach of a man, with open bill, and strike furious and dangerous blows. Let me now, Reader, assure you that unless you had seen the sight witnessed by my party and myself that day, you could not form a correct idea of the impression it has to this moment left on my mind.

The extent of the southward migration of the Gannet, after it has reared its young, is far greater perhaps than has hitherto been supposed. I have frequently seen it on the Gulf of Mexico, in the latter part of autumn and in winter; and a few were met with, in the course of my last expedition, as far as the entrance of the Sabine River into the Bay of Mexico. Being entirely a maritime species, it never proceeds inland, unless forced by violent gales, which have produced a few such instances in Nova Scotia and the State of Maine, as well as the Floridas, where I saw one that had been found dead in the woods two days after a furious hurricane. The greater number of the birds of this species seen in these warm latitudes during winter are young of that or the preceding year. My friend JOHN BACHMAN has informed me that during one of his visits to the Sea Islands off the shores of South Carolina, on the 2d of July 1836, he observed a flock of Gannets of from fifty to an hundred, all of the colouring of the one in my plate, and which was a bird in its first winter plumage. They were seen during several days on and about Cole's Island, at times on the sands, at others among the rolling breakers. He also mentions having heard Mr GILES, an acquaintance of his, who knows much about birds, say, that in the course of the preceding summer he had seen a pair of Gannets going to, and returning from, a nest in a tree! This is in accordance with the report of Captain NAPOLEON COSTE, who commanded the United States Revenue Cutter, the Campbell, placed at my disposal during my visit to the Texas, and who was Lieutenant as well as Pilot of the Marion. He stated that he had found a breeding place on the coast of Georgia, occupied by a flock of old, and therefore White Gannets, the nests of all of which were placed upon trees. No one can be greatly surprised at these reports, who knows, as I do, that the Brown Gannet, *Sula fusca*, breeds both on trees and on dry elevated sand bars. During winter months I have generally observed single birds at some considerable distance from the shore out at sea, sometimes indeed beyond what mariners call soundings, but rarely young ones, they generally keeping much nearer to the shores, and procuring their food in shallower water.[5]

The flight of the Gannet is powerful, well sustained, and at times extremely elegant. While travelling, whether in fine or foul weather, they fly low over the surface of the water, flapping their wings thirty or forty times in succession, in the manner of the Ibis and the Brown Pelican, and then sailing about an equal distance, with the wings at right angles to the body, and the neck extended forwards. But, Reader, to judge of the elegance of this bird while on wing, I would advise you to gaze on it from the deck of any of our packet ships, when her commander has first communicated the joyful news that you are less than three hundred miles from the nearest shore, whether it be that of merry England or of my own beloved country. You would then see the powerful fisher, on well-spread pinions, and high over the water, glide silently along, surveying each swelling wave below, and coursing with so much ease and buoyancy as to tempt you to think that had you been furnished with equal powers of flight, you might perform a journey of eighty or ninety miles without the slightest fatigue in a single hour. But perhaps at the very moment when these thoughts have crossed your mind, as they many times have crossed mine on such occasions, they are suddenly checked by the action of the bird, which, intent on filling its empty stomach, and heedless of your fancies, plunges headlong through the air, with the speed of a meteor, and instantaneously snatches the fish which its keen sight had discovered from on high. Now perchance you may see the snow-white bird sit buoyantly for a while on the bosom of its beloved element, either munching its prey, or swallowing it at once. Or perhaps, if disappointed in its attempt, you will see it rise by continued flappings, shaking its tail sideways the while, and snugly covering its broad webbed feet among the under coverts of that useful rudder, after which it proceeds in a straight course, until its wings being well supplied by the flowing air, it gradually ascends to its former height, and commences its search anew.

In severe windy weather, I have seen the Gannet propelling itself against the gale by sweeps of considerable extent, placing its body almost sideways or obliquely, and thus alternately, in the manner of Petrels and Guillemots; and I have thought that the bird then moved with more velocity than at any other time, except when plunging after its prey. Persons who have seen it while engaged in procuring food, must, like myself, have been surprised when they have read in books that Gannets "are never known to dive," and yet are assured that they "have been taken by a fish fastened to a board sunk to the depth of two fathoms, in which case the neck has either been found dislocated, or the bill firmly fixed in the wood." With such statements before him, one might think that his own vision had been defective, had he not been careful to note down at once the result of his observations. And as this is a matter of habit with me, I will offer you mine, good Reader, not caring one jot for what has been said to you before on the subject.[6]

I have seen the Gannet plunge, and afterwards remain under the surface of the water for at least one minute at a time. On one occasion of this kind, I shot one just as it emerged, and which held a fish firmly in its bill, and had two others half-way down its throat. This has induced me to believe that it sometimes follows its prey in the water, and seizes several fishes in succession. At other times I have observed the Gannet plunge amidst a shoal of launces so as scarcely to enter the water, and afterwards follow them, swimming, or as it were running, on the water, with its wings extended upwards, and striking to the right and left until it was satiated. While on the Gulf of Mexico, I wounded a Gannet, which, on falling to the water, swam so fast before the boat, that we rowed about a quarter of a mile before we reached it, when it suddenly turned towards us, opened its bill, as if intent on defending itself, but was killed with the stroke of an oar by one of the sailors. When shot at without even being touched, these birds often disgorge their food in the manner of Vultures; and this they always do when wounded, if their stomach and gullet happen to be full. Sometimes, after being wounded in the wings, they will float and allow you to take them, without making any attempt to escape. Nay, my young friend, GEORGE C. SHATTUCK, M.D., of Boston, while with me at Labrador, caught one which he found walking amongst a great number of Guillemots, on a low and rocky island.[7]

When they are on their favourite breeding rocks, and about to fly, they elevate their head, throw it backward, open the bill, and emit a loud prolonged cry, before launching themselves into the air, in doing which they waddle a few paces with their wings partially extended. After starting, their first motion is greatly inclined downwards, but they presently recover, and seem to support themselves with ease. When they are twenty or thirty yards off, you observe them shaking the tail sideways, and then hiding their feet among the under coverts of the tail. At other times they suddenly open their feet, moving them as if for the purpose of grasping some object below, in the same manner as some hawks, but only for a few moments, when again the tail is shaken, and the feet hidden as before. They beat their wings and sail alternately, even when flying around their breeding places.

On the ground the movements of the Gannet are exceedingly awkward, and it marches with hampered steps, assisting itself with the wings, or keeping them partially open, to prevent its falling. Their walk, indeed, is merely a hobble. When the sun shines, they are fond of opening their wings and beating them in the manner of Cormorants, shaking the head meanwhile rather violently, and emitting their usual uncouth guttural notes of *cara, karew, karow*. You may well imagine the effect of a concert performed by all the Gannets congregated for the purpose of breeding on such a rock as that in the Gulf of St Lawrence, where, amidst the uproar produced by the repetition of these notes, you now and then distinguish the loud and continued wolfish howling-like sounds of those about to fly off.

The newly-finished nest of this bird is fully two feet high, and quite as broad externally. It is composed of seaweeds and maritime grasses, the former being at times brought from considerable distances. Thus, the Gannets breeding on the rocks in the Gulf of St Lawrence, carry weeds from the Magdeleine Islands, which are about thirty miles distant. The grasses are pulled or dug up from the surface of the breeding place itself, often in great clods consisting of roots and earth, and leaving holes not unlike the entrances to the burrows of the Puffin. The nests, like those of Cormorants, are enlarged or repaired annually. The single egg, of a rather elongated oval form, averages three inches and one-twelfth in length, by two inches in its greatest breadth, and is covered with an irregular roughish coating of white calcareous matter, which on being scraped off, leaves exposed the pale greenish-blue tint of the under layer.

The birds usually reach the rock when already paired, in files often of hundreds, and are soon seen billing in the manner of Cormorants, and copulating on the rocks, but never, like the birds just mentioned, on the water, as some have supposed. The period of their arrival at their breeding grounds appears to depend much on the latitude of the place; for, on the Bass Rock, in the Firth of Forth, which I had the pleasure of visiting in the agreeable company of my learned friend WILLIAM MACGILLIVRAY and his son, on the 19th of August 1835, the Gannets are first seen in February, whereas in the Gulf of St Lawrence they rarely reach the Great Rock until the middle of April or beginning of May; and at Chateau Beau in the Straits of Belle Isle, not until a fortnight or three weeks later. Like the members of most large communities, the Gannets, though so truly gregarious at this season, shew a considerable degree of animosity towards their more immediate neighbours as soon as incubation commences. A lazy bird perhaps, finding it easier to rob the nest of its friend of weeds and sods, than to convey them from some distant place, seizes some, on which the other resents the injury, and some well-directed thrusts of their strong bills are made, in open day and in full view of the assembled sitters, who rarely fail to look on with interest, and pass the news from one to another, until all are apprized of the quarrel. The time however passes on. The patient mother, to lend more warmth to her only egg, plucks a few of the feathers from some distance beneath her breast. In sunny weather, she expands those of her upper parts, and passing her bill along their roots, destroys the vile insects that lurk there.

Should a boisterous gale or a thick cold fog mar the beauty of the day, she gathers her apparel around her, and shrinks deeper into her bed; and should it rain, she places her body so as to prevent the inundation of her household. How happy, Reader, must she be when now and then her keen eyes distinguish in the crowd her affectionate mate, as he returns from the chase, with loaded bill, and has already marked her among the thousand beauties all equally anxious for the arrival of their lords! Now by her side he alights as gently as is in his nature, presents her with a welcome repast, talks perhaps cheeringly to her, and again opening his broad wings departs in search of a shoal of herrings. At length, the oval chest opens, and out crawls the tender young; but lo! the little thing is black. What a strange contrast to the almost pure white of the parent! Yet the mother loves it, with all the tenderness of other mothers. She has anxiously expected its appearance, and at once she nurses it with care; but so tender is it that she prefers waiting a while before she feeds it. The time however soon comes, and with exceeding care she provides some well macerated morsels which she drops into its open mouth; so well prepared are they that there is no instance on record of a Gannet, even of that tender age, having suffered from dyspepsia or indigestion.[8]

The male Gannet assists in incubating, though he sits less assiduously than the female; and, on such occasions, the free bird supplies the other with food. The sight of the young Gannet just after birth might not please the eye of many, for it is then quite naked, and of a deep bluish-black, much resembling a young Cormorant. Its abdomen is extremely large, its neck thin, its head large, its eyes as yet sightless, its wings but slightly developed. When you look at it three weeks afterwards, it has grown much, and almost entirely changed its colour, for, now, with the exception of certain parts of the neck, the short thighs, and the belly, it is covered with yellowish soft and thick down. In this state it looks perhaps as uncouth as at first, but it grows so rapidly that at the end of three weeks more, you find its downy coat patched with feathers in the most picturesque manner imaginable. Looking around you, you observe that all the young are not of the same growth; for all the Gannets do not lay on the same day, and probably all the young are not equally supplied with food. At this period, the great eyrie looks as if all its parts had become common property; the nests, which were once well fashioned are trampled down; the young birds stand everywhere or anywhere; lazy-looking creatures they are, and with an appearance of non-chalance which I have never observed in any other species of bird, and which would lead you to think that they care as little about the present as the future. Now the old birds are freed of part of their cares, they drop such fish as they have obtained by the side of their young, and, like Cormorants, Pelicans, or Herons, seldom bring a supply oftener than once a-day. Strange to say, the young birds at this period do not appear to pay the least attention to the old ones, which occasionally alight near them, and drop fish for them to feed upon.

Gannets do not feed, as some have supposed, and as many have believed, on herring only; for I have found in their stomachs codlings eight inches in length, as well as very large American mackerels, which, by the way, are quite different from those so abundantly met with on the coasts of Europe.

The young never leave the spot on which they have been reared until they are well able to fly, when they separate from the old birds, and do not rejoin them until at least a year after. Although I have in a few instances found individuals yet patched with dark-grey spots, and with most of their primary quills still black, I am confident that it is not until the end of two years that they acquire their full plumage. I have seen some with one wing almost pure black, and the tail of that colour also; others with the tail only black; and several with pure black feathers interspersed among the general white plumage.

I know of no other bird that has so few formidable enemies as the Gannet. Not one of the species of Lestris with which I am acquainted, ever attempts to molest it; and, although I have seen the Frigate Pelican in quest of food within a short distance of it, I never saw it offer injury. The insular rocks on which it breeds are of course inaccessible to quadrupeds. The only animals, so far as I know, that feed on the eggs or young, are the *Larus marinus* and *Larus glaucus*. It is said that the Skua, *Lestris Catarractes*, sometimes pursues the Gannets, but that species does not exist in North America; and I am inclined to doubt the truth of this statement, for I have never seen a Lestris of any kind attack a bird equal to itself in size and strength.[9]

Soon after the young Gannets are able to fly, all the birds of the species leave the breeding place, and absent themselves until the following season. While at Newfoundland, I was told that the English and French fishermen who inhabit that country salt young Gannets for winter provision, as is done in Scotland; but I saw none there. In my estimation, the flesh of this bird is so bad that, as long as any other can be procured, it ought to be rejected.

It is a curious fact, that the Gannets often procure mackerels or herrings four or five weeks before the fishermen fall in with them on our coast; but this is easily explained by their extensive wanderings. Although this bird is easily kept in captivity, it is far from being a pleasant pet. Its ordure is abundant, disagreeable to the eye as well as the nose; its gait is awkward; and even its pale owl-like eyes glare on you with an unpleasant expression. Add to this, the expense of its food, and I can easily conceive that you will not give it a place in your aviary, unless for the mere amusement of seeing it catch the food thrown to it, which it does like a dog.

The feathers of the lower parts of the Gannet differ from those of most other birds, in being extremely convex externally, which gives the bird the appearance of being covered beneath with light shell-work, exceedingly difficult to be represented in a drawing.[10]

Notes

1. First published in *OB* 4 (1838), 223–40. Audubon's "Common Gannet," or just "Gannet" (plate 12; Havell 326;), is now known as the northern gannet (*Morus bassanus*). For an introduction to the *Ripley* and this voyage to Labrador, see the headnote to the Labrador journal. Gannet Rock consists of two islets, Rocher aux Oiseaux and the associated Rochers aux Margaulx (which in turns consist of separate rocks), all collectively known as Bird Rocks (see figs. 29, 33, 35). Located about twelve miles northeast of the Magdalen Islands archipelago, these sandstone islets, about half a mile apart, emerge from the sea at the edge of the Laurentian channel in the middle of the Gulf of St. Lawrence. Northern gannets are considered species of Least Concern today (IUCN, 2018). See Environment and Climate Change Canada–Quebec Region, "Bird Rocks Migratory Bird Sanctuary" (accessed December 15, 2020), https://www.canada.ca/en/environment-climate-change/services/migratory-bird-sanctuaries/locations/bird-rocks.html; John W. Chardine, Jean-François Rail, and Sabina Wilhelm, *Journal of Field Ornithology* 84, no. 2 (2013): 190.

2. Thomas ("Tom") Lincoln (1812–1883) was a farmer and naturalist, son of Judge Theodore Lincoln, of Dennysville, near Eastport, Maine, at whose house Audubon spent several weeks in the later summer of 1832. Lincoln accompanied Audubon on his 1833 expedition to Labrador. Audubon named the "Lincoln Finch" (Lincoln's sparrow, *Melospiza lincolnii*) after him.

3. Godwin, a Nova Scotia native, had worked as a commercial egger collecting seabird eggs from breeding communities along the Labrador coast, selling his spoils in markets in New-

foundland and Nova Scotia. His navigational skills, or lack thereof, turned out to be a persistent problem during the Labrador trip.

4. Brion (Bryon) is northeast of the islands in the Magdalen archipelago (see fig. 35). Using Godwin's estimates as represented in this entry in *Ornithological Biography*, in 1943 Fisher and Vevers calculated there might have been between 100,000 and 125,000 pairs of northern gannets on Bird Rocks in the 1830s, which would have made this by far the largest northern gannet colony in the world at the time. A century later, there were only about 1,250 pairs. As of 2009, however, Bird Rocks, now a protected sanctuary, hosts colonies numbering over 30,000 pairs and increasing, with space to grow, even considering significant erosion since Audubon's day. James Fisher and H. G. Vevers, "The Breeding Distribution, History and Population of the North Atlantic Gannet (*Sula bassana*), Part 1, A History of the Gannet's Colonies, and the Census in 1939," *Journal of Animal Ecology* 12, no. 2 (November 1943): 202, 204; Jean-François Rail, Louise Champoux, Raphaël A. Lavoie, and Gilles Chapdelaine, "Monitoring of the Population and Contamination of the Northern Gannet in Quebec, 1966–2009," Canadian Wildlife Service, Technical Report Series no. 528 (2013), 14, 16, 17.

5. Audubon's "Brown Gannet," which he elsewhere calls "Booby Gannet" (Havell 207), is now the brown booby, *Sula leucogaster*. Napoleon Coste had sailed earlier with Audubon aboard the *Marion* (see notes to first "Florida Keys" essay). The US revenue cutter *Campbell* (1834), only 40 tons displacement, with two cannon, would be active in the Second Seminole War soon after this trip and then was sold in 1839 in Baltimore.

6. The statement that gannets "are never known to dive" is from Prideaux John Selby, *Illustrations of British Ornithology*, vol. 2, *Water-Birds* (Edinburgh: W. H. Lizars, 1833), 454, 458. The illustrations for the work of Selby (1788–1867), issued in ten parts over a period of thirteen years (1821–1834), were etched by Audubon's first engraver, William Home Lizars. They were also of double elephant folio size, like Audubon's; only very large species were reduced in size.

7. George Cheyne Shattuck (1813–1893), a member of Audubon's Labrador team, acquired his MD from Harvard in 1835. He was a visiting physician at Massachusetts General Hospital from 1849 to 1855, when he was appointed professor of clinical medicine at Harvard, and in 1859 became the Hersey Professor of Theory and Practice of Physick and dean of the Faculty of Medicine in 1864. He also founded St. Paul's School in Concord, New Hampshire. Ornithologists today confirm that gannets definitely plunge-dive and capture fish underneath the water.

8. William MacGillivray was Audubon's main collaborator on *Ornithological Biography*. His son John MacGillivray (1821–1867) became a naturalist, too, notable for his participation in the voyages of HMS *Rattlesnake*. Even today, Bass Rock off the east coast of Scotland has one of the largest breeding colonies of gannets worldwide. At the time of Audubon's visit, up to two thousand birds were taken annually for food and feathers; John Chalmers, *Audubon in Edinburgh and His Scottish Associates* (Edinburgh: National Museums of Scotland/Royal College of Surgeons, 2003), 166.

9. Audubon's "Lestris" are usually jaegers. "Frigate Pelicans" are frigatebirds (see "The Frigate Pelican"; plate 3). *Larus marinus* is the great black-backed gull (see ""Black Backed Gull"; plate 14). *Larus glaucus* is Audubon's "Burgomaster Gull" (Havell 396), now more commonly known as the glaucous gull, *Larus hyperboreus*. The "Skua," or *Lestris catarractes*, now the great skua (*Stercorarius skua*), appears thus in C. J. Temminck, *Manuel d'Ornithologie*, pt. 2, 2nd ed. (Paris: Chez Gabriel Dufour, 1820), 792–93. The great skua now breeds mainly in Iceland and on islands in the Atlantic north of Great Britain but does, according to modern ornithologists, range into the waters of New England, Atlantic Canada, and throughout the

open North Atlantic. (The similar-looking South Polar skua, *Stercorarius maccormicki*, is also found occasionally on the North American East and West Coasts).

10. Ornithologists who study gannets on Bird Rocks today confirm much of Audubon and Godwin's observations, notably the regularity of the nest placement, the weight of the chicks, and that adult plumage isn't acquired until years after fledging. The nest height, however, which Audubon did not see for himself, is more often a third the size described (which Godwin observed correctly). Males provide nest material but not food to the female; "yellowish" plumage in chicks was more likely grime on the white down. And gannets do not spread their wings to dry them, as do cormorants; this behavior, which can look similar, is more likely about showing ownership over the nest. The greens, blues, and grays in Audubon's painting of the eyes and facial skin of the gannets are not exactly accurate to life, which might be due to the bird's rapid changes after death, Audubon's artistic license, and/or oxidation of the paint he used over time. Jean-François Rail, personal communications, October 2 and November 16, 2020, and Roberta J. M. Olson, personal communication, October 22, 2020.

THE EGGERS OF LABRADOR

THE distinctive appellation of Eggers is given to certain persons who follow, principally or exclusively, the avocation of procuring the eggs of wild birds, with the view of disposing of them at some distant port. Their great object is to plunder every nest, whenever they can find it, no matter where, and at whatever risk. They are the pest of the feathered tribes, and their brutal propensity to destroy the poor creatures after they have robbed them, is abundantly gratified whenever an opportunity presents itself.[1]

Much had been said to me respecting these destructive pirates before I visited the coast of Labrador, but I could not entirely credit all their cruelties until I had actually witnessed their proceedings, which were such as to inspire no small degree of horror. But you shall judge for yourself.

See yon shallop shyly sailing along;—she sneaks like a thief, wishing as it were to shun the very light of heaven. Under the lea of every rocky isle some one at the tiller steers her course. Were his trade an honest one, he would not think of hiding his back behind the terrific rocks that seem to have been placed there as a resort to the myriads of birds that annually visit this desolate region of the earth, for the purpose of rearing young, at a distance from all disturbers of their peace. How unlike the open, the bold, the honest mariner, whose face needs no mask, who scorns to skulk under any circumstances! The vessel herself is a shabby thing:—her sails are patched with stolen pieces of better canvass, the owners of which have probably been stranded on some inhospitable coast, and have been plundered, perhaps murdered, by the wretches before us. Look at her again!—Her sides are neither painted, nor even pitched; no—they are daubed over, plastered and patched with stripes of seal-skins, laid along the seams. Her deck has never been washed or sanded, her hold—for no cabin has she,—though at present empty, sends forth an odour pestilential as that of a charnel-house. The crew, eight in number, lie sleeping at the foot of their tottering mast, regardless of the repairs needed in every part of her rigging. But see! she scuds along, and as I suspect her crew to be bent on the commission of some evil deed, let us follow her to the first harbour.[2]

There rides the filthy thing! The afternoon is half over. Her crew have thrown their boat overboard; they enter and seat themselves, each with a rusty gun. One of them skulls the skiff towards an island for a century past the breeding place of myriads of Guillemots, which are now to be laid under contribution. At the approach of the vile thieves, clouds of birds rise from the rock and fill the air around, wheeling and screaming over their enemies. Yet thousands remain in an erect posture, each covering its single egg, the hope of both parents. The reports of several muskets loaded with heavy shot are now heard, while several dead and wounded birds fall heavily on the rock or into the water. Instantly all the sitting birds rise and fly off affrighted to their companions above, and hover in dismay over their assassins, who walk forward exultingly, and with their shouts mingling oaths and execrations. Look at them! See how they crush the chick within its shell, how they trample on every egg in their way with their huge and clumsy boots. Onward they go, and when they leave the isle, not an egg that they can find is left entire. The dead birds they collect and carry to their boat. Now they have regained their filthy shallop; they strip the birds by a single jerk of their feathery apparel, while the flesh is yet warm, and throw them on some coals, where in a short time they are broiled. The rum is produced when the guillemots are fit for eating, and after stuffing themselves with this oily fare, and enjoying the pleasure of beastly intoxication, over they tumble on the deck of their crazed craft, where they pass the short hours of night in turbid slumber.

The sun now rises above the snow-clad summit of the eastern mount. "Sweet is the breath of morn" even in this desolate land. The gay Bunting erects his white crest, and gives utterance to the joy he feels in the presence of his brooding mate. The Willow Grous on the rock crows his challenge aloud. Each floweret, chilled by the night air, expands its pure petals; the gentle breeze shakes from the blades of grass the heavy dewdrops. On the Guillemot Isle the birds have again settled, and now renew their loves. Startled by the light of day, one of the Eggers springs on his feet and rouses his companions, who stare around them for a while, endeavouring to recollect their senses. Mark them, as with clumsy fingers they clear their drowsy eyes! Slowly they rise on their feet. See how the filthy lubbers stretch out their arms and yawn; you shrink back, for verily "that throat might frighten a shark."[3]

But the master, soon recollecting that so many eggs are worth a dollar or a crown, casts his eye towards the rock, marks the day in his memory, and gives orders to depart. The light breeze enables them to reach another harbour a few miles distant, one which, like the last, lies concealed from the ocean by some other rocky isle. Arrived there, they re-act the scene of yesterday, crushing every egg they can find. For a week each night is passed in drunkenness and brawls, until, having reached the last breeding place on the coast, they return, touch at every isle in succession, shoot as many birds as they need, collect the fresh eggs, and lay in a cargo. At every step each ruffian picks up an egg so beautiful that any man with a feeling heart would pause to consider the motive which could induce him to carry it off. But nothing of this sort occurs to the Egger, who gathers and gathers, until he has swept the rock bare. The dollars alone chink in his sordid mind, and he assiduously plies the trade which no man would ply who had the talents and industry to procure subsistence by honourable means.

With a bark nearly half filled with fresh eggs they proceed to the principal rock, that on which they first landed. But what is their surprise when they find others there helping themselves as industriously as they can! In boiling rage they charge their guns, and ply their oars. Landing on the rock, they run up to the Eggers, who, like themselves, are desperadoes. The first question is a discharge of musketry, the answer another. Now, man to man, they fight like tigers. One is carried to his boat with a fractured skull, another limps with a shot in his leg, and a third feels how many of his teeth have been driven through the hole in his cheek. At last, however, the quarrel is settled; the booty is to be equally divided; and now see them all drinking together. Oaths and curses and filthy jokes are all that you hear; but see, stuffed with food, and reeling with drink, down they drop one by one; groans and execrations from the wounded mingle with the snorings of the heavy sleepers. There let the brutes lie.

Again it is dawn, but no one stirs. The sun is high; one by one they open their heavy eyes, stretch their limbs, yawn, and raise themselves from the deck. But see, here comes a goodly company. A hundred honest fishermen, who for months past have fed on salt meat, have felt a desire to procure some eggs. Gallantly their boats advance, impelled by the regular pull of their long oars. Each buoyant bark displays the flag of its nation. No weapons do they bring, nor any thing that can be used as such save their oars and fists. Cleanly clad in Sunday attire, they arrive at the desired spot, and at once prepare to ascend the rock. The Eggers, now numbering a dozen, all armed with guns and bludgeons, bid defiance to the fishermen. A few angry words pass between the parties. One of the Eggers, still under the influence of drink, pulls his trigger, and an unfortunate sailor is seen to reel in agony. Three loud cheers fill the air. All at once rush on the malefactors; a horrid fight ensues, the result of which is, that every Egger is left on the rock beaten and bruised. Too frequently the fishermen man their boats, row to the shallops, and break every egg in the hold.

The Eggers of Labrador not only rob the birds in this cruel manner, but also the fishermen, whenever they can find an opportunity; and the quarrels they excite are numberless. While we were on the coast, none of our party ever ventured on any of the islands which these wretches call their own, without being well provided with means of defence. On one occasion, when I was present, we found two Eggers at their work of destruction. I spoke to them respecting my visit, and offered them premiums for rare birds and some of their eggs; but although they made fair promises, not one of the gang ever came near the Ripley.

These people gather all the eider down they can find; yet so inconsiderate are they, that they kill every bird that comes in their way. The eggs of Gulls, Guillemots, and Ducks are searched for with care; and the

Puffins and some other birds they massacre in vast numbers for the sake of their feathers. So constant and persevering are their depredations, that these species, which, according to the accounts of the few settlers I saw in the country, were exceedingly abundant twenty years ago, have abandoned their ancient breeding places, and removed much farther north in search of peaceful security. Scarcely, in fact, could I procure a young Guillemot before the Eggers had left the coast, nor was it until late in July that I succeeded, after the birds had laid three or four eggs each, instead of one, and when nature having been exhausted, and the season nearly spent, thousands of these birds left the country without having accomplished the purpose for which they had visited it. This war of extermination cannot last many years more. The Eggers themselves will be the first to repent the entire disappearance of the myriads of birds that made the coast of Labrador their summer residence, and unless they follow the persecuted tribes to the northward, they must renounce their trade.

Had not the British Government long once passed strict laws against these ruthless and worthless vagabonds, and laid a heavy penalty on all of them that might be caught in the act of landing their cargoes in Newfoundland or Nova Scotia, I might perhaps have been induced to have ere this humbly prayed in behalf of the feathered tribe before the authorities in England for the extinction of the wasteful if not criminal barbarity of the Eggers of Labrador.[4]

Notes

1. "The Eggers of Labrador" was first published in *OB* 3 (1835), 82–86.

2. A "shallop" was a general term for any open or partially decked oar- or sailboat, built primarily for coastal fishing.

3. Eve's words to Adam from Milton's *Paradise Lost*, book IV, lines 641–642: "Sweet is the breath of morn, her rising sweet / With charm of earliest birds." The avian reference explains why these lines would have stuck in Audubon's mind. "Willow Grous or Large Ptarmigan" (Havell 191) is now known as the willow ptarmigan (*Lagopus lagopus*). The origin of "that throat might frighten a shark" is not clear. However, Jules Verne echoed it decades later: "Ned Land did not speak, but he opened his jaws wide enough to frighten a shark." Verne, *Twenty Thousand Leagues under the Seas: A World Tour Underwater* [*Vingt mille lieues sous les mers: Tour du monde sous-marin*] (1872; Boston: Geo. M. Smith & Co., 1873), 262 (chap. 17).

4. Audubon's published text abruptly ends after "might." The rest of the sentence has been restored from the manuscript, which, riddled with corrections, might have proved too dif-

ficult for Audubon's printer to read. See Albert E. Lownes, "Notes on Audubon's Ornithological Biography," *Auk* 52, no. 1 (January 1935): 103 (Lownes was in possession of the manuscript). For an introduction to the connections with fisheries and human impacts on seabirds for food and feathers, see W. Jeffrey Bolster, *The Mortal Sea: Fishing the Atlantic in the Age of Sail* (Cambridge, MA: Belknap, 2012), 82–86.

THE FOOLISH GUILLEMOT

THIS bird [plate 13] is seldom found farther south than the entrance of the Bay of New York, where, however, it appears only during severe winters, for being one of the most hardy inhabitants of the northern regions, its constitution is such as to enable it to bear without injury the rigours of their wintry climates. About the bays near Boston the Guillemots are seen every year in greater or less numbers, and from thence to the eastward they become gradually more abundant. A very old gunner whom I employed while at Boston, during the winter of 1832–3, assured me, that when he was a young man, this species bred on many of the rocky islands about the mouth of the bay there; but that for about twenty years back none remained after the first days of April, when they departed for the north in company with the Thick-billed Guillemot, the Common Auk, the Puffin, and the Eider and King Ducks, all of which visit these bays in hard weather. In the Bay of Fundy, the Foolish Guillemot is very numerous, and is known by the name of *Murre*, which it retains among all the eggers and fishermen of Newfoundland and Labrador, where it breeds in myriads. To those countries, then, I must lead you, good Reader, as there we can with ease study the habits of these birds.[1]

Stay on the deck of the Ripley by my side this clear and cold morning. See how swiftly scuds our gallant bark, as she cuts her way through the foaming billows, now inclining to the right and again to the left. Far in the east, dark banks of low clouds indicate foul weather to the wary mariner, who watches the approach of a northern storm with anxiety. Suddenly the wind changes; but for this he has prepared; the topsails are snugged to their yards, and the rest are securely reefed. A thick fog obscures all around us. The waters suddenly checked in their former course, furiously war against those which now strike them in front. The uproar increases, the bark is tossed on every side; now a sweeping wave rushes against the bows, the vessel quivers, while down along her deck violently pour the waters, rolling from side to side, seeking for a place by which they may escape. At this moment all about you are in dismay save the Guillemots. The sea is covered with these intrepid navigators of the deep. Over each tumultuous billow they swim unconcerned on the very spray at the bow of the vessel, and plunging as if with pleasure, up they come next moment at the rudder. Others fly around in large circles, while thousands contend with the breeze, moving directly against it in long lines, towards regions unknown to all, save themselves and some other species of sea-birds.

The Guillemots pair during their migrations;—many of them at least do so. While on my way toward Labrador, they were constantly within sight, gambolling over the surface of the water, the males courting the females, and the latter receiving the caresses of their mates. These would at times rise erect in the sea, swell their throats, and emit a hoarse puffing guttural note, to which the females at once responded, with numerous noddings to their beaux. Then the pair would rise, take a round in the air, re-alight, and seal the conjugal compact; after which they flew or swam together for the season, and so closely, that among multitudes on the wing or on the waves, one might easily distinguish a mated pair.

Not far from Great Mecatina Harbour[2] lie the Murre Rocks [see fig. 33], consisting of several low islands, destitute of vegetation, and not rising high from the waters. There thousands of Guillemots annually assemble in the beginning of May, to deposit each its single egg, and raise its young. As you approach these islands, the air becomes darkened with the multitudes of birds that fly about; every square foot of the ground seems to be occupied by a Guillemot planted erect as it were on the granite rock, but carefully warming its cherished egg. All look toward the south, and if you are fronting them, the snowy white of their bodies produces a very remarkable effect, for the birds at some distance look as if they were destitute of head, so much does that part assimilate with the dark hue of the rocks on which they stand. On the other hand, if you approach them in the rear, the isle appears as if covered with a black pall.

Now land, and witness the consternation of the settlers! Each affrighted leaves its egg, hastily runs a few steps, and launches into the air in silence. Thrice around you they rapidly pass, to discover the object of your unwelcome visit. If you begin to gather their eggs, or, still worse, to break them, in order that they may lay others which you can pick up fresh, the Guillemots all alight at some distance, on the bosom of the deep, and anxiously await your departure. Eggs, green and white, and almost of every colour, are lying thick over the whole rock; the ordure of the birds mingled with feathers, with the refuse of half-hatched eggs partially sucked by rapacious Gulls, and with putrid or dried carcasses of Guillemots, produces an intolerable stench; and no sooner are all your baskets filled with eggs, than you are glad to abandon the isle to its proper owners.

On one occasion, whilst at anchor at Great Mecatina, one of our boats was sent for eggs. The sailors had eight miles to pull before reaching the Murre Islands, and yet ere many hours had elapsed, the boat was again alongside, loaded to a few inches of the gunwale, with 2500 eggs! Many of them, however, being addle, were thrown overboard. The order given to the tars had been to bring only a few dozens; but, as they said, they had forgotten!

The eggs are unaccountably large for the size of the bird, their average length being three inches and three-eighths, and their greatest breadth two inches. They are pyriform or elongated, with a slight compression towards the smaller end, which again rather swells and is rounded at the extremity. They afford excellent food, being highly nutritive and palatable, whether boiled, roasted, poached, or in omelets. The shell is rough to the touch, although not granulated. Some are of a lively verdigris colour, others of different tints, but all curiously splashed, as it were, with streaks or blotches of dark umber and brown. My opinion, however, is, that, when first dropped, they are always pure white, for on opening a good number of these birds, I found several containing an egg ready for being laid, and of a pure white colour. The shell is so firm that it does not easily break, and I have seen a quantity of these eggs very carelessly removed from a basket into a boat without being damaged. They are collected in astonishing quantities by "the eggers," to whom I have already given a character, and sent to distant markets, where they are sold at from one to three cents each.[3]

Although the Guillemots are continually harassed, their eggs being carried off as soon as they are deposited, and as long as the birds can produce them, yet they return to the same islands year after year, and, notwithstanding all the efforts of their enemies, multiply their numbers.

The Foolish Guillemot, as I have said, lays only a single egg, which is the case with the Thick-billed Guillemot also. The Razor-billed Auk lays two, and the Black Guillemot usually three. I have assured myself of these facts, not merely by observing the birds sitting on their eggs, but also by noticing the following circumstances. The Foolish Guillemot, which lays only one, plucks the feathers from its abdomen, which is thus left quite bare over a roundish space just large enough to cover its single egg. The Thick-billed Guillemot does the same. The Auk, on the contrary, forms two bare spots, separated by a ridge of feathers. The Black Guillemot, to cover her three eggs, and to warm them all at once, plucks a space bare quite across her belly. These observations were made on numerous birds of all the species mentioned. In all of them, the males incubate as well as the females, although the latter are more assiduous. When the Guillemots are disturbed, they fly off in silence. The Auks, on the contrary, emit a hoarse croaking note, which they repeat several times, as they fly away from danger. The Foolish Guillemot seldom if ever attempts to bite, whereas the Razor-billed Auk bites most severely, and clings to a person's hand until choked. The plumage of all the birds of this family is extremely compact, closely downed at the root, and difficult to be plucked. The fishermen and eggers often use their skins with the feathers on as "comforters" round their wrists. The flesh is dark, tough, and not very palatable; yet many of these birds are eaten by the fishermen and sailors.[4]

The young, which burst the egg about the beginning of July, are covered with down of a brownish-black colour. When eight or ten days old they are still downy, but have acquired considerable activity. As they grow up, they become excessively fat, and seem to be more at ease on the water than on the land. About the middle of August they follow their parents to the open sea, the latter being then seldom able to fly, having dropped their quills; and by the middle of September scarcely any of these birds are to be found on or near the islands on which they breed, although great numbers spend the winter in those latitudes.

There is no perceptible difference between the sexes as to colour, but the males are larger than the females. The white line that encircles the eye and extends toward the hind head is common to both sexes, but occurs only in old birds. Thousands of these Guillemots however breed, without having yet acquired it, there merely being indications of it to be seen on parting the feathers on the place, where there is a natural division.

The flight of the Foolish Guillemot is rapid and greatly protracted, being performed by quick and unintermitted beatings. They move through the air either singly or in bands, in the latter case seldom keeping any very regular order. Sometimes they seem to skim along the surface for miles, while at other times they fly at the height of thirty or forty yards. They are expert divers, using their wings like fins, and under water looking like winged fishes. They frequently plunge at the flash of the gun, and disappear for a considerable time. Before rising, they are obliged to run as it were on the water, fluttering for many yards before they get fairly on wing.

Those which I kept alive for weeks on board the Ripley, walked about and ran with ease, with the whole length of their tarsus touching the deck. They took leaps on chests and other objects to raise themselves, but could not fly without being elevated two or three feet, although when they are on the rocks, and can take a run of eight or ten yards, they easily rise on wing.

The islands on which the Guillemots breed on the coast of Labrador, are flattish at top, and it is there, on the bare rock, that they deposit their eggs. I saw none standing on the shelvings of high rocks, although many breed in such places in some parts of Europe. Their food consists of small fish, shrimps, and other marine animals; and they swallow some gravel also.

Notes

1. First published in *OB* 3 (1835), 142–47. Audubon's "Foolish Guillemot" (plate 13; Havell 218) is now known as the common murre (*Uria aalge*). He painted them in Labrador in June 1833; see "Journal of a Collecting Voyage," June 17. Common murres are considered a species of Least Concern (IUCN, 2018). Ornithologists today agree with Audubon that, in eastern North America, the common murre rarely winters south of Long Island; most remain between Cape Cod and Newfoundland, though there are vagrant instances of the birds having been found in Virginia. The "Thick-billed Guillemot" mentioned here is Audubon's

"Large-Billed Guillemot" (Havell 245), now the thick-billed murre (*Uria lomvia*). Another former name was Brünnich's guillemot, after the Danish zoologist Morten Thrane Brünnich.

2. Audubon published this spelling as "Macatina" in *Ornithological Biography*, and it was spelled "Mecatine" in the Lucy Audubon edition of the Labrador journal. To reduce confusion, we have changed it throughout to the more common historical and current spelling of "Mecatina."

3. Ornithologists know today that eggs pick up their markings during their final descent, from pigments supplied by the cell walls of the oviduct.

4. Ornithologists today report that "Black Guillemots" (Havell 219), *Cepphus grylle*, typically lay only one- or two-egg clutches.

THE GREAT BLACK-BACKED GULL

HIGH in the thin keen air, far above the rugged crags of the desolate shores of Labrador, proudly sails the tyrant Gull [plate 14], floating along on almost motionless wing, like an eagle in his calm and majestic flight. On widely extended pinions, he moves in large circles, constantly eyeing the objects below. Harsh and loud are his cries, and with no pleasant feeling do they come on the winged multitudes below. Now onward he sweeps, passes over each rocky bay, visits the little islands, and shoots off towards the mossy heaths, attracted perhaps by the notes of the Grous or some other birds. As he flies over each estuary, lake, or pool, the breeding birds prepare to defend their unfledged broods, or ensure their escape from the powerful beak of their remorseless spoiler. Even the shoals of the finny tribes sink deeper into the waters as he approaches; the young birds become silent in their nests or seek for safety in the clefts of the rocks; the Guillemots and Gannets dread to look up, and the other Gulls, unable to cope with the destroyer, give way as he advances. Far off among the rolling billows, he spies the carcass of some monster of the deep, and, on steady wing, glides off towards it. Alighting on the huge whale, he throws upwards his head, opens his bill, and, louder and fiercer than ever, sends his cries through the air. Leisurely he walks over the putrid mass, and now, assured that all is safe, he tears, tugs, and swallows piece after piece, until he is crammed to the throat, when he lays himself down surfeited and exhausted, to rest for a while in the feeble sheen of the northern sun. Great, however, are the powers of his stomach, and ere long the half-putrid food which vulture-like he has devoured, is digested. Like all gluttons, he loves variety, and away he flies to some well-known isle, where thousands of young birds or eggs are to be found. There, without remorse, he breaks the shells, swallows their contents, and begins leisurely to devour the helpless young. Neither the cries of the parents, nor all their attempts to drive the plunderer away, can induce him to desist until he has again satisfied his ever-craving appetite. But although tyrannical, the Great Gull is a coward, and meanly does he sneak off when he sees the Skua fly up, which, smaller as it is, yet evinces a thoughtless intrepidity, that strikes the ravenous and merciless bird with terror.[1]

If we compare this species with some other of its tribe, and mark its great size, its powerful flight, and its robust constitution, we cannot but wonder to find its range so limited during the breeding season. Few individuals are to be found northward of the entrance into Baffin's Bay, and rarely are they met with beyond this, as no mention is made of them by Dr RICHARDSON in the Fauna Boreali-Americana. Along our coast, none breed farther south than the eastern extremity of Maine. The western shores of Labrador, along an extent of about three hundred miles, afford the stations to which this species resorts during spring and summer; there it is abundant, and there it was that I studied its habits.

The farthest limits of the winter migrations of the young, so far as I have observed, are the middle portions of the eastern coast of the Floridas. While at St Augustine, in the winter of 1831, I saw several pairs keeping company with the young Brown Pelican, more as a matter of interest than of friendship, as they frequently chased them as if to force them to disgorge a portion of their earnings, acting much in the same manner as the Lestris does toward the smaller Gulls, but without any effect. They were extremely shy, alighted only on the outer edges of the outer sandbars, and could not be approached, as they regularly walked off before my party the moment any of us moved towards them, until reaching the last projecting point, they flew off, and never stopped until out of sight. At what period they left that coast I am unable to say. Some are seen scattered along our sea-shores, from the Floridas to the Middle States, there being but few old birds among them; but the species does not become abundant until beyond the eastern extremities of the Connecticut and Long Island, when their number greatly increases the farther you proceed. On the whole of that extensive range, these birds are very shy and wary, and those which are procured are merely "chance shots." They seldom advance far up the bays, unless forced to do so by severe weather or heavy gales; and although I have seen this bird on our great lakes, I do not remember having ever observed an individual on any of our eastern rivers, at a distance from the sea, whereas the *Larus argentatus* is frequently found in such places.[2]

Towards the commencement of summer, these wandering birds are seen abandoning the waters of the ocean to tarry for a while on the wild shores of Labrador, dreary and desolate to man, but to them delightful as affording all that they can desire. One by one they arrive, the older individuals first. As they view from afar the land of their birth, that moment they emit their loud cries, with all the joy a traveller feels when approaching his loved home. The males sooner or later fall in with the females of their choice, and together they proceed to some secluded sand-bar, where they fill the air with their furious laughs until the rocks echo again. Should the student of nature happen to be a distant spectator of these meetings, he too must have much enjoyment. Each male bows, moves around his mate, and no doubt discloses to her the ardour of his love. Matters are managed to the satisfaction of all parties, yet day after day for a while, at the retreat of the waters, they meet as if by mutual agreement. Now you see them dressing their plumage, now partially expanding their wings to the sun; some lay themselves comfortably down on the sand, while others, supported by one foot, stand side by side. The waters again advance, and the Gulls all move off in search of food. At length the time has arrived; small parties of a few pairs fly towards the desert isles. Some remain in the nearest to prepare their nests, the rest proceed, until each pair has found a suitable retreat, and before a fortnight has elapsed, incubation has commenced.

The nest of this species is usually placed on the bare rock of some low island, sometimes beneath a projecting shelf, sometimes in a wide fissure. In Labrador it is formed of moss and seaweeds carefully arranged, and has a diameter of about two feet, being raised on the edges to the height of five or six inches, but seldom more than two inches thick in the centre, where feathers, dry grass, and other materials are added. The eggs are three, and in no instance have I found more. They are two inches and seven-eighths in length, by two inches and one-eighth in breadth, broadly ovate, rough but not granulated, of a pale earthy greenish-grey colour, irregularly blotched and spotted with brownish-black, dark umber, and dull purple. Like those of most other Gulls, they afford good eating. This species lays from the middle of May to that of June, and raises only one brood in the season. The birds never leave their eggs for any length of time, until the young make their appearance. Both sexes incubate, the sitting bird being supplied with food by the other. During the first week, the young are fed by having their supplies disgorged into their bill, but when they have attained some size, the food is dropped beside or before them. When they are approached by man, they walk with considerable speed towards some hiding place, or to the nearest projecting ledge, beneath which they squat. When five or six weeks old, they take to the water, to ensure their escape, and swim with great buoyancy. If caught, they cry in the manner of their parents. On the 18th of June, several small ones were procured and placed on the deck of the Ripley, where they walked with ease and picked up the food thrown to them. As soon as one was about to swallow its portion, another would run up, seize it, tug at it, and if stronger, carry it off and devour it. On the 23d of that month, two individuals, several weeks old, and partly fledged, were also brought on board. Their notes, although feeble, perfectly resembled those of their parents. They ate greedily of every thing that was offered to them. When fatigued they sat with their tarsi placed on the ground and extended forward, in the manner of all the Herons, which gave them a very ludicrous appearance. Ere a month had elapsed, they appeared to have formed a complete acquaintance with the cook and several of the sailors, had become quite fat, and conducted themselves much like Vultures, for if a dead Duck, or even a Gull of their own species, were thrown to them, they would tear it in pieces, drink the blood, and swallow the flesh in large morsels, each trying to rob the others of what they had torn from the carcass. They never drank water, but not unfrequently washed the blood and filth from their bills, by immersing them and then shaking the head violently. These birds were fed until they were nearly able to fly. Now and then, the sailors would throw them overboard while we were in harbour. This seemed to gratify the birds as well as the sailors, for they would swim about, wash themselves, and dress their plumage, after which they would make for the sides, and would be taken on board. During a violent gale, one night, while we were at anchor in the harbour of Bras d'Or, our bark rolled heavily, and one of our pets went over the side and swam to the shore, where, after considerable search next day, it was found shivering by the lee of a rock. On being brought to its brothers, it was pleasant to see their mutual congratulations, which were extremely animated. Before we left the coast, they would sometimes fly of their own accord into the water to bathe, but could not return to the deck without assistance, although they endeavoured to do so. I had become much attached to them, and now and then thought they looked highly interesting, as they lay panting on their sides on the deck, although the thermometer did not rise above 55°. Their enmity to my son's pointer was quite remarkable, and as that animal was of a gentle and kindly disposition, they would tease him, bite him, and drive him fairly from the deck into the cabin. A few days after leaving St George's Bay in Newfoundland, we were assailed by a violent gale, and obliged to lie-to. Next day one of the Gulls was washed overboard. It tried to reach the vessel again, but in vain; the gale continued; the sailors told me the bird was swimming towards the shore, which was not so far off as we could have wished, and which it probably reached in safety. The other was given to my friend Lieutenant GREEN of the United States Army, at Eastport in Maine. In one of his letters to me the following winter, he said that the young *Larus marinus* was quite a pet in the garrison, and doing very well, but that no perceptible change had taken place in its plumage.[3]

On referring to my journal again, I find that while we were at anchor at the head of St George's Bay, the sailors caught many codlings, of which each of our young Gulls swallowed daily two, measuring from eight to ten inches in length. It was curious to see them after such a meal: the form of the fish could be traced along the neck, which for a while they were obliged to keep stretched out; they gaped and were evidently suffering; yet they would not throw up the fish. About the time the young of this species are nearly able to fly, they are killed in considerable numbers on their breeding grounds, skinned and salted for the settlers and resident fishermen of Labrador and Newfoundland, at which latter place I saw piles of them. When they are able to shift for themselves, their parents completely abandon them, and old and young go separately in search of food.

The flight of the Great Black-backed Gull is firm, steady, at times elegant, rather swift, and long protracted. While travelling, it usually flies at the height of fifty or sixty yards, and proceeds in a direct course, with easy regulated flappings. Should the weather prove tempestuous, this Gull, like most others, skims over the surface of the waters or the land within a few yards or even feet, meeting the gale, but not yielding to it, and forcing its way against the strongest wind. In calm weather and sunshine, at all seasons of the year, it is fond of soaring to a great height, where it flies about leisurely and with considerable elegance for half an hour or so, in the manner of eagles, vultures, and ravens. Now and then, while pursuing a bird of its own species, or trying to escape from an enemy, it passes through the air with rapid boundings, which, however, do not continue long, and as soon as they are over it rises and slowly sails in circles. When man encroaches on its domains, it keeps over him at a safe distance not sailing so much as moving to either side with continued flappings. To secure the fishes on which it more usually preys, it sweeps downwards with velocity, and as it glides over the spot, picks up its prey with its bill. If the fish be small, the Gull swallows it on wing, but if large, it either alights on the water, or flies to the nearest shore to devour it.

Although a comparatively silent bird for three-fourths of the year, the Great Black-backed Gull becomes very noisy at the approach of the breeding season, and continues so until the young are well fledged, after which it resumes its silence. Its common notes, when it is interrupted or surprised, sound like *cack cack cack*. While courting, they are softer and more lengthened, and resemble the syllables *cawah*, which are often repeated as it sails in circles or otherwise, within view of its mate or its place of abode.

This species walks well, moving firmly and with an air of importance. On the water it swims lightly but slowly, and may soon be overtaken by a boat. It has no power of diving, although at times, when searching for food along the shores, it will enter the water on seeing a crab or a lobster, to seize it, in which it at times succeeds. I saw one at Labrador plunge after a large crab in about two feet of water, when, after a tug, it hauled it ashore, where it devoured it in my sight. I watched its movements with a glass, and could easily observe how it tore the crab to pieces, swallowed its body, leaving the shell and the claws, after which it flew off to its young and disgorged before them.

It is extremely voracious, and devours all sorts of food excepting vegetables, even the most putrid carrion, but prefers fresh fish, young birds, or small quadrupeds, whenever they can be procured. It sucks the eggs of every bird it can find, thus destroying great numbers of them, as well as the parents, if weak or helpless. I have frequently seen these Gulls attack a flock of young Ducks while swimming beside their mother, when the latter, if small, would have to take to wing, and the former would all dive, but were often caught on rising to the surface, unless they happened to be among rushes. The Eider Duck is the only one of the tribe that risks her life, on such occasions, to save that of her young. She will frequently rise from the water, as her brood disappear beneath, and keep the Gull at bay, or harass it until her little ones are safe under some shelving rocks, when she flies off in another direction, leaving the enemy to digest his disappointment. But while the poor Duck is sitting on her eggs in any open situation, the marauder assails her, and forces her off, when he sucks the eggs in her very sight. Young Grous are also the prey of this Gull, which chases them over the moss-covered rocks, and devours them before their parents. It follows the shoals of fishes for hours at a time, and usually with great success. On the coast of Labrador, I frequently saw these birds seize flounders on the edges of the shallows; they often attempted to swallow them whole, but, finding this impracticable, removed to some rock, beat them, and tore them to pieces. They appear to digest feathers, bones, and other hard substances with ease, seldom disgorging their food, unless for the purpose of feeding their young or mates, or when wounded and approached by man, or when pursued by some bird of greater power. While at Boston in Massachusetts, one cold winter morning, I saw one of these Gulls take up an eel, about fifteen or eighteen inches in length, from a mud bank. The Gull rose with difficulty, and after some trouble managed to gulp the head of the fish, and flew towards the shore with it, when a White-headed Eagle made its appearance, and soon overtook the Gull, which reluctantly gave up the eel, on which the Eagle glided towards it, and, seizing it with its talons, before it reached the water, carried it off.

This Gull is excessively shy and vigilant, so that even at Labrador we found it difficult to procure it, nor did we succeed in obtaining more than about a dozen old birds, and that only by stratagem. They watched our movements with so much care as never to fly past a rock behind which one of the party might be likely to lie concealed. None were shot near the nests when they were sitting on their eggs, and only one female attempted to rescue her young, and was shot as she accidentally flew within distance. The time to surprise them was during violent gales, for then they flew close to the tops of the highest rocks, where we took care to conceal ourselves for the purpose. When we approached the rocky islets on which they bred, they left the place as soon as they became aware of our intentions, cackled and barked loudly, and when we returned, followed us at a distance more than a mile.

They begin to moult early in July. In the beginning of August the young were seen searching for food by themselves, and even far apart. By the 12th of that month they had all left Labrador. We saw them afterwards along the coast of Newfoundland, and while crossing the Gulf of St Lawrence, and found them over the bays of Nova Scotia, as we proceeded southward. When old, their flesh is tough and unfit for food. Their feathers are elastic, and good for pillows and such purposes, but can rarely be procured in sufficient quantity.

The most remarkable circumstance relative to these birds is, that they either associate with another species, giving rise to a hybrid brood, or that when very old they lose the dark colour of the back, which is then of the same tint as that of the *Larus argentatus*, or even lighter. This curious fact was also remarked by the young gentlemen who accompanied me to Labrador; and although it is impossible for me to clear up the doubts that may be naturally entertained on this subject, whichever of the two suppositions is adopted, the fact may yet be established and accounted for by persons who may have better opportunities of watching them and studying their habits. No individuals of *Larus argentatus* were, to my knowledge, seen on that coast during the three months which I passed there, and the fishermen told us that the "saddle-backs were the only large Gulls that ever breed there."

This bird must be of extraordinary longevity, as I have seen one that was kept in a state of captivity more than thirty years.

Notes

1. First published in *OB* 3 (1835), 305–16. Audubon's "Great Black-backed Gull," *Larus marinus* (plate 14; Havell 241), was presumably based on a bird killed near Boston in 1832. It is one of only three Audubon paintings featuring birds injured or killed by humans (the others are the "Esquimaux Curlew," Havell 208, and the "Golden-eye Duck," Havell 342). This gull is considered a species of Least Concern today, though populations appear to be declining (IUCN, 2018).

2. *Larus argentatus* is the herring gull (Havell 291).

3. George S. Greene (1801–1899) was a West Point graduate, civil engineer, and Union general, who despite his age distinguished himself on Civil War battlefields, including Gettysburg. While stationed at Fort Sullivan in Eastport, during the winter of 1832–1833, Greene lost his wife and all three of their children within seven months, by all accounts due to tuberculosis.

THE WANDERING SHEARWATER

I HAVE found this species [plate 15] ranging from the Gulf of St Lawrence to that of Mexico, but have very seldom seen it near the coast. While sailing round Nova Scotia, on my way to Labrador, early in June, I observed one evening about sunset, a great number flying from the rocky shores, which induced me to think that they bred there. Scarcely one was to be seen during the day, and this circumstance strengthened my opinion, as I was aware that these birds are in the habit of remaining about their nests at that time. In September the case is very different; for they are then seen far out at sea, at all hours by day and through the night.[1]

In calm weather, they are fond of alighting on the water, in company with the Fulmars, and are then easily approached. They swim buoyantly, and have a graceful appearance while playing among themselves. Two that had been caught with hooks, walked as well as Ducks, and made no pretence of sitting on their rumps, as some writers have said they do. On being approached, they opened their bills, raised their feathers, and squirted an oily substance through their nostrils, which they continued to do when held in the hand, at the same time scratching with their sharp claws and bills. They refused all sorts of food; and as they were unpleasant pets, they were set at liberty. To my great surprise, instead of flying directly off, as I expected, they launched toward the water, dived several yards obliquely, and on coming to the surface, splashed and washed themselves for several minutes before they took to wing, when they flew away with their usual ease and grace.[2]

The flight of this wanderer of the ocean is extremely rapid and protracted. When it blows hard, it skims along the troughs of the waves on extended wings in large curves, shewing its upper and lower parts alternately, evidently with the view of being aided by the wind. In calm weather its flight is much lower and less rapid, and it rarely throws its body sideways, but seems to feed more abundantly than during boisterous weather. Like the small Petrels, it frequently uses its feet to support itself on the surface, without actually alighting. In the stomach of those which I opened, I found fishes, portions of crabs, sea-weeds, and oily substances. It does not appear that this species goes far north, as was formerly supposed; for none of the late northern voyagers mention having seen it, although they found the Fulmar abundant.[3]

Notes

1. First published in *OB* 3 (1835), 555–57. Audubon's "Wandering Shearwater/Cinerous Petrel" (plate 15; Havell 283), now known as the great shearwater (*Ardenna gravis*), was painted during his Labrador expedition. These large seabirds breed almost exclusively on the Falkland and Tristan da Cunha Islands in the South Atlantic but range widely throughout the Atlantic, even up to Greenland, according to modern records, during the rest of the year. There are no historical breeding sites for any shearwaters in Nova Scotia, as Audubon surmised. The great shearwater is considered a species of Least Concern globally (IUCN, 2018). See Peter Harrison, *Seabirds: An Identification Guide* (1985), 258–59; C. Carboneras, F. Jutglar, and G. M. Kirwan, "Great Shearwater," v. 1.0 (2020), birdsoftheworld.org.

2. This "squirting of an oily substance through the nostrils," more often from the bird's mouth, according to modern ornithologists, is a defense mechanism, evolved in some seabirds to eject the stomach contents to appease or distract a predator. This concentrated fluid also feeds young at the nest ashore.

3. This alternating flight, in "large curves" during strong winds, without flapping, is known today as "dynamic soaring" and still excites ornithologists: "The dynamic soaring of the *Pterodroma* petrels is one of the most thrilling sights in birding," write Edward S. Brinkley and Alec Humann, in Chris Elphick, John B. Dunning Jr., and David Allen Sibley, *The Sibley Guide to Bird Life & Behavior* (2001), 141.

COD-FISHING

ALTHOUGH I had seen, as I thought, abundance of fish along the coasts of the Floridas, the numbers which I found in Labrador quite astonished me. Should your surprise while reading the following statements be as great as mine was while observing the facts related, you will conclude, as I have often done, that Nature's means for providing small animals for the use of larger ones, and *vice versa*, are as ample as is the grandeur of that world which she has so curiously constructed.[1]

The coast of Labrador is visited by European as well as American fishermen, all of whom are, I believe, entitled to claim portions of fishing-ground, assigned to each nation by mutual understanding. For the present, however, I shall confine my observations to those of our own country, who, after all, are probably the most numerous. The citizens of Boston, and many others of our eastern sea-ports, are those who chiefly engage in this department of our commerce. Eastport in Maine sends out every year a goodly fleet of schooners and "pickaxes" to Labrador, to procure cod, mackerel, halibut, and sometimes herring, the latter being caught in the intermediate space. The vessels from that port, and others in Maine and Massachusetts, sail as soon as the warmth of spring has freed the gulf of ice, that is, from the beginning of May to that of June.[2]

A vessel of one hundred tons or so, is provided with a crew of twelve men, who are equally expert as sailors and fishers, and for every couple of these hardy tars, a Hampton boat is provided, which is lashed on the deck, or hung in stays. Their provision is simple, but of good quality, and it is very seldom that any spirits are allowed, beef, pork, and biscuit, with water, being all they take with them. The men are supplied with warm clothing, waterproof oiled jackets and trowsers, large boots, broad-brimmed hats with a round crown, and stout mittens, with a few shirts. The owner or captain furnishes them with lines, hooks, and nets, and also provides the bait best adapted to ensure success. The hold of the vessel is filled with casks of various dimensions, some containing salt, and others for the oil that may be procured.

The bait generally used at the beginning of the season, consists of mussels salted for the purpose; but as soon as the capelings reach the coast, they are substituted to save expense; and in many instances, the flesh of gannets and other sea-fowl is employed. The wages of fishermen vary from sixteen to thirty dollars per month, according to the qualifications of the individual.[3]

The labour of these men is excessively hard, for, unless on Sunday, their allowance of rest in the twenty-four hours seldom exceeds three. The cook is the only person who fares better in this respect, but he must also assist in curing the fish. He has breakfast, consisting of coffee, bread, and meat, ready for the captain and the whole crew, by three o'clock every morning, excepting Sunday. Each person carries with him his dinner ready cooked, which is commonly eaten on the fishing-grounds.

Thus, at three in the morning, the crew are prepared for their day's labour, and ready to betake themselves to their boats, each of which has two oars and lugsails. They all depart at once, and either by rowing or sailing, reach the banks to which the fishes are known to resort. The little squadron drop their anchors at short distances from each other, in a depth of from ten to twenty feet, and the business is immediately commenced. Each man has two lines, and each stands in one end of the boat, the middle of which is boarded off to hold the fish. The baited lines have been dropped into the water, one on each side of the boat; their leads have reached the bottom, a fish has taken the hook, and after giving the line a slight jerk, the fisherman hauls up his prize with a continued pull, throws the fish athwart a small round bar of iron placed near his back, which forces open the mouth, while the weight of the body, however small the fish may be, tears out the hook. The bait is still good, and over the side the line again goes, to catch another fish, while that on the left is now drawn up, and the same course pursued. In this manner, a fisher busily plying at each end, the operation is continued until the boat is so laden, that her gunwale is brought within a few inches of the surface, when they return to the vessel in harbour, seldom distant more than eight miles from the banks.

During the greater part of the day, the fishermen have kept up a constant conversation, of which the topics are the pleasure of finding a good supply of cod, their domestic affairs, the political prospects of the nation, and other matters similarly connected. Now the repartee of one elicits a laugh from the other; this passes from man to man, and the whole

FIGURE 30. Cod-fishers hand-lining off the coast of Newfoundland, engraved from a drawing by D. C. Hitchcock in John Mullaly *A Trip to Newfoundland; Its Scenery and Fisheries* (New York: T. W. Strong, 1855), 43. Courtesy of Williams College.

flotilla enjoy the joke. The men of one boat strive to outdo those of the others in hauling up the greatest quantity of fish in a given time, and this forms another source of merriment. The boats are generally filled about the same time, and all return together.

Arrived at the vessel, each man employs a pole armed with a bent iron, resembling the prong of a hay-fork, with which he pierces the fish, and throws it with a jerk on deck, counting the number thus discharged with a loud voice. Each cargo is thus safely deposited, and the boats instantly return to the fishing-ground, when, after anchoring, the men eat their dinner and begin a-new. There, good reader, with your leave, I will let them pursue their avocations for a while, as I am anxious that you should witness what is doing on board the vessel.

The captain, four men, and the cook, have, in the course of the morning, erected long tables fore and aft the main hatchway, they have taken to the shore most of the salt barrels, and have placed in a row their large empty casks, to receive the livers. The hold of the vessel is quite clear, except a corner where is a large heap of salt. And now the men having dined precisely at twelve, are ready with their large knives. One begins with breaking off the head of the fish, a slight pull of the hand and a gash with the knife effecting this in a moment. He slits up its belly, with one hand pushes it aside to his neighbour, then throws overboard the head, and begins to doctor another. The next man tears out the entrails, separates the liver, which he throws into a cask, and casts the rest overboard. A third person dexterously passes his knife beneath the vertebræ of the fish, separates them from the flesh, heaves the latter through the hatchway, and the former into the water.

Now, if you will peep into the hold, you will see the last stage of the process, the salting and packing. Six experienced men generally manage to head, gut, bone, salt and pack, all the fish caught in the morning, by the return of the boats with fresh cargoes, when all hands set to work, and clear the deck of the fish. Thus their labours continue until twelve o'clock, when they wash their faces and hands, put on clean clothes, hang their fishing apparel on the shrouds, and, betaking themselves to the forecastle, are soon in a sound sleep.

At three next morning comes the captain from his berth, rubbing his eyes; and in a loud voice calling "all hands, ho!" Stiffened in limb, and but half awake, the crew quickly appear on the deck. Their fingers and hands are so cramped and swollen by pulling the lines, that it is difficult for them to straighten even a thumb; but this matters little at present; for the cook, who had a good nap yesterday, has risen an hour before them, and prepared their coffee and eatables. Breakfast dispatched, they exchange their clean clothes for the fishing-apparel, and leap into their boats, which had been washed the previous night, and again the flotilla bounds to the fishing-ground.

As there may be not less than 100 schooners or pickaxes in the harbour, 300 boats resort to the banks each day; and, as each boat may procure 2000 cods per diem, when Saturday night comes about 600,000 fishes have been brought to the harbour.[4] This having caused some scarcity on the fishing-grounds, and Sunday being somewhat of an idle day, the Captain collects the salt ashore, and sets sail for some other convenient harbour, which he expects to reach long before sunset. If the weather be favourable, the men get a good deal of rest during the voyage, and on Monday things go on as before.[5]

I must not omit to tell you, reader, that, while proceeding from one harbour to another, the vessel has passed near a rock, which is the breeding place of myriads of Puffins. She has laid to for an hour or so, while part of the crew have landed, and collected a store of eggs, excellent as a substitute for cream, and not less so when hard boiled as food for the fishing-grounds. I may as well inform you also, how these adventurous fellows distinguish the fresh eggs from the others. They fill up some large tubs with water, throw in a quantity of eggs, and allow them to remain a minute or so, when those which come to the surface are tossed overboard, and even those that manifest any upward tendency, share the same treatment. All that remain at bottom, you may depend upon it, good reader, are perfectly sound, and not less palatable than any that you have ever eaten, or that your best guinea-fowl has just dropped in your barn-yard. But let us return to the cod-fish.

The fish already procured and salted, is taken ashore at the new harbour, by part of the crew, whom the captain has marked as the worst hands at fishing. There, on the bare rocks, or on elevated scaffolds of considerable extent, the salted cods are laid side by side to dry in the sun. They are turned several times a-day, and in the intervals the men bear a hand on board at clearing and stowing away the daily produce of the fishing-banks. Towards evening they return to the drying grounds, and put up the fish in piles resembling so many hay-stacks, disposing those towards the top in such a manner that the rain cannot injure them, and placing a heavy stone on the summit to prevent their being thrown down should it blow hard during the night. You see, reader, that the life of a Labrador fisherman is not one of idleness.

The capelings have approached the shores, and in myriads enter every basin and stream, to deposit their spawn, for now July is arrived. The cods follow them, as the blood-hound follows his prey, and their compact masses literally line the shores. The fishermen now adopt another method: they have brought with them long and deep seines, one end of which is, by means of a line, fastened to the shore, while the other is, in the usual manner, drawn out in a broad sweep, to inclose as great a space as possible, and hauled on shore by means of a capstan. Some of the men in boats support the corked part of the net, and beat the water to frighten the fishes within towards the land, while others, armed with poles, enter the water, hook the fishes, and fling them on the beach, the net being gradually drawn closer as the number of fishes diminishes. What do you think, reader, as to the number of cods secured in this manner at a single haul?—thirty, or thirty thousand? You may form some notion of the matter when I tell you that the young gentlemen of my party, while going along the shores, caught cod-fish alive, with their hands, and trouts of many pounds weight with a piece of twine and a mackerel-hook hung to their gun-rods; and that, if two of them walked knee-deep along the rocks, holding a handkerchief by the corners, they swept it full of capelings. Should you not trust me in this, I refer you to the fishermen themselves, or recommend you to go to Labrador, where you will give credit to the testimony of your eyes.

The seining of the cod-fish, I believe, is not *quite* lawful, for a great proportion of the codlings which are dragged ashore at last, are so small as to be considered useless; and, instead of being returned to the water, as they ought to be, are left on the shore, where they are ultimately eaten by bears, wolves, and ravens. The fishes taken along the coast, or on fishing-stations only a few miles off, are of small dimensions; and I believe I am correct in saying, that few of them weigh more than two pounds, when perfectly cured, or exceed six when taken out of the water. The fish are liable to several diseases, and at times are annoyed by parasitic animals, which in a short time render them lean and unfit for use.

Some individuals, from laziness, or other causes, fish with naked hooks, and thus frequently wound the cod without securing them, in consequence of which the shoals are driven away, to the detriment of the other fishers. Some carry their cargoes to other parts before drying them, while others dispose of them to agents from distant shores. Some have only a pickaxe of fifty tons, while others are owners of seven or eight vessels of equal or larger burden; but whatever be their means, should the season prove favourable, they are generally well repaid for their labour. I have known instances of men, who, on their first voyage, ranked as "boys," and in ten years after were in independent circumstances, although they still continued to resort to the fishing; for, said they to me, "how could we be content to spend our time in idleness at home!" I know a person of this class who has carried on the trade for many years, and who has quite a little fleet of schooners, one of which, the largest and most beautifully built, has a cabin as neat and comfortable as any that I have ever seen in a vessel of the same size. This vessel took fish on board only when perfectly cured, or acted as pilot to the rest, and now and then would return home with an ample supply of halibut, or a cargo of prime mackerel. On another occasion, I will offer some remarks on the improvements which I think might be made in the cod-fisheries of the coast of Labrador.[6]

Notes

1. "Cod-Fishing" was first published in *OB* 2 (1834), 522–27. The Atlantic cod (*Gadus morhua*) is a large-bodied, commercially iconic groundfish.

2. American schooners had gone cod-fishing off Labrador since 1794. Audubon provides one of the first references to the type of small boat they used, the Hampton boat, made in Seabrook, New Hampshire, a partially decked, clinker-built, sailing or rowing double-ended craft (i.e., the edges of hull planks overlap each other and the boat is pointy at both ends). The design made them nimble for all kinds of fishing, including whaling. They were launched from larger schooners, which sometimes carried five of these smaller boats, and often sold them at the end of the fishing season to local fishermen; see Wayne M. O'Leary, *The Tancook Schooners: An Island and Its Boats* (Montreal: McGill-Queen's University Press, 1994), 24–25. Audubon's "pickaxe" is likely a "pinky," a type of smaller schooner popular for fishing at the time, common out of Gloucester, Massachusetts.

3. Note the range of ecological impact of the cod-fisheries, as fishermen took seabirds, shellfish, and other fish species for bait. Audubon's "capelings" are capelin, or caplin (*Mallotus villosus*), a small fish of the smelt family, a favorite prey of whales, seals, Atlantic cod, and seabirds. These fish still arrive in massive shoals to spawn along shorelines in early summer.

4. Audubon represents 600,000 as the weekly total, but the numbers given in the passage suggest that this may have been the daily catch.

5. Audubon observed this density of fishermen in Bradore Harbor, near the Strait of Belle Isle; Peter Logan, *Audubon: America's Greatest Naturalist and His Voyage of Discovery to Labrador* (San Francisco: Ashbryn Press, 2016), 235–37.

6. Though Audubon described a remarkable abundance of cod in this account of fishing in the Strait of Belle Isle region in the mid-1830s, he was right to question whether it could last, especially with the catching of these smaller cod. In less than two decades, fishermen working throughout the region would begin to document depletion as they felt the need to turn to new technologies, such as dory fishing throughout Atlantic Canada and on the Grand Banks and the use of long-lines (tub trawls), purse seines, and cod traps. Stocks of cod in the Northwest Atlantic have all but collapsed in recent times due to overfishing. In the Gulf of St. Lawrence and Eastern Scotian Shelf, where cod have been fished since the sixteenth century and possibly longer, stocks reached their lowest abundances in the early 1990s, and the fishery was subsequently closed. Since then, increased natural mortality due in part to predation by grey seals (*Halichoerus grypus*) has prevented recovery, and some scientists predict cod will be extirpated from the region by 2050, even with a closed fishery. Matthew McKenzie, personal communication, July 23, 2020; W. Jeffrey Bolster, *The Mortal*

Sea: Fishing the Atlantic in the Age of Sail (Cambridge, MA: Belknap, 2012), 121–25, 133–42; Rachel D. Neuenhoff et al., "Continued Decline of a Collapsed Population of Atlantic Cod (*Gadus morhua*) Due to Predation-Driven Allee Effects," *Canadian Journal of Fisheries and Aquatic Sciences* 76, no. 1 (2019), 1.

THE RAZOR-BILLED AUK

A FEW birds of this species [plate 16] occasionally go as far south as New York during winter; but beyond that parallel I never met with one. From Boston eastward many are seen, and some breed on the Seal Islands off the entrance of the Bay of Fundy. These Auks generally arrive on our Atlantic coast about the beginning of November, and return northward to breed about the middle of April. During their stay with us, they are generally seen singly, and at a greater distance from the shores than the Guillemots or Puffins; and I have no doubt that they are able to procure shell-fish at greater depths than these birds. I have observed them fishing on banks where the bottom was fifteen or eighteen fathoms from the surface, and, from the length of time that they remained under water, felt no doubt that they dived to it. On my voyage round Nova Scotia and across the Gulf of St Lawrence, we saw some of them constantly. Some had eggs on the Magdeleine Islands, where, as the inhabitants informed us, these birds arrive about the middle of April, when the Gulf is still covered with ice. As we proceeded towards Labrador, they passed us every now and then in long files, flying at the height of a few yards from the water, in a rather undulating manner, with a constant beat of the wings, often within musket-shot of our vessel, and sometimes moving round us and coming so close as to induce us to believe that they had a wish to alight. The thermometer indicated 44°. The sight of these files of birds passing swiftly by was extremely pleasing; each bird would alternately turn towards us the pure white of its lower parts, and again the jetty black of the upper. As I expected ere many days should pass to have the gratification of inspecting their breeding grounds, I experienced great delight in observing them as they sped their flight toward the north.[1]

After we had landed, we every day procured Auks, notwithstanding their shyness, which exceeded that of almost all the other sea-birds. The fishermen having given me an account of their principal breeding places, the Ripley proceeded toward them apace. One fair afternoon we came in view of the renowned Harbour of Whapati Guan, and already saw its curious beacon, which, being in form like a huge mounted cannon placed on the elevated crest of a great rock, produced a most striking effect. We knew that the harbour was within the stupendous wall of rock before us, but our pilot, either from fear or want of knowledge, refused to guide us to it, and our captain, leaving the vessel in charge of the mate, was obliged to go off in a boat, to see if he could find a passage. He was absent more than an hour. The Ripley stood off and on, the yards were manned on the look-out, the sea was smooth and its waters as clear as crystal, but the swell rose to a prodigious height as it passed sluggishly over the great rocks that seemed to line the shallows over which we floated. We were under no apprehension of personal danger, however, for we had several boats and a very efficient crew; and besides, the shores were within cannon shot; but the idea of losing our gallant bark and all our materials on so dismal a coast haunted my mind, and at times those of my companions. From the tops our sailors called out "Quite shallow here. Sir." Up went the helm, and round swung the Ripley like a duck taken by surprise. Then suddenly near another shoal we passed, and were careful to keep a sharp look-out until our commander came up.[2]

Springing upon the deck, and turning his quid rapidly from side to side, he called out, "All hands square the yards," and whispered to me "All's safe, my good Sir." The schooner advanced towards the huge barrier, merrily as a fair maiden to meet her beloved; now she doubles a sharp cape, forces her way through a narrow pass; and lo! before you opens the noble harbour of Whapati Guan. All around was calm and solemn; the waters were smooth as glass, the sails fell against the masts, but the impetus which the vessel had received urged her along. The lead was heaved at every yard, and in a few minutes the anchor was dropped.

Reader, I wish you had been there, that you might yourself describe the wild scene that presented itself to our admiring gaze. We were separated from the rolling swell of the Gulf of St Lawrence by an immense wall of rock. Far away toward the east and north, rugged mounds innumerable rose one above another. Multitudes of frightened Cormorants croaked loudly as they passed us in the air, and at a distance fled divers

Guillemots and Auks. The mossy beds around us shone with a brilliant verdure, the lark piped its sweet notes on high, and thousands of young codfish leaped along the surface of the deep cove as if with joy. Such a harbour I had never seen before; such another, it is probable, I may never see again; the noblest fleet that ever ploughed the ocean might anchor in it in safety. To augment our pleasures, our captain some days after piloted the Gulnare into it. But, you will say, "Where are the Auks, we have lost sight of them entirely." Never fear, good reader, we are in a delightful harbour, and anon you shall hear of them.

Winding up the basin toward the north-east, Captain EMERY, myself, and some sailors, all well armed, proceeded one day along the high and precipitous shores to the distance of about four miles, and at last reached the desired spot. We landed on a small rugged island. Our men were provided with long poles, having hooks at their extremities. These sticks were introduced into the deep and narrow fissures, from which we carefully drew the birds and eggs. One place, in particular, was full of birds; it was a horizontal fissure, about two feet in height, and thirty or forty yards in depth. We crawled slowly into it, and as the birds affrighted flew hurriedly past us by hundreds, many of their eggs were smashed. The farther we advanced, the more dismal did the cries of the birds sound in our ears. Many of them, despairing of effecting their escape, crept into the surrounding recesses. Having collected as many of them and their eggs as we could, we returned, and glad were we once more to breathe the fresh air. No sooner were we out than the cracks of the sailors' guns echoed among the rocks. Rare fun to the tars, in fact, was every such trip, and, when we joined them, they had a pile of Auks on the rocks near them. The birds flew directly towards the muzzles of the guns, as readily as in any other course, and therefore it needed little dexterity to shoot them.[3]

When the Auks deposit their eggs along with the Guillemots, which they sometimes do, they drop them in spots from which the water can escape without injuring them; but when they breed in deep fissures, which is more frequently the case, many of them lie close together, and the eggs are deposited on small beds of pebbles or broken stones raised a couple of inches or more, to let the water pass beneath them. Call this instinct if you will:—I really do not much care; but you must permit me to admire the wonderful arrangements of that Nature from which they have received so much useful knowledge. When they lay their eggs in such a horizontal cavern as that which I have mentioned above, you find them scattered at the distance of a few inches from each other; and there, as well as in the fissures, they sit flat upon them like Ducks, for example, whereas on an exposed rock, each bird stands almost upright upon its egg. Another thing quite as curious, which I observed, is, that, while in exposed situations, the Auk seldom lays more than one egg, yet in places of greater security I have, in many instances, found two under a single bird. This may perhaps astonish you, but I really cannot help it.[4]

The Razor-billed Auks begin to drop their eggs in the beginning of May. In July we found numerous young ones, although yet small. Their bill then scarcely exhibited the form which it ultimately assumes. They were covered with down, had a lisping note, but fed freely on shrimps and small bits of fish, the food with which their parents supply them. They were very friendly towards each other, differing greatly in this respect from the young Puffins, which were continually quarrelling. They stood almost upright. Whenever a finger was placed within their reach, they instantly seized it, and already evinced the desire to bite severely so cordially manifested by the old birds of this species, which in fact will hang to your hand until choked rather than let go their hold. The latter when wounded threw themselves on their back, in the manner of Hawks, and scratched fiercely with their claws. They walked and ran on the rocks with considerable ease and celerity, taking to wing, however, as soon as possible. When thus disturbed while breeding, they fly round the spot many times before they alight again. Sometimes a whole flock will alight on the water at some distance, to watch your departure, before they will venture to return.

This bird lays one or two eggs, according to the nature of the place. The eggs measure at an average three inches and one-eighth, by two and one-eighth, and are generally pure white, greatly blotched with dark reddish-brown or black, the spots generally forming a circle towards the larger end. They differ considerably from those of the Common and the Thick-billed Guillemots, being less blunted at the smaller end. The eggs afford excellent eating; the yolk is of a pale orange colour, the white pale blue. The eggers collect but few of the eggs of this bird, they being more difficult to be obtained than those of the Guillemot, of which they take vast numbers every season.

The food of the Razor-billed Auk consists of shrimps, various other marine animals, and small fishes, as well as roe. Their flesh is by the fishers considered good, and I found it tolerable, when well stewed, although it is dark and therefore not prepossessing. The birds are two years in acquiring the full size and form of their bill, and, when full grown, they weighed about a pound and a half. The stomach is an oblong sac, the lower part of which is rather muscular, and answers the purpose of a gizzard. In many I found scales, remnants of fish, and pieces of shells. The intestines were upwards of three feet in length.

Immediately after the breeding season, these birds drop their quills, and are quite unable to fly until the beginning of October, when they all leave their breeding grounds for the sea, and move southward. The young at this period scarcely shew the white streak between the bill and the eye; their cheeks, like those of the old birds at this time, and the fore part of the neck, are dingy white, and remain so until the following spring, when the only difference between the young and the old is, that the former have the bill smaller and less furrowed, and the head more brown. The back, tail, and lower parts do not seem to undergo any material change.

Notes

1. First published in *OB* 3 (1835), 112–17. Audubon's "Razor Bill/Razor-billed Auk" (plate 16; Havell 214), now known as the razorbill (*Alca torda*), was apparently painted from birds collected during the Labrador expedition in June 1833. Razorbills are considered Near Threatened and decreasing as a result of unmitigated harvesting for food, eggs, and feathers through the early 1900s, from which their recovery has remained slow, likely due to overfishing and climate change (IUCN, 2018). Modern ornithologists record a similar range of the razorbill in North America, with regular winter birds as far south as Long Island and New Jersey and even, rarely, as far south as Florida. Razorbills still return to their breeding rookeries in Maine and the Atlantic Canada in mid-April. Audubon's record of ice cover in mid-April for the Gulf of St. Lawrence is worth noting, as that is the average time of ice breakup in recent decades. Government of Canada, "30-year Ice Atlas: East Coast," https://iceweb1.cis.ec.gc.ca/30Atlas.

2. The "Harbour of Whapati Guan" is on the Ouapitagone Archipelago, a group of granite rock islands off the north shore of the Gulf of St. Lawrence (see fig. 33). The name is said to have its origins in an Innu word meaning "whetstone"; another explanation traces it to a word for cormorant, whose nesting grounds were nearby.

3. Captain Henry T. Emery (1808–1840) died less than a decade later of yellow fever in the West Indies. The 106-ton schooner *Ripley* was lost in Bay Chaleur, New Brunswick, off the Gulf of St. Lawrence. Mary Durant and Michael Harwood, *On the Road with John James Audubon* (New York: Dodd, Mead, 1980), 416–18, confuse the son with the father. But see the conclusive evidence offered by Peter Logan, *Audubon: America's Greatest Naturalist and His Voyage of Discovery to Labrador* (San Francisco: Ashbryn Press, 2016), 576n79.

4. Ornithologists today maintain that razorbills always lay one egg per year and that "occasional reports of birds with 2 eggs, may be a result of layings by 2 females, egg-napping following disturbance, or laying of first and (intended) replacement eggs by 1 female." J. Lavers, J. M. Hipfner, and G. Chapdelaine, "Razorbill," v. 1.0 (2020), birdsoftheworld.org.

THE COMMON CORMORANT

LOOK at the birds before you [plate 17], and mark the affectionate glance of the mother, as she stands beside her beloved younglings! I wish you could have witnessed the actions of such groups as I did while in Labrador. Methinks I still see the high rolling billows of the St Lawrence breaking in foaming masses against the huge cliffs, on the shelves of which the Cormorant places its nest. I lie flat on the edge of the precipice some hundred feet above the turbulent waters, and now crawling along with all care, I find myself only a few yards above the spot on which the parent bird and her young are fondling each other, quite unconscious of my being near. How delighted I am to witness their affectionate gratulations, hear their lisping notes, mark the tremulous motions of their expanded throats, and the curious vacillations of their heads and necks! The kind mother gently caresses each alternately with her bill; the little ones draw nearer to her, and, as if anxious to evince their gratitude, rub their heads against hers. How pleasing all this is to me! But at this moment the mother accidentally looks upward, her keen eye has met mine, she utters a croak, spreads her sable wings, and in terror launches into the air, leaving her brood at my mercy. Far and near, above and beneath me, the anxious parent passes and repasses; her flight is now unnatural, and she seems crippled, for she would fain perform those actions in the air, which other birds perform on the ground or on the water, in such distressing moments of anxiety for the fate of their beloved young. Her many neighbours, all as suspicious as herself, well understand the meaning of her mode of flight, and one after another take to wing, so that the air is in a manner blackened with them. Some fly far over the waters, others glide along the face of the bold rock, but none that have observed me realight, and how many of those there are I am pretty certain, as the greater number follow in the track of the one most concerned. Meanwhile little ones, in their great alarm, have crawled into a recess and there they are huddled together. I have witnessed their pleasures and their terrors, and now, crawling backwards, I leave them to resume their ordinary state of peaceful security.[1]

It was on the 3d of July 1833, about three in the morning, that I had the pleasure of witnessing the scene described above. I was aware before that a colony of Cormorants had nestled on the ledges of the great rocky wall that separated our harbour of Whapati Guan from the waters of the Gulf of St Lawrence. A strong gale had ruffled the sea, and the waves dashed with extreme violence against the rocks, to which circumstance, I believe, was owing my having remained a while unseen and unheard so near the birds, which were not more than four or five yards below me. The mother fondled and nursed her young with all possible tenderness, disgorged some food into the mouth of each, and coaxed them with her bill and wings. The little ones seemed very happy, billed with their mother, and caressed her about the breast. When the parent bird flew off on observing me, the young seemed quite frightened, squatted at once on their broad nest, and then crawled with the aid of their bills until they reached a recess where they remained concealed.[2]

On another occasion, my young friends LINCOLN and COOLEDGE, along with my son, went to the same rocks, for the purpose of bringing me a nest and some of the young Cormorants. They reported that, in one instance, they surprised the parent birds close beneath them, apparently asleep, resting on their rumps in an upright position, with the head thrust under the wing, and that, had they had a noose attached to their poles, they might have secured at least one of them, but that after a few minutes one drew out her head, stretched her neck, and after looking around flew off croaking, so as to alarm all her neighbours.

We saw no nests of this species placed in any other situations than the highest shelves of the precipitous rocks fronting the water and having a southern exposure. No other Cormorants bred on the spots of which this kind had taken possession; but Ravens and Peregrine Falcons were observed to have nests on the same rocks, and in some instances close to them. The nests were formed of a quantity of small dry sticks, matted in a rude manner with a large quantity of weeds and moss, to a thickness of four or five inches in new nests, and in others to that of a foot or more; for we observed that this species, as well as the Double-crested and the Florida Cormorants, repair and enlarge their tenements each season, and return to the same rocks many years in succession, as was shewn by their places of resort remaining whitewashed with excrements through the winter, in which condition we saw them previous to the arrival of the birds that season. The nests varied in breadth according to the space on which they were placed; where there was ample room, they measured at the base from thirty to thirty-six inches in diameter; others were scarcely large enough to hold the young, which nevertheless seemed as contented as their neighbours. On some shelves, eight or ten yards in extent, the nests were crowded together; but more usually they were placed apart on every secure place without any order; none, however, were below a certain height on the rocks, nor were there any on the summit. The nests being covered with filth, were offensive to the eye, and still more so to the nose. The eggs, three or four in number, more frequently the former, average two inches and five-eighths in length, by one inch and three quarters in breadth, the shell of a uniform pale bluish-green colour, mostly coated over with calcareous matter.[3]

The young are at first of a dark purplish livid colour, and have a very uncouth appearance, their legs and feet seeming enormous. In less than a fortnight they become covered on all the upper parts with brownish-black down, but the abdomen remains bare much longer than the rest. They increase rapidly in size, and are fledged in six or seven weeks. Some that were weighed when about a month old, averaged three pounds, and others almost able to fly six pounds, the young of this species, as of most water birds, being much heavier than the parent at the time of leaving the nest. We procured several of different sizes, which we kept on the deck. Whenever a person approached them, they raised their heads, stretched their necks, and opened their bills, so as to expand the skin of the throat, which they made to vibrate, while they uttered a sort of hissing mutter of a very strange character, but resembling that of the young of the Brown Pelican. They crawled sluggishly about, aiding themselves in their progress with their bills, and at all times looked extremely clumsy. They took food very readily, ate a prodigious quantity, certainly more than their own weight each day, and appeared always ready to receive more. When thrown overboard, they swam off under water, like the old birds, with considerable speed, moving their unfledged wings all the while. Some would not rise for twenty or thirty yards, but few went farther under water than that distance, and they were soon fatigued. On one occasion, some half-grown young birds threw themselves from their nest, or were pushed off by their parents while in the agonies of death, they having been shot at. As they passed quickly downwards through the air, they moved their wings with great rapidity, and the instant they reached the water they disappeared beneath the surface.[4]

This Cormorant swims at times with astonishing speed, keeping itself deeply immersed. Now and then, should it apprehend danger, it sinks so far as to shew only the head and neck, in the manner of the Anhinga. When searching for food in clear shallow water, they frequently swim with the rump rather elevated, and the head under, in the manner of the Shoveller Duck on such occasions, as if they were looking for prey on the bottom; but I never observed them act thus when the depth of water exceeded a few yards. They secure their prey by diving and pursuing it under water, with the wings partially extended and employed as paddles, while the tail directs their course, and checks or accelerates their speed. I have observed this in the Florida Cormorant, as well as in the present species. I never saw one while flying plunge after its prey; but I have repeatedly seen them drop from a rock headlong into the sea when shot at for the purpose of observing their actions.[5]

Cormorants, Pelicans, Ducks, and other water birds of various kinds, are, like land birds, at times infested with insects which lodge near the roots of their feathers; and to clear themselves of this vermin, they beat up the water about them by flapping their wings, their feathers being all the while ruffled up, and rub or scratch themselves with their feet and claws, much in the same manner as Turkeys and most land birds act, when scattering up the dry warm earth or sand over them. The water birds after thus cleansing themselves remove, if perchers, and able to fly, to the branches of trees, spread out their wings and tail in the sun, and after a while dress their plumage. Those which are not perchers, or whose wings are too wet, swim to the shores, or to such banks or rocks as are above water, and there perform the same process. The Florida Cormorant is especially addicted to this practice, and dives and plumes itself several times in the day. The Double-crested and the present species, which inhabit colder regions, seem to be satisfied with less frequent trimming, and go through the operation only once a-day, at the warmest period. I never observed any of these birds in their natural free state perform these actions in rainy or even cloudy weather, but have frequently seen Cormorants in a state of captivity do so on small artificial ponds, such as those of the London Zoological Gardens.[6]

When they have landed after cleansing themselves by washing, they usually extend their wings, and flap them for a while, in the manner of young birds of any kind when trying the strength of their wings before leaving the nest. They are extremely regular in returning to the same places to roost, at the approach of night, when hundreds appear to congregate on their way there, as they pass over the different fishing grounds. Those that have no broods, spend the night apart from the rest, standing nearly erect in files on the most elevated shelves, to which they ascend in the manner of some Hawks, when about to perch on any elevated spot. In winter, however, I observed some near Boston roosting singly, and immediately over their fishing places, which are usually the eddies under the projecting points of rocky islands. They are shy and wary at all periods; but when congregated in the day, it is almost impossible to approach them while fishing, for they dive and return to the surface one after another, so that one or more are constantly on the watch, and act as sentinels. It is in general quite useless to pursue one that has been wounded.

The flight of this species is strong, swift, and remarkably sustained. They usually fly in long strings, now and then forming angles, at a moderate elevation in the air. When on the rocks, they stand erect on their rump, with the neck gracefully curved, and resting between the shoulders. You may see them in hundreds, when they look like a crowd of black dominoes. If alarmed, they extend their neck to its full length, and move their head sideways to observe your motions; and if you approach them, they gradually raise and extend their wings, elevate the tail, incline the body forwards, and fly off in silence.

All our Cormorants feed principally on fish of various kinds. When they have seized one that is too large to be swallowed entire, they carry it to the shore, or to the branch of a tree, and there thrash and tear it to pieces. Some fishes which they have swallowed evidently incommode them, and on such occasions I have sometimes seen them shake their heads with great violence, and disgorge the fish, or pass it downwards into the stomach. The young ones which we kept several weeks at Labrador, performed both actions, but generally the first. All the species are expert at tossing up a fish inconveniently caught, a foot or so above their head, and receiving it in their extended gullet, in the same manner as the Frigate Pelican, of which an account will be given in the present volume. Some which I have observed in a domesticated state, were so expert at receiving a fish thrown to them from the distance of several yards, by a sudden and precise movement of the neck and head, as seldom to miss one in a dozen.

The courtship of this species is so similar to that of the Florida Cormorant, that I consider it unnecessary to describe it, as I should merely repeat what has been said with respect to that species.[7] I have seen them act in the same manner, both on the shelves on which the nests were placed, and on the water. They begin to lay about the first of June, on the islands near the Bay of Fundy, about a fortnight later in Labrador; and it is my opinion that the younger birds spend their breeding season in the former places.

The Common Cormorant walks in a waddling and awkward manner, but at a good pace, and leaps from one stone to another, assisting itself with its wings, and occasionally with the tail, which acts as a kind of spring. I am unable to say at what age this species attains the full dress of the love season, but it cannot be in less than three years, as some which I have known to have been kept in a state of constant captivity, did not shew the white patch on the thigh, nor the slender white feathers around the head and part of the neck, until the middle of May, in the fifth year. That the younger birds of this and other Cormorants, breed before they have acquired the full beauty of their plumage, is a fact which I have had many opportunities of ascertaining. The Common Cormorant is found breeding, both near the entrance of the Bay of Fundy, and along the coast of Labrador, in flocks of fifty or more pairs, of which not an individual shews any white unless on the sides of the head, and along the throat, but much duller on these parts than even in the female represented in the plate, which was yet what may be termed an immature bird. No differences appear in the garb of the sexes, in their different states of plumage, and perfect specimens of both are equally beautiful in the breeding season, being then similar to the male of which I have endeavoured to present a good portrait. I have observed a greater difference in size between individuals of this species, than those of any other.

The white markings observed on the old birds of this species, during the period of courtship, incubation, and rearing of the young until they are able to fly, and which extends to two months and a half, begin to disappear from the moment incubation has fairly begun, and at the time when the young leave the nest scarcely any remain, unless on the sides of the head. In autumn and winter the feathers of the head are similar to those of the neck, and the plumage in general has lost much of its vernal and æstival beauty. The entire crest also falls off in autumn. The white markings and the crest are renewed in the wild state about the end of February; but in birds kept in domestication rarely before May. The young do not exhibit the crest until the second spring, at which period, being yet destitute of white markings on the head and thighs, they might readily be mistaken for a different species, by a person unacquainted with their habits.

The singular fact that the young of the three species of Cormorant described in this volume, have *open nostrils* until they are nearly half-grown, may surprise you as much as it surprised me. Having observed it in many individuals, I preserved one in spirits, and of it you will find a description beneath.[8]

The Common Cormorant is rarely seen farther south than the extreme limits of Maryland; but from Chesapeake Bay eastward, it becomes more plentiful; and in severe winters, I have seen it exposed for sale in the New York market. They are abundant in winter around the islands of the Bay of Boston, and on the coasts of Massachusetts and Maine, where most of them remain during autumn, winter, and the early part of spring, as well as on the Bay of Fundy and along the shores of Nova Scotia. I am unable to say how far north they go beyond Labrador, to breed, or what may be the limits of their range on the St Lawrence in autumn. I have never seen one on a tree, or on fresh water. The flesh of this species is dark, tough, and fishy, its eggs also do not furnish agreeable food, and it is seldom that either are eaten, even by epicures.[9]

Notes

1. First published in *OB* 3 (1835), 458–69. Audubon's "Common Cormorant," *Phalacrocorax carbo* (plate 17; Havell 266), is known today as the great cormorant. Audubon hunted and painted these birds, the largest of North American cormorants, in the summer of 1833 during his Labrador expedition. Great cormorants are considered a species of Least Concern globally (IUCN, 2019), and their worldwide population seems to be increasing, although, as Audubon describes, their rookeries are vulnerable to disturbance and subsequent predation on their chicks. Great cormorants are one of the most adaptable species of seabirds in the world, capable of living in freshwater, feeding at depths and the surface, and living at elevation and in a range of latitudes from equatorial to subpolar. Cormorants, perhaps because of their dark color, snakelike necks, and predation of commercially valuable fish, have long been demonized in popular culture, since well before Audubon, so it is especially intriguing that Audubon begins this entry in awe of these birds and their chicks, which are altricial—at first gray-pink, featherless, and lizardlike—not exactly "cute" by common white American standards.

2. Audubon's spying on the great cormorant and her young is depicted in his original watercolor, now at the New-York Historical Society (NYHS 1863.17.266), and *The Birds of America* plate (Havell 266), although his vantage point is not "above" but to the right side of the nest.

3. Audubon described and recognized five different cormorant species in North America: the "Common Cormorant" (now the great cormorant, *Phalacrocorax carbo*); the "Violet-green Cormorant" (Havell 412), now the pelagic cormorant, *Urile pelagicus*, found only on the Pacific coast; the "Townsend's Cormorant" (Havell 412), now the Brandt's cormorant, *Urile penicillatus*, found only on the Pacific coast; the "Florida Cormorant" (Havell 252), now the double-crested cormorant subspecies, *Nannopterum auritum floridanum*; and the "Double-crested Cormorant" (Havell 257), now another subspecies, *Nannopterum auritum auritum*. Regarding these two subspecies of double-crested cormorant (of which there are five currently recognized in North America and the northern Caribbean), Audubon's confusion was a reasonable one, since he saw them each breeding separately in Florida and in Atlantic Canada; see Linda Wires, *The Double-crested Cormorant: Plight of a Feathered Pariah* (New Haven, CT: Yale University Press, 2014), 35–39. A Pacific coast cormorant species of which Audubon missed receiving a skin was the red-faced cormorant (*Urile urile*), which rarely makes it south of Alaskan waters; and there is also the neotropic cormorant (*Nannopterum brasilianum*), which is found occasionally along the coasts and inland waterways of the Gulf of Mexico and Baja.

4. One of the historical and current human grievances against cormorants is that they have slightly larger appetites than other birds their size, perhaps due to their metabolism and deep-diving behavior. Audubon fuels that stereotype here, reporting the cormorants "ate a prodigious quantity."

5. Audubon's "Shoveller Duck" (Havell 327) is now more commonly known as the northern shoveler (*Spatula clypeata*).

6. Cormorant wing-spreading behavior remains the subject of some debate among ornithologists, although it is generally accepted that it is done primarily to dry the wings and regulate

body temperature after foraging under the surface, since cormorants' feathers absorb more water than those of other birds, allowing them to dive deeper for fish.

7. In "The Florida Cormorant" (*OB* 3 [1835]: 390), Audubon shares his observations of mating Florida Cormorants (double-crested cormorants) near one of the Florida Keys: "The males while swimming gracefully round the females, would raise their wings and tail, draw their head over their back, swell out their neck for an instant, and with a quick forward thrust of the head utter a rough guttural note, not unlike the cry of a pig. The female at this moment would crouch as it were on the water, sinking into it, when her mate would sink over her until nothing more than his head was to be seen, and soon afterwards both sprung up and swam joyously round each other, croaking all the while. Twenty or more pairs at a time were thus engaged."

8. The anatomical section of this biography is found in *OB* 3 (1835), 464–69, which extensively discusses the upper mandible and the nostrils.

9. Audubon's description of the range of the great cormorant along the North American East Coast remains generally true. It is unclear how far south this species nested in the eighteenth and nineteenth centuries and if they were forced to abandon their breeding sites along the coast of New England and most of Atlantic Canada. There was nesting in Maine in the late twentieth century, but as of 2020 this has been contracted significantly to about thirty pairs at two sites, in part due to loss of safe rookeries and predation by eagles (John Drury, personal communication, June 27, 2020). Great cormorants still breed in the general areas where Audubon observed them during his Labrador expedition. See Jeremy J. Hatch, et al., "Great Cormorant," v. 1.0 (2020), birdsoftheworld.org.

THE PUFFIN

THE Sea Parrot [plate 18], as this bird is usually called on the eastern coasts of the United States, as well as by the fishermen of Newfoundland and Labrador, sometimes proceeds as far south as the entrance of the River Savannah in Georgia, where I saw a good number in the winter of 1831–32. It is by no means, however, common with this species to extend its southward migrations so far, and I suspect it does so only in very severe weather. It is never plentiful off Long Island, but becomes more abundant the farther you proceed eastward, until you reach the entrance to the Bay of Fundy, where it is quite common, and on the Islands of which many breed, although not one perhaps now for a hundred that bred there twenty years ago. Those which proceed farther north leave the United States about the middle of April, and move along the coast, none ever crossing over the land to any extent. On my voyage to Labrador I observed Puffins every day; but although we reached that country in the early part of June, none had then begun to breed. As we approached the shores of that inhospitable land, we every now and then saw them around the vessel, now floating on the swelling wave, now disappearing under the bow, diving with the swiftness of thought, and sometimes rising on wing and flying swiftly, but low, over the sea. The nearer we approached the coast the more abundant did we find the Puffins, and sometimes they were so numerous as actually to cover the water to the extent of half an acre or more. At first we paid little attention to them, but as soon as I became aware that they had begun to breed, I commenced an investigation, of which I now proceed to lay before you the result.[1]

The first breeding place which I and my party visited was a small island, a few acres in extent, and pleasant to the eye, on account of the thick growth of green grass with which it was covered. The shores were exceedingly rugged, the sea ran high, and it required all the good management of our captain to effect a safe landing, which, however, was at length accomplished at a propitious moment, when, borne on the summit of a great wave, we reached the first rocks, leaped out in an instant, and held our boat, while the angry waters rolled back and left it on the land. After securing the boat, we reached with a few steps the green sward, and directly before us found abundance of Puffins. Some already alarmed flew past us with the speed of an arrow, others stood erect at the entrance of their burrows, while some more timid withdrew within their holes as we advanced towards them. In the course of half an hour we obtained a good number. The poor things seemed not at all aware of the effect of guns, for they would fly straight towards us as often as in any other direction; but after a while they became more knowing, and avoided us with more care. We procured some eggs, and as no young ones were yet to be found, we went off satisfied. The soil was so light, and so easily dug, that many of the burrows extended to the depth of five or six feet, although not more than a few inches below the surface, and some of the poor birds underwent a temporary imprisonment in consequence of the ground giving way under our weight. The whole island was perforated like a rabbit-warren, and every hole had its entrance placed due south, a circumstance which allowed the birds to emerge in our sight almost all at once, presenting a spectacle highly gratifying to us all. Our visit to this island took place on the 28th of June 1833.

On the 12th of August, the day after my son procured the two Jer

Falcons mentioned in the second volume of this work, our Captain, my friends GEORGE SHATTUCK and WILLIAM INGALLS, with four sailors, and another boat in company, went on a visit to "Perroket Island," distant about two miles from the harbour of Bras d'Or. The place is known to all the cod-fishers, and is celebrated for the number of Puffins that annually breed there. As we rowed towards it, although we found the water literally covered with thousands of these birds, the number that flew over and around the green island seemed much greater, insomuch that one might have imagined half the Puffins in the world had assembled there. This far-famed isle is of considerable extent, its shores are guarded by numberless blocks of rock, and within a few yards of it the water is several fathoms in depth. The ground rises in the form of an amphitheatre to the height of about seventy feet, the greatest length being from north to south, and its southern extremity fronting the Straits of Belle Isle. For every burrow in the island previously visited by us there seemed to be a hundred here, on every crag or stone stood a Puffin, at the entrance of each hole another, and yet the sea was covered and the air filled by them. I had two double-barrelled guns and two sailors to assist me; and I shot for one hour by my watch, always firing at a single bird on wing. How many Puffins I killed in that time I take the liberty of leaving you to guess.[2]

The burrows were all inhabited by young birds, of different ages and sizes, and clouds of Puffins flew over our heads, each individual holding a "lint" by the head. This fish, which measures four or five inches in length, and is of a very slender form, with a beautiful silvery hue, existed in vast shoals in the deep water around the island. The speed with which the birds flew made the fish incline by the side of their neck. While flying the Puffins emitted a loud croaking noise, but they never dropped the fish, and many of them, when brought down by a shot, still held their prey fast. I observed with concern the extraordinary affection manifested by these birds towards each other; for whenever one fell dead or wounded on the water, its mate or a stranger immediately alighted by its side, swam round it, pushed it with its bill as if to urge it to fly or dive, and seldom would leave it until an oar was raised to knock it on the head, when at last, aware of the danger, it would plunge below in an instant. Those which fell wounded immediately ran with speed to some hole, and dived into it, on which no further effort was made to secure them. Those which happened to be caught alive in the hand bit most severely, and scratched with their claws at such a rate that we were glad to let them escape. The burrows here communicated in various ways with each other, so that the whole island was perforated as if by a multitude of subterranean labyrinths, over which one could not run without the risk of falling at almost every step. The voices of the young sounded beneath our feet like voices from the grave, and the stench was extremely disagreeable, so that as soon as our boats were filled with birds we were glad to get away.[3]

During the whole of our visit, the birds never left the place, but constantly attended to their avocations. Here one would rise from beneath our feet, there, within a few yards of us, another would alight with a fish, and dive into its burrow, or feed the young that stood waiting at the entrance. The young birds were far from being friendly towards each other, and those which we carried with us kept continually fighting so long as we kept them alive. They used their yet extremely small and slender bills with great courage and pertinacity, and their cries resembled the wailings of young whelps. The smaller individuals were fed by the parents by regurgitation, or received little pieces of fish which were placed in their mouths; the larger picked up the fish that were dropped before them; but almost all of them seemed to crawl to the entrance of the holes for the purpose of being fed. In all the burrows that communicated with others, a round place was scooped out on one side of the avenue, in the form of an oven; while in those which were single, this oven-like place was found at the end, and was larger than the corridor. All the passages were flattish above, and rounded beneath, as well as on the sides. In many instances we found two birds sitting each on its egg in the same hole.

The Puffin never lays more than one egg, unless the first may have been destroyed or taken away; nor does it raise more than a single young one in the season. The time of incubation is probably from twenty-five to twenty-eight days, although I have not been able to ascertain the precise period. Both birds work in digging the hole, using their bills and feet; they also sit alternately on their egg, although the female engages more industriously in this occupation, while the male labours harder at the burrow. The egg is pure white when first deposited, but soon becomes soiled by the earth, as no nest is formed for its reception. It generally measures two and a half inches by one and three-fourths, but varies in size according to the age of the bird, as well as in shape, some being considerably more rounded at the smaller end than others. When boiled, the white is of a livid-blue colour. The captain and myself were the only persons of our party who tried to eat some. The eggs are certainly very bad, and are never collected by "The Eggers." The flesh of the birds is very dark, tough, and so fishy, as to be eatable only in cases of great want. Two Italians who had come to Labrador to purchase cod-fish, and were short of provisions, fed upon Puffins daily, to the great amusement of our party. The fishermen at times, when bait is scarce along the coast, destroy a great number of these birds, which they skin like rabbits, and then cut the flesh into slices.

The flight of the Puffin is firm, generally direct, now and then pretty well sustained. It is able to rise at once from the water or the land, although at times it runs on both before taking to wing. This depends much on necessity, for if pushed it flies at once from the ground, or plunges under the surface of the water. There they swim, with the wings partially opened, at a small depth, passing along in the manner of Divers; and by this means they catch their prey; but at other times they dive to the bottom, many fathoms deep, for shell-fish and other objects.

During the love season, the males chase each other in the air, on the water, or beneath its surface, with so much quickness as to resemble the ricochets of a cannon-ball. Having kept several for about a week, I threw them overboard in the harbour where we were at anchor, and where the water was beautifully clear. On leaving my gloved hand, they plunged through the air, entered the water, and swam off, assisting themselves by their wings to the distance of from fifty to an hundred yards. On coming up, they washed their plumage for a long time, and then dived in search of food. While on board, they ran about from the dark towards the light, keeping themselves erect, and moving with great briskness, until at times close to my feet, when they would watch my motions like hawks, and if I happened to look towards them, would instantly make for some hiding-place. They fed freely and were agreeable pets, only that they emitted an unpleasant grunting noise, and ran about incessantly during the night, when each footstep could be counted. When on rocky shores, or islands with large stones, I observed that the Puffins often flew from one crag or stone to another, alighting with ease, and then standing erect.

The young, while yet covered with down, are black, with a white patch on the belly. Their bills do not acquire much of the form which they ultimately have for several weeks; nor do they assume their perfect shape for years. I have examined many hundred individuals, among which I have found great differences in the size and form of the bill. In fact, the existence of this diversity has induced many persons to think that we have several species of Puffin on our coasts; but, after having examined many specimens in Europe, I am decidedly of opinion that this species is the same that occurs in both continents, and that we have only one more at all common on our eastern coasts. The sexes differ in no perceptible degree, only that the males are somewhat larger. When two years old they may be considered of their full size, although the bill continues to grow and acquires furrows, until it becomes as you see it in the Plate.

Notes

1. First published in *OB* 3 (1835), 105–11. Audubon's "Puffin" (plate 18; Havell 213) is known today as the Atlantic puffin (*Fratercula arctica*). In his painting, drawn during the Labrador expedition in 1833, Audubon shows the birds in breeding plumage with the female in a burrow, the male to the right. Today, Atlantic puffins are classified as Vulnerable and their populations are decreasing, having historically suffered intense habitat damage and unchecked persecution for their flesh and feathers (IUCN, 2018). Especially in regions where forage fish populations have either collapsed or moved poleward as a result of climate change, adult puffins must now travel farther than ever to gather food for their young. This forces them to expend a great deal of energy, and if they are unsuccessful, their chicks may not survive.

2. The "12th of August" appears to be in error, since Audubon's party left Bradore on August 11; Peter Logan, *Audubon: America's Greatest Naturalist and His Voyage of Discovery to Labrador* (San Francisco: Ashbryn Press, 2016), 620n182. "Perroket," now Perroquet Island, is 1.7 miles east of Bradore; the Bradore Bay Migratory Bird Sanctuary, established in 1925, includes Perroquet and Greenly Island. Puffins here, at the largest colony in Quebec, have suffered dramatic declines but still number between fifteen and twenty thousand individuals; Environment and Climate Change Canada-Quebec Region, "Baie de Brador Migratory Bird Sanctuary," www.canada.ca/en/environment-climate-change/services/migratory-bird-sanctuaries/locations/brador-bay.html (accessed January 20, 2021). The "second volume of this work" refers to *OB* 2 (1834), 554; see "Journal of a Collecting Voyage," August 10. William Ingalls (1813–1903), a member of Audubon's Labrador team, trained with his father, William Ingalls, MD, and later was a surgeon at the Chelsea Marine Hospital. After the Civil War, during which he worked as brigadier-surgeon in the artillery, he was appointed a visiting surgeon at Boston City Hospital.

3. "Lint" is possibly a historical term, according to the description, for the sand lance or sand eel (*Ammodytes spp.*), a staple in a puffin's diet.

GREAT AUK

THE only authentic account of the occurrence of this bird on our coast that I possess, was obtained from Mr HENRY HAVELL, brother of my Engraver, who, when on his passage from New York to England, hooked a Great Auk [plate 19] on the banks of Newfoundland, in extremely boisterous weather. On being hauled on board, it was left at liberty on the deck. It walked very awkwardly, often tumbling over, bit every one within reach of its powerful bill, and refused food of all kinds. After continuing several days on board, it was restored to its proper element.[1]

When I was in Labrador, many of the fishermen assured me that the "Penguin," as they name this bird, breeds on a low rocky island to the south-east of Newfoundland, where they destroy great numbers of the young for bait; but as this intelligence came to me when the season was too far advanced, I had no opportunity of ascertaining its accuracy. In Newfoundland, however, I received similar information from several individuals. An old gunner residing on Chelsea Beach, near Boston, told me that he well remembered the time when the Penguins were plentiful about Nahant and some other islands in the Bay.[2]

The egg is very large, measuring five inches in length, and three in its greatest breadth. In form it resembles that of the Common Guillemot; the shell is thick and rather rough to the touch; its colour yellowish-white, with long irregular lines and blotches of brownish-black, more numerous at the larger end.

Notes

1. First published in *OB* 4 (1838), 316–17. Henry Augustus Havell (1803–1845) prepared many of the proofs or color guides for *The Birds of America*, traced many paintings, and supervised the staff of colorists. See Joseph Goddu, *John James Audubon and Robert Havell, Jr.: Artist Proofs for* The Birds of America (New York: Hirschl & Adler, 2002), 25.

2. Audubon used the scientific name *Alca impennis* for the great auk (plate 19, fig. 1; Havell 341), but today this is usually accepted as *Pinguinus impennis*, the generic name reflecting what Audubon observes: that the great auks were often known as "penguins" (the original penguins, in fact, before European explorers went south). Audubon's secondhand record of

great auks in Massachusetts Bay has been confirmed by archaeological research and represented part of their presumed winter migrations from Icelandic waters and north to as far south as New England and Spain. The great auk was officially extinct by 1844; see introduction. Great auks were flightless and might have weighed more than eleven pounds. The "low rocky island" off to the southeast of Newfoundland that Audubon hoped to search for these birds was probably Funk Island (fig. 33), which ornithologists believe might once have hosted more than two hundred thousand great auks; it is assumed they were largely, if not entirely, extirpated from those rocks decades before Audubon's voyage. Once common throughout Atlantic Canada and the New England coast, great auks were also known to breed in historically large numbers on the Magdalen Islands, which Audubon did visit (see "Journal of a Collecting Voyage," June 12; figs. 33, 35). W. A. Montevecci and D. A. Kirk, "Great Auk," v. 1.0 (2020), birdsoftheworld.org.

WILSON'S PETREL

A LONG voyage would always be to me a continued source of suffering, were I restrained from gazing on the vast expanse of the waters, and on the ever-pleasing inhabitants of the air that now and then appear in the ship's wake. The slightest motion of the vessel effectually prevents me from enjoying the mirth of my fellow passengers, or sympathizing with them in their sickness. When the first glimpse of day appears, I make my way on deck, where I stand not unlike a newly hatched bird, tottering on feeble legs. Let the wind blow high or not, I care little which, provided it waft me toward the shores of America. If the sky be clear, the first sight of the sun excites emotions of gratitude towards the Being by whose power it was formed, and sent forth to shed its benign influence on surrounding worlds. Silent adoration occupies my soul, and I conclude with ardent wishes for the happiness of friends left far behind, and those toward whom I am proceeding. But now, ever flapping its wing-lets, I have marked the little bird [plate 20], dusky all over save a single spot, the whiteness of which contrasts with the dark hue of the waters and the deep tone of the clear sky. Full of life and joy it moves to and fro, advances toward the ship, then shoots far away, gambols over the swelling waves, dives into their hollows, and twitters with delight as it perceives an object that will alleviate its hunger. Never fatigued, the tiny Petrels seldom alight, although at times their frail legs and feet seem to touch the crest of the foaming wave. I love to give every creature all the pleasure I can confer upon it, and towards the little things I cast over the stern such objects as I know they will most prize. Social creatures! would that all were as innocent as you! There are no bickerings, no jealousies among you; the first that comes is first served; it is all the result of chance; and thus you pass your lives. But the clouds gather, the gale approaches, and our gallant bark is trimmed. Darkness spreads over the heavens, and the deep waters send back a blacker gloom, broken at intervals by the glimmer of the spray. You meet the blast, and your little wings bear you up against it for a while; but you cannot encounter the full force of the tempest; and now you have all come close beneath me, where you glide over the curling eddies caused by the motion of the rudder. You shall have all possible attention paid you, and I will crawl to the camboose, in search of food to support your tiny frames in this hour of need. But at length, night closes around, and I bid you farewell.[1]

The gale is over; the clear blue of the sky looks clearer than ever, the sun's rays are brighter, on the quiet waters the ship seems to settle in repose, and her wings, though widely spread, no longer swell with the breeze. At a distance around us the dusky wanderers are enjoying the bright morning; the rudder-fish, yesterday so lively, has ended its career, so violently was it beaten by the waves against the vessel; and now the Petrels gather around it, as it floats on the surface. Various other matters they find; here a small crab, there the fragments of a sea-plant. Low over the deep they range, and now with little steps run on the waters. Few are their notes, but great their pleasure, at this moment. It is needless for me to feed them now, and therefore I will return to my task.[2]

It would be extremely difficult for any individual to determine the extent of the movements of the three species of Petrel seen on the waters of the Atlantic. My opinion is that until their breeding places are repeatedly visited by naturalists, little can be known respecting the range of their flight. I have crossed the ocean many times, and have always paid more or less attention to these birds; yet I am as ignorant of their migrations as my predecessors. I have rarely seen Wilson's Petrel farther to the eastward than the Azores, and beyond these islands it generally abandoned the vessel. Along the American coast, I have not met with it to the northward beyond the 51st degree of latitude; while to the southward I have rarely observed many on the Gulf of Mexico; nor do I believe that any breed on the shores of the Floridas, or on the Bahama Islands, as alleged by WILSON, who, it would appear, stated so from report. Petrels are rarely destroyed by men, quadrupeds, or rapacious birds, when breeding; to the former they are of no value as an article of food, and by the latter they are seldom sought after; consequently they are more likely to return to their breeding places than most other birds, many of which are frequently induced to abandon them on account of the persecutions to which they are subjected. I have found the Forked-tailed Petrel breeding on our coast, in the fissures of rocks above the reach of the spray, and Wilson's digging for itself burrows in the sand or loose earth on low islands. The *Thalassidroma pelagica* I have never found breeding on any part of our coast; but it is well known that it resorts to holes on certain of the Shetland Islands, among the blocks and stones of which the beaches are formed; though it appears that in some spots, where the fishermen are in the habit of destroying them, many resort to the elevated fissures of the rocks, where also a few of the Forked-tailed species occasionally breed. The latter then, though more abundant in America, belongs to Europe also. WILSON was not aware that the species now named after him was any thing else than "the Stormy Petrel, *Procellaria pelagica* of LINNÆUS;" and he remarks that it "is found over the whole Atlantic ocean, from Europe to North America, at all distances from land, and in all weathers."[3]

To my learned friend the PRINCE OF MUSIGNANO, the scientific world is indebted for a Memoir on Petrels, in which he has clearly shewn the specific differences of the three species mentioned above, of which he has also given figures, as well as those of the bills and feet nearly of the natural size [fig. 31]. But the artist who drew these birds for him, or the engraver, committed an error in representing the present bird as the largest of the three.[4]

Wilson's Petrel breeds on some small islands situated off the southern extremity of Nova Scotia, and called "Mud Islands," but which are formed of sand and light earth, scantily covered with grass. Thither the birds resort in great numbers, about the beginning of June, and form burrows of the depth of two or two and a half feet, in the bottom of which is laid a single white egg, a few bits of dry grass, scarcely deserving the name of a nest, having been placed for its reception. The egg measures an inch and a half in length, by seven-eighths of an inch in breadth, is almost equally rounded at both ends, and has a pure white

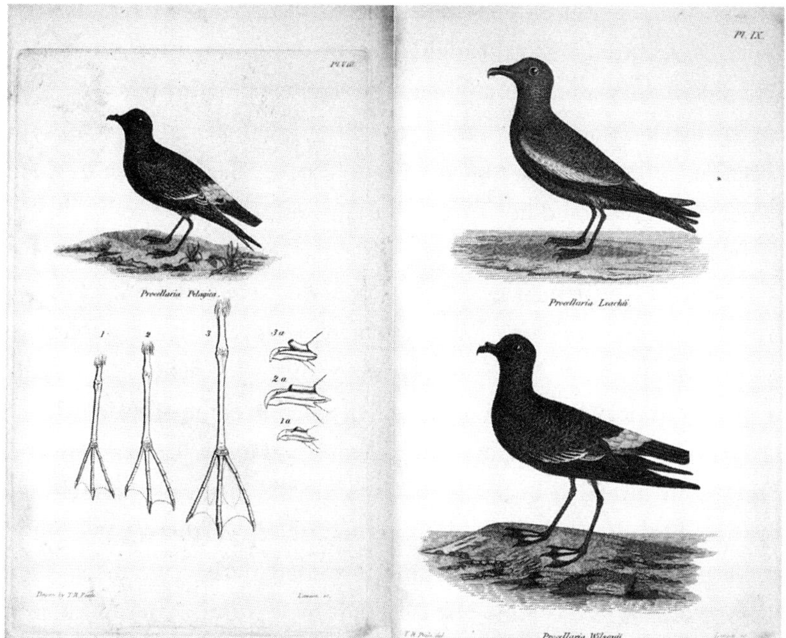

FIGURE 31. The illustrations of storm-petrels that Audubon critiques, as published in Prince Charles-Lucien Bonaparte's "An Account of Four Species of Stormy Petrels," *Journal of the Academy of Natural Sciences of Philadelphia* 3, no. 2 (1824): plates VIII and IX. Courtesy of Williams College.

colour. These Petrels copulate on the water, in the same manner as the Hyperborean Phalarope. By the beginning of August the young follow their parents to sea, and are then scarcely distinguishable from them. During incubation, they remain in the burrows, or at their entrance, rarely going to seek for food before the dusk.[5]

On wing this species is more lively than the Forked-tailed, but less so than the Common Stormy Petrel. It keeps its wings nearly at right angles with its body, and makes considerable use of its feet, particularly during calm weather, when it at times hops or leaps for several feet, or pats the water, whilst its wings are extended upwards with a fluttering motion, and it inclines its head downwards to pick up its food from the water, and I have observed it immerse the whole head beneath the surface, to seize on small fishes, in which it generally succeeded. It can walk pretty well on the deck of a vessel, or any other flat surface, and rise from it without much difficulty. Its notes are different from that of the

Forked-tailed Petrel, and resembles the syllables *kee-re-kee kee*. They are more frequently emitted at night than by day. I never could ascertain whether or not these birds alight on the rigging at night, but my opinion is that they do not, for the sailors, to whom I had offered premiums for catching some of them, told me that although they flew about them while aloft, they could not see one standing anywhere.

In my journal written on board the packet ship Columbia, commanded by my worthy friend JOSEPH DELANO, Esq., I find the following memorandums: "Wilson's Petrel was first seen, this voyage, about two hundred miles from England, and *alone* until we reached the middle of the Atlantic, when the Forked-tailed came in sight, after which the latter was most plentiful, and the pelagica by far the least numerous." During my several visits to the coasts of the Floridas, I saw scarcely any of these birds in the course of several months spent there, but I found them pretty abundant on returning towards Charleston. This species, like the others, feeds on mollusca, small fishes, Crustacea, marine plants, excrements of cetaceous animals; and the greasy substances thrown from vessels. When caught, they squirt an oily substance through the nostrils, and often disgorge the same. The sexes are similar in their external appearance.[6]

Notes

1. First published in *OB* 3 (1835), 486–90. Audubon's "Wilson's/Stormy Petrel" (plate 20; Havell 270) is known today as Wilson's storm-petrel (*Oceanites oceanicus*). Audubon was apparently too seasick to finish his drawings at sea and executed his painting years later. Wilson's storm-petrel, a species of Least Concern, can be found on all the world's oceans today and is potentially "one of the most abundant birds in the world." IUCN, 2018; J. Drucker, C. Carboneras, F. Jutglar, and G. M. Kirwan, "Wilson's Storm-Petrel," v. 1.0 (2020), birdsoftheworld.org. The word *petrel* is perhaps derived from "Petrello," Italian for little Peter, since the birds, as Audubon explains, pitter over the surface of the sea for food, evoking the biblical story of St. Peter walking on water. The nickname "Mother Carey's Chickens," which Audubon included in his plate for this species (see "Journal of a Sea Voyage," April 26 and July 9) derived, perhaps sarcastically, from the Latin "Mater Cara" for the Virgin Mary, a patron of sailors, since storm-petrels were often regarded as harbingers of bad weather. Mariner opinions had varied over the centuries, however, on whether storm-petrels brought good or ill fortune in relation to storms. The crew on the *Delos* saw them in positive terms, as does Audubon here, describing these smallest of ocean seabirds as vulnerable in a gale, finding a ship in their "hour of need."

2. Storm-petrels have long been known to mariners for following in the wake of vessels. Perhaps they benefit from food stirred up in the vessel's wake. In Audubon's time, some

naturalists thought storm-petrels drank and ate whale and fish oils off the surface. Audubon explains that he fed them some type of food from the ship's on-deck galley, the "camboose." Modern ornithologists agree that Wilson's storm-petrels subsist mostly on planktonic crustaceans such as krill, small fish and squids, and dead marine mammals. Audubon's storm-petrels would more likely have been picking up organisms living in and around the "marine plants," such as a species of *Sargassum*, than feeding on the algae itself.

3. In addition to Wilson's storm-petrel, the other two North Atlantic storm-petrels mentioned by Audubon are his "Fork-tail/Fork-tailed Petrel" (Havell 260), now the Leach's storm-petrel (*Hydrobates leucorhous*), and the "Common Stormy Petrel/Least Stormy-Petrel" (Havell 340), now the European storm-petrel (*Hydrobates pelagicus*). Modern ornithologists have confirmed in part Audubon's distribution and observations, although Wilson's storm-petrel can be found through the North Atlantic south of Greenland and the UK, and they breed only on islands in the Southern Ocean and along the coast of Antarctica. Audubon's "Forked-tailed" (Leach's) petrels do indeed breed in Atlantic Canada, including at the Mud Islands off Nova Scotia—Audubon seems to have received incorrect information about Wilson's breeding there—and the Leach's breeding range indeed still "belongs to Europe also." (Just to add modern confusion, there is still a storm-petrel with the common name "fork-tailed," but this species is found today only in the North Pacific, *Oceanodroma furcata*). See Derek Onley and Paul Scofield, *Albatrosses, Petrels & Shearwaters of the World* (2007), 218–36; Peter Logan, *Audubon: America's Greatest Naturalist and His Voyage of Discovery to Labrador* (San Francisco: Ashbryn Press, 2016), 149. Audubon cited Wilson's comments on the storm-petrel from *American Ornithology*, vol. 7 (Philadelphia: Bradford and Inskeep, 1814), 91; Sabina Wilhelm, personal communication, August 11, 2020.

4. In 1824 Prince Charles-Lucien Bonaparte named the bird *Procellaria wilsonii* but the German naturalist Heinrich Kuhl had already described it; see Edward H. Burtt Jr., "The Birds of Alexander Wilson: Wilson's Storm-Petrel (*Oceanites oceanicus*)," *Wilson Journal of Ornithology* 125, no. 2 (June 2013): 441; Bonaparte, "An Account of Four Species of Stormy Petrels," *Journal of the Academy of Natural Sciences of Philadelphia* 3, no. 2 (1824): 230–31.

5. Audubon's "Hyperborean Phalarope" (Havell 215) is today the red-necked phalarope (*Phalaropus lobatus*).

6. Any journals Audubon might have kept during his two voyages aboard the packet ship *Columbia*, from Portsmouth, England, to New York in 1829 and in 1831, no longer exist. The *Columbia* was a packet ship, equipped for a fairly new type of transatlantic passage that left on a schedule and emphasized speed and the carrying of mail ("packets"), newspapers, and passengers, rather than a tramp-style vessel, which waited until filled to carry cargo and might visit multiple ports. Captain Joseph C. Delano of New Bedford (1796–1886) had been captain of the *Columbia* (built 1821, 492 tons) since at least 1826. In 1830, between Audubon's two passages, which each took about a month, Delano made a record westbound transatlantic run of fifteen days and eighteen hours. Yet Audubon wrote in "Forked-tailed Petrel" that Delano promised to allow him to lower boats in calm conditions in order to retrieve birds (*OB* 3 [1835], 434). Matthew Fontaine Maury (1806–1873), one of the founders of modern oceanography, once wrote that Delano was "one of the best navigators and most intelligent men who ever sailed out of the port of New York." Delano's paternal uncle was Franklin Delano Roosevelt's great-grandfather. See Joan Druett, *Hen Frigates: Wives of Merchant Captains under Sail* (New York: Touchstone, 1998), 25–30; Carl C. Cutler, *Greyhounds of the Sea* (Annapolis: United States Naval Institute Press, 1930), 457; and Lewis J. Darter, "Federal Archives Relating to Matthew Fontaine Maury," *American Neptune*, 1, no. 2 (April 1941): 155.

III

Journal of a Collecting Voyage from Eastport to Labrador Aboard the *Ripley* (1833)

In June 1833, Audubon, who said he wanted to go where the loon went for the summer, set out for "the granitic rocks of Labrador," the easternmost section of the Canadian Shield ("The Red-throated Diver," *OB* 3 [1835], 20). He had chosen men less than half his age to accompany him: his twenty-year-old son John Woodhouse; two medical students from Boston, William Ingalls and George Shattuck; and two young men from Maine, Thomas Lincoln and Joseph Coolidge. Only John Woodhouse and Tom Lincoln had some prior ornithological expertise; the others Audubon had promised to instruct. Lucy stayed behind at her brother-in-law's house in New York, where, unable to communicate with her husband and son, she felt increasingly uncomfortable.[1]

After several discouraging weeks of waiting in Eastport, Maine (there was snow on the ground!), the *Ripley*, a 105-ton schooner chartered for $350 a month, finally set off for Nova Scotia. They rounded the coast, passed by Cape Breton Island, and entered the Gulf of Lawrence, heading first to the Magdalen Islands and then to the coast of Labrador (modern day Quebec; fig. 33). On the return voyage, Audubon stopped in Newfoundland, arriving back in Eastport on August 30, which, as far as he was concerned, wasn't a day too soon: "Seldom in my life have I left a country with as little regret as this," he had written on August 11.

A son of the tropics, used to stalking his birds in the sweltering heat of Louisiana, Audubon was not prepared for the cold that awaited him in Labrador, the misty rains, choppy waters, strong winds, and ubiquitous smell of codfish. And he felt his age: at forty-eight, barely recovered from a stroke he had suffered a few months earlier, he did not appreciate the mossy landscapes of the Labrador coast, where mosquitoes attacked travelers by the thousands and even the smallest birds, such as the newly discovered "Lincoln Finches" (Lincoln's sparrows) he had named after his young assistant, immediately became hostile and pugnacious (*OB* 3 [1835], 540). Labrador "chilled the heart," Audubon wrote in his journal (July 18). We have come far from the "swiftness of thought" expressed in the earlier journals: Audubon's ability to find uplift in the contemplation of any land- or seascape and in each bird a source of delight now appears severely diminished. The damp, "dirty" subarctic weather (July 8, July 16) dampened his spirits, too. When Audubon noted, on July 20, that "the country of Labrador deserves credit for one fine day," he was only partly joking. A day earlier, he'd imagined how their ship, tossed against the shore by waves up to fifty feet high, might be "dashed to pieces."

Seabirds they found aplenty. The choppy waters were covered with murres, "playing in the very spray under our bow, plunging as if in fun under it, and rising like spirits close under our rudder" (June 17). When he looked up, the air darkened with velvet ducks flying by. And the armies of northern gannets circling "Great Gannet Rock," a forbidding plateau rising from the sea near Cape St. Mary's, Newfoundland, to Audubon seemed like falling snowflakes, shrouding the view in a "thick, foggy-like atmosphere" (June 14).

But such natural abundance was under constant threat even then. Since joining Newfoundland in 1809, Labrador had become a kind of white man's larder, with supplies still outstripping demand. In the harbor of Bradore, Audubon saw the carcasses of fifteen hundred seals piled up, with dogs tearing into the offal: "The stench filled the air for half a mile around" (July 27). To Audubon, the fishermen who killed thousands of guillemots in a day, plucking their feathers and throwing the bodies into the sea (July 23), must have seemed monstrous caricatures of himself and his pursuits. Then there were occasions when Audubon glimpsed what would happen when all that abundance ran out. On June 18, for example, the apocalyptic carnage inflicted on the colonies of nesting murres by eggers hoping to sell their loot in the markets of Halifax left nothing behind for him to collect (fig. 32). "I remained all day on board drawing."[2]

Working conditions aboard the *Ripley* were far from ideal. Audubon and his men toiled and rested in the bowels of the ship. Even when the hatch was closed to keep out the constant rain, water would drip onto Audubon's sheets, spread out on the large table where he made his drawings. Not surprisingly, the artistic and scientific tally of the voyage was, by Audubon's standards, modest: 173 skins, a handful of newly discovered species, and twenty-five finished drawings. But the chilling experience of Labrador's emptiness inspired some of Audubon's best art as well as some of his best writing. His journal notes found their way into some

FIGURE 32. Rosamond Purcell, *Collector's Box of Murre Eggs*, photograph, in *Egg & Nest* (2008). A contemporary photographer based in Medford, Massachusetts, Purcell has long been attracted to natural history collections and museums, turning displays marked by death and decay into photographs and installations of transcendent and haunting beauty. The murre eggs in this box, with their different shapes and collector's labels, were collected at different sites and randomly reassembled by Purcell. The markings on each egg are unique to the bird that laid it.

of the most memorable essays and stories collected in part II of our anthology—see the references to his journals in "The Brown Pelican," "Black Skimmer or Razor-billed Shearwater," "The Sooty Tern," "St John's River in Florida," "The Great Black-backed Gull," and "Wilson's Petrel." In terms of the artistic yield, consider Audubon's magnificent representation of two northern gannets (plate 12), a tender father-and-son portrait that, according to the novelist Katherine Govier, mirrors Audubon's reinvigorated relationship with his son John. Audubon's emotional investment in the scene is evident in the care he put even into his representation of Great Gannet Rock in the background of his composition (see fig. 29).[3]

Audubon's original journal from the trip has not survived. A few years after his death, Lucy, with the help of a friend, the Reverend Charles Coffin Adams, assembled her husband's papers, including excerpts she had copied from his original Labrador journal, into a monster of a manuscript, which she sent to a publisher in England. Sampson Low, Son & Marston asked a young poet, Robert Williams Buchanan (1841–1901), to turn the unwieldy thing into a book. Buchanan radically cut Lucy's manuscript, removed much of the ornithological information, and added a few unsolicited tidbits of his own, including an assessment of Audubon, whom he had never met ("He prattled about himself like an infant, gloried in his long hair, admired the fine curve of his nose"). *The Life and Adventures of John James Audubon, the Naturalist* was published in 1868 and reprinted both in England and the United States. Buchanan's hatchet job annoyed Lucy Audubon, but since he never returned her manuscript, she was faced with the choice of starting again, from scratch, or republishing Buchanan's version minus his offending comments. Lucy's *The Life of John James Audubon, the Naturalist, Edited by His Widow*, completed with the help of New York editor James Grant Wilson (1832–1914), was published by G. P. Putnam and Sons in 1869. Despite these problems, the excerpts from the Labrador journal included in Lucy Audubon's biography are, as Peter Logan has argued, more reliable than the text edited by Maria Rebecca Audubon, who created her own version from Audubon's journal, which had remained in the family, injecting her environmental beliefs, before she, presumably, destroyed the original—which thus shared, in a final ironic twist, the fate of so many of the birds her grandfather had encountered.[4]

Notes

1. On Lucy Audubon's situation, see Peter Logan, *Audubon: America's Greatest Naturalist and His Voyage of Discovery to Labrador* (San Francisco: Ashbryn Press, 2016), 222–23.

2. Rosamond Purcell, Linnea S. Hall, and René Corado, *Egg & Nest* (Cambridge, MA: Belknap, 2008), 207.

3. On collections from this voyage, see John James Audubon to Victor Audubon, September 9, 1833, American Philosophical Society; Logan, *Audubon*, 621n3. For Katherine Govier's description of the painting of the gannets, see *Creation* (Toronto: Random House, 2002), 44.

4. On Maria R. Audubon and conservation, see Daniel Patterson, "Maria Rebecca Audubon, Her Grandfather's 1843 Missouri River Journals, and 'The Great Auk Speech,'" in *The Missouri River Journals of John James Audubon*, ed. Patterson (Lincoln: University of Nebraska Press, 2016), 3–23. In 1897, the prominent ornithologist Elliott Coues, who collaborated with Maria on her edition of *Audubon and His Journals*, reported that, while several of Audubon's original journals had "perished, by fire or otherwise," Maria still had nine originals in her possession, among them "the Labrador journal of 1833," likely the last time it was seen by anyone (Patterson, 7). Acting, with her family's support, as the guardian of their reputation, Maria was unabashed about her role in discarding those of her grandfather's manuscripts that she didn't want to be read by others: "fire was our only surety that many family details should be put beyond the reach of vandal hands" (quoted in Stanley Clisby Arthur, *Audubon: The Intimate Life of the American Woodsman* [1937; New Orleans: Pelican, 2000], 243).

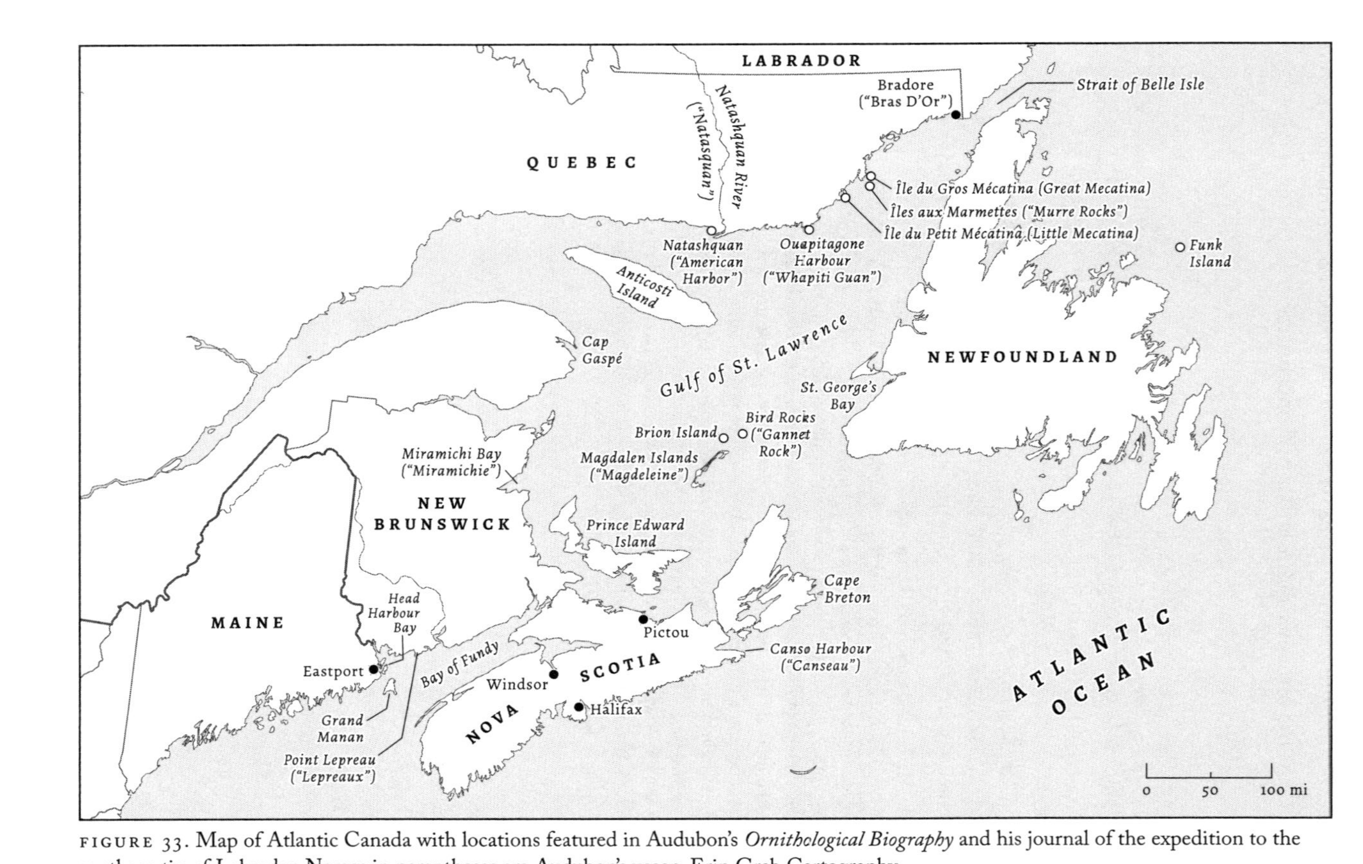

FIGURE 33. Map of Atlantic Canada with locations featured in Audubon's *Ornithological Biography* and his journal of the expedition to the southern tip of Labrador. Names in parentheses are Audubon's usage. Erin Greb Cartography.

Journal of a Collecting Voyage from Eastport to Labrador aboard the Ripley *(1833)*

Here [in Boston], I was witness to the melancholy death of the great Spurzheim, and was myself suddenly attacked by a short but severe illness, which greatly alarmed my family; but thanks to Providence and my medical friends, Parkman, Shattuck, and Warren, I was soon enabled to proceed with my labor—a sedentary life and too close application being the cause assigned for my indisposition. I resolved to set out again in quest of fresh materials for my pencil and pen. My wishes directing me to Labrador, I returned eastward with my youngest son, and had the pleasure of being joined by four young gentlemen, all fond of natural history, and willing to encounter the difficulties and privations of the voyage—George Shattuck, Thomas Lincoln, William Ingalls, and Joseph Coolidge.[1]

June 4, 1833. The day has been fine, and I dined with Captain Childs, commanding the United States troops here. We had a pleasant dinner, but I am impatient to be under weigh for Labrador. The vessel is being prepared for our reception and departure; and we have concluded to ship two extra sailors, and a boy, to be a sort of major-domo, to clean our guns, hunt for nests and birds, and assist in skinning them, &c. While rambling in the woods this morning I discovered a crow's nest with five young ones in it, and as I climbed the tree the parents came to the rescue of their children, crying loudly and with such perseverance, that in fifteen minutes more than fifty pairs of these birds had joined in their vociferations, although I saw only a single pair when I began to climb the tree.[2]

June 6. We sailed from Eastport about one o'clock P.M. [fig. 34], and the whole male population seemed to have turned out to witness our departure, just as if no schooner of the size of the Ripley had ever gone from this mighty port to Labrador; our numerous friends came with the throng, and we all shook hands as if we were never to meet again; and as we pushed off with a trifling accident or so, the batteries of the garrison and the cannon of the revenue cutter in the stream saluted us with stout, loud, and oft-repeated reports. Captain Coolidge accompanied us, and was, indeed, our pilot, until we passed Lubec. The wind was light and ahead, and yet with the assistance of the tide we drifted twenty-five miles down to Little River during the night.

June 7. This morning found us riding at anchor near some ugly-looking rocks, the sight of which caused our captain to try to get out of their way, and the whole morning was spent in trying to get into Little

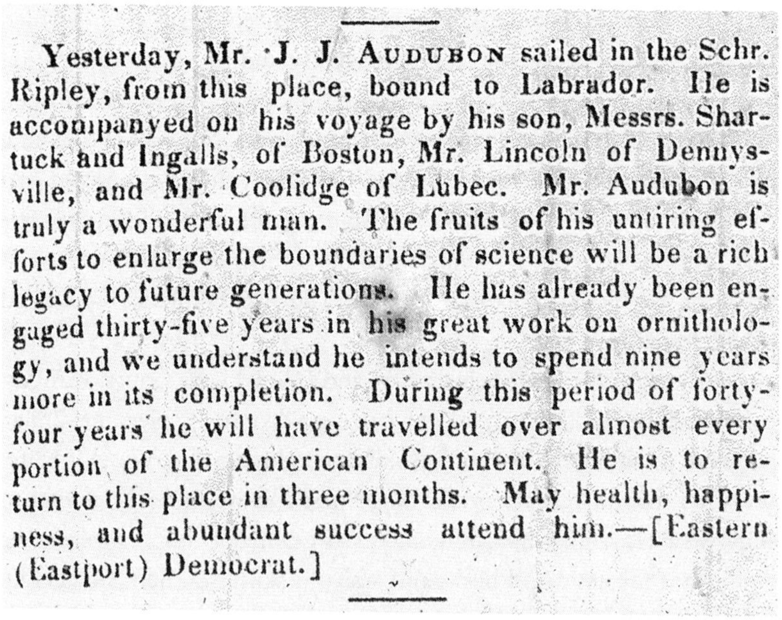

Yesterday, Mr. J. J. AUDUBON sailed in the Schr. Ripley, from this place, bound to Labrador. He is accompanyed on his voyage by his son, Messrs. Shartuck and Ingalls, of Boston, Mr. Lincoln of Dennysville, and Mr. Coolidge of Lubec. Mr. Audubon is truly a wonderful man. The fruits of his untiring efforts to enlarge the boundaries of science will be a rich legacy to future generations. He has already been engaged thirty-five years in his great work on ornithology, and we understand he intends to spend nine years more in its completion. During this period of forty-four years he will have travelled over almost every portion of the American Continent. He is to return to this place in three months. May health, happiness, and abundant success attend him.—[Eastern (Eastport) Democrat.]

FIGURE 34. Report of Audubon's departure on the *Ripley* from Eastport. Maine. *Eastern Argus* (Portland, ME), June 10, 1833. Courtesy of Williams College.

River, but the men were unable to tow us in. We landed for a few minutes and shot a hermit thrush, but the wind sprang up, and we returned to the vessel and tried to put out to sea; we were for a time in danger of drifting upon the rocks, but the wind increased, and we made our way out to sea. Suddenly, however, the fog came drifting in, and was so thick that we could hardly see the bowsprit, and the night was spent in direful apprehension of some impending evil; although, about twelve, squalls of wind decided in our favor, and when day dawned the wind was blowing fresh from the north, and we were driving on the waters, all sea-sick, and crossing that worst of all dreadful bays, the Bay of Fundy.

June 8. We sailed between Seal and Mud Islands. In the latter the procellaria (a species of gull) breed abundantly; their nests are dug in the sand to the depth of two feet or more, and the whole island is covered with them, looking like rat holes. They lay three white eggs.[3]

[. . .]

[*June 11.*] To day there has been cold, rain and hail, but the frogs are piping in the pools. By-and-by the weather became beautiful, and the wind fair, and we were soon under way, following in the wake of the whole fleet, which had been anchored in the harbor of Canseau, and gliding across the great bay under full press of sail. The land locked us in, the water was smooth, the sky serene, and the thermometer at 46°, and the sunshine on deck was very agreeable. After sailing twenty-one miles we entered the real Gut of Canseau; passing one after another every vessel of the fleet with which we had sailed.[4]

The land on each side now rose in the form of an amphitheatre, and on the Nova Scotia side to a considerable height; dwellings appeared here and there, but the country is too poor for comfort: the timber is small, and the land too stony; a small patch of ploughed land planted, or ready for potatoes, was all the cultivation we saw. Near one house we saw a few apple trees, which were not yet in bloom. The general appearance of this passage reminded me of some parts of the Hudson River, and, accompanied as we were by thirty sail of vessels, the time passed agreeably. Vegetation appeared as forward as at Eastport: saw a few chimney swallows, and heard a few blue jays. As we passed Cape Porcupine, a high rounding hill, we saw some Indians in birch-bark canoes, and clearing Cape George we were soon in the Gulf of St. Lawrence. From this place, on the 20th of May last year, the sea was a sheet of ice as far as the eye could reach with the aid of a good spy-glass.

We ran down the west coast of Cape Breton Island, and the country looked well in the distance; large undulating hills were covered with many hamlets, and patches of cultivated land were seen. It being calm when we neared Jestico Island, about three miles from Cape Breton, I left the vessel and landed on it. It was covered with well-grown grass, and filled with strawberry vines in full bloom. The sun shone brightly, the weather was pleasant, and we found many northern birds breeding there; the wild gooseberries were plentiful, about the size of a pea, and a black currant also. The wind arose, and we hurried back to the vessel; on the way my son John and some of the sailors nearly killed a seal with their oars.[5]

[*June 12.*] This morning at four o'clock we came in sight of the Magdalene Islands [fig. 35], distant about twenty miles. The morning was dull, and by breakfast-time a thick fog obscured the horizon, and we lost sight of the islands; the wind rose sluggishly and dead ahead, and several ships and brigs loaded with timber from the Miramichie came near us beating their way to the Atlantic. At nine o'clock we dropped

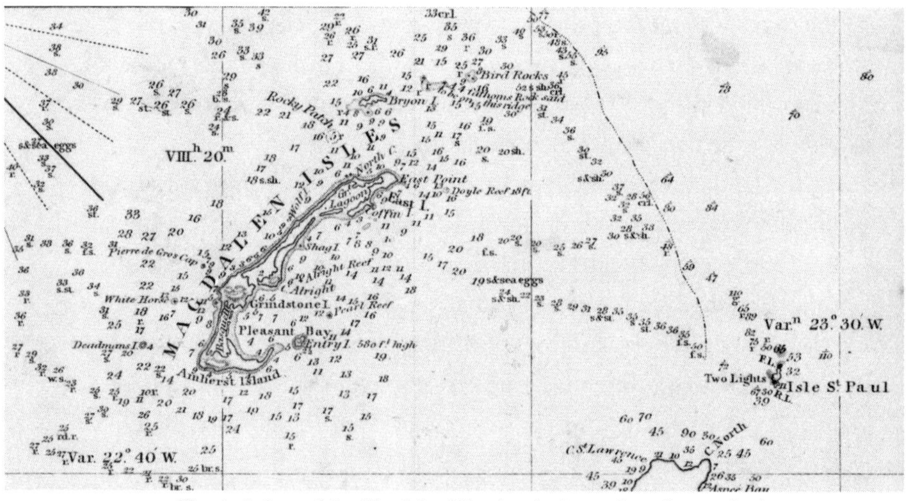

FIGURE 35. Nautical chart of the Magdalen Islands, which are about forty miles long, with the Bird Rocks, known to Audubon as "Gannet Rock," to the north of this detail (New York: E. & G. W. Blunt, 1844, rev. 1852). Note Pleasant Bay and Entry Island to the south, Bryon [Brion] to the north, and the "sea eggs" to the east, which likely meant sea urchins on the bottom. Courtesy of McMaster University.

anchor, being partly land-locked between Breton Island and the Highlands, and within a quarter of a mile of an Island, which formed a part of the group. The pilot, who is well acquainted here, informed me that the islands are all connected by dry sand-bars, and with no channel between them except the one we are in, called Entree Bay, which is formed by Entree Island and a long sand-spit connecting it with the mainland. The island is forty-eight miles long, and three in breadth; the formation is a red rough sandy soil, and the north-west side is constantly wearing away by the action of the sea. Guillemots were seated upright along the projecting shelvings in regular order, resembling so many sentinels on the look-out; many gannets also were seen on the extreme points of the island. On one of the islands were many houses, and a small church, and on the highest land a large cross, indicating the religion of the inhabitants. Several small vessels lay in the harbor called Pleasant Bay, but the weather is so cold we cannot visit them until to-morrow.[6]

[*June 13.*] Magdalene Islands, Gulf of St. Lawrence. It is one week since we left Eastport, and we breakfasted with the thermometer at 44° in our cabin, and on deck it feels like mid-winter. We landed on the island next to us so chilled that we could scarcely use our hands; two large bluffs frowned on each side of us, the resort of many sea-birds, and some noble ravens which we saw. Following a narrow path we soon came upon one of God's best finished jewels, a woman. She saw us first, for women are always keenest in sight and perception, in patience and fortitude and love, in faith and sorrow, and, as I believe, in everything else which adorns our race. She was hurrying towards her cottage, with a child in her arms, having no covering but a little shirt. The mother was dressed in coarse French homespun, with a close white cotton nightcap on her head, and the mildest-looking woman I had seen in many a day. At a venture I addressed her in French, and it answered well, for she replied in an unintelligible jargon, about one-third of which I understood, which enabled me to make out that she was the wife of a fisherman who lived there.

[. . .]

[*June 14.*] Day dawned with the weather dull, but the wind fair, and we pulled up anchor and left the Magdalene Islands for Labrador, the ultimatum of our present desires. About ten o'clock we saw on the distant horizon a speck, which I was told was the Rock; the wind now freshened, and I could soon see it plainly from the deck, the top apparently covered with snow. Our pilot said that the snow, which seemed two or three feet thick, was the white gannets which resort there. I rubbed my eyes, and took my spy-glass, and instantly the strange picture stood before me. They were indeed birds, and such a mass of birds, and of such a size as I never saw before. The whole of my party were astonished, and all agreed that it was worth a voyage across the Bay of Fundy and the Gulf of St. Lawrence to see such a sight. The nearer we approached, the greater was our surprise at the enormous number of these birds, all calmly seated on their eggs, and their heads turned to the windward towards us. The air for a hundred yards above, and for a long distance around, was filled with gannets on the wing, which from our position made the air look as if it was filled with falling snowflakes, and caused a thick, foggy-like atmosphere all around the rock. The wind was too high to allow us to land, but we were so anxious to do so that some of the party made the attempt. The vessel was brought to, and a small whaleboat launched, and young Lincoln and John pushed off with clubs and guns; the wind increased and rain set in, but they gained the lee of the rock, but after an hour's absence returned without landing. The air was filled with birds, but they did not perceptibly diminish the numbers on the rock. As the vessel drifted nearer the rock, we could see that the birds sat so close as almost to touch one another in regular lines, looking like so many mole-hills. The discharge of a gun had no effect on those which were not touched by the shot, for the noise of the birds stunned all those out of reach of the gun. But where the shot took effect the birds scrambled and flew off in such multitudes and such confusion that, whilst eight or ten were falling in the water dead or wounded, others shook down their eggs, which fell into the sea by hundreds in all directions. The sea became rougher, and the boat was compelled to return, bringing some birds and some eggs, but without the party being able to climb the rock.[7]

The top of the main rock is a quarter of a mile wide from north to south, and a little narrower from east to west; its elevation above the sea is between three and four hundred feet. The sea dashes around it with great violence: except in long calms it is extremely difficult to land on it, and much more difficult to climb to its platform. The whole surface was perfectly covered with nests, about two feet apart, in rows as regular as a potato field. The fishermen kill these birds and use their flesh for bait for cod-fish. The crews of several vessels unite, and, armed with clubs, as they reach the top of the rock the birds rise with a noise like thunder, and attempt to fly in such hurried confusion as to knock each other down, often piling one on another in a bank of many feet thickness. The men beat and kill them until they have obtained a supply, or wearied themselves. Six men in this way have killed five or six hundred in one hour. The birds are skinned and cut into junks, and the bait keeps good for a fortnight. Forty sail of fishermen annually supply themselves with bait from this rock in this way. By the twentieth of May the birds lay their eggs, and hatch about the twentieth of June.

[*June 15.*] The wind is blowing a gale, and nearly all my party is deadly sick. Thermometer 43°, and raining nearly all day. We laid to all night, and in the morning were in sight of Anticosti Island, distant about twenty miles. It soon became thick, and we lost sight of it.

[*June 16.*] The weather is calm, beautiful, and much warmer. We caught many cod-fish, which contained crabs of a curious structure. At six P.M. the wind sprung up fair, and we made all sail for Labrador.

[*June 17.*] I was on deck at three o'clock A.M., and although the sun was not above the horizon it was quite light. The sea was literally covered with foolish guillemots playing in the very spray under our bow, plunging as if in fun under it, and rising like spirits close under our rudder. The wind was fair, and the land in sight from aloft, and I now look forward to our landing on Labrador as at hand, and my thoughts are filled with expectation of the new knowledge of birds and animals which I hope to acquire there. The Ripley sails well, but now she fairly skipped over the water. The cry of land soon made my heart bound with joy; and as we approached it we saw what looked like many sails of vessels, but we soon found that they were snow-banks, and the air along the shore was filled with millions of velvet ducks and other aquatic birds, flying in long files a few yards above the water.[8]

We saw one vessel at anchor, and the country looked well from the distance; and as we neared the shore the thermometer rose from 44° to 60°, yet the appearance of the snow-drifts was forbidding. The shores appeared to be margined with a broad and handsome sand-beach, and we saw imaginary bears, wolves and other animals scampering away on the rugged shore. About thirty boats were fishing, and we saw them throwing the fish on deck by thousands.

We soon reached the mouth of the Natasquan River, where the Hudson Bay Company have a fishing establishment, and where no American vessel is allowed to come. The shore was filled with bark-covered huts, and some vessels were anchored within the sand-point which forms one side of the entrance to the river. We sailed on four miles further to the American harbor, and came to anchor in a beautiful bay, wholly secure from any winds.

And now we are positively at Labrador, lat. 50°, and farther north than I ever was before on this continent. But what a country! When we landed and reached the summit we sank nearly up to our knees in mosses of different sorts, producing such a sensation as I never felt before. These mosses in the distance look like hard rocks, but under the feet they feel like a velvet cushion. We rambled about and searched in vain for a foot of square earth; a poor, rugged, and miserable country; the trees are wiry and scraggy dwarfs; and when the land is not rocky it is boggy to a man's waist. All the islands about the harbor were of the same character, and we saw but few land birds, one pigeon, a few hawks, and smaller birds. The wild geese, eider-ducks, loons, and many other birds breed here.

[*June 18.*] The boats went off to neighboring islands in search of birds and eggs, and I remained all day on board drawing. Eggers from Halifax had robbed nearly all the eggs.

The eider-ducks build their nests under the scraggy boughs of the fir-trees, which here grow only a few inches above the ground. The nests are scraped a few inches deep in the rotten moss which makes the soil, and the boughs have to be raised to find the nests. The eggs are deposited in down, and covered with down, and keep warm a long time in absence of the duck. They commonly lay six eggs.[9]

[*June 19.*] The vessel rolls at her anchorage, and I have drawn as well as I could. Our party has gone up the Natasquan in search of adventures and birds. It seems strange to me that in this wonderfully wild country all the wild birds should be so shy.

[*June 20.*] To-day I went four miles to the falls of the little Natasquan

River. The river is small, its water dark and irony, and its shores impenetrable woods, except here and there a small interval overgrown with a wiry grass, unfit for cattle, and of no use if it were, for there are no cattle here. We saw several nets in the river for catching salmon; they are stretched across the river, and the fish entangle their fins in trying to pass them, and cannot get away. We visited the huts of the Canadian fishermen of the Hudson Bay Company. They are clothed and fed, and receive eight dollars a year besides, for their services. They have a cow, an ox, and one acre of potatoes planted. They report seven feet of snow in winter, and that only one-third as many salmon are taken now as ten years ago; one hundred barrels now is regarded as a fair season. This river is twelve miles long, has three rapids, is broad, swift, and shallow, and discharges a quantity of fine gravelly sand.[10]

[*June 20.*] Drew all day. Thermometer 60° at twelve. We are so far north that we have scarcely any darkness at night. Our party visited some large ponds on a neighboring island; but they had neither fish, shells, nor grass about them; the shore a reddish sand: saw only a few toads, and those pale-looking and poor. The country a barren rock as far as the eye could reach, and mosses of several species were a foot in depth. So sonorous is the song of the fox-colored sparrow, that I heard it to-day while drawing in the cabin, from the distance of a quarter of a mile. The mosquitoes and black gnats are bad on shore.[11]

[. . .]

June 23. We met here two large boats loaded with Mountaineer Indians, about twenty, old and young, male and female. The boats had small canoes lashed to their sides, like whale boats, for seal fishing. The men were stout and good-looking, and spoke tolerable French; their skins were redder and clearer than any other Indians I have ever seen. The women also appeared cleaner than usual, their hair was braided, and dangled over their shoulders, like so many short ropes. They were all dressed in European costumes except their feet, on which coarse moccasins made of seal skin supplied the place of shoes.[12]

On leaving the harbor this morning, we saw a black man-of-war-like looking vessel entering it, bearing the English flag; it proved to be the Quebec cutter. I wrote a note to the commander, sent him my card, and requested an interview. He proved to be Captain Bayfield of the Royal

Navy, the vessel was the Gulnare, and he replied that he would receive me in two hours. After dinner, taking some credentials in my pocket, I went aboard of the Gulnare, was politely received, and introduced to the surgeon, who seemed a man of ability, and is a student of botany and conchology. Thus the lovers of nature meet everywhere, but surely I did not expect to meet a naturalist on the Labrador station. The first lieutenant is a student of ornithology, and is making collections. I showed a letter from the Duke of Sussex to the captain, and after a pleasant hour, and a promise from him to do anything in his power to aid us, I returned to our vessel.[13]

June 24. It was our intention to leave this harbor to-day for one fifty miles east, but the wind is ahead, and I have drawn all day. Shattuck and I took a walk over the dreary hills towards evening, and we found several flowers in bloom, among which was a small species of the Kulnua Glauca.[14] We visited the camp of the Mountaineer Indians about half a mile from us, and found them skinning seals, and preparing their flesh for use. We saw a robe the size of a good blanket made of seal skin, and tanned so soft and beautiful with the hair on, that it was as pleasant to the touch as a fine kid glove. They refused to sell it. The chief of this party is well informed, talks French so as to be understood, is a fine-looking fellow, about forty years old, and has a good-looking wife and baby. His brother also is married, and has several sons between fourteen and twenty. The whole group consists of about twenty persons. They came and saluted us soon after we landed, and to my astonishment offered us a glass of rum. The women were all seated outside of their tents, unpacking bundles of clothing and provisions. We entered one tent, and seated ourselves before a blazing fire, the smoke of which escaped through the top of the apartment. To the many questions I put to the chief and his brother, the following is the substance of his answers.

The country from this place to the nearest settlement of the Hudson Bay Company is as barren and rocky as this about us. Very large lakes of water abound two hundred miles inland from the sea: these lakes contain carp, trout, white fish, and many mussels unfit to eat; the latter are described as black outside and purple within, and are no doubt "unios." Not a bush is to be met with; and the Indians who now and then cross that region carry their tent-poles with them, and also their canoes, and burn moss for fuel. So tedious is the travelling said to be, that not more than ten miles a day can be accomplished, and when the journey is made in two months, it is considered a good one. Wolves and black bears abound, but no deer nor caraboos are seen, and not a bird of any kind except wild geese and brants about the lakes, where they breed. When the journey is undertaken in winter, they go on snow shoes, without canoes. Fur animals are scarce, but a few beavers and otters, martins and sables, are caught, and some foxes and lynxes, while their numbers yearly diminish. Thus the Fur Company may be called the exterminating medium of these wild and almost uninhabitable regions, which cupidity or the love of money alone would induce man to venture into. Where can I now go and find nature undisturbed?[15]

[*June 24.*] Drawing all day until five o'clock, when I went to dine on board the Gulnare; quite a bore to shave and dress in Labrador. The company consisted of the captain, doctor, and three other officers; we had a good sea dinner, cod and mutton, good wine and some excellent snuff, of which I took a pinch or two. Conversation turned on botany, politics, and the Established Church of England, and ranged away to hatching eggs by steam. I saw the maps the officers are making of the coast, and was struck with the great accuracy of the shape of our perfect harbor. I returned to our vessel at ten in the evening; the weather is warm, and the mosquitoes abundant and hungry.

[*June 25–26.*] We have now been waiting five days for a fair wind to take us eastward in our explorations. The waters of all the streams we have seen are of a rusty color, probably derived from the decomposing mosses which form the soil on the rocks. The rivers seem to be the drain from swamps fed by rain and melting snow; the soil in the low grounds is of quite a peaty nature. The freshets take down sand and gravel from the decomposed rocks, and form bars at the mouths of all the rivers. Below the mouth of each stream is the best fishing ground for codfish. They accumulate there to feed on the fry which run into the rivers to deposit their spawn, and which they follow again to sea, when they return to strike out into deep water.

It is quite remarkable how shy the agents of the Fur Company here are of strangers. They refused to sell me a salmon: and one of them told me he would be discharged if it were known he had done so. They evade all questions respecting the interior of the country, and indeed tell the most absurd things, to shock you, and cut short inquiries. This is probably to prevent strangers from settling here, or interfering with their monopoly.

June 27. The morning dawned above rain and fogs, which so enveloped us below that we could scarcely discern the shore, distant only a hundred yards. Drawing all day.

June 28. The weather shocking, rainy, foggy, dark, and cold. Began drawing a new finch I discovered, and outlined another. At twelve the wind suddenly changed, and caused such a swell and rolling of the vessel, that I had to give up my drawing. After dinner the wind hauled to the south-west, and all was bustle, heaving up anchor, loosing sails, and getting ready for sea. We were soon under weigh and went out of the harbor in good style; but the sea was high, and we were glad to go to our beds.[16]

June 29. At three o'clock this morning we were about fifteen miles from land, and fifty from American Harbor. The thermometer was 54°, and the wind light and favorable; at ten the breeze freshened, but our pilot did not know the land, and the captain had to find a harbor for himself. We passed near an island covered with foolish guillemots, and came to for the purpose of landing on it, which we did through a great surf; there we found two eggers searching the rocks for eggs. They told us they visited all the islands in the vicinity, and obtained fresh eggs every day. They had eight hundred dozen, and expected to increase them to two thousand dozen before they returned to Halifax. The quantities of broken eggs on this and all the islands where eggs are obtained, causes a stench which is scarcely endurable. From this island we went to another about a mile distant, and caught many birds and collected many eggs.

June 30. I have drawn three birds to-day since eight o'clock. Thermometer 50°.

July 1. The thermometer 48°, and the weather so cold that it has been painful for me to draw, but I worked all day.

July 2. A beautiful day for Labrador. Went ashore and killed nothing, but was pleased with what I saw. The country is so grandly wild and desolate, that I am charmed by its wonderful dreariness. Its mossy gray-clad rocks, heaped and thrown together in huge masses, hanging on smaller ones, as if about to roll down from their insecure resting-places into the sea below them. Bays without end, sprinkled with thousands of rocky inlets of all sizes, shapes, and appearances, and wild birds everywhere, was the scene presented before me.

[. . .]

July 3. We have had a stiff easterly wind all day, rainy, and the water so rough we could not go ashore, for plants to draw, until late in the afternoon. The view of the sea from the highest rocks was grand, the small islands were covered with the foam and surf thrown up by the agitated ocean. Thank God that we are not tossing on its billows.

July 4. Two parties went out to-day to get birds and plants, and I remained on board all day drawing. Captain Bayfield sent us a quarter of mutton for our fourth of July dinner, and I dare say it is a rarity on this coast of Labrador, even on this day.

[. . .]

July 6. Thermometer 48°. At noon my fingers were so cold that I could no longer hold my pencil to draw, and I was compelled to go on shore for exercise. The fact is I am growing old too fast, alas! I feel it, and yet work I will, and may God grant me life to see the last plate of my mammoth work finished.

July 7. Drawing all day; finished the female grouse and five young ones, and preparing the male bird.[17]

July 8. Rainy, dirty weather, wind east, thermometer 48°. Began drawing at half-past three A.M., but my condition very disagreeable in such weather. The fog collects and falls in large drops from the rigging on my table, and now and then I am obliged to close the sky-light, and work almost in darkness. Notwithstanding, I have finished my plate of the cock ptarmigan.

July 9. The wind east, wet, disagreeable, and foggy. This is the most wonderful climate in the world; the thermometer 52°, mosquitoes in profusion, plants blooming by millions, and at every step you tread on flowers such as would be looked on in more temperate climates with pleasure. I only wish I could describe plants as well as I can the habits of birds. I have drawn all day on the loon, a most difficult bird to imitate.[18]

July 10. Thermometer 54°. Could I describe one of those dismal gales which blow ever and anon over this dismal country, it would probably be interesting to any one unacquainted with the inclemency of this climate.

Nowhere else are the north-east blasts, which sweep over Labrador, felt as they are here. But I cannot describe them. All I can say is, that while we are safe in a land-locked harbor, their effects on our vessel are so strong, that they will not allow me to draw, and sometimes send some of us to our beds. And what the force of these horrid blasts outside of the harbor at sea is I can hardly imagine; but it seems as if it would be impossible for any vessel to ride safely before them, and that they will rend these rocky islands asunder. The rain is driven in sheets, and falls with difficulty upon its destination of sea or land. Nay, I cannot call it rain, as it is such a thick cloud of water, that all objects at a distance are lost sight of at intervals of three or four minutes, and the waters around us come up and beat about in our rock-bound harbor, as a newly caught and caged bird beats against the wire walls of his prison cage.

July 11. The gale or hurricane of yesterday subsided about midnight, and at sunrise this morning the sky was clear and the horizon fiery red. It was my intention to have gone one hundred miles further north, but our captain says I must be content here.

On rambling over the numerous bays and inlets, which are scattered by thousands along this coast, as pebbles are on a common sand beach, one sees immense beds of round stones (boulders?) of all sizes, and some of large dimensions, rolled side by side, and piled up in heaps, as if cast there by some great revolution of nature.[19] I have seen many such places, and always look on them with astonishment, because they seem to have been vomited up by the sea, and cast hundreds of yards inland, by its powerful retchings; and this gives some idea of what a hurricane at Labrador can do.

July 12. Thermometer 48°, and it is raining hard, and blowing another gale from the east, and the vessel rocks so much that I am unable to finish my drawing.

July 13. Rose this morning at half-past three, and found the wind north-east, and but little of it. The weather is cloudy and dull, as it is always here after a storm. I was anxious to stay on board, and finish the drawing of a grouse I had promised to Dr. Kelley of the Gulnare. But at seven the wind changed, and we prepared to leave our fine harbor.[20] We beat out to sea, and made our course for the harbor of Little Mecatina, distant forty-three miles. By noon the wind died away, but the sea rolled, and we were all sea-sick, and glad to go to our berths.

July 14. Awoke this morning to find a cold north-east wind blowing, and ourselves twenty miles from our destination, a heavy sea beating against the vessel's bows, as she is slowly beating tack after tack against the wind. We are in despair of reaching our destination to-day. Towards evening however the wind favored us, and as we approached the island, it proved the highest land we have seen, and looked rugged and horrid.

When we came within a mile and a half of the shore we took a small boat, and pushed off for the land. As we came near it, the rocks appeared stupendously high and rough, and frowned down on our little boat, as we moved along and doubled the little cape which made one side of the entrance of Mecatina's Harbor, but it looked so small to me, that I doubted if it were the place; and the shores were horribly wild, fearfully high and rough, and nothing but the croaking of a pair of ravens was heard mingling with the dismal sound of the surge which dashed on the rocky ledges, and sent the foaming water into the air.

By the time we reached the shore the wind began to freshen, the Ripley's sails now swelled, and she cut her way through the water, and rounded the point of land which formed part of the harbor, and shot ahead towards the place where we were standing. Our harbor represents the bottom of a large bowl, in the centre of which our vessel is anchored, surrounded by rocks full a thousand feet high, and the wildest looking place I was ever in.

[. . .]

July 15. We rose and breakfasted at three o'clock, every one being eager to go ashore and explore this wild country. But the wind was east, and the prospects of fine weather not good. But two boats' crews of young men rowed off in different directions, while I renewed my drawing. By ten the rain poured, and the boats returned.

July 16. Another day of dirty weather, and obliged to remain on board nearly all the day. Thermometer 52°, mosquitoes plenty. This evening the fog is so thick, that we cannot see the summit of the rocks around us.

July 17. Mosquitoes so annoyed me last night that I did not close my eyes. I tried the deck of the vessel, and although the fog was as thick as fine rain, the air was filled with these insects, and I went below and fought them until daylight, when I had a roaring fire made and got rid of them. I have been drawing part of the day, and besides several birds, I have outlined one of the mountainous hills near our vessel, as a background to my willow grouse.

July 18. After breakfast, all hands except the cook left the Ripley, in three boats, to visit the main shore, about five miles off. The fog was thick, but the wind promised fair weather, and soon fulfilled its promise. Directly after landing our party found a large extent of marsh land, the first we have seen in this country; the soil was wet, our feet sank in it, and walking was tire-some. We also crossed a large savannah of many miles in extent. Its mosses were so wet and spongy, that I never in my life before experienced so much difficulty in travelling. In many places the soil appeared to wave and bend under us like old ice in the spring of the year, and we expected at each step to break through the surface, and sink into the mire below. In the middle of this quagmire we met with a fine small grove of good-sized white birch trees, and a few pines full forty feet high, quite a novelty in this locality.

From the top of a high rock I obtained a good view of the most extensive and dreary wilderness I ever beheld. It chilled the heart to gaze on these barrens of Labrador. Indeed I now dread every change of harbor, so horridly rugged and dangerous is the whole coast and country to the eye, and to the experienced man either of the sea or the land. Mosquitoes, many species of horse-flies, small bees, and black gnats fill the air. The frogs croaked, and yet the thermometer was not above 55°. This is one of the real wonders of this extraordinary country. The parties in the boats, hunting all day, brought back but nineteen birds, and we all concluded that no one man could provide food for himself here from the land alone.

July 19. Cold, wet, blowing, and too much motion of the vessel for drawing. In the evening it cleared up a little, and I went ashore, and visited the hut of a seal-fisher. We climbed over one rocky precipice and fissure after another, holding on to the moss with both hands and feet, for about a mile, when we came to the deserted hut of a Labrador seal-catcher. It looked snug outside, and we walked in; it was floored with short slabs, all very well greased with seal oil. A fire-oven without

FIGURE 36. Jaeger in Labrador. Robert Havell Jr. after John James Audubon, "Arctic Yager" (long-tailed jaeger), 1835 (detail). Aquatint engraving. *The Birds of America*, plate 267. Courtesy of the Lilly Library. Audubon expected to see this seabird breeding in the region but never did. He painted the bird in the foreground standing on a pile of rocks, while Havell, who had never been to Labrador, added the crashing surf, the boats, and the tall cliffs in the background.

a pipe, a salt-box hung to a wooden peg, a three-legged stool for a table, and wooden box for a bedstead, were all its furniture. An old flour-barrel, containing some hundreds of seine floats, and an old seal seine, comprised the assets of goods and chattels. Three small windows, with four panes of glass each, were still in pretty good order, and so was the low door, which swung on wooden hinges, for which I will be bound the maker had asked for no patent. The cabin was made of hewn logs, brought from the mainland, about twelve feet square, and well put together. It was roofed with birch bark and spruce, well thatched with moss a foot thick; every chink was crammed with moss, and every aperture rendered air-tight with oakum. But it was deserted and abandoned. The seals are all caught, and the sailors have nothing to do now-a-days. We found a pile of good hard wood close to the cabin, and this we hope to appropriate to-morrow. I found out that the place had been inhabited by two Canadians, by the chalk marks on the walls, and their almanac on one of the logs ran thus: L 24, M 25, M 26, I 27, V 28, S 29, D 30, giving the first letter of the day of the week. On returning to the vessel, I stopped several times to look on the raging waves rolling in upon the precipitous rocks below us, and thought how dreadful it would be for any one to be wrecked on this inhospitable shore. The surges of surf which rolled in on the rocks were forty or fifty feet high where they dashed on the precipices beneath us, and any vessel cast ashore there must have been immediately dashed to pieces.[21]

July 20. The country of Labrador deserves credit for one fine day. This has been, until evening, calm, warm, and really such a day as one might expect in the Middle States about the middle of May. I drew until ten o'clock, and then made a trip to the island next to us, and shot several birds. We passed several small bays, where we found vast quantities of stones thrown up by the sea, and some of them of enormous size. I now think that these stones are brought from the sea on the thick drift ice, or icebergs, which come down from the arctic regions, and are driven in here and broken by the jagged rocks; they are stranded, and melt, and leave these enormous pebbles in layers from ten to one hundred feet deep.[22]

July 21. I write now from a harbor which has no name, for we have mistaken it for the one we were looking for, which lies two miles east of this. But it matters little, for the coast of Labrador is all alike, comfortless, cold, and foggy. We left the Little Mecatina this morning at five o'clock, with a stiff south-west breeze, and by ten dropped anchor where we now are. As we doubled the cape of the island called Great Mecatina, we had the pleasure of meeting the officers of the Gulnare, in two boats, engaged in surveying the coast. We made an excursion into the island, but found nothing of interest.[23]

In the evening we visited the officers of the Gulnare, encamped in tents on shore, living in great comfort; the tea-things were yet on the iron bedstead which served as a table, the trunks formed their seats, and the clothes-bags their cushions and pillows. Their tent was made of tarred cloth, which admitted neither wind nor rain. It was a comfortable camp, and we were pleased to find ourselves on the coast of Labrador in company with intelligent officers of the royal navy of England, gentlemen of education and refined manners; it was indeed a treat, a precious one. We talked of the wild country around us, and of the enormous destruction of everything which is going on here, except of the rocks; of the aborigines, who are melting away before the encroachments of a stronger race, as the wild animals are disappearing before them. Some one said, it is rum which is destroying the poor Indians. I replied, I think not, they are disappearing here from insufficiency of food and physical comforts, and the loss of all hope, as he loses sight of all that was abundant before the white man came, intruded on his land, and his herds of wild animals, and deprived him of the furs with which he clothed himself. Nature herself is perishing. Labrador must shortly be depopulated, not only of her aboriginal men, but of every thing and animal which has life, and attracts the cupidity of men. When her fish, and game, and birds are gone, she will be left alone like an old worn-out field.

July 22. This morning Captain Bayfield and his officers came alongside to bid us good-bye, to pursue their labors further westward. After breakfast we manned three boats, and went to explore a small harbor about one mile east of our anchorage. There we found a whaling schooner, fifty-five tons burthen, from Cape Gaspe. We found the men employed in boiling blubber in a large iron vessel like a sugar-boiler. The blubber lay in heaps on the shore, in junks of six or eight pounds each, looking filthy enough. The captain or owner of the vessel appeared to be a good sensible man of his class, and cut off for me some strips of the whale's skin from under the throat, with large and curious barnacles attached to the skin. They had struck four whales, and three had sunk, and were lost to them. This, the men said, was a very rare occurrence. We found, also, at this place, a French Canadian seal-catcher, from whom I gathered the following information.[24]

This portion of Labrador is free to any one to settle on, and he and another person had erected a cabin, and had nets and traps to catch seals and foxes, and guns to shoot bears and wolves. They take their quarry to Quebec, receiving fifty cents a gallon for seal oil, and from three to five guineas for black and silver fox skins, and others in proportion. In the months of November and December, and indeed until spring, they kill seals in large numbers; seventeen men belonging to their party killed twenty-five hundred seals once in three days. This great feat was done with short sticks, and each seal was killed with a single blow on the snout, whilst lying on the edges of the floating or field ice. The seals are carried home on sledges drawn by Esquimaux dogs, which are so well trained that, on reaching home, they push the seals from the sledges with their noses, and return to the killers with regular despatch. (This, reader, is hearsay!) At other times the seals are driven into nets, one after another, until the poor animals become so hampered and confined, that they are easily and quickly dispatched with guns. The captain showed me a spot, within a few yards of his log cabin, where last winter he caught six fine large silver-gray foxes. Bears and caraboos abound during winter, and also wolves, hares and porcupines. The wolves are of a dun color, very ferocious and daring; a pack of thirty followed a man to his cabin, and they have several times killed his dogs at his own door. I was surprised at this, because his dogs were as large as any wolves I have ever seen. These dogs are extremely tractable, so much so that, when geared into a sledge, the leader immediately starts at the word of command for any given course, and the whole pack gallop off at the rate of seven or eight miles an hour. The Esquimaux dogs howl like wolves, and are not at all like our common dogs. They were extremely gentle, and came to us, and jumped on and caressed us as if we were old acquaintances. They do not take to the water, and are fit only for draught and the chase of caraboos; and they are the only dogs which can at all near the caraboo while running.

As soon as winter storms and thick ice close the harbors and the intermediate spaces between the mainland and the sea islands, the caraboos are seen moving on the ice in great herds, first to the islands, where the snow is most likely to be drifted, because there in the shallows—from which the snow has blown away—he easily scrapes down to the mosses, which at this season are the only food they can find. As the severity of winter increases, these animals follow the coast northwest, and gradually reach a comparatively milder climate. But notwithstanding all this, on their return in the spring, which is as regular as the migration of the birds, they are so poor and emaciated, that the men take pity on them, and will not kill them. Merciful beings, these white men! They spare life when the flesh is off from their bones, and there is no market for their bones at hand.

The otter is tolerably abundant here. These are chiefly trapped at the foot of the waterfalls, to which they resort, being the latest to freeze and the earliest to thaw in spring. A few martins and sables are caught, but every year reduces their number. This Frenchman receives his supplies from Quebec, where he sends his furs and oil. The present time he calls "the idle season," and he loiters about his cabin, lies in the sunshine like a seal, eats, drinks, and sleeps his life away, careless of the busy world, and of all that is going on there. His partner has gone to Quebec, and his dogs are his only companions until he returns; and the dogs, perhaps, are the better animal of the two. He has selected a delightful site for his castle, under the protection of an island, and on the south side, where I found the atmosphere quite warm, and the vegetation actually rank, for I saw plants with leaves twelve inches broad, and grasses three feet high.[25]

This afternoon the wind has been blowing a tremendous gale, and our anchors have dragged with sixty fathoms of chain out. Yet one of the whaler's boats came with six men to pay us a visit. They wished to see some of my drawings, and I gratified them; and in return they promised to show me a whale before it was cut up, should they catch one before we leave this place for Bras d'Or.

July 23. We visited to-day the seal establishment of a Scotchman, named Robertson, about six miles east of our anchorage. He received us politely, addressed me by name, and told me he had received information of my visit to this country through the English and Canadian newspapers. This man has resided here twenty years, and married a Labrador lady, the daughter of a Monsieur Chevalier of Bras d'Or; has a family of six children, and a good-looking wife.[26] He has a comfortable house, and a little garden, in which he raises a few turnips, potatoes, and other vegetables. He appeared to be lord of all these parts, and quite contented with his lot. He told me that his profits last year amounted to three thousand dollars. He does not trade with the Indians, of whom we saw about twenty of the Mountaineer tribe, and he has white men-servants. His seal-oil tubs were full, and he was then engaged in loading a schooner bound to Quebec. He complained of the American fishermen, and said they often acted as badly as pirates towards the Indians, the white settlers, and the eggers, all of whom have more than once retaliated, when bloody combats have followed. He assured me that he had seen a fisherman's crew kill thousands of guillemots in a day, pluck off their feathers, and throw their bodies into the sea.

Mr. Robertson also told me that, during mild winters, his little harbor is covered with thousands of white gulls, and that they all leave on the approach of spring. The travelling here is altogether over the ice, which is covered with snow, and in sledges drawn by Esquimaux dogs, of which this man keeps a famous pack. He often goes to Bras d'Or, seventy-five miles distant, with his wife and children on one sledge, drawn by ten dogs. Scarcely any travelling is done on land, the country is so precipitous and broken. Fifteen miles north of here he says there is a lake, represented by the Indians as four hundred miles long and one hundred broad, and that this sea-like lake is at times as rough as the ocean in a storm. It abounds with fish, and some water-birds resort there, and breed by millions along its margin. We have had a fine day, but Mr. R. says that the summer has been unusually tempestuous. The caraboo flies drove our hunters on board to-day, and they looked as bloody as if they had actually had a gouging fight with some rough Kentuckians. Here we found on this wonderful wild coast some newspapers from the United States, and received the latest intelligence from Boston to be had at Labrador.

July 26. We left our anchorage, and sailed with a fair wind to visit the Chevalier's settlement, called Bonne Espérance, forty-seven miles distant. When we had gone two-thirds of the distance the wind failed us; calms were followed by severe squalls, and a tremendous sea rolled, which threatened to shake our masts out. At eight o'clock, however, we came abreast of the settlement, but as our pilot knew nothing of the harbor, the captain thought it prudent to stand off, and proceed on to Bras d'Or. The coast here, like all that we have seen before, was dotted with rocky islands of all sizes and forms, and against which the raging waves dashed in a frightful manner, making us shudder at the thought of the fate of the wretched mariners who might be thrown on them.[27]

July 27. At daylight this morning we found ourselves at the mouth of Bras d'Or Harbor, where we are now snugly moored. We hoisted our colors, and Captain Billings, of American Harbor, came to us in his Hampton boat, and piloted us in. This Bras d'Or is the grand rendezvous of almost all the fishermen, that resort to this coast for cod-fish; and we found here a flotilla of one hundred and fifty sails, principally fore-and-aft schooners, and mostly from Halifax and the eastern parts of the United States.[28]

There was a life and bustle in the harbor which surprised us, after so many weeks of wilderness and loneliness along the rocky coast. Boats were moving to and fro over the whole bay, going after fish, and returning loaded to the gunwale; some with seines, others with capelings, for bait, and a hundred or more anchored out about a mile from us, hauling the poor cod-fish by thousands, and hundreds of men engaged in cleaning and salting them, and enlivening their work with Billingsgate slang, and stories, and songs.[29]

[. . .]

We saw also to-day the carcasses of fifteen hundred seals stripped of their skins, piled up in a heap, and the dogs feeding on them. The stench filled the air for half a mile around. They tell us the dogs feed on this filthy flesh until the next seal season, tearing it piecemeal when frozen in winter.

Mr. Jones's house was being painted white, his oil-tubs were full, and the whole establishment was perfumed with odors which were not agreeable to my olfactory nerves. The snow is to be seen in large patches on every hill around us, while the borders of the water-courses are fringed with grasses and weeds as rank as any to be found in the Middle States in like situations. I saw a small brook with fine trout, but what pleased me more was to find the nest of the shore-lark; it was embedded in moss, so exactly the color of the bird, that when the mother sat on it, it was impossible to distinguish her. We see Newfoundland in the distance, looking like high mountains, whose summits are far above the clouds at present. Two weeks since the harbor where we now are was an ice-field, and not a vessel could approach it; since then the ice has sunk, and none is to be seen far or near.[30]

July 31. Another horrid hurricane, accompanied by heavy rain, and the vessel rolling so that I cannot go on with my drawing.

August 1. The weather has quite changed, the wind blows from the south-west; it is dry, and I have used the time in drawing. At noon we were visited by an iceberg, which was driven by the easterly wind and storm of yesterday to within three miles of us, and grounded at the entrance of the bay. It looks like a large man-of-war, dressed in light greenish muslin instead of canvas; and when the sun shines on it, it glitters most brilliantly.

When these transient monuments of the sea happen to tumble or roll over, the fall is tremendous, and the sound produced resembles that of loud distant thunder. These icebergs are common here all summer, being wafted from the lower end of the straits with every heavy easterly wind or gale. And as the winds generally prevail from the south and south-west, the coast of Newfoundland is more free from them than Labrador;

and the navigation along the straits is generally performed along the coast of Newfoundland. My time and our days now weigh heavily on our hands; nothing to be seen, nothing to be shot, therefore nothing to be drawn. I have now determined on a last thorough ransack of the mountain tops, and plains, and ponds, and if no success follows, to raise anchor and sail towards the United States once more; and blessed will the day be when I land on those dear shores where all I long for in this world exists and lives, I hope.

August 2. Thermometer 58° at noon. Thank God it has rained all day. I say thank God, though rain is no rarity, because it is the duty of every man to be thankful for whatever happens by the will of the Omnipotent Creator; yet it was not so agreeable to any of my party as a fine day would have been. We had an arrival of a handsome schooner, called the Wizard, from Boston to-day [fig. 37], but she brought neither papers nor letters; but we learned that all our great cities have a healthy season, and we thanked God for this. The retrograde movement of many land and water birds has already commenced, especially of the lesser species.[31]

August 3. The Wizard broke her moorings and ran into us last night, causing much alarm but no injury. The iceberg of which I have spoken

"WIZARD" OF BOSTON, WM. WILLCOMB, COMMANDER.

FIGURE 37. Schooner *Wizard.* This "handsome" schooner from Boston, at about seventy-four feet long on deck, was of similar size and rig to the *Ripley*, to which it fetched up while at anchor in Bradore Bay. Painting reproduced in Oliver Clifton Willcomb, *Genealogy of the Willcomb Family of New England* (Lynn, MA, 1902), 73. Courtesy of Williams College.

has been broken into a thousand pieces by the late gale, and now lies stranded along the coast. One such monster deposits hundreds of tons of rocks, and gravel, and boulders, and so explains the phenomena which I have before mentioned as observable along the coast.

August 4. It is wonderful how quickly every living thing in this region, whether animal or vegetable, attains its growth. In six weeks I have seen the eggs laid, the birds hatched, and their first moult half gone through; their association into flocks begun, and preparations for leaving the country.

That the Creator should have ordered that millions of diminutive, tender creatures, should cross spaces of country, in all appearance a thousand times more congenial for all their purposes, to reach this poor, desolate, and deserted land, to people it, as it were, for a time, and to cause it to be enlivened with the songs of the sweetest of the feathered musicians, for only two months at most, and then, by the same extraordinary instinct, should cause them all to suddenly abandon the country, is as wonderful as it is beautiful and grand.[32]

Six weeks ago this whole country was one sheet of ice; the land was covered with snow, the air was filled with frost, and subject to incessant storms, and the whole country a mere mass of apparently useless matter. Now the grass is abundant, and of rich growth, the flowers are met with at every step, insects fill the air, and the fruits are ripe. The sun shines, and its influence is as remarkable as it is beautiful; the snow-banks appear as if about to melt, and here and there there is something of a summerish look. But in thirty days all is over; the dark northern clouds will come down on the mountains; the rivulets and pools, and the bays themselves, will begin to freeze; weeks of snow-storms will follow, and change the whole covering of these shores and country, and Nature will assume not only a sleeping state, but one of desolation and death. Wonderful! wonderful! But it requires an abler pen than mine to paint the picture of this all-wonderful country.

August 5. This has been a fine day! We have had no new hurricane, and I have finished the drawings of several new birds. It appears that northern birds come to maturity sooner than southern ones; this is reversing the rule in the human species.[33] The migration of birds is much more wonderful than that of fishes, because the latter commonly go feeling their way along the shores, from one clime to another, and return to the very same river, creek, or even hole, to deposit their spawn, as the birds do to their former nest or building-ground as long as they live. But the latter do not feel their way, but launching high in the air, go at once, and correctly, too, across immense tracts of country, seemingly indifferent to them, but at once stopping, and making their abode in special parts heretofore their own, by previous knowledge of the advantages and comforts which they have enjoyed, and which they know await them there.[34]

August 10. I now sit down to post up my poor book, while a furious gale is blowing without. I have neglected to make daily records for some days, because I have been so constantly drawing, that when night came, I was too weary to wield my pen. Indeed, all my physical powers have been taxed to weariness by this little work of drawing; my neck and shoulders, and most of all my fingers, have ached from the fatigue; and I have suffered more from this kind of exertion than from walking sixty-five miles in a day, which I once did.

To-day I have added one more new species to the "Birds of America" the Labrador falcon; and may we live to see its beautiful figure multiplied by Havell's graver.[35]

August 11. At sea, Gulf of St. Lawrence. We are now fully fifty miles from the coast of Labrador. Fresh water was taken on board, and all preparations were made last evening, and this morning we bid adieu to the friends we had made at Labrador.

Seldom in my life have I left a country with as little regret as this; next in order would come East Florida, after my excursion up the St. John's River. As we sailed away I saw probably for the last tune the high and rugged hills, partly immersed in large banks of fog, that usually hang over them.

Now we are sailing before the wind in full sight of the south-west coast of Newfoundland, the mountains of which are high, spotted with drifted snow-banks, and cut horizontally with floating strata of fogs extending along the land as far as the eye can reach. The sea is quite smooth, or else I have become a better sailor by this rough voyage. Although the weather is cloudy, it is such as promises in this region a fair night. Our young men are playing the violin and flute, and I am scribbling in my book.

It is worth telling that during the two months we have spent on the coast of Labrador, moving from one harbor to another, or from behind one rocky island to another, only three nights have been passed at sea. Twenty-three drawings have been commenced or finished, and now I am anxious to know if what remains of the voyage will prove as fruitful; and only hope our Creator will permit us all to reach our friends in safety and find them well and happy.

August 13. Harbor of St. George's Bay, Newfoundland. By my dates you will see how long we were running, as the sailors call it, from Labrador to this place, where we anchored at five this evening. Our voyage here was all in sight of, and indeed along the north-west side of Newfoundland; the shores presenting the highest lands we have yet seen. In some places the views were highly picturesque and agreeable to the eye, although the appearance of vegetation was but little better than at Labrador. The wind was fair for two-thirds of the distance, and drew gradually ahead and made us uncomfortable.

This morning we entered the mouth of St. George's Bay, which is about forty miles wide and fifty miles deep, and a more beautiful and ample basin cannot be found; there is not a single obstruction within it. The north-east shores are high and rocky, but the southern are sandy, low, and flattish. It took us until five o'clock to ascend it, when we came to anchor in sight of a small village, the only one we have seen in two months; and we are in a harbor with a clay bottom, and where fifty line-of-battle ships could snugly and safely ride.

The village is built on an elongated point of sand or sea wall, under which we now are, and is perfectly secure from all winds except the north-east. The country on ascending the bay became gradually more woody and less rough in shape. The temperature changed quite suddenly this afternoon, and the weather was so mild that we found it agreeable lolling on deck, and it felt warm even to a southron like myself. Twenty-two degrees difference in temperature in two days is a very considerable change.[36]

We found here several sail of vessels engaged in the fisheries, and an old hulk from Hull in England, called Charles Tennison, which was wrecked near here four years ago, on her way from Quebec to Hull. As we sailed up the bay two men boarded us from a small boat and assisted us as pilots. They had a half barrel of fine salmon, which I bought from them for ten dollars. As soon as we dropped anchor our young men went ashore to buy fresh provisions, but they returned with nothing but two bottles of milk, though the village contains two hundred inhabitants. Mackerel, and sharks of the man-eating kind, are said to be abundant here. Some signs of cultivation are to be seen across the harbor, and many huts of Michmaes Indians adorn the shores. We learn that the winters are not nearly as severe here as at Quebec, yet not far off I could see dots of snow of last year's crop. Some persons say birds are plenty, others say there are none hereabouts.[37]

The ice did not break up, so that this bay was not navigable until the 17th of May, and I feel confident that no one can enter the harbors of Labrador before the 10th or middle of June.

[. . .]

August 15. We have had a beautiful day. This morning some Indians came alongside of our vessel with half a reindeer, a caraboo, and a hare of a species I had never seen before. We gave them twenty-one pounds of pork for forty-four pounds of venison, thirty-three pounds of bread for the caraboo, and a quarter of a dollar for the hare. The Indians showed much cleverness in striking the bargain. I spent part of the day drawing, and then visited the wigwams of the Indians across the bay. We found them, as I expected, all lying down pell-mell in their wigwams, and a strong mixture of blood was perceptible in their skins, shape, and deportment: some were almost white, and sorry I am to say, that the nearer they were to our nobler race the filthier and the lazier they were. The women and children were particularly disgusting in this respect. Some of the women were making baskets, and others came in from collecting a fruit called here the baked apple (*Rubus chamaemorus*), and when burnt a little it tastes exactly like a roasted apple. The children were catching lobsters and eels, of which there are a great many in the bay, as there are in all the bays of the island, whilst at Labrador this shell-fish is very rare. The young Indians found them by wading to their knees in eel grass.[38]

We bargained with two of the hunters to go with our young men into the interior to hunt for caraboos, hares, and partridges, which they agreed to do for a dollar a day. The Indians cook lobsters by roasting them in a pile of brushwood, and eat them without any salt or other condiment. The caraboos are at this date in "velvet," their skins are now light gray, and the flesh poor but tender. The average weight of this animal, when in good condition, is four hundred pounds. In the early part of March they leave the hilly grounds, where no moss or any other food can be obtained, and resort to the shores of the sea to feed on kelp and other sea grasses cut up by the ice and cast up by the waves along the shore. Groups of several hundreds may be seen at one time thus feeding: their flesh here is not much esteemed; it tastes like indifferent, poor, but very tender venison.

August 17. We should now be ploughing the deep had the wind been fair, but it has been ahead, and we remain here *in statu quo*. The truth is, we have determined not to leave this harbor without a fair prospect of a good run, and then we shall trust to Providence after that.

[. . .]

Several flocks of golden-winged plovers passed over the bay this forenoon, and two lestris pomerania came in this evening. The ravens abound here, but no crows have yet been seen; the great tern are passing south by thousands, and a small flock of Canada geese were also seen. The young of the golden-crested wren were shot. A muscicapa was killed, which is probably new. I bought seven Newfoundland dogs for seventeen dollars: two bitches, four pups, and a dog two years old. With these I shall be able to fulfill promises made to friends to bring them dogs.[39]

On the 18th of August at daylight the wind promised to be fair, and although it was rather cloudy we broke our anchorage, and at five o'clock were under weigh. We coasted along Newfoundland until evening, when the wind rose to a tempest from the south-west, and our vessel was laid to at dark, and we danced and kicked over the waves the whole of that night and the next day. The next day the storm abated, but the wind was still so adverse that we could not make the Gannet Rock or any part of Newfoundland, and towards the latter we steered, for none of us could bear the idea of returning to Labrador. During the night the weather moderated, and the next day we laid our course for the Straits of Canseau; but suddenly the wind failed, and during the calm it was agreed that we would try and reach Pictou in Nova Scotia, and travel by land. We are now beating about towards that port, and hope to reach it early to-morrow morning. The captain will then sail for Eastport, and we, making our way by land, will probably reach there as soon as he. The great desire we all have to see Pictou, Halifax, and the country between there and Eastport is our inducement.

August 22. After attempting to beat our vessel into the harbor of Pictou, but without succeeding, we concluded that myself and party should be put on shore, and the Ripley should sail back to the Straits of Canseau, the wind and tide being favorable. We drank a parting glass to our wives and friends, and our excellent little captain took us to the shore, whilst the vessel stood up to the wind, with all sails set, waiting for the captain.

We happened to land on an island called Ruy's Island, where, fortunately for us, we met some men making hay. Two of them agreed to carry our trunks and two of our party to Pictou for two dollars. Our effects were put in a boat in a trice, and we shook hands heartily with the captain, towards whom we all now feel much real attachment, and after mutual adieus, and good wishes for the completion of our respective journeys, we parted, giving each other three most hearty cheers.

We were now, thank God, positively on the main shore of our native land; and after four days' confinement in our berths, and sea-sickness, and the sea and vessel, and all their smells and discomforts, we were so refreshed, that the thought of walking nine miles seemed nothing more than figuring through a single quadrille. The air felt uncommonly warm, and the country, compared with those we had so lately left, appeared perfectly beautiful, and we inhaled the fragrance of the new mown grass, as if nothing sweeter ever existed. Even the music of crickets was delightful to my ears, for no such insect is to be found either at Labrador or Newfoundland. The voice of a blue jay sounded melody to me, and the sight of a humming-bird quite filled my mind with delight.

We were conveyed to the main, only a very short distance, Ingalls and Coolidge remaining in the boat; and the rest took the road, along which we moved as lightly as if boys just released from school. The road was good, or seemed to be so; the woods were tall timber, and the air, which circulated freely, was all perfume; and every plant we saw brought to mind some portion of the United States, and we all felt quite happy. Now and then as we crossed a hill, and cast our eyes back on the sea, we saw our beautiful vessel sailing freely before the wind, and as she diminished towards the horizon, she at last appeared like a white speck, or an eagle floating in the air, and we wished our captain a most safe voyage to Quoddy.

Notes

1. Johann Spurzheim (1776–1832), influential German promoter of phrenology, died of typhoid fever in Boston. His brain, skull, and heart were removed and displayed publicly. Clearly, Audubon thinks he has similar public importance, though he is obviously glad that, after his stroke, all his organs are still in place. George Parkman, MD (1790–1849), a wealthy Boston physician with a particular interest in insanity, gained posthumous fame after the Erving Professor of Chemistry, Dr. John W. Webster, killed him in 1849 and hid the remains in his lab. George Cheyne Shattuck Sr. (1783–1854) was a Boston physician and the father of Audubon's assistant George Shattuck. The surgeon John Collins Warren (1778–1856) pioneered the use of anesthesia in the United States and was the first dean of Harvard Medical School. Joseph A. Coolidge (1815–1901) was the son of an Eastport revenue cutter captain and a member of Audubon's Labrador team, later a merchant in San Francisco.

2. Captain Thomas Wells Childs (1796–1853) was at the time commander of the garrison at Fort Sullivan in Eastport, Maine.

3. On "the procellaria (a species of gull)," see Audubon's journal entries on storm-petrels in his "Journal of a Sea Voyage" (June 20); "Wilson's Petrel"; plate 20 (Havell 270).

4. Lucy Audubon or her editor Robert W. Buchanan misdated several entries when they published their selections from the Labrador journal; dates in brackets are the corrected dates; see Peter Logan, *Audubon: America's Greatest Naturalist and His Voyage of Discovery to Labrador* (San Francisco: Ashbryn Press, 2016), 442n18. Canso Harbor, next to Chenabucto Bay, is protected by the Canso Islands off the mainland of Nova Scotia. The "Gut of Canseau" is the Strait of Canso, connecting Chedabucto Bay on the Atlantic Ocean to St. George's Bay on the Northumberland Strait.

5. Jestico Island is now Henry Island, Nova Scotia. The "seal" here could be a harbor seal (*Phoca vitulina*) or a grey seal (*Halichoerus grypus*), both common today in the summer months, or perhaps the hooded seal (*Cystophora cristata*) or harp seal (*Pagophilus groenlandicus*).

6. "Miramichie," now Miramichi Bay, is on the west coast of the Gulf of St. Lawrence. "Entree Island" is Pleasant Bay and Entry Island (French: Île-d'Entrée), eight miles east of the main harbor of the Magdalen Islands (figs. 33, 35). In Lucy Audubon's edition of the Labrador journal, these appear as the "Magdalene" Islands. In *Ornithological Biography*, Audubon spelled them most often as "Magdeleine."

7. The "white gannets" are Audubon's "Common Gannet," now known as the northern gannet (see notes to "Common Gannet"; plate 12).

8. Audubon's painting and biography of the "Foolish Guillemot" (plate 13; Havell 218), now known as the common murre (*Uria aalge*), was largely derived from this visit. His "millions of velvet ducks" ("Velvet Duck," Havell 247), are now commonly referred to as white-winged

scoter ducks (*Melanitta deglandi*). White-winged scoters are a species of Least Concern, but their populations appear to be decreasing dramatically (IUCN, 2018). A 2004 study estimated about a hundred thousand individuals on the Atlantic coast, while more recent information suggests that numbers currently wintering on the Atlantic coast are only in the tens of thousands. P. W. Brown and L. H. Fredrickson, "White-winged Scoter," v. 1.0 (2020), birdsoftheworld.org.

9. Audubon's "eider-ducks" seem to be the common eider (Havell 246); see notes to "The Bay of Fundy."

10. The "salmon" fished here were Atlantic salmon (*Salmo salar*), which are now almost entirely extirpated from their historic range in the northeastern US and had been recognized as overfished in Atlantic Canada as early as the 1780s. Atlantic salmon populations in eastern Canada remain fishable today, although the 2019 harvest was estimated to be an "all-time low." Atlantic Salmon Foundation, "Status of North American Atlantic Salmon Populations, May 2019," www.asf.ca/assets/files/state-of-popn-2019v2.pdf.

11. Audubon's "Fox-coloured Sparrow" (Havell 108) is now the fox sparrow (*Passerella iliaca*). See *OB* 2 (1834), 59: "Would that I could describe the sweet song of this Finch; that I could convey to your mind the effect it produced on my feelings, when wandering the desolate shores of Labrador!"

12. Audubon's "Mountaineer Indians" are the Montagnais (and Naskapi), the Innu First Nation who lived throughout regions of present-day Quebec and Labrador. One of the first northern indigenous groups to encounter Europeans, the Innu were a migratory hunting, fishing, and sealing tribe when they met and allied with Samuel de Champlain and then French Jesuits in the early seventeenth century, becoming active in trading with Europeans and as intermediaries with other tribes.

13. Henry Wolsey Bayfield (1795–1885), born in Kingston-upon-Hull, Yorkshire, was appointed admiralty surveyor for North America; surveying Lake Superior, Lake Erie, Lake Huron, and the St. Lawrence River became his life's project and resulted in a book later published as *The St. Lawrence Pilot*. The schooner HMS *Gulnare* was a wooden gun vessel of 351 tons, launched at Chatham Dockyard in 1833, renamed HMS *Gleaner* in 1838, and scrapped in 1849. The figurehead, a serpent, is preserved at the National Maritime Museum, Royal Museums in Greenwich. Bayfield wrote about his encounter with Audubon in his journal; see *The Lawrence Survey Journals of Captain Henry Wolsey Bayfield*, 2 vols., ed. Ruth McKenzie (Toronto: Champlain Society, 1984). The *Gulnare*'s first lieutenant was Augustus Frederick Bowen, but, as a later entry confirms (July 13), the bird enthusiast was the ship's surgeon, Dr. William Kelley. The letter from Augustus Frederick, Duke of Sussex, ordered British officials in North America to assist Audubon in his work; see Maria R. Audubon, ed., *Audubon and His Journals* (New York: Charles Scribner's Sons, 1897), 1:376–77.

14. The "Kulnua Glauca" (Buchanan must have had trouble deciphering Lucy's handwriting) is the *Kalmia glauca* (now *Kalmia polifolia*), the bog laurel, the flowering plant on the right drawn by Audubon for the botanical background of his "Lincoln Finch" (Havell 193; now Lincoln's sparrow, *Melospiza lincolnii*).

15. Audubon's "unios" were freshwater mussels of the genera *Unionoida*, "caraboos" were caribou (*Rangifer tarandus*), and "wild geese" were probably Canada geese (*Branta canadensis*). The "martins" were American martens (*Martes americana*), and his "sables" could be a variety of mustelids found in Atlantic Canada, including weasels, minks, and fishers. True sables are similar to martens but live only in northern Asia.

16. The "new finch" is, again, Audubon's "Lincoln Finch" (Lincoln's sparrow).

17. Audubon was drawing his two "Willow Grous/Large Ptarmigan" (now willow ptarmigan, *Lagopus lagopus*) and her five chicks (Havell 191; original watercolor at the New-York Historical Society, NYHS 1863.17.191). The male bird he refers to here is the same as the "cock ptarmigan" he mentions in his July 8 entry in this journal.

18. The bird on the right of Audubon's painting of his "Great Northern Diver/Loon" (Havell 306; original watercolor at the New-York Historical Society, NYHS 1863.17.304), now most often the common loon (*Gavia immer*), was painted from one of the birds they killed in Labrador. The young bird in winter plumage on the left was, according to what he wrote in *OB* 4 (1838), 48, painted separately in October 1819 from "a specimen obtained on the Ohio."

19. "Boulders?" might have been an editorial comment in the manuscript that was accidentally included in the printed journal. In Maria Audubon's edition (*Audubon and His Journals*, 1:395), the word appears later in the same passage: "If those great boulders are brought from the bottom of the sea . . ." Incidentally, Lucy's version of that later sentence ("seem to have been vomited up by the sea") seems indeed closer to Audubon's diction than Maria's likely sanitized rendition.

20. In Maria Audubon's slightly different version of the same passage, Audubon wants to spend the day aboard the *Gulnare* to "draw at the ground of the grouse" (*Audubon and His Journals*, 1:395). However, on July 17, he is still working on that background, reason enough to assume that he didn't "finish" his drawing on July 17 (Logan therefore finds Maria's rendition more authentic than Lucy's; Logan, *Audubon*, 603n136). However, the entry in Lucy's biography reprinted here also mentions that "the wind changed," which likely means that Audubon was interrupted. If Audubon's ptarmigan portrait was indeed for Dr. Kelley, it seems he *wasn't* finished in time to present the work to his new friend. The original, which served as the basis for Havell 191, is now held by the New-York Historical Society. "Willow Grous or Large Ptarmigan" is one of Audubon's more involved undertakings, since it shows the female ptarmigan with seven chicks, against a botanical background that includes beach-pea, roseroot, and Labrador-tea. On July 22 (see below), Captain Bayfield and his men departed west.

21. The names of the days in French, from *L* (Lundi, Monday) to *D* (Dimanche, Sunday), with *I* indicating Jeudi (Thursday).

22. Theories on glaciation and ice ages were just emerging in the late 1830s, *after* this expedition, championed by Louis Agassiz (1807–1873). The boulders that Audubon described in this part of Atlantic Canada were indeed deposited by ice, by glacial moraines, not by drifting ice or hurricane waves. What made Audubon change his initial thoughts from a week earlier, in his July 11 entry, where he thought erratic boulders had been "vomited up" by the sea? He picks up the topic again on August 4, regarding deposits from an iceberg. See Christoph Irmscher, *Louis Agassiz: Creator of American Science* (Boston: Houghton Mifflin, 2013), 64–76.

23. The pilot had mistakenly guided them into Mutton Bay (originally Baie du Portage), Quebec, so named because of the sheep that fishing vessels would bring onshore to graze.

24. "Cape Gaspe" is Cap Gaspé, Quebec (see fig. 33). The whales they caught from here, the primary whaling port of the region at the time, especially at this time of year, were likely the now critically endangered North Atlantic right whale (*Eubalaena glacialis*), which even by the 1830s were in such severe decline that it is possible that, as Scoresby writes in the 1820s, whalemen of the Gulf of St. Lawrence more often caught other types of baleen whales, perhaps minkes, humpbacks, or fin whales. Whale hunters brought the whales ashore and boiled out the blubber for oil for illumination. William Scoresby Jr., *An Account of the Arctic Regions* (Edinburgh: Archibald Constable and Co., 1820), 2:134–38. Right whales received their name, it is commonly believed today, because they were the "right" whales to catch—

slow enough swimmers that hunters could get close enough with oar or sail power (the other baleen whales are much faster). In another current interpretation, these whales were preferred, or "right," because they were said to rarely sink after being harpooned—a problematic assumption, as perhaps affirmed by Audubon's description here (if these were indeed *Eubalaena glacialis*). The names "black whale" and "Greenland whale" were also in use in the nineteenth century. The names "black whale" and "Greenland whale" were also current in the nineteenth century, used as well for the closely related bowhead whale. The seal hunters' targets in this region would have included harp seals, hooded seals, harbor seals, and grey seals. By the time of Audubon's visit, colonists had been hunting seals in the Gulf of St. Lawrence for over a century. The 1830s appear to have been near the peak, with some 600,000 animals killed each year. K. Ronald and David M. Lavigne, "Sealing," *The Canadian Encyclopedia* (February 7, 2006, rev. March 4, 2015): https://www.thecanadianencyclopedia.ca/en/article/sealing#, accessed December 22, 2021.

25. Audubon's "otter" is the North American river otter (*Lontra canadensis*), known then as the "Canada" or "American Otter." Otters were valued for their pelts. Audubon and Bachman later wrote about them at length, explaining they were "nearly extirpated in our Atlantic States east of Maryland," but still found to the south and west, and "a considerable number are also annually obtained in the British provinces." J. J. Audubon and John Bachman, *The Viviparous Quadrupeds of North America* (New York: V. G. Audubon, 1851), 2:11. Due to water quality improvements throughout North America, as well as modern restoration efforts, North American river otters are now considered a species of Least Concern (IUCN, 2014), though regulated fur harvests still exist.

26. The man is Samuel Robertson; see notes to "The Long-billed Curlew."

27. The settlement was on the St. Paul's River (Rivière-Saint-Paul), called Esquimaux River at the time.

28. Captain Billings is William Billings of Eastport, Maine (1794–1856).

29. "Billingsgate slang" refers to foul language, associated with the fish market in London.

30. "Mr. Jones" is William Randall Jones; see notes to "The Long-billed Curlew." Audubon's "Shore Lark" (Havell 200) is today known as the horned lark (*Eremophila alpestris*).

31. The *Wizard* (fig. 37) was a 105-ton vessel launched a year earlier in Essex, Massachusetts, seventy-four feet in length and almost nineteen feet in breadth, under the command of William Wilcomb of Ipswich, MA (Logan, *Audubon*, 250).

32. In his Labrador journal, Audubon a few times openly connects his wonder at nature with God, casting everything in nature as purposeful parts of the "Creator's sublime system" ("Introductory Address," *OB* 1 [1831], xix). Writing and exploring before *On the Origin of Species* (1859), Audubon's study of birds and the natural world easily fit hand in glove with recognition of a divine purpose: his exuberant celebrations of American nature paralleled those of Ralph Waldo Emerson and Louis Agassiz. See also, for example, Audubon's discussion of the "oil bag" in "The White Ibis," *OB* 3 (1835), 177.

33. Audubon refers to the belief, propagated by Buffon and others, that, for example, girls in southern climates reach maturity sooner than in the cold countries of the North. Georges-Louis Leclerc Buffon, *Histoire naturelle générale et particulière* (Paris: de l'Imprimerie Royale, 1749), 3:490.

34. Audubon's confident discussion of the wonders of intentional seasonal migration over oceans and coasts, which he explores throughout his biographies, is notable. While the concept of bird migration (rather than, say, hibernation) had been known for thousands of years

in a range of cultures around the world (Wilson recognized the phenomenon regularly in his work, too), it had not been definitively proven and mapped directly in Western circles until anecdotal evidence emerged, like that of the white stork found in Germany in 1822 with an African spear still in its neck, and systematic international collaborations began, like the first international ornithological conference in 1884 in Vienna. As a young man in Pennsylvania, according to his own, perhaps dubious account, Audubon famously tied thread "rings" on the legs of his pewee flycatcher, now the eastern phoebe (*Sayornis phoebe*), observing that individuals came back the following season, as he describes in *OB* 2 (1834), 126–27. See also, in this volume, "The Turtlers," in relation to sea turtle movements.

35. Audubon's "Labrador Falcon" (Havell 196) is now the gyrfalcon (*Falco rusticolus*). In *Ornithological Biography*, Audubon calls the bird the "Iceland or Jer Falcon" (*OB* 2 [1834], 552–58). See also journal entry for August 12. The circumstances of Audubon's drawing on board the *Ripley* of a male and female falcon, the first of this species Audubon had seen, are explained in *OB* 2 (1834), 554: "one of the severest tasks I ever performed. The next day it rained for hours, and the water fell on my paper and colours all the while from the rigging of the Ripley." It took Audubon seventeen hours to complete the drawing (now held by the New-York Historical Society, NYHS 1863.17.195). A later drawing of white-faced gyrfalcons (NYHS 1863.17.366; Havell 366) was executed in London ca. 1835–1836 from birds held in captivity; see Roberta J. M. Olson, *Audubon's Aviary* (New York: New York Historical Society/ Rizzoli, 2012), 342. On plumage phases and misperceptions of separate species, see Susanne M. Low, *A Guide to Audubon's* Birds of America, 2nd ed. (1988; New Haven, CT: William Reese Co. and Donald A. Heald, 2002), 120, 186.

36. "The village" is Sandy Point, on what was formerly a peninsula but is now an island (abandoned since the 1970s).

37. The "Michmaes Indians" are the people of the Mi'kmaq First Nation, who had lived in Atlantic Canada and Maine for centuries before European contact, tracing their ancestors in this region back thirteen thousand years; there is some current debate about the length of their presence in Newfoundland. Like the Montagnais-Naskapi, they traded and integrated with the earliest French immigrants. Audubon's "man-eating" sharks could be a few species in this area, such as the porbeagle shark (*Lamna nasus*), great white shark (*Carcharodon carcharias*), or shortfin mako shark (*Isurus oxyrinchus*), all in decline globally.

38. On Audubon's racist portrayal of Indigenous people, see the introduction. Compare this depiction to his noble-savage description of the solitary Seminole hunter and paddler in "St John's River in Florida." The white-flowered cloudberry, *Rubus chamaemorus* (spelled "chamænrous" in Lucy Audubon's edition) featured in the center of the botanical background to the "Lincoln Finch" (Havell 193), now Lincoln's sparrow, *Melospiza lincolnii*. Audubon wrote that the Eskimo curlew (now Critically Endangered, IUCN, 2019) came north "in clouds" to feed on the cloudberry (*OB* 2 [1834], 542). At that time, American lobster (*Homarus americanus*) populations remained robust anywhere beyond the reach of a small boat's sail from large urban markets like New York and Boston. Canning technologies, which arrived in Maine in the 1840s and 1850s and in Newfoundland in the 1870s and 1880s, enabled the subsequent crash of lobster populations. Meanwhile, eels, along with salmon, were some of the first fisheries to be regulated in Atlantic Canada, beginning in the late 1780s, in response to noticeably declining stocks. See Joseph Gough, *Managing Canada's Fisheries: From Early Days to the Year 2000* (Georgetown, ON: Fisheries and Oceans Canada, 2006), 123–24; W. Jeffrey Bolster, *The Mortal Sea: Fishing the Atlantic in the Age of Sail* (Cambridge, MA: Belknap, 2012), 213–15. The *Ripley* had previously gathered plentiful lobsters at the Gut of Canso (Logan, *Audubon*, 151–52).

39. Audubon's "Golden Plover" (Havell 300) is now the American golden-plover (*Pluvialis dominica*). The "lestris pomerania," likely migrating south from Arctic breeding sites, were his "Jager" (pomarine jaeger, *Stercorarius pomarinus*): "This bird I never had an opportunity of examining until I visited Labrador" (*OB* 3 [1835], 396). See also detail of fig. 36, the other jaeger species in the region, as well as the second "Florida Keys" essay. Audubon's "Great Tern" (Havell 309) is now known as the common tern (*Sterna hirundo*), and his "Golden-crested Wren" as the golden-crowned kinglet (*Regulus satrapa*). This latter species that he shot in Labrador had heads of a "uniform tint with the upper parts of the body," which distinguished them from southern representatives of the species, featured in his painting (Havell 183). Audubon identified the "muscicapa," a flycatcher, as *Muscicapa Richardsonii*, calling it a "Short-legged Pewee/Short-legged Pewitt Flycatcher" (*OB* 5 [1839], 299). His painting of this species (as *M. phoebe*), among other flycatchers (Havell 434), is based on a specimen provided later from Townsend's collection of western birds. Today, this "new" flycatcher is considered the Alder flycatcher (*Empidonax alnorum*).

Coda

John James Audubon is an ambiguous hero at best, which is also why he remains endlessly fascinating. Whatever you assert about him, you can, with almost equal authority and assuredness, state the exact opposite. Take his recent biographer William Souder, who, explaining Audubon's almost industrial-style shooting of birds, asserts that he wasn't a modern man, only to tell us, a page or two later, that he really *was*, in some respects, since modern ornithologists, when in the field, still wield shotguns in much the same way.[1]

The contradictions began with Audubon's birth, illegitimate by the standards of his time, in Haiti. Audubon was born into the most ruthless slave economy in the world, which subsequently became the first nation in the world to abolish slavery. He entered another slave economy when, at age eighteen, he left France for the United States. In Henderson, Kentucky, where Audubon, beginning in 1811, ran a general store, enslaved people cooked, gardened, and even dug a pond for him. And in 1830, the Audubons passed on a woman and her two sons "yet belonging to us" to friends before they departed for England.[2] Approving accounts of how Audubon would neglect his business, preferring to scour the woods around Henderson for more birds to draw, gloss over the fact that he could do so only because enslaved humans did his work for him. Yet Audubon genuinely admired Black people for being good cooks and excellent shots (as he thought he was too), although such affirmations of their worth, troubled anyway by Audubon's penchant for stereotypical labels such as "the sons of Africa" (in "The Brown Pelican"), evaporate when we remember where he was when he made such remarks—in places like Bulowville, Florida, where he was the plantation owner's special guest.[3]

Similar contradictions characterize Audubon's references to Native Americans. When he toured the drawing rooms of Britain, he readily posed as an expert on Native American cultures, imitating not only, as one would expect from a naturalist, authentic bird calls ("I . . . hooted like the Barred Owl, and cooed like the doves"), but also the "Indian Yell."[4] But when he encountered the Innu of Labrador, he was appalled by their unkempt appearance even though he fully recognized the role imperialism and ecocide had played in their current situation ("they are disappearing here from insufficiency of food and physical comforts," he wrote in a July 21, 1833, journal entry). In "The Bay of Fundy," Audubon recoiled from the way local tribes would kill the marine birds that hadn't migrated for the summer because they were too old to reproduce—startling them first with "horrific yells," they walked among them with cudgels "until all are destroyed." But remember how Audubon would frequently describe himself, too: as given to precisely such violent excesses, surrounding himself with heaps of dead bird bodies wherever he went, a "two-legged monster, armed with a gun" (*OB* 3 [1835], 477). In Labrador, specifically, the members of Audubon's crew fully participated in the killing of murres, filling their boat with fifteen hundred eggs in one visit (twenty-five hundred, according to Audubon's later account).[5] If he was genuinely concerned about nature perishing, why then did he represent himself, on so many occasions, as contributing to the problem? Why give us, in the episodes added to *Ornithological Biography*, a gallery of additional unappealing characters, men who not only use violence but use it *too much*: a pirate, turtlers, eggers, and cod fishermen collecting gutted fish "in piles resembling so many hay-stacks"?

No amount of contextualizing will allow us to airbrush Audubon into the St. Francis of the animal world. Yet we would do well to remember, too, that we have done more damage to nature in a shorter period of time than Audubon did over his four decades or so of active fieldwork. It is true that Audubon's Great Gannet (a.k.a. Bird) Rock and Murre Rocks are now bird sanctuaries, subject to the Migratory Birds Convention Act and monitored by the Canadian Wildlife Service, home to tens of thousands of gannets, kittiwakes, murres, and other seabirds during the breeding season. But waterbirds, the subject of the selections in this anthology, face a "litany of threats" today, from overfishing, to microplastics, to oil and gas development, to polluted and disrupted food sources due to warming water temperatures.[6] An estimated one million common murres died of starvation in the Gulf of Alaska during the 2014–2016 heatwave (hundreds of thousands more suffered a similar fate in the California Current).[7] No one has counted the seabirds killed each year by illegal oil discharges from ships in the Northwest Atlantic. And when we consider that one of the primary sources of the mortality of diving seabirds is entanglement and drowning in fishing gear, the picture Audubon paints of the exploitation of an environment that he came to believe, during his Labrador trip, was never meant for white people suddenly becomes more relevant.[8]

In *Origin of Species*, Darwin invited his readers to look at nature as a "yielding surface, with ten thousand sharp wedges packed close together and driven inwards by incessant blows, sometimes one wedge being struck, and then another with greater force."[9] That was already Audubon's view. But unlike Darwin, he already recognized that nature was no longer a self-organizing system, that human impact on it was on the verge of permanently altering a balance that, as Rachel Carson lamented in *Silent Spring* (1962), had lasted for hundreds of millions of years.[10] Humans, to Audubon, were "disturbing agents," to use a phrase coined, a decade or so after Audubon's death, by one of the earliest American ecologists, the Vermont lawyer and diplomat George Perkins Marsh.[11] The provocation of Audubon's work is that he does not exempt himself from that charge. He noticed that local bird populations were diminishing, that forests were receding, and that even waterbirds such as the osprey, "on account of frequent disturbance, or attempts at destruction," were building their nests a mile from any river or ocean. Yet he hunted them too, frequently gathering more than he needed for his art. In Labrador, the "enormous destruction" wrought by fishermen and hunters on the ocean and land alike was immediately evident to him (as noted in his July 21 journal entry), though Audubon and his men, as we have seen, contributed their share as well to the universal devastation. Traveling up the Missouri in 1842, he deplored the slaughter of the buffalo, whose lives were being "needlessly ended" (never mind that he went on a hunt, too). By then, however, nature's diminishment had begun to parallel his own: Audubon died fewer than ten years after that final expedition, on January 27, 1851, in New York City, his brain addled by dementia.[12]

In his writings, Audubon paints an intentionally complex portrait of himself, one that amounts to so much more than that of a man constantly in search of birds. Note that he called his volumes not *Ornithological Biographies* but *Ornithological Biography*; while the essays tell many different stories, the underlying narrative, complex as it is, remains the same: it is a story about the inevitable entanglement of nonhuman and human lives on this planet. Audubon's water-bound outlaw characters, his pirates, eggers, turtlers, and fishermen killing their way through the world, are grotesquely magnified versions of Audubon himself and, for that matter, of ourselves. For, while most of us are not personally engaged in exterminating the albatrosses of the world, the piece of plastic that will kill just one of them could very well have come from the bottle we bought, against our better judgment, at the corner convenience store. Audubon already knew that the "Water Bird, which sweeps afar over the wide ocean, hovers above the surges, or betakes itself for refuge to the inaccessible rocks on the shore" (*OB* 3 [1835], x–xi), was more challenging to the naturalist than its landbound relative. But what he gradually came to accept, too, is an insight we are still grappling to understand today: that our destructiveness might end the world as we know it. Seabirds, precisely because they are so elusive, are a more reliable indicator than landbirds of the reach of human influence on nature; they are, as we would say today, bellwethers of environmental damage. In *Moby-Dick*, published the year Audubon died, Melville asserted what Audubon had also seen, that human acquisitiveness extends far beyond the confines of *terra firma*, that the oceans are humanity's final and potentially fatal frontier.

We are in the middle of a public reassessment of John James Audubon. Spearheaded by the Audubon Society, this new reckoning with Audubon's personal failings was preceded and inspired by the public embarrassment the Sierra Club expressed about its cofounder, John Muir. If Muir used slurs to refer to Black people, Audubon enslaved them, as Drew Lanham points out in a powerful piece written for *Audubon Magazine.*[13] Sure enough, Muir and Audubon were "men of their time," as the usual exculpatory narrative goes, but they failed to be "men ahead of their time," Lanham observes before asking the decisive question: "The stories of icons and heroes are critical, but what happens when truth rubs the shine off to reveal tarnished reality?" Confronting Audubon's complicity in white supremacy is essential, a prerequisite for diversifying a field still dominated by white naturalists. At the same time, it would seem only fair to acknowledge that the shine didn't just come off Audubon recently. He was a disappointment even to his contemporaries—to his father, who wanted him to be a sailor; to his wife Lucy, who had to raise their sons on her own during their father's frequent absences; to fellow naturalists, who lamented his errors and excoriated his plagiarisms; to his granddaughter, who assiduously scrubbed his prose and burned his journals; to modern environmentalists, chagrined over his mass killings of birds that undermined those passages in his writings in which he spoke out in favor of conservation. An unlikely and unseemly patron saint, he did not, we should remind ourselves, foist his name on the society that was named for him; that credit belongs to George Bird Grinnell, who had spent the formative years of his childhood roaming Audubon Park in the Upper Bronx, admiring Audubon's "beautiful and spirited paintings."[14] Audubon was, one suspects, a disappointment even to himself, his ambition constantly outpacing his artistic skills and financial means. Just take a look at the last volume of *The Birds of America*, which peters out in a series of plates featuring multiple birds jumbled together, a mess that belies the proud one-bird-per-plate principle to which he had adhered in the preceding volumes. His final work, *The Viviparous Quadrupeds of North America*, had to be completed by his collaborator, John Bachman.

Audubon at Sea shows us an Audubon who is truly at sea, physically and emotionally. Especially when he writes about waterbirds and their watery habitats, Audubon's writings guide us to a far more difficult place than any simple narrative of personal redemption through environmental awareness could reach. At sea, the "Birds of America" emerge in their full strangeness, mocking the human observer's limited understanding and commenting, if obliquely, on the quixotic attempt to kill them so that they can be recreated on paper "as if still alive."[15] The superiority of man over nature or, for that matter, of white over black, master over slave—they depend, as Herman Melville knew, on the notion that boundaries must exist and therefore must be kept intact. Yet, as Melville's Ahab, radicalized by a life at sea, demonstrates, with "eyes of red murder, and foam-glued lips," the only way we know how to keep them intact is through violence, thus inviting precisely what we had hoped to avoid: chaos.[16] This is the paradox Audubon, Melville's spiritual ancestor, constantly revisits. Audubon leads us across the water to the edge of things, to the place where life and death meet. We are used to imagining him roaming the woods, rifle in hand. But he might be even more relevant to us to today when he is riding the waves on wind-tossed boats toward some rocky island where he will be watching the murres cry out in helpless pain over the eggs that are being taken from their nests, his revulsion qualified by the recognition that he has contributed to that pain himself. Audubon doesn't show us a way out of our modern predicament. But at least shows us what it (still) is.

Notes

1. William Souder, *Under a Wild Sky: John James Audubon and the Marking of* The Birds of America (2004; Minneapolis: Milkweed, 2014), 97, 99.

2. Lucy Audubon, *The Life of John James Audubon, the Naturalist* (New York: Putnam, 1869) 203.

3. According to Gregory Nobles, who offers this summary, biographers have not addressed Audubon's complicity in the system of slavery; see Nobles, *John James Audubon: The Nature of the American Woodsman* (Philadelphia: University of Pennsylvania Press, 2017), 307n60, 202–3.

4. August 6 and October 13, 1826, Audubon's "Journal of a Sea Voyage from New Orleans to Liverpool aboard the *Delos*" (1826), Field Museum, Chicago.

5. See Peter Logan, *Audubon: America's Greatest Naturalist and His Voyage of Discovery to Labrador* (San Francisco: Ashbryn Press, 2016), 610n59.

6. Jeremy Hance, "After 60 Million Years of Extreme Living, Seabirds Are Crashing," *Guardian*, September 22, 2015.

7. John F. Piatt, Julia K. Parrish, Heather M. Renner, Sarah K. Schoen, et al., "Extreme Mortality and Reproductive Failure of Common Murres Resulting from the Northeast Pacific Marine Heatwave of 2014–2016," *PLOS ONE* 15, no. 1 (2020): e0226087.

8. William A. Montevecchi, H. Chaffey, and C. Burke, "Hunting for Security: Changes in the Exploitation of Marine Birds in Newfoundland and Labrador," in *Resetting the Kitchen Table: Food Security, Culture, Health, and Resilience in Coastal Communities*, ed. Christopher Parrish et al. (New York: Nova, 2007), 99–114, 109.

9. Darwin, *Origin*, 97.

10. Rachel Carson, *Silent Spring* (1962; Boston: Mariner, 2002), 6–7.

11. George Perkins Marsh, *Man and Nature; or, Physical Geography as Modified by Human Action* (1864; Cambridge, MA: Belknap, 1965), 36.

12. See, for example, Daniel Patterson on Audubon's "conservation ethic," in *The Missouri River Journals of John James Audubon*, ed. Patterson (Lincoln: University of Nebraska Press, 2016), esp. 260–97; and Christoph Irmscher, "Audubon Goes North," in *Cultural Circulation: Dialogues between Canada and the American South*, ed. Waldemar Zacharasiewicz and Christoph Irmscher (Vienna: Austrian Academy of Sciences, 2013), 77–97, esp. 91–92.

13. J. Drew Lanham, "What Do We Do about John James Audubon?," *Audubon Magazine*, Spring 2021, https://www.audubon.org/magazine/spring-2021/what-do-we-do-about-john-james-audubon.

14. See Carolyn Merchant, *Spare the Birds! George Bird Grinnell and the First Audubon Society* (New Haven, CT: Yale University Press, 2016), 26–27.

15. "Myself," in Audubon, *Writings and Drawings*, ed. Christoph Irmscher (New York: Library of America, 1999), 793.

16. See Melville, "The Whiteness of the Whale," in *Moby-Dick; or, The Whale*, ed. Harrison Hayford, Hershel Parker, and G. Thomas Tanselle (Evanston, IL: Northwestern University Press/Newberry Library, 1988), 188–95, and "eyes of red," 223.

Acknowledgments

Our work on this anthology was supported by Williams College–Mystic Seaport research assistants Eleanore MacLean, Rachel Earnhardt, and Sarah Dohan and later by Dominick Leskiw. Nathan Schmidt at Indiana University Bloomington provided editing and research during the final stages of the anthology.

We would like to thank the staff of the Field Museum in Chicago, especially Gretchen Rings; Joel Silver, director of the Lilly Library; Zach Downey, the Lilly's former digitization manager, who photographed the plates featured in this edition; Jody Mitchell, the Lilly's current digitization manager; and Alison O'Grady at Williams College Libraries. We gratefully acknowledge support from the Indiana University Presidential Arts and Humanities Program, the Textbook and Academic Authors Association Publication Grant, and a Furthermore Publication Grant (J. M. Kaplan Fund). Several scholars graciously helped with matters of interpretation, including Jim Carlton, Drew Lanham, Roberta Olson, Hugh Powell, Captain J. B. Smith, and Caleb Spiegel.

Thank you to Stephen Hull, formerly at the University Press of New England. At the University of Chicago Press. a wonderful team led by our editor Karen Merikangas Darling shepherded our book into print. Apart from Karen, we are deeply indebted to editorial associate Tristan

Bates; manuscript editor Joel Score, whose thoughtful suggestions vastly improved our text; and designer Isaac Tobin, who made our efforts look beautiful. Thank you also to June Sawyers for undertaking the complex indexing of the book. And our deep gratitude for the helpful readings by Charles Hansford Adams (University of South Florida) and by our peer reviewers, whose suggestions helped us fix details and clarify the overall purpose of the volume. And an enormous thank you to professor, artist, and activist Subhankar Banerjee for writing the foreword to *Audubon at Sea* and donating one of his extraordinary photographs.

General Index

Modern spellings are used for this index. When different, the spellings used by Audubon are cross-referenced and/or set in parentheses and quotation marks following the modern name. Italicized references indicate illustrations.

Ornithological Index

Bird names at the time of publication follow the Cornell Lab of Ornithology's Birds of the World (birdsoftheworld.com). Common names used by Audubon and his contemporaries are cross-referenced to current usage and appear in parentheses following current names, usually capitalized per his usage. Where Audubon uses a name for which modern usage can't reliably be given, the original name appears in quotation marks. Italicized references indicate illustrations.